CAMP

BY L. C. ROSEN

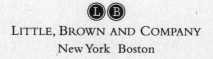

LITTLE, BROWN AND COMPANY
New York Boston

Copyright © 2020 by Lev Rosen
Interior camp tent © DMaryashin/Shutterstock.com
Interior sun icon © BullsStock/Shutterstock.com

Cover art copyright © 2020 by MDI Digital. Wooden background © 10 FACE/Shutterstock.com. Cover design by Angelie Yap.
Cover copyright © 2020 by Hachette Book Group, Inc.

Little, Brown and Company
Hachette Book Group
1290 Avenue of the Americas, New York, NY 10104
Visit us at LBYR.com

Simultaneously published in 2020 by Penguin Random House UK in Great Britain
First U.S. Edition: May 2020

Little, Brown and Company is a division of Hachette Book Group, Inc.
The Little, Brown name and logo are trademarks of Hachette Book Group, Inc.

The publisher is not responsible for websites (or their content) that are not owned by the publisher.

Library of Congress Cataloging-in-Publication Data
Names: Rosen, Lev AC., author.
Title: Camp / by L. C. Rosen.
Description: First edition. | New York : Little, Brown and Company, 2020. | Audience: Ages 14+. | Summary: At Camp Outland, a camp for LGBTQIA+ teens, sixteen-year-old Randall "Del" Kapplehoff's plan to have Hudson Aaronson-Lim fall in love with him succeeds, but both are hiding their true selves.
Identifiers: LCCN 2019034949 | ISBN 9780316537759 (hardcover) | ISBN 9780316537742 (ebook) | ISBN 9780316537926 (library edition ebook)
Subjects: CYAC: Camps—Fiction. | Gays—Fiction. | Lesbians—Fiction. | Gender-nonconforming people—Fiction. | Dating (Social customs) —Fiction. | Love—Fiction. | Secrets—Fiction.
Classification: LCC PZ7.1.R67 Cam 2020 | DDC [Fic]—dc23
LC record available at https://lccn.loc.gov/2019034949

ISBNs: 978-0-316-53775-9 (hardcover), 978-0-316-53774-2 (ebook)

Printed in the United States of America

LSC-C

10 9 8 7 6 5 4 3 2

For Robin,
who brings summer with her
wherever she goes

ONE

The smell wraps around me like a reunion between old friends when I step off the bus. That dark soil smell, but mixed with something lighter. Something green that immediately makes me think of leaves in rain, or trees in the wind. I love this smell. I love it every summer. It's the smell of freedom. Not that stupid kayaking-shirtless-in-a-Viagra-commercial freedom. That's for straight people. This is different. It's the who-cares-if-your-wrists-are-loose freedom. The freedom from having two seniors the table over joke about something being "so gay" at lunch.

Several tables are set out next to the parking lot, a big banner hanging over them: WELCOME TO CAMP OUTLAND.

This year, I admit, it smells a little different. Maybe not quite as free. But I knew it would be like this when I came

up with my plan. This smell, I hope—slightly less pine, a bit more grass, the barest whiff of daisy, which I could be imagining—this is the smell of love.

"Keep it moving, keep it moving," Joan, the camp director, calls out to us as we step off the bus we've been traveling in for the last several hours, waving her hands like a traffic cop. "Tables are by age—find your age, go to that table to register."

I look for the table that says 16 and wait in line. I run my hands over my newly shortened hair. Until two days ago, it had been chin length and wavy and super cute, if I do say so myself, but I needed to lose it for the plan to work. The line of campers moves forward and I'm at the front, staring down at Mark, the theater counselor—*my* counselor. I think he's in his forties, gray at the temples, skin that's a little too tan for a white guy, wearing the Camp Outland polo, big aviator sunglasses, and a pin that says THEATER GAY in sparkly rainbow letters. This will be the big test. He looks up at me, and for a moment, there's a flash, like he recognizes me, but then he squints, confused.

"What's your name, honey?" he asks.

I smile. Not my usual big grin; I've been working on changing it. Now it's more like a smirk.

"Randall," I say. "Randall Kapplehoff."

"Randy?" He practically shouts it, looking me over again as he stands up. "Oh my god, what happened to you?"

"Puberty," I say, now smiling my real smile. I look around, bring it back to smirk.

"Honey, you were a baritone last summer, this isn't puberty," he says. "I barely recognized you."

Good, I think. That's the point.

"I just thought it was time for a change," I say.

"Were you being bullied?" he asks, concerned eyes peeking over his sunglasses.

"No." I shake my head. "Just…wanted to try something new."

"Well," Mark says, sitting down. "It's certainly new. I hope you haven't changed so much you're not auditioning for the show this summer, though."

"We'll see," I say.

He frowns and flips through the pages on his clipboard. "Well, at least you'll still be hanging out with us. You're in cabin seven." He takes a name tag label out from the back of his clipboard and writes a big *R* on it before I think to stop him.

"Actually," I say, putting out a hand, "it's Del now."

He peeks up at me over the sunglasses again. "Del?"

"Yeah." I nod, chin first. "I'm Del."

"Okay," he says like he doesn't believe me, and writes it out on a new name tag sticker and hands it to me. I press it over my chest, rubbing it in, hoping it will stick. "Well, I'm going to have to talk to my therapist about this later," he says to himself. Then he glances at his watch and turns back to

me. "Flagpole meet-up is at eleven. So, go pick a bunk and be there in twenty minutes."

"Thanks," I say.

"Later...Del," he says.

I walk back over to the bus where our bags have been unloaded and pick up the big military surplus bag I bought online. The purple wheely bag with the stickers of cats wearing tiaras on it wasn't going to work this summer. Neither was having my parents drop me off. I think that made them a little sad. Camp Outland had been their idea four years ago, after I came out. Not many other twelve-year-olds were talking about how dreamy and cute Skylar Astin was in *Pitch Perfect 2*, and how I hoped my boyfriend would look like him someday, so they thought it would be good for me to meet some other queer kids, and they found Camp Outland—a four-week sleepaway summer camp for LGBTQIA+ teens nestled in the woods of northern Connecticut.

And let's be honest. It was an amazing idea. Every summer has been better than the last. But this summer is going to be the best. Because this summer, Hudson Aaronson-Lim is going to fall in love with me.

I hoist the military bag onto my shoulder, not flinching as the scratchy, cheap canvas brushes my ear, and follow the other campers down the path through the woods. The camp is built like a waterfall feature. At the top is the parking lot, then follow the stairs down and you end up at the administrative section—Joan the camp director's office, the infirmary,

the big meeting hall for movie nights. Then another flight down and you have a big open field lined with cabins. The tier below that is the last one—the real camp—and has the dining hall, pool, drama cabin, obstacle course, capture the flag field, arts and crafts cabin, and a boathouse next to the river. I stop at the cabin-lined field, surrounded by the woods. There's a flagpole in the center of the field for morning camp-wide meet-ups and evening bonfires. Breakfast is at nine, lunch is at one, and dinner is at six, then lights-out at ten. Otherwise, we pretty much make our own schedules. Sign up for pool time, sports, waterskiing, or just drop by the arts and crafts cabin and spend all day gossiping and weaving friendship bracelets. My favorite thing every year, though, has been the drama cabin. Mark puts on a show, and you have to audition but it's not like school where the pretty blond girl lands the lead every year. They don't care about gender or appearance when casting, they just want everyone to have fun, and we always do. Last year, I was Domina in *Funny Thing*, and I got a standing ovation after "That Dirty Old Man."

But this year, no theater. This year…sports. I manage not to shiver as I think about it.

"Hey," a voice behind me says. A voice I know. It's low and a little breathy. I turn around and there he is, Hudson Aaronson-Lim, in all his glory. Tall, with muscular arms bulging in his white tee, and equally appealing bulging in his black gym shorts. He has a broad, square face, shadowed

by prominent cheekbones and a little stubble. His short black hair is swept to the side, but messy, like he doesn't care. He is, without a doubt, the most attractive man I've ever seen in real life. And more attractive than half the men I've seen on-screen. He's got a killer smile, and he unleashes it on me now, crooked and a little sleazy, but only enough to make it sexy. I get that feeling I get around him, like I'm filled with stars and can be anything I want, do anything I want— conquer the world. Checking in on his Instagram never really gives me the same feeling. It's a high I've missed all year.

"Hi," I say after too long a silence. I hope I'm not blushing.

"You new?" he asks.

I smirk. He barely noticed me before, so it's not surprising he wouldn't recognize me. Now I have his attention.

"You could say that," I answer, not wanting to outright lie.

He steps closer. I coordinated my outfit perfectly for this meeting. Brown flannel button-down with short sleeves, untucked; olive-green shorts; yellow sneakers that pick out the yellow in the flannel. I've also lost twenty pounds, cut my hair off, and studied the "bros" at school all year. I am, I think, Hudson's dream boy. A masc fantasy. Sure, I watch everything I do now, and I won't be able to be in the show this summer, but it'll all be worth it for love.

I smell him as he steps closer—this sort of faded lightning

smell, like day-old deodorant and maple. I work hard to keep my knees from shaking.

"I'm Hudson," he says.

"Del," I say, keeping my voice low.

"So, what cabin are you in?" He's really close now. I can feel the heat off his body and I wonder if he can feel it off mine, like we're touching.

"Seven," I say.

"Oh." He raises an eyebrow. "So, did you pick that?"

"It's my lucky number," I say.

"Well, I'm cabin fourteen," he says. "So maybe your luck is changing."

"Something wrong with seven?" I ask.

"Nah, they're good people," he says. "But I think you'd have more fun with me—in my cabin. Folks like us." He waves his finger back and forth between us, almost like a question, a "We going to do this?" and I have to take a deep breath to keep from nodding.

"Well, it's just where I'm sleeping, right?" I say.

"Yeah," he laughs, and reaches out and gives my shoulder a squeeze. This is the first time he's intentionally touched me and it's something I've wanted for years and it's hard not to melt right away, but instead I just lock eyes with him and smile. Remember, I tell myself, you want him to fall in love with you. If I just wanted to screw him, I could probably do that right now—but I'm going to be the guy who finally

gets Hudson to commit. No one else has done it, but I will. Because I have a plan.

"Well," he says, dropping his hand, his eyes closing just a little, like he's curious, "I'll see you around, I hope."

"I hope so," I say, and he grins, and I wonder for a moment if it was too much, but no, I think, as I turn around and head for my cabin, that was just enough. I look back after a few steps and he's still watching me and smiles when he sees me watching and then heads for his own cabin.

Okay, I say in my head, walking slowly, breathe in, breathe out. My legs feel like jelly, my heart is racing. Okay. Okay okay okay. Step one, done. It worked. IT WORKED. Maybe this whole thing could work? Maybe I didn't give up carbs and cut off my hair and spend hours working on my walk and voice and learning not to talk with my hands or quote a show tune every sentence for nothing. Maybe I can really win my dream guy.

I walk into the cabin and George starts screaming. "OH MY GOD," he says, giving me a hug. "I was watching from the window, and I almost didn't recognize you—I mean, I saw the photos on Snapchat, of course, darling, and everything you texted me, but I didn't think you'd really be going through with the wardrobe and styling changes." He reaches up and pets the air where my hair used to be. "Poor hair," he says solemnly. "But you just talked to him, and he totally checked out your ass as you walked away! Could you feel his dark, sexy eyes just burrowing into you?" He wiggles his eyebrows.

"Hey," Ashleigh says from her top bunk on the side of the room, where she's flipping through a comic.

I let my bag drop, and I take one long dramatic breath.

"I think it's going to work," I say.

George screams again, one big drag queen shriek.

I grin, and look them both over. My two best camp friends. Two best friends, really. It feels sad saying that about people I only see for four weeks out of the year, but we e-mail and text, and watch *Drag Race* together while in a group chat, and it's not like I have other queer friends. There's not even a GSA at my tiny school in eastern Ohio. Like, I'm sure there are other queer kids, and maybe they're even out, a little, like I am, to a few friends and their parents, but no one is talking about it. Once you start talking about it, other people join the conversation, and in eastern Ohio, they don't always say nice things.

My transformation at school didn't go unnoticed, though. I was still a theater kid (always the chorus, never a lead—there, anyway), but suddenly the girls were looking at me differently, asking me to hang out. I pretended to be sick a lot. My parents gave me weird looks a lot, too, and asked if everything was okay, but I just smiled and told them things were great. It was definitely strange. But worth it if I can go back to school with my phone lock screen as a photo of Hudson and me making out.

"So," George says when he's done screaming, "what's the timeline on this? You're still going to be able to hang out with

us, right? Mark says they're going to do *Bye Bye Birdie* this year, and I am so excited! Darling, you know I'm going to cut some bitches to play Kim, so don't even think of going up against me."

George spreads his fingers out in front of him, his nails painted in green and gold to spell B CAMP @ CAMP. I've been so focused on my own physical changes over the school year, I guess I didn't notice his on Snapchat and Instagram. He doesn't look that different. He's still "stocky," as we call ourselves (well, called, in my case, I guess), but his face is a little more angular, and the stubble and chest hair peeking out from the collar of his purple V-neck give his sandy-colored complexion more maturity. His black curly hair is still shaved at the sides and big on top, but it looks less like a kid's haircut and more like a man's. He's gone from looking too young for his age to looking a little older than the rest of us. And he's wearing it well. Ashleigh hasn't changed at all. Same denim cutoffs, same black-and-white flannel wrapped around her waist and black tank top. Same rough-looking undercut, one side of her head shaved, the other side's unwashed wavy hair falling over her thin, pale face. She's the ultimate theater techie. Lights, sound, stage managing—she does it all, way better than anyone else.

"I don't know if I can be in the musical," I say, trying not to sound as sad as I feel about it.

"Darling, no," George says, shaking his head. "I know you have this plan and all, but there's always time for theater!" He does jazz hands.

Ashleigh looks up from her comic, a worn-out copy of *Deadly Class*. "You're giving up theater for this guy?" she asks. "Really?"

"That's the plan," I say. "And he's not just some guy. He's Hudson. THE Hudson. The perfect man." As I say it, a few more old friends come into the bunk—other theater kids. We say hi, give each other hugs, some tell me they like my haircut. Jordan does a double take and says, "Whoa, didn't recognize you. Cool look, though," with slightly worried eyes before grabbing a bed. I take the bunk next to George's, under Ashleigh.

"I thought you'd be taking the top bunk with that new hair," George says.

"Calm down," I say. "It's just a haircut."

"And no theater," Ashleigh says.

"What are you going to do all summer?" George asks.

"Sports, I guess," I say, not really sure which ones I mean. "Obstacle course stuff, arts and crafts."

"Well, at least we'll have that," George says.

"I just don't get this, Randy," Ashleigh says. "Like, I get you have a crush on the guy, but—"

"It's more than a crush," I say. "He makes me feel...different. He's special."

Ashleigh sighs above me, and I see George stare up at her, exchanging a look.

"And call me Del now," I add. "At least in public."

"Del." George tries it out. "I don't hate it."

"I do," Ashleigh says. "It's not your name."

"It's the other part of Randall," I say, taking out my sheets—plain gray this year, not the rainbow unicorn sheets I usually bring—and making my bed. "It's fine. I'm not forgetting who I am. I'm just changing the way other people see me."

"To be more masculine." Ashleigh says it with disgust. She hops down from her bunk and helps me tuck the corners of my sheet in. "As if that means anything. Gender essentialist nonsense."

"It's a type," George says, shrugging.

"It's what Hudson likes," I say, sitting down on my made bed and smoothing out the gray sheets. They're high thread count, at least. They may look different, but they feel the same.

"And you're sure all this is worth it?" Ashleigh asks.

"Absolutely," I say.

TWO

We gather around the flagpole in a semicircle, staring up at Joan, who's looking at her clipboard and making that face she makes all the time, with her mouth twisted to one side. I sit next to George and Ashleigh. I can still be friends with them—that won't hurt the plan. I decided if he didn't like me being friends with them, then he wasn't the guy I thought he was, the one who believes we're all special and can do anything. He might not know how we're old, close friends, but that's not important. Besides, I'm going to need their help.

I spot Hudson on the other side of the circle and he waves at me. I smile. Next to him is his best friend, Brad—tall, lanky, shaved head, and dark skin. He's like Hudson, in that he's into sports and doesn't wear nail polish, but strangely,

Brad has never been one of Hudson's conquests. No one is sure why—it's one of the great mysteries of camp, like whether someone really died in cabin three, or why the cabins aren't gender-exclusive but the changing rooms by the pool are.

"I'm going to need you to show me the tree later," I tell George and Ashleigh.

"You've seen the tree," Ashleigh says. She's already been down to the arts and crafts cabin and raided it for string and is weaving a bracelet.

"Randy has," I say. "Del hasn't. Del needs to see the tree while Hudson is watching so I can say I'd never want to be with a playboy like that."

"Playboy?" George says. "Darling, this isn't the sixties. We don't talk like that."

"I'm more worried about how he talked about himself in the third person, and as two different people," Ashleigh says.

"It helps me distinguish," I say. "Del is like a role."

"Method actors," George says, his voice dripping disdain. "All right, all right, I'll help you out—but I don't know how you're going to get him to eavesdrop on us."

"Just take me to see the tree when I ask you to, okay?"

"Attention, please!" Joan is standing at the flagpole in the center of the cabins, holding her hand up. "When the hand goes up!" she says.

"The mouth goes shut!" shout about half the campers in

response. Some people keep talking, but Joan keeps her hand raised and eventually everyone quiets down.

"Thank you," Joan says. Joan always seems like she hasn't gotten enough sleep. She's maybe in her fifties, with short curly hair and big plastic glasses I swear she's had since the seventies on a chain around her neck, always in the purple camp polo and cargo shorts. "Hello, and welcome to Camp Outland!" she says with half-hearted enthusiasm and a smile that would probably be big if she had the energy. "I'm Joan Ruiz, and I run the camp. I'll be leading meetings here every morning at eight, and I handle our LGBTQIA+ history activities on Monday nights. Otherwise, you're probably only going to be hearing my voice if you get in trouble, so let's talk about how not to do that. First—no cell phones, no computers, no smart watches or belts or whatever they have these days. We have boom boxes in each cabin, if you need music, but otherwise, no technology. If we catch you with a phone or anything else, you'll be put on kitchen cleanup for a week, and we will confiscate the phone. You won't get it back until you go home. It'll be dead by then, so you won't be able to immediately get on the Internet, where I know you'll want to be. That also means you have to write letters—Real Mail, I call it—if you want to talk to your friends or family back home. Next: food! You have to be at all three meals a day. If you're vegan or vegetarian or kosher or halal, you should have told us already and we're prepared for you, but if for some reason you didn't,

come see me after flagpole. You eat what you're given. It's not so bad, I promise. Yes, you can be sent candy and snacks from home, but only things that follow the rules—nothing with peanuts or sesame seeds or anything anyone is deathly allergic to—your counselors have a list. When you get food from home, your cabin counselor will go through it to make sure it meets the rules. Don't leave food out! That's how you get ants. More ants. And if you're going to gamble with candy, just do it over cards. No betting on who's going throw up after eating too much or who's going to drop the egg during the egg race. That's just mean. No drinking! If we catch you with drugs or alcohol, you'll be kicked out. Same if you're caught outside your cabin after curfew."

I pluck the grass as Joan goes on, stealing glances at Hudson, who I'm pleased to see is stealing glances at me. We lock eyes once and I grin. This might be going too smoothly. The issue now is making sure he knows I'm not just going to be another conquest. That's what he does. A different boy every two weeks at camp. A week of wooing, a week of holding hands and sneaking out to the Peanut Butter Pit, and then, inevitably, a breakup with some tears.

They always stay friends, though. Hudson is the master of staying friends—and that makes sense. He's nice about it, he never cheats on them, they always just…consciously uncouple.

But I'm going to knock all those other bitches out of the water. 'Cause Hudson is going to stay with me all summer.

And beyond that, too. We're going to be boyfriends and share a tent on the canoe trip the second-to-last weekend of camp.

When Joan is done talking, she introduces the nurse, Cosmo, a skeletal man in his sixties with long gray hair to his shoulders.

"Just stay healthy, everybody," he says by way of his speech. "Like, water, sunscreen. You know." He waves at us and walks away. Joan frowns a little, then hoists the big rainbow flag on the flagpole, running it up to the top, where it starts flapping in the breeze. Everyone watches in silence, but with smiles. I admit, I grow a little teary-eyed at it every year—can you blame me? This is our special home. The scent of the wind rushes back, heavy with that smell—definitely freedom—and I close my eyes. I can't tear up this year. Hudson is watching, and butch boys don't cry in public.

"Okay," Joan says, after the flag is raised. "Go unpack, make your schedules with your bunk counselors, then there'll be some group time, some free swim, and then dinner. After dinner, the counselors are going to put on a talent show for you folks. Go with pride!" she shouts, the official dismissal.

Everyone scatters up and heads back toward their cabins, but I see Hudson coming in my direction. George and Ashleigh look at me, as if waiting for something.

"I'll see you at the cabin," I say. George gives me some side-eye as they walk away.

"Hey," Hudson says, arriving just as they leave. "So, your bunkmates showing you the ropes?"

"Yeah," I say. "It all seems so awesome."

"It is," Hudson says. "Like, could you ever imagine a place like this when you were closeted? No people calling you names, no people asking if you've tried being straight, putting you down. None of that bullying crap. It's amazing."

"I can't imagine anyone bullying you," I say, looking him over.

"Well, not anymore," he says. "My trick is to beat them at their own game." I don't know what he means, but I nod like I do. "So, anyway, I just wanted to tell you you should sign up for the adventure elective."

"Yeah?" I ask.

"Yeah, I always do. It rocks. We mess around on the obstacle course and hike and stuff. Oh, and I try to take my swim class period before lunch...if you want to see me in a bathing suit." He grins, all wolfish charm, and I feel a heat flash down my spine and legs to my toes.

"Okay," I say.

"And, so, let's try to hang out—just us—when we have some free time." He bites the side of his lower lip as he looks at me, like he's nervous.

"Yeah," I manage to squeak out.

"Cool," he says. "See you later." He jogs off and I watch him go, feeling my heart rise and fall in rhythm to his legs.

"Later," I say, after he's way out of earshot. Then I turn around and head back to my cabin.

Inside, music is playing. A sort of vintage doo-wop vibe,

but no vocals. It makes me think of really old-fashioned dancing, like where they twist their hips with their arms bent. And apparently, I'm not the only one thinking of that, because several of my bunkmates are dancing just like that.

"Randy," Mark says as I come in. He's our cabin counselor. "So nice of you to join us."

"Del," I say.

"Right," he says, "sorry. Anyway, as I was just telling everyone, the musical this summer is *Bye Bye Birdie*, and to make sure we're really living that retro vibe, I'll be playing nothing but fifties and sixties music in this cabin. I encourage you to dance to it." He gestures at the campers, who have managed to get themselves in synch—a semi-choreographed routine with hip swivels and tossing back their heads. "It'll give you a feel for the music."

"And it inspires me!" Crystal says. She's the other cabin counselor and plays choreographer to Mark's director. She has wavy blond hair to her shoulders and always wears loose-fitting skirts and peasant blouses. Right now she's dancing... but not to the music, near as I can tell. Just... to something in her head.

"Okay," I say. And I can feel my feet tapping—I want to join in. I want to dance with the rest of them. I take a step forward. Hudson is in his own cabin. He won't see me.

So I start dancing with them. The swivels, the arms up, the head tosses. We add in a few step-forward-back moves,

19

too. It feels so good. All year I've been making sure my movements are casual, clumsy, rough. I've thought about how apes move, swinging their arms. It's so nice to have a little elegance back in my step. To have some rhythm. To feel like myself.

Mark turns off the stereo as the song ends and claps his hands.

"All right!" he says. "None of you are new, so we don't need to do two truths and a lie or anything. Let's get right to schedules. The theater elective is the first half of the day, and auditions are tomorrow, so I hope you all came prepared. As for what you want to do the rest of the day—that's up to you. You know the drill. Put down your choices and we'll figure it out if there's too many campers in anything."

Crystal hands out clipboards with the various electives on them for us to choose from. I look down at my clipboard. Outdoor Adventure is the first activity of the day—just like theater. I take a deep breath and circle it with my pencil. I miss theater the moment I do it, but I know this has to be part of the plan. I'll miss singing, dancing, backstage chaos... last year floods my mind for a moment, all wild joy in my blood. But I'll have it again next year. This year, I'll give it up for Hudson. Otherwise, I won't see Hudson as much.

George looks over and tsks. "Whatever you want, darling," he says.

"Hudson asked me to," I say.

"And you want to make him happy," George says. "Sure."

20

I circle the swim class period before lunch and then try to think of what Hudson would circle—sports, probably, which means a lot of touch football and kickball. That's okay, I've been practicing, or at least actively participating in gym class. Luckily there's still room for arts and crafts after lunch—the same time as George and Ashleigh. And the whole camp does a free pool time at the end of the day. When I give my clipboard back to Crystal, she looks at it confused.

"You forgot to circle theater," she says, handing it back.

"I'm..." The words make my throat dry and I cough. "I'm not doing theater this year."

Crystal looks like I've confessed to murdering her pet rabbit. She turns pink and her mouth opens and she looks behind her at Mark, then back at me, then back at Mark, until he walks over and looks at the clipboard, then frowns at me.

"Okay, Del." He pauses, frowning, but then makes his expression soft. He looks worried. "What is...all this?" He gestures at me. "Are you okay? Did you hit your head? Is someone making you act like this? My therapist says sudden changes like these are usually the result of trauma."

"What?" I say. "No. I just...wanted to change."

"He's doing it for a boy," Ashleigh says.

"A boy?" Mark practically shouts. "And based on your makeover, I'm guessing he's one of those 'straight-acting' types? Honey, if he's suck—" He pauses, smiles. "If he's kissing you, he's not acting straight. No offense, Jen," he says

to one of the campers. "Bisexual folks can act straight and still be super queer. But we're talking about men who don't want anyone to think they're gay until they have a di—" He pauses again, smiles. Mark's gotten in trouble before for his overly graphic language. "Until they're making out with a boy. They hate themselves, and they hate you, too. They're not worth the time of day, much less an entire wardrobe change." By now his voice is loud enough it can probably be heard outside. "I'm going to need to book a double with Dr. Gruber," he says much softer to himself.

"He's not straight-acting," I say.

"He's masc4masc," George says.

"Oh, what's the difference?" Mark asks. "And who even says that? He tells people that over the campfire?"

"We found his BoyDate profile," George says. Which is true. Last summer, when my parents picked me up, they brought my phone and I turned it on—just to see, just to check if I could find his profile, and save it, and maybe there'd be photos—and there it was: HudsonRocks, five eleven, athletic build, masc4masc. As if we didn't know that from all the boys he'd gotten with at camp.

Mark sighs and takes my shoulders in his hands, bending down to look me in the eyes. "Look, Del, Randy, I don't care what you call yourself. I just want you to be happy. Are you happy? Don't you want to wear that same purple sweater you bring every summer? Don't you want to sing in the show?"

"I..." I take a deep breath. I do. But I also want something else, and I can't have both. "I want Hudson."

Mark lets go of my arms and stands up straight. "Well, it's your choice. But, honey, I've been around the block a lot more than you have, and I promise you, a man who makes you change to be with him isn't worth it."

"He is," I say softly.

Mark ignores me and claps his hands. "Everyone turned their clipboards back in? Great. Now let's get back to dancing!" He turns the music on and everyone is dancing again, but I sit down on my bed, my head in my hands, and try to shake the feeling that even though I know this plan will work, I'm letting everybody else down. I take a deep breath. Hudson is worth it, I remind myself. Everything I'm giving up is worth it for him.

THREE

LAST SUMMER

Normally, I don't care for the camp-wide color wars. Three days when all the usual activities are replaced by relay races and capture the flag and making banners and worthless points stacking up like condom wrappers at the boathouse? Not fun. Mark loathes it—says the break from rehearsal and all the screaming damaging our vocal cords is just Joan trying to sabotage the show. The whole camp is divided up into two teams—no splitting up bunkmates, though, to prevent inter-cabin fighting—and this year, we're Green. Not my favorite color, or one I usually gravitate to, sartorially speaking, but I have a great pair of white shorts trimmed in green lace. That and a black shirt, and I think I'm showing my team spirit in a very fashionable way. And at least I'm not on Orange. I don't know what I'd wear for that.

And besides, Hudson is on our team. Not just on it—he's a captain: one of the eight campers chosen to lead their color into battle, four per team. They're like army generals and cheerleaders rolled into one. Hudson has taken to it like it was a mission delivered unto him by God herself. He's standing onstage with the other three generals, in a bright green polo and not-at-all-matching khaki-green shorts. His face is painted with green stripes under his eyes, like a football fantasy come to life, and he's even sprayed his hair with a light coating of bright green wash-out dye. And he's waving a green flag in the air, screaming.

"Go Mean Green!" he shouts with the other generals. Across the soccer field from us, team Orange glares. Another reason I'm happy to be on green: Nothing rhymes with *orange*.

George sits to my right, in green eye shadow and a forest-green romper studded with gold stars. Ashleigh is to my left, in a black tank top and denim cutoffs. A green bandanna that one of the counselors gave her sticks out of her pocket.

"I feel like we're in a cult," Ashleigh says.

"An army," George corrects. "That means a cult that's openly fighting another cult. As opposed to secretly fighting everyone."

"It'll be fun," I say, watching Hudson jump up and down onstage. "I wonder if his underwear is green."

"If that boy owns anything beyond 'funny' boxers with pictures of bacon or something, I'll eat my own underwear,"

George says. "Though I will say those streaks under his eyes are expertly applied. Perfect edges. I wonder who did them?"

"Green briefs," I say, still thinking aloud. "I'm going to picture him in green briefs."

"Gross," Ashleigh says. "I don't need to hear what you're going to be fantasizing about."

"Sweetie, you were the one who did a five-minute monologue on Janice's purple bikini today," I say.

Ashleigh turns to the grass in front of her and pulls out a few blades. I keep watching Hudson. "He's so pretty," I say. "Even in that outfit."

"Darling, that's his thing," George says. "Pretty, masculine, straight-acting, whatever you want to call it. And he only hooks up with other boys like him."

"I mean, I could go butch."

"Randy," Ashleigh says, "come on. You wear women's tank tops, nail polish, sometimes lipstick. You've got long hair and a soft body. No body-shaming, I think you're perfect, but even if you could do the 'straight-acting' thing all of a sudden, you'd still need to change your wardrobe, cut your hair off, lose some weight, get some muscle...."

"I could devote myself to the part," I say. "Go Method."

"And then he'd break up with you two weeks later," George says. "Just like he does with all the others. So even if you could suddenly go butch overnight, it would be for what, a week of making out and then some screwing at the Peanut Butter Pit before he forgot your name?" The Peanut

Butter Pit was under the rope swing at the obstacle course—dug deep enough to afford some privacy for two horizontal bodies in it, and a favorite spot of Hudson's for being horizontal. Or whatever angles are involved for cowboy and doggie style.

"He's not really like that," I say, plucking a blade of grass and twirling it between my fingers. "I mean, he acts like he is, but he's more than that."

"And you know all this how? From looking deep into his eyes?"

"No," I say. "We were in the same cabin my first year. His grandma had just died and Hudson cried in his sleep, had these sad dreams about her. I woke him up once and we talked a little. About his dream. About how to remember her. About how to be the best versions of ourselves. It was... deep." I look down. I haven't told anyone about that night before. It's a special memory, and I know they'll tear it down, but they have to understand: Hudson isn't just hot. He's the only one I know who can make me feel like I'm not just free to be myself here, where it's safe, but I'm free to be myself anywhere I want, and screw anyone who tells me differently.

"Did he even see your face?"

"The lights were out," I say, maybe a little defensively. "But he's a nice guy. He's just never met a guy who's captured his attention long enough to become a real boyfriend."

"Oh," George says. "Sure. And that's going to be you?"

"Yeah," I say, willing it into the universe. "It is."

"We're gonna kick their orange asses!" Hudson says, taking center stage. "So, I know, you probably think it's just a relay race, just some stupid points for a stupid game. And I get that. But guess what? We're going to rock at it anyway. Why? Because we rock! We, queer people, are amazing. And I know out in the real world, it's people telling you to be like this or be like that, and it's bullying and it's people calling you names and keeping you down. People saying we'll never win because of who we are. But here is where we gather our strength. Here is where we work on being everything they say we're not. Here is where we prove to ourselves how much we rock so that out there we can prove it to them and beat them in whatever contests and competitions they throw at us! How we can be anything we want! How we are special!" he says, and he locks eyes with me for a moment, his gaze so intense, it feels like he's talking just to me. I can be anything I want. I can do anything I want. "And yeah, maybe today that means running with an egg in a spoon and not dropping it, but so what? Succeeding here is just preparing to succeed out there, even if it is at something silly like a relay race. So let's get out there and show them all what we can do!"

Everyone cheers. Me included. I don't know if it's that I'm better around him, or just that he can make me realize it, but it's like all my anxieties—being the only queer kid in school, having no close friends outside of camp, my parents being supportive but also treating me like an alien, always watching everything I say, or making sure no one pays attention to

me—all of that is thrown off like a drag queen's reveal, and suddenly, here I am, some new amazing superhero: Queer Randy. And all I want to do when that happens is kiss him. Because no one else has ever made me feel like that.

Ashleigh and George make me feel loved. So do my parents, and Mark and Crystal. But Hudson gives me something I don't really get from anywhere else. He makes me feel *special*. Like who I am here—where I don't close my hands on the bus when some jocks pass by so they don't see the nail polish, and have a comeback for anything anyone says to me—can be who I am out there, too.

And I know Hudson isn't talking to me specifically, but it feels like he is. And I think he would, if it were just me in the audience. I think he believes in me, and that makes me feel like I have a thousand stars—a galaxy—inside me, glowing brightly.

"So get in line, and let's run some eggs!" Hudson shouts, and I jump up and cheer and run to be first in line during the relay.

FOUR

The dancing in the cabin eventually changes into putting on our swimsuits for the camp-wide free swim. I'm proud of the swim trunks I found. They're black with white trim, a little tight. I take them out and Ashleigh does a double take.

"Look," she says, putting her hand on my shoulder. "I'm not saying I approve of this crazy plan, but if you're going to do it, you should do it right."

"What?" I ask. "What's wrong with my swimsuit?"

"Trunks," Ashleigh says. "Your trunks. And your shoes."

"I love these shoes."

"That should be your first clue right there," she says. "You're doing like . . . campy straight. The plaid that matches the shoes? The swim trunks that look like something Sean

Connery would have worn in an old Bond film? It's like you're playing straight in a show."

"You can take the queer out of the theater," George says, coming up to us, "but not the theater out of the queer." George is in a white Speedo with a rainbow over the butt. Without his shirt on, I can see that the hint of hair I saw before is a full-on forest over his chest and belly.

"So how do I fix it?" I ask. "I have these in black and red and blue. That's it."

"They should be okay," Ashleigh says. "But let's see the rest of the wardrobe."

I lead them to the cubby I have for my clothes, where everything has been neatly folded and arranged by color.

"See," Ashleigh says. "This could work. You just need to put it together differently. Less thought out."

"Are we going to have a fashion show?" George says. Everyone else who's been getting ready in the cabin pauses and looks over, wide-eyed.

"Fashion show?" asks Montgomery, a thin redhead a year older than us who, when telling stories of his school year in LA, has already described himself as "that bitch" four times.

"Don't tease," says Paz, also a year older than us, with a shaved head and dark skin.

"Fashion show!" chant the other campers. "Fashion show!"

Ashleigh grins, and she and George start rifling through my clothes, throwing things at me.

"Montage!" Montgomery shouts, and for the next twenty minutes I'm modeling different outfits for them, to calls of "Ooh, honey, butch!" and "She almost passes!" Even Mark, who seems annoyed by all of this, eventually gets into it—although it also feels like he's mocking me as he puts on "How Lovely to Be a Woman." But maybe that's just because it's from the show. Even with the counterintuitive soundtrack, though, I'm loving it, modeling each of the outfits with all the masculinity I've been practicing over the year—legs apart as I walk, hips forward, nods with my chin. I even flash my abs and show off the guns I've managed to build up. Some of the boys stare at me a bit differently after that—like I'm someone new. Which, I guess is the whole point.

When the little fashion show is over, I have a different selection of outfits. They're...no fun, frankly. I get it—they're kind of sexy in a threw-it-on-that-morning sort of way. But nothing matches, nothing is neat, everything just feels haphazard. If there's a style here, I don't see it, or at least, it's not for me. Still, everyone assures me that they'll get the job done. And what are clothes, really, next to love?

"Well, now that that's over, let's get to the pool," Mark says. "Come on. No one left behind."

I change into the black swimsuit and grab my towel and follow everyone else down the stairs to the bottom level of the camp. This is where the camp feels huge. I don't know

exactly how big it is, but it's got to be a few miles in each direction. You can't see the river—the far end—from the steps, though I guess you can see the dining hall from the drama cabin, which are at the two other farthest ends of the oval that encompasses camp. The pool is right by the stairs, though, and is already filled with campers shrieking and splashing. The water looks great, but as we get close, Ashleigh grabs George's and my arms. I look over at her. She's staring at the lifeguard. I look, too. Then I see who it is.

"Janice," Ashleigh says in a whisper.

"Darling, it's fine," George says.

Almost all the staff at Camp Outland is queer—except the lifeguards and kitchen staff. They need to be certified by the state, and it's hard enough finding local queer staff (at least, this is how Mark explained it a few years back), so Joan uses a company that brings people in. Joan keeps an eye on all of them, of course. "She can spot a homophobe from a hundred yards," Mark says. "Why do you think she looks so tired all the time?"

Most of the lifeguards are straight, though. Even Janice Uncas, with her long lavender curls and lip ring, and who's only a year older than us, so it's totally okay, as Ashleigh has pointed out. Last summer, Ashleigh grew really close with her. Not sexy close, but close enough she fell a little in love. And a little in love with a straight girl, near as I can tell, meant a lot of pain all summer.

"It's okay," I tell Ashleigh. "She's your friend. You're over her, right?" Ashleigh had sent us a long e-mail in November about how over her she was.

"Yeah," Ashleigh says. "I just…didn't think she'd be back. I thought she was going to spend the summer with her grandparents, doing Mohegan Tribe stuff. That's what she said."

"I guess things changed," I say.

"She's waving at us," George says. "Wave back."

We all wave back, and then start walking again.

"I just don't want to do this again," Ashleigh says. "I'm going to keep my distance. Stay polite, but not, like, best friends, like last summer."

"Good plan," I say.

"We'll hold you to it," George says.

"Okay," Ashleigh says, pulling at the straps on her black one-piece, which is dotted with skulls. We walk past the safety fence around the pool and past the changing rooms to the pool itself, where George jumps in. I immediately spot Hudson, in a blue swimsuit—trunks, I mean. I hop in before he sees me, up past the waist so he doesn't see the not-quite-masc-enough trunks. The water is a little cold, but the air is warm, so it's nice, and a moment later I dip down to my neck.

"Darling, show off the abs," George says. "Here he comes."

Hudson is indeed swimming over, his dark hair plastered

across his forehead. Brad is with him, and in a moment they're standing in front of me, George, and Ashleigh. There's a long moment where I check out Hudson without his shirt on—the carved but not too carved abs, the strong shoulders that would probably be perfect for sleeping on—and I realize he's checking me out, too, tracing the trail of hair from my belly button down. I blush and dive under to hide it, popping up again a second later.

"You two done admiring each other?" George asks.

"I was admiring you," Brad says to George.

"You grow a little body hair and suddenly they notice you," George says to Ashleigh. Ashleigh is just staring at Janice, though, oblivious to us.

"I've noticed you before, George," Brad says. George looks a little surprised he knows his name. "But yeah . . . the hair looks good on you. I'd like to lick—"

"Sometimes less is more, darling," George interrupts. "But thank you." He smiles and bats his eyelashes. Brad bites on his lower lip, smiling.

"You're welcome. How was everyone's year?" Brad asks, and Hudson looks confused.

"Bro, Del is new," he says to Brad.

"Del?" Brad asks.

"Darling," George says suddenly, "why don't you and I go talk more about the wonders puberty has worked on my body over in the deep end?"

"Yeah?" Brad grins. "Sure." I shoot George a thank-you

35

with my eyes. Hopefully he can keep Brad from ruining the plan.

They swim off, and Ashleigh, still staring at Janice, starts to swim away, too.

"I'm going to go talk to Janice," she says.

"No, you said—" I start to say, but then Hudson has his arm on my shoulder—my naked shoulder—and I can't speak for a moment. I turn to look at him. He smiles. His eyes are dark gray with just a hint of blue, and the water flashes on them like sequins.

"So," he says. "I'm glad they left us alone."

"Yeah," I say.

"Relatively speaking," he says, gesturing at the rest of the camp swimming around us.

I laugh. "Yeah."

"So, did you just come out recently?" he asks, leaning against the side of the pool and sliding down to his neck. I copy him, and it feels more intimate—our heads above the water, our bodies under it, blurred by the surface, so it looks like we're touching.

"No," I say. "I came out when I was twelve." That's the truth. Easier to stick to the truth.

"So, your parents just didn't want to send you to a queer camp, then? Afraid it would be, like, all orgies and drag shows? Mine were freaked out about that."

"Something like that," I say. That's a lie. My parents were great about sending me here. They were the ones who found

the camp and suggested it four years ago. But I can explain that later. For now, he thinks this is my first year, and I'm keeping it that way.

"I just told them, it's like any other camp, but no one is going to be afraid to get in a pool with me or anything."

"Afraid to get in a pool with you?" I ask. "Who thinks like that?"

"Just some kids from my school. I came out when I was twelve, too. Outed, kind of, except to my folks. It didn't go well. School in the suburbs of western Virginia isn't exactly super liberal. So here, it's like...a vacation, you know?"

"Yeah. In Ohio, too," I say. "I don't think I have it as bad as that, though. People mostly just ignore me."

"Hard to imagine that." Hudson wiggles his eyebrows, and under the water, his knee brushes mine and I look down to cover my blushing.

"Well, it happens," I say. "I'm sorry you were bullied, though."

"Not bullied, really," he says. "I don't like that word—it sounds so dramatic, or like I'm a victim or something. But let's not talk about it. We're at queer camp now! Everything rocks."

"Yeah," I say, our knees now firmly against each other. "Everything is perfect."

We're suddenly splashed as George does a cannonball a few feet from us, Brad doing another right after him. George swims over to us, narrowing his eyes.

"Where's Ashleigh?" he asks.

"She went..." I remember and it hits me so hard, I think I might sink. "She's talking to Janice. I tried to stop her." But not enough.

"Not that hard, by the looks of it," he says, now swimming to the edge of the pool and hoisting himself out. "Come on, we have to stop her."

"Wait, what?" Hudson says.

"Sorry," I say, following George. "She made us promise."

"Should I come?" he asks.

"No," George says. "You'll just be a distraction."

"Come back soon," Hudson says, crossing his arms over the edge of the pool and resting his chin on them.

"I will," I say. "Or I'll see you at dinner."

"Okay," he says as I follow George around the side of the pool.

"Brad will keep his mouth shut, you're welcome," George says quietly as we walk—no running by the pool. "I told him you hit your head."

"What?" I half whisper, half shout.

"It was what came to mind, after what Mark said," he says, hands up in mock defense. "You have some memories, but not all of them. And reminding you of stuff could make you have a meltdown. So we decided it's best if Hudson thinks you're new."

"Why would you say that?" I ask, but we've reached where Ashleigh is sitting next to Janice, their feet dipped into

the very deep end. Janice isn't in the lifeguard chair (some older guy is manning it), but she has sunglasses on and keeps her eyes on the pool. She's focused, but she smiles as Ashleigh talks, and they both laugh at something as we approach them.

"That's so funny," Janice says as we sit down next to Ashleigh. Ashleigh looks over at us and frowns a little.

"What's so funny?" George asks.

"Ashleigh was telling me about this guy who kept trying to ask her out at school," Janice says. "You should tell it."

"Oh, so he just wouldn't get the hint," Ashleigh says. "So finally I just grabbed my closest straight friend and said, 'Can we just make out in front of him until he goes away?' and she was like, 'okay,' and so next time he came over to bother me, I started making out with her and he was all offended! He said, 'You should have said something.' As if repeatedly telling him I was a demisexual lesbian wasn't enough? Then he called us dykes and ranted about me on Instagram—but at least he stopped asking me out."

"Yeah, that's funny," George says, throwing me a look. We both know a story about her making out with a straight girl is probably not something that just came up. "But, Ashleigh, we have to go back to our cabin—remember what we talked about?"

Ashleigh frowns, knowing we have nothing to go back to.

"Remember?" I say. "You made us promise."

"Yeah," she says. "Sorry, Janice, I'd better get back."

"That's okay. See you later."

"Later," Ashleigh says as we get up. We all start walking back to the other side of the pool. I'm about to jump in and rejoin Hudson, but Ashleigh tugs on my arm. "We said we were going back to the cabin. She'll know I'm avoiding her if we don't."

"Right," I say with a sigh. I catch Hudson's eye and frown and shrug, letting myself be dragged away by Ashleigh. He waves at me, a sad look on his face.

We trudge back up to the cabin, Ashleigh frowning. "Sorry," she says. "Sorry, sorry. I know I said I wasn't going to do it, but, like, there aren't many girls here I really click with enough to want to…"

"Darling, you're at a queer camp. Have you tried clicking with the other girls?"

"Well…," she says. "Daphne, two years ago."

"She's gone," I say. No campers over eighteen allowed. Everyone keeps in touch—we just don't see them during the summer anymore. It's kind of sad, but then we hear stories about them going off to college and living every day like it's camp, and it's more like they've escaped than they've left.

"I know, but, like, I need to know someone, really like them, before I want to… you know. I don't just think 'she's hot' about some girl and then try to go after her. And it feels like no one wants to get to know me."

"That's idiotic," George says.

"Hard agree," I say. "Not everyone is demisexual. Plenty of the girls want to get to know you."

Ashleigh laughs. "Yeah, but then what if I don't like them?"

"Then walk away," George says. "But promise me you'll talk to someone besides the straight girl this summer?"

"Yeah," Ashleigh says as we reach our cabin. "Yeah, thanks, guys."

"What was going on with you and Brad?" I ask George as we hop in the showers. The bathroom has four sinks and six showers, each with their own stall and towel hook so no one can see us naked, but we can still talk. We shout over the water.

"That sort of thing has been happening a lot lately," George calls back. "I got hairy, now everybody is into me all of a sudden. The boys at school barely noticed me before; now I've slept with three of them."

"You've had sex?" I ask, happy he can't see me blushing red in the shower. I have not. I mean, made out, sure, and it's not like I don't know how it feels when another guy's body is against yours and he's horny. Two summers ago, Carter Monroe kind of implied he wanted to get naked with me after we spent some time making out, but I want my first time to be special. And with Hudson.

"Mmm-hm," George answers.

"Why didn't you tell us?" Ashleigh asks.

"It didn't seem like that big a deal," George says. "I'm from Manhattan, darlings. Sex is just something you do sometimes."

I blush again and force myself to laugh.

"Oh, don't try that jaded act with us," Ashleigh says. "We know you. You're supposed to tell us this stuff."

"I guess...," George says, his voice a little hard to hear under the water. I finish washing and turn the faucet off, then start drying myself with my towel. "Look," he says, "it was...embarrassing. Like, suddenly I look more adult and people want me and I jump into bed with the first of them who offers? I didn't want you guys to think I was a slut."

"Why would we think that?" I ask, wrapping my towel around my waist.

"Well, you're holding out for Hudson, and Ashleigh is only into girls if she has a real bond with them, and here I am, screwing a guy whose last name I don't remember."

"Was it fun?" Ashleigh asks.

"A little," George says, turning the water off. "The first time was awkward. But then it was fun. Lots of fun. Highly recommended."

Ashleigh and I both laugh.

"I don't think you're a slut," I say, doing my hair in the mirror. Styling it to look like I don't care how it looks is very difficult.

"Me neither," Ashleigh says, coming out of the stall, already dressed in denim cutoffs and a black tank top. She

runs her hands through her hair, then heads back into the main cabin.

"Thank you, darlings. But remember, if anyone cute asks, I'm a complete whore." He pushes open his shower curtain and steps out, his huge pink towel wrapped around his chest and still almost hitting the floor.

"How about Brad?" I ask.

"Maybe," George says, tilting his head and shaking a can of hairspray in front of the mirror. "He's cute. But it's only the first day."

I finish in the mirror and go back into the cabin to get out one of the pre-selected masc-enough outfits, this one a white T-shirt and blue shorts, then come back to the bathroom, hop into the stall, and change. When I step out, George is scrunching his hair, and Ashleigh is back, applying dark lipstick in the mirror.

"So," I say. "After dinner, can you show me the tree? Make sure Hudson is following us—but at a distance."

"How are you going to arrange that?" Ashleigh asks.

"I think if we all eat with them, and then after, as we're leaving, you pull me aside or something and you're like, 'We need to show you something,' and head toward the obstacle course, he'll follow."

"He'll follow without being seen?" George asks. "I'm as much for wacky hijinks as the next homo, but this feels like a stretch."

"It doesn't really matter if he follows us—he just has to

know we went off to see it. But if he does follow, then I can talk about how I'd never be just another conquest for a man like that," I say, putting my hand to my chest and looking like a Victorian woman who's just been offended.

"Maybe not like that if you want to keep this charade up," George says.

Ashleigh snorts a laugh.

"I just need a reason to be cold to him," I say. "Make it clear I want a real relationship."

"And what makes you think he won't just move on to an easier guy?" George asks.

"Who else fits his profile?" I ask. "Who he hasn't already taken to the Peanut Butter Pit, I mean."

"There might be some new guys," Ashleigh says.

"Or who knows, maybe he'll repeat."

"We have a connection," I say. "He's already made his move. He's not looking at anyone else, and he likes a challenge. He might fake the long-term-relationship-guy thing at first, but he'll take it slow. And slow is all I need to make him really fall in love."

George shoots a glance at Ashleigh in the mirror. They both have the "our friend is nuts" look on their faces. Behind us, the other campers start to come in. Jordan walks in just as George and Ashleigh are looking at each other and giggles.

"Maybe you could tell Brad, too," I say to George. "Let him know I'm a romantic, not just another mark on the tree,

and Hudson will have to really woo me. Y'know, since my head injury."

George rolls his eyes. "Well, I do like a bigger role," he says. "Though I usually prefer comedies to outright farce."

"Did you hurt your head?" Jordan asks, hopping in the shower.

"No," I reply quickly.

"It's just part of the plan, darling!"

"The romance plan?" Jordan asks, sticking their head out of the shower. They have very short blunt bangs and the rest of their head is nearly shaved, giving their face a very punk vibe, which always amuses me, because Jordan is a giant softie who has seen every romantic comedy movie ever, multiple times. "I LOVE the plan! It's like *Pillow Talk!*" They pop back into the shower. "Or *How to Marry a Millionaire*, what with the planning. How to marry a masc-ulaire!" They giggle.

"Everyone knows?" I ask George and Ashleigh.

"The cabin does." Ashleigh shrugs. "Did you think no one would notice? Or figure it out?"

I laugh. "Okay. That doesn't matter, because it'll be great," I say. "It will work great." I hope. I've turned over all the ways to do this during the course of the year. Getting Hudson's attention was straightforward, but holding it for longer than two weeks is the hard part. But this should work. Not just saying I'm an LTR kind of guy, but making myself

a challenge for him. He's never had one of those before, not really, but everyone knows how competitive he is. Always has to be on the winning team in capture the flag. Always has to run through the obstacle course the fastest. Well, he wouldn't give up on a guy he liked, right? Just another challenge. And a challenge means time, time together, which leads to us falling in love. It's a solid plan, or so I tell myself as George and Ashleigh exchange another look and George goes to change. Definitely not a plan I got watching too many old romantic comedies.

"So I have to be the bad guy, then?" Ashleigh says, crossing her arms and leaning against the bathroom wall. "Lead you to the tree, warn you of Hudson's manizing ways?"

"Yeah, if that's okay."

"I'm not an actor, you know. I'm a techie."

"No acting required," I say. "You clearly think this is a bad idea."

"Look," she says, walking back into the cabin, where George has slipped on a bright green satin robe with big flowing sleeves, embroidered with blue carnations. I have a matching purple one with gold-and-white lilies—we both bought them at the same time when I found the link online and sent it to him two years ago, between summers, and brought them last year. But I left mine at home this summer. "It's not that I don't want you to get with him, if you think that'll make you happy. It's just...this whole plan. Pretending to be someone else. Where does it end?"

"We fall in love," I say, following her.

"And then what?" she asks. "You keep being Del the rest of your life?"

I shrug. "Once we're in love, I'll gradually turn back into Randy."

"The guy he didn't fall in love with," Ashleigh says. "You see where I'm confused? This script is all over the place."

"It's all about how you play it," I say. "Besides, what's the worst that happens? I don't get the guy?" Please let that not happen. Please, please, please. I force myself to smile. "Then all this will be over, and you won't have anything to worry about."

"Except your broken heart," she says.

"Well, then you can say you told me so." Please oh please let her not have a reason to tell me she told me so.

"Darlings, let's not fight. Randy has a plan, and he's asking us to help, and if it all goes sideways, then at least it will be a story to tell people, right? It's only love, no need to take it so seriously."

"Right," I say, but I'm holding my smile so tightly, my jaw aches.

"Fine, fine," Ashleigh says. "I just want it on record that I don't see this ending well, and I don't like you changing who you are just for some guy. You can find a guy who loves you for you."

"But they won't be Hudson," I say. "If you just had to change your wardrobe a little to make Janice fall for you, would you?"

Ashleigh climbs into her bed. "Yeah, okay, I get it," she says.

Mark walks in just as she finishes talking. "What?" he asks. "Pool time too boring for you? Too much gossip you didn't want the camp to hear?"

"Something like that," George says, plucking a sandal-wood fan from under his pillow and opening it. "Plus my hair needs time to air-dry before dinner."

"Well, at least that's a decent excuse," Mark says, going into the counselor's room (we've seen inside; it's miniscule, with two twin beds and a nightstand, but I guess counselors have earned a little more privacy). "Dinner is at six, so be dressed by then."

A moment later, the other campers start coming in, showering off and changing into their dinner best. Even George, after his hair is dry enough, changes into a purple T-shirt with a picture of Ariana Grande as the Virgin Mary on it and a pair of very short black shorts. Someone puts on the *Bye Bye Birdie* soundtrack and everyone sings along, practicing for their auditions tomorrow. I smile and listen and sometimes sing along, even though tomorrow will be very different for me.

FIVE

LAST SUMMER

He is so pretty," I say again, lying in the grass and watching Hudson run across the green. It's capture the flag during color wars, and George, Montgomery, and I have gotten ourselves captured so we can sit on the sidelines and watch. Montgomery is in green cutoffs, so short you can see his ass from the bottom, and a black crop top. George and I didn't want to recycle our outfits, so we're in pink and purple, respectively—but our nails are painted green, and conveniently the silk fan I brought from home is a pretty chartreuse, so I've been carrying it around in my back pocket, and now I'm fanning myself with it. Hudson has his shirt off and he gleams with sweat as he runs across the soccer field. I might be drooling a little. But the fan covers it.

"Darling, you have got to get over this crush," George says. "Or come up with a plan for getting his attention."

"I'm working on it, sweetie," I say. "I have some ideas." I pluck a stray daisy and tuck it behind my ear.

"Oh, really?" Montgomery asks. "Like what?"

"Like I just have to make him want to talk to me," I say, tucking another daisy behind the other ear. "If I can make him feel half as good as he makes me feel, just by talking, I know he won't want to give that up after two weeks."

Suddenly, as if he can hear us talking, Hudson runs over to us. George and I exchange a worried look, but he taps us each on the shoulder, and then runs back to his side. He looks behind him and grins a big goofy smile.

"C'mon, dudes!" he shouts. "I freed you!"

The three of us shrug, then stand up and run over back to his side of the line. I tuck my hair behind my ears and wait next to Hudson, who's smiling at us.

"So, no thank-you?" he says.

"Thanks," I say.

"Darling, it was a waste of a trip," George says. "We're useless at this game."

"Nah," Hudson says, looking right at me. "I know you'll be good at it. Just give it a try." I smile back at him, this stupid, doofy smile, because I can feel this warmth in my chest, this feeling like when I did a tequila shot that one time, and I feel looser and stronger. No one has ever believed I could be good at anything athletic. I'm a theater kid, a sissy, I can

barely throw a ball. Even my dad said maybe it "wasn't our thing" the first time we tried playing catch in the backyard and the neighbors snickered at us. And Hudson can see all that. He can see my painted nails and loose wrists, and he can still believe I'd be good at it if I tried.

And then he runs off. I turn to George.

"See?" I say. "He's divine."

Montgomery watches Hudson running. "He's got a great ass, at least," he says, folding his arms.

"I'm going to go for the flag," I say, slapping my fan closed and tucking it in my back pocket. "Cover me?"

"What?" George says.

"Are you nuts?" Montgomery asks, but I'm across the line into enemy territory before I have time to answer, dodging the other campers as they try to tag me, going for the bright orange flag on top of the hill on their side of the camp. And suddenly I realize I CAN do it. I can do whatever I want, really, and I'm close to the hill and I can see Hudson ahead of me, too, and I get close, like we're going to do this together, we're going to steal this flag as a duo, and he looks over and flashes me that smile.

And I trip. Fall on my face. Someone tags me right away, but Hudson manages to steal the flag, and he's running with it before someone tags him, too. He walks into jail and sits on the grass next to me, grinning, sweat pouring off him. He smells like dirt and the sun.

"Thanks for that distraction, bro," he says, raising his fist.

51

I realize I'm supposed to bump it, and do, though it feels forced and stupid.

"Yeah." I nod. "I did that on purpose."

"You were really going out there," he says, and I can't tell if he believes my lie. "I told you you'd be good at it if you tried."

"I guess so," I say.

He grabs some grass out of the ground in a handful, then puts it back down, patting it into the earth. "You know," he says. "We don't have to be whatever they say we are. We can be athletes and superheroes. We can be strong and fast and kick ass. We just have to put our fingers in our ears and stop listening to them, and just let ourselves want to be those things. Want to be greater. Then we can be anything."

"Yeah," I say, and I feel that warm feeling inside me again, like stars. I wonder if he can sense it. I wonder how I can make him feel this way.

"Come on, losers," Ashleigh says, walking up to us slowly, like she doesn't care, and tagging us each on the shoulder. Ashleigh actually loves capture the flag but says she prefers to be a "spy"—make them think she doesn't care about playing, sidle up to the flag, stuff it in her pocket, and just walk back. It's never worked, but she says one day it will.

"See you later, man," Hudson says, running back to our side before launching himself at the enemy's flag again.

"Later," I say.

"You're smiling like a chorus boy who chugged a Red Bull before the big number," Ashleigh says.

SIX

At dinner, Brad and Hudson sit down with us without my even waving them over. Everything is going so much better than I ever could have hoped. The only disappointment is the actual food—dry hamburgers and weirdly soft french fries, like they're wet. But no one really minds the bad food here—not when there's so much ambiance.

The dining hall is...amazing. There's no other word for it. A huge log cabin from the outside, but inside, every log painted a different stripe of the rainbow. Instead of fluorescent lights, there are strings of rainbow Christmas lights, and then big dangling white lamps that Joan (who's a metalworker) made. They're each the size of a beach ball and look like stars. Sure, the lighting is a little dim, but who wants to see the food too clearly anyway? Under the stars, dark wooden tables are

set up in a square and we can all sit and eat wherever we want. Platters of food and pitchers of bug juice and water are passed around, family style, and folks with dietary restrictions can go to the kitchen door and are handed their meals. It's astounding. Every time we eat, it's a family meal under the night sky. And sitting next to Hudson, the dim light making his skin glow, it feels like a romantic date.

"Sucks you had to leave the pool early," he says. The clatter of people talking around us is loud enough that by talking softly, no one else can hear. He pushes his thigh up against mine.

"Yeah, sorry," I say.

"No worries, I get it. So, how are you liking everything?" he asks. "It rocks, right?"

"It really does," I say. "I feel so . . ."

"Free?" he asks.

"Exactly."

George elbows me, and I turn. He's holding out a tray of fries and I take it, scooping some off onto my plate, and pass it to Hudson, who passes it on.

He sticks a fry in his mouth and I watch his lips close around it and suddenly feel very thirsty. I turn as the bug juice pitcher comes my way, and I pour for myself and for Hudson and then the tray of burgers is in front of me, looking like reheated McDonald's. But it's food. I take one.

"When I first came here," he says, taking the tray and a burger, "it was just . . . like I could breathe? But I hadn't

known I'd been holding my breath? And there are so many different types of queer people here, too. I'm the only one I know at home. Before here, I thought that aside from me, they were all like the ones on television."

I laugh. "What, *Will and Grace* reruns?"

"And *Queer Eye*," he says. "That teen rom-com that came out a few months ago didn't play anywhere near me, so I have to wait until it's on Netflix. Maybe they'll show it here, actually. We do movie nights when it's raining."

"Yeah?" I turn away from him so he can't tell I already knew that, and bite into my burger. It tastes like cardboard.

"Yeah," he says, leaning into me slightly. "We should go together."

"You asking me out?" I ask.

"Yeah." He grins. "I am. You interested?"

"Yes." I nod, feeling warm all over. "I will definitely go on a date with you next time it rains."

He laughs. "I better find a way to make it rain, then," he says.

I almost choke on the fry I'm eating, suddenly picturing him in a thong, gyrating onstage as dollar bills rain down around him.

"You okay?" he asks, patting me on the back. He hands me my cup of bug juice and I take a sip.

"Thanks, sorry," I say. "You just said make it rain, and I thought of strippers."

"Oh." He smiles, a little tightly. "Yeah, ha."

"Sorry, should I not have said strippers?"

He laughs. "No. You can say strippers. But I'm not wearing body glitter for you. I don't think that's hot."

"Yeah." I nod, though I think it sounds very hot. "That's not what I meant."

He puts his hand on my thigh and squeezes, briefly, then pulls it back. "But play your cards right and I'll tell you what does sound hot," he says, leaning into my ear. I must flush scarlet, because across from me, Ashleigh raises her eyebrows. She's doing what she promised and is talking to Paz, who broke up with her girlfriend over the school year.

"I should tell you," I say to Hudson. "I'm...not...that is, I'm...I think you're really cute, and you seem great, and we click, but a date first," I say. "You know what I mean?"

He leans back slightly, but he's smiling, looking at me a little differently. Before he was almost predatory, but now he looks sweeter. "I get exactly what you mean. I promise, we can take it easy. First I have to work on that rain, right?"

I laugh. "Maybe stripping is the way to do it, though."

His smile changes again, wolfish. His gray-blue eyes narrow and his eyebrows wiggle. "I would have said that, but I thought you wanted to take it easy."

I lean into him, knocking our shoulders. "I do. I'm just offering helpful suggestions. I want it to rain, too."

"So, maybe," he says, like he's just coming up with it, "we try going and hanging out together—a date-like situation— even if it doesn't rain?"

"That's such an interesting idea," I say, playing along. "I think I could go for that. Though, I'm new. What would we do, if we can't watch a movie?"

"We have time after dinner before the talent show. There's plenty to do—people like to hang out at the boat-house, or there's a bonfire at the flagpole, sometimes. Or…" He lights up. "I could give you a tour. Since you're new."

"That sounds nice," I say. "I'd love to see the sights."

He laughs. "In fact, since we wouldn't want it to rain for that—we could do it right after dinner. Tonight. Before the counselor talent show."

"Tonight?" I ask. This is really going way too well. "I…" I glance over at Ashleigh, who's smiling at Paz. "Ashleigh said she wanted to show me something. A tree? But after that, I'm all yours."

I turn back to him, and his perfect skin has colored slightly—the palest of pink. "Tree?" he asks. "A special tree?"

I shrug and use all my acting skills not to smile. "That's what she said."

"You can skip that, though, right?" He turns to his food and starts gobbling it down. I finally found his one flaw: He's not a cute eater. Why does that make him generally cuter?

"Seems rude," I say. "She's my bunkmate, and she's made a real effort to become my friend. You want to come? Do you know what tree she means?"

"Yeah," he says. "I think I do."

I stare at him in silence, and take another bite of my

burger, another fry. To my right, I hear Brad and George cackling in unison at something.

"Something wrong?" I ask gently.

"It's fine," he says. "Just...you should know. The tree. There was this guy, Hal. And he looked kind of like me. And his name is on the tree. A lot."

It takes every inch of training not to let my eyes widen in shock. This is not where I thought this would go. He's actively pretending to be someone else.

Well...that makes two of us.

"There are names on the tree?" I ask.

"Yeah." He smiles, takes a long drink of water. He seems more relaxed. Apparently he's happy with his own plan. "But that's all I'll say. Keep it a surprise. It's really...like, amazing. Nothing you'd see anywhere else."

"Okay...." I try to sound suspicious. But inwardly, I'm freaking out. This is not part of the plan. I take a long drink of juice and finish my burger just as the dessert platter comes around—cupcakes, very slightly burnt.

Our thighs press together as we eat—chocolate is chocolate, burnt or not—and when Joan dismisses us, we walk together outside, where Ashleigh is waiting for me.

"Come on," she says with absolutely no inflection. "I'm going to show you the tree I told you about now." She waves. The acting is far worse than I could have imagined. I glance up at Hudson, worried she's just given everything away, but he's smiling, apparently not seeing anything wrong.

"Okay," I say. "Hudson is coming, too."

"He is?" she asks.

"Yeah," he says. "I know some people think I'm on there. But that was Hal. He looks like me, but he's not here anymore."

Ashleigh starts to laugh. "What?" she asks.

"I'm just saying…" He pauses, sees George and Brad, and waves them over. "Brad, bro, you know me, right? I'm not on the tree, right?" Brad furrows his brow, confused. "But Hal, the guy who isn't here anymore—he is. And he looks a lot like me, so people thought…"

Ashleigh keeps laughing, but she's trying to hide it at least now. I can't blame her. This is what happens when non-theater people try to do improv.

"Riiiiight," Brad says after a long moment of Hudson and Brad staring at each other. "Hal. Yeah. Hudson's never been on the tree."

"What is this tree?" I ask—my acting being the best going on in the immediate area.

Ashleigh stops trying to hide the laugh and bends over. "I can't," she says. "I…George."

George immediately steps in front of her. "I'll show you the tree, darling," he says, keeping a perfectly calm face. "Ashleigh seems to be having one of her moments."

"Yeah," I say, "that sounds great, thanks." It's so nice to have a professional scene partner.

George turns around and I follow him, along with

Hudson, Brad, and a still-giggling Ashleigh. George leads us past the kickball field, and the soccer field, into the woods. We follow a trail and come to a huge tree, wide around enough that four or five people would have to link hands to encircle it. It's dark, but not so dark I can't see what's carved into its bark—what I'm supposedly here to see. Hearts, lots of them, and in the hearts, names and initials. Tom and Steven, Becky and Jessica, LR and CS. Hundreds of them. And lots of them—lots—are HAL and . . . well, some boy. HAL. Hudson Aaronson-Lim. Except nope, not anymore. Now it's Hal. An imaginary person. I walk forward and run my hands over the carvings.

"See?" Hudson says. "All this love. All this queer love. Doesn't it just . . . rock?"

"Yeah," I say.

"I hope one day I have someone special enough to carve my name with," he says, and looks at me in the dim light, his eyes wide and sweet.

Behind him, Ashleigh barks another laugh.

SEVEN

LAST SUMMER

Think if I faked drowning myself, she'd give me mouth-to-mouth?" Ashleigh asks, staring at Janice from across the pool like a cat at a bird out the window.

"I think you'd have to stop breathing for that, sweetie," I say.

"And she'd probably do that thing where she pressed down on your chest really hard," George adds.

"She could press anything she wanted as hard as she wanted."

"I don't know female anatomy well enough to understand that," I say. "But I suspect it's too much information."

"Oh, sure, you can dream about what kind of underwear Hudson wears but one reference to Janice's hand on my clit is too much."

George and I stare at her wide-eyed.

"Darling, let's not talk about anything under the under-wear," George says after a minute. "New rule."

Ashleigh chuckles. "Fine. Prudes."

"It could work, though," I say.

"No," George says.

"Not the mouth-to-mouth, but, like, a rescue, adrenaline pumping, bodies intertwined..."

"Don't encourage her," George says.

"It's a good scene!" I say. "A rescue, a thank-you, a look."

"A scene from what? A straight porn?" George asks. "Come on, darling."

"No, no. It's a meet-cute. Now Ashleigh has a reason to try to pay Janice back for saving her life, and they spend loads of time together and fall in love!" I clasp my hands.

"You've sold me," Ashleigh says. "I'm doing it."

"What?" George says.

"Wait, you have to do it safely," I say, but she's already swum out to the middle of the deep end and has started to flail. I sigh. "These things need planning."

"If she dies, I'm blaming you," George says.

I look across the pool at Janice, whose eyes scan the water but don't take any note of Ashleigh's dramatic splashing. But someone else does. Hudson dives in next to us, paddles out to Ashleigh, and grabs her around the waist, then tries to pull her over to us. I suddenly wish I had faked drowning.

"Heroic," George says with a snicker.

"Hey, it really is," I say.

Hudson is trying to pull Ashleigh, but she doesn't want to be rescued by him, so she fights, kicking to get back to the center of the pool. He looks at her, confused. Janice blows the whistle at them.

"Stop roughhousing!" she shouts.

I can see Ashleigh's mortified face even under the hair plastered over it. She swims back over to us, Hudson following her.

"Dude," she says, pushing the hair out of her face, "what was that?"

"I was trying to help," Hudson says, his face all confusion. "You looked like you were in trouble."

"I mean, that was the idea," I say to Ashleigh.

Ashleigh sighs.

"What?" Hudson asks.

"Never mind," Ashleigh says, then grudgingly adds, "Thanks."

"I just...we have to look out for each other, right?"

"Right," Ashleigh says.

"Right," I say at the same time, with much more enthusiasm.

Hudson grins at all of us. This big goofy grin where he knows he's missed something and doesn't care, because he tried to help and thinks maybe he did.

"Stay safe," he says, and swims over to where Brad and some other folks are trying to keep a beach ball in the air.

"Come on," I say. "He just swooped in to rescue you. It's

not even a sex thing, he's just that good a guy. You can't be mad at him."

"I can be mad at anyone I want," Ashleigh says, rolling her eyes.

"It was heroic," George says. "Even I had a bit of a flutter in my pants. But don't worry, darling, he's still all yours."

"Fine, yes, it was very heroic, he's wonderful, he's perfect, and he totally ruined my plan," Ashleigh concedes.

I laugh. "Should have planned it better. Can't try it again now."

"It probably wouldn't have worked anyway, right?" Ashleigh says. "I mean, crazy plans to win someone's heart never work."

"I think that depends," I say, smiling and watching Hudson jump out of the pool to tap the beach ball into the air. "If they're crazy enough, they might."

That night, we have a big campfire and make s'mores and sing songs. Mark has been trying to get the whole camp to sing "I'm Coming Out," but it doesn't work so well with only an acoustic guitar, and we all know it, so we only participate half-heartedly. George is painting Jordan's nails, and Ashleigh has a system going with five sticks speared with marshmallows, all set up at angles, roasting over the fire, which she runs between, rotating.

"Did she really try to fake drowning today?" Jordan asks,

looking down at their nails. They asked if George could do patterns, and George was willing to try, so he's currently painting black hearts over the sparkly pink base.

"The things we do for love," I say.

"See, the faking it is the problem," they say. "In a rom-com, you have to unintentionally almost drown and be saved, and maybe lose your memory in the process. You can't just splash around. They try that in all the teen beach movies, and it never works right."

"Not to be that bitch," Montgomery says from where he sits on a log watching George paint, "but how is it *ever* going to work? Straight people don't go gay because they rescued one. If that worked, I'd set fire to our apartment on a regular basis until I'd worked my way through all the men from the LA's finest firemen calendar."

"Darling, don't make me laugh or I'll screw up Jordan's nails," George says, chuckling.

I grab a marshmallow from one of the bags lying on the ground, wipe the ants off, and impale it with my twig, approaching the fire. Hudson is standing there, roasting two on one stick. His flavor of the week, whose name I've forgotten, is standing nearby, talking to Brad.

"Thanks," I say to Hudson as I stick my marshmallow out over the flames. "Ashleigh won't say it, but what you did was really brave."

He looks at me and grins. "The pool? So, what was that even about, bro?"

I wave my hand. "It wasn't a well-thought-out plan, but suffice to say, it was for love."

"Awww, then I'm sorry I ruined it," he says. "I love love." I notice he does not glance over at his current paramour, and that I've suddenly gotten very warm, even for standing next to the fire.

"Who doesn't?" I ask. "But I think this was love that wasn't meant to be."

"What? Now you're just bringing me down, dude. I only like happy love stories."

"It just seems a very unlikely pairing," I say.

"Aw, don't count her out. If she's really in love, she should go for it, y'know? Get back in there, take out the competition or dive over the obstacles, and win." He pauses and gazes at the fire, the flames reflecting in his eyes. "I think... I think love is special, especially for us queer people, but we have to try harder. Even if it seems unlikely. Because if you feel a connection with someone. If someone makes you feel special... we don't get that so much. We don't get it as much as straight people. So... it has to be worth it. Even if it is doomed or whatever. You just gotta go for it."

I grin into the fire. "Maybe you're right."

"Hey, babe." Hudson's beau comes over. "Is my s'mores done yet?"

"S'more," I say. "Singular."

"Right," he says, rolling his eyes. "I just want something sweet in my mouth."

"Well, I can give you that," Hudson says, grabbing his boyfriend around the waist and pulling him in for a kiss. My marshmallow starts to crackle over the fire, the skin turning black. I pull it out.

"Later," I say to them. They don't even notice as I walk away.

EIGHT

You are officially in the most ridiculous situation of all time, darling. And I am HERE. FOR. IT," George says, fanning himself on his bed back in the bunk after our visit to the tree. "I mean, I knew this would be ridiculous, but I didn't realize how much fun it would be to watch."

"This is not the plan," I say, grabbing a baseball cap and a sweatshirt.

Ashleigh snorts from the bunk above me.

"Would you stop?" I ask. "It's fine, though. I mean, so, he's pretending he's not this big…"

"Playboy," George says. "I've decided we're bringing it back."

"That just works in my favor," I say. "It means he'll try to get close to me."

"I guess your makeover really made the right impression if he pulled that story out of nowhere," George says. "Who knew little boy butch was a closet drama diva? I mean, can you imagine what he could bring to the stage with those improv skills and that level of commitment?"

"I don't know how he thinks we won't tell you," Ashleigh says.

"After your giggling fit, I wouldn't be surprised if he thinks you're too amused by it," George says. "Or he doesn't think we know about his love life enough to comment."

"Are you really going to go through with this?" Ashleigh asks, her voice a little hoarse from laughing. "I mean, you playing Del, him playing Hudson-not-Hal? Neither of you will get to know each other."

"I already know him," I say. "And he'll know me. Just me in different clothes."

"With different mannerisms and interests," Ashleigh says.

"Plus a very slightly lower pitch to your voice and a slower way of speaking—nice touch, by the way. Oscar worthy."

"Thanks," I say, feeling a little proud, though I'm trying to be annoyed at how much they're making fun of me. I put the baseball cap on. I feel my smile trying to force its way off my face, it's so big. I let out a little shriek and stomp my feet. "It's going perfectly. He can feel how right we are for each other—that's why he doesn't want me to know it's him on the tree."

George and Ashleigh stare at me like I've just told them about the joys of breasts. George nods.

"Look," Ashleigh says. "I don't want to be the downer here, but just keep in mind, he's a player."

"Playboy," George corrects.

"Sure. Playboy. And maybe he's just saying he's not Hal to get in your pants because he thinks you want someone who isn't a playboy."

"Or maybe he just was waiting for someone he felt a real connection with," I say.

Ashleigh sighs. "Sure, maybe. But...you told me not to drive headlong into heartbreak again this summer, so I'm telling you the same."

"It'll be fine," I say, checking myself in the mirror. I brush a stray hair. Do I put on the sweatshirt or carry it? I'll carry it for now. It's not that cool out. "Okay, I have to go. I said I'd meet him by the flagpole after I grabbed my sweatshirt. I'll see you guys at the talent show."

"He probably needed time to tell his cabin about his new identity," George says. Ashleigh snorts again.

"This is great," I say, heading for the screen door out of the cabin. "See you later!" I push open the creaking screen door and run out to the flagpole for my date.

I'm there first, but I'm happy about it. I wanted to get out of the cabin and have just a moment to enjoy what's happening. Hudson already likes me enough that he's pretending to be a romantic! George and Ashleigh might think it's funny, and okay, it is, a little, but it's also sweet. He's being the guy I know he always wanted to be, and would be, with

the right guy, and it's like he already knows that that's me. It's not about just trying to get in my pants. That would be way more work than it's worth. He's doing this because he feels something. And that means that this was the right idea, that all the work over the year, skipping the show this summer, it's all exactly what I needed to do. It has to be. It just *has* to.

I look up at the sky. The sun is mostly down now and the horizon is blue and orange and purple, but right above me, the sky is dark and the stars are aligning perfectly in the sky. They wink down at me.

"Hey," comes Hudson's voice behind me, a little softer than it needs to be. I turn around. He's put an old green sweatshirt on over his T-shirt, but it's tight enough that it hugs his stomach and shoulders, almost more revealing than the tee was. I have my sweatshirt in my hand, I realize, and I suddenly wonder if I should put it over my shoulders or my waist, or is that too femme? I should just wear it, so I put it on quickly as he walks toward me, but I knock my hat off, and as I pull the sweatshirt down over my face, suddenly Hudson is close, in front of me, and kneeling to pick up my hat. He offers it to me and I have to bite back a joke about him being a prince and this being a glass slipper, which would definitely result in me singing some *Cinderella* (Rogers and Hammerstein, not Disney).

"Thanks," I say, and shove the hat on. "Sorry, I just got cold."

"Yeah, it can get chilly here at night," he says. "I don't

know if you have that in the summer in Ohio. It's like really hot during the day, but sometimes at night…cool."

"Yeah," I say. We stare at each other in silence and I wonder if he realizes we're just talking about the weather like two idiots or if he's looking into my eyes and wanting to kiss me. I'm feeling both.

"So, tour time," he says, smiling that big, kind of wolf grin he has. When he does it, his tongue is just barely visible, poking between the small gap in his teeth at the top corner of his mouth. "Obviously, this is the flagpole," he says. "There'll be a bonfire here in like fifteen minutes. People will roast marshmallows and make s'mores and stuff. That"— he points, and steps closer to me, to line up his finger with my eyes—"is cabin fourteen. My cabin. Just in case you want to visit sometime."

"We can just do that?" I ask. "Stop by?"

"Yeah," he says. "Until curfew anyway. After that… well, you gotta sneak, so the counselors don't catch you. There's a window at the very back of the cabin, opens onto my bed."

"Top or bottom?" I ask, blushing the moment it comes out and happy that the dark hides it. "I mean—sorry, I don't mean—"

"Vers," he says before I can go on, and winks at me. "Bottom bunk, though. I like being able to just collapse into bed at the end of the day."

"Me too," I say, which is like half true, because who

doesn't like that, but also the first year I took the top bunk and Ashleigh was under me and then I was painting my nails and some dripped on her, so we switched.

"So you can just knock on the window, you know, and I can climb out of it. If there's any reason for that," he says.

I laugh. These are totally the lines he uses every year. I can tell, they're so practiced. But he's using them on me. And it doesn't mean he's still a playboy. He might just know how they work and he wants to connect with me. Ashleigh was being unromantic, is all. I look up again, at the stars.

"Okay," I say. "All good information to have…potentially. But not much of a tour thus far." There. That cooled it down.

"Thus?" he says.

"Thus," I say adamantly.

"Okay, well, thusly, let us commence to the next stop wheretofore is the infirmary," he says, in a terrible British accent.

"Wheretofore," I say.

"Absolutely," he says, walking toward the stairs. The stairs are carved wood stuck into the ground, and they curve up, like mushrooms on a tree. In some places they're narrow, and some wide, and in the dark, they're a little hard to navigate.

"Careful," he says. "These stairs are tricky in the dark. Want to hold my hand for support?"

I take a deep breath before I say, "Sure," and reach out. His

hand takes mine and I feel my dick get hard almost immediately. His hand is warm and a little rough—like maybe I should lend him some moisturizer—but also soft, and when he tightens it around my hand, it's just the right amount of squeeze.

"Didn't think you'd go for that," he says as we walk up the stairs.

"I was trying to call your bluff."

"Well, we definitely just skipped ahead, date-wise. Now we're hand holders," he says. "We're the guys who hold hands within the first five minutes of their first date."

"Only because of these very dangerous steps, though," I say.

"Right," he says, and I can hear how happy he is. "Only 'cause of that."

We reach the top of the stairs and neither of us lets go, even when a mosquito lands on my wrist and starts sucking. Hudson looks at it and swats it away for me. I almost expect him to make a joke about how he's the only one who'll be sucking on me tonight, but if he did I would probably burst into a fit of uncomfortable giggles and run away.

We walk down the path a little to a small clearing where he uses his free hand to point at the three buildings. "So, that's the infirmary," he says. "Cosmo is kind of weird, but also really cool, too. You can go there whenever, and you can just lie down, or he can give you aspirin or Band-Aids if you hurt yourself. Nurse stuff. But he's also just cool to talk to, and he has great stories about Stonewall—he was actually

there. I mean, if you care about that stuff. I know not all of us do. My mom says it's not important, but it's still like...cool to hear about, y'know? He also has bowls of condoms, and lube, just sort of on the desk for anyone to take."

"Just on the desk?" I ask, like I haven't taken some before.

"He says trying to act like no one is going to screw is the dumbest thing he's ever heard, so he wants to make sure we do it safely."

"So people have sex here?" I ask. "In the cabins with people watching?" If I turn the conversation to sex, then I can scale it back, too. If he is just being a playboy like Ashleigh said—and I don't think he is—then I just have to tease and pull back, tease and pull back, until he knows me and we fall in love, and then tease and NOT pull back. Del is a tease.

"No!" Hudson says, then laughs. "I've heard some people have tried—real quiet, under the covers, people sleeping—but they always get caught. And then made fun of for the rest of the summer."

"Do people come here just to hang out—no romance?" I ask, pulling it back.

"Oh, sure. It's camp. Tennis, swimming, waterskiing... but that's all down the hill. So let me finish up here. I take my tour guide responsibilities seriously."

"Okay," I say, laughing.

"Here's the office." He points at the small white building that I've seen every summer, more like a house than a cabin. I nod as though I'm seeing it for the first time. "Joan is there

most of the time. She and her wife live there all year, but her wife is a lawyer, so she's not around the camp much, except for dinner, sometimes."

"Okay," I say, getting a little bored with all the stuff I know already. But I gotta play the part.

"Oh, and this." He runs for the meeting hall, dropping my hand. I frown a little, but I guess we had to stop at some point. "This is the meeting hall." I follow him, trying to act impressed.

"What's it for?"

"Rainy days—movie nights, any outdoor electives that can't meet in the rain might use it, and sometimes..." He swings open the screen door, then tries the heavy wood door behind it. "Oh well. Sometimes they leave it open. This cabin people have definitely had sex in." He grins at me. I grin back, then turn away. Remember, Del is a tease, I tell myself. No pushing him against the cabin and kissing his very soft-looking lips. Not yet.

"But they have to be quiet," he says, "'cause Joan is right there. Last year, these two girls moaned so loud, she heard them and they got kicked out that night."

"For sex?" I ask.

"For being out of their cabins after curfew," he says, closing the screen door and leaning against the cabin wall. It's dark now and the few electric lights have turned on, but most of the light is coming from Joan's place and the infirmary. "It's a queer camp, so they want to stay sex positive,

like not shaming anyone for wanting sex, you know? But the rules are meant to make it difficult to find alone time. But the difficulty is half the fun." He does that smile again where his tongue finds the upper corner of his mouth and presses against the gap between his teeth there.

He takes my hand again and for a moment I think he's going to pull me in for a kiss, but instead he leads me back to the stairs, and down them, back to the cabins and flagpole, where some folks are trying to start a bonfire, and then to the other set of steps, down to the main part of camp.

"So let's see," he says as we walk. He drops my hand when we see some other people on the tennis courts. It makes me a little sad, but I get it—we don't want to look too ridiculous on day one. A slow burn is always more respectable. "So those are the tennis courts," he says. "Do you play tennis?"

"Yeah," I say. Tennis had been one of the easier ways to get fit during the year. Dad set up a net in the backyard. "My dad likes to play, too."

"Cool. I'm pretty bad at it, I have an awful serve."

"I can give you some pointers, maybe."

I can see him smile in the dark. "Maybe." He turns back to the tour and we walk along the grass, taking in the camp. It smells so green and the night has made it smell wet, too— the faint fishiness coming off the lake, but not, like, gross fishy. Other campers are running around with flashlights, scaring each other in the dark, and some counselors are around, watching them. By the drama cabin I see Ashleigh

watching George and my other bunkmates practicing dance moves for auditions.

"So, you saw the dining hall, obviously," Hudson says as we walk. He points. "That's the arts and crafts cabin. The counselor who runs it, Marguerite, is this weird conceptual artist in the real world. I think she has stuff in museums? I don't usually go there; I have zero artistic talent."

"Zero? Really?" I ask. I don't mention he's wildly under-stating Marguerite's weirdness.

"I..." He pauses. It's hard to read his face by just the stars and few electric lights, but he looks almost sad for a moment. But then it's gone, and I decide it's just the dark. "Nah, nothing really. But it's cool if you do. I'm super jealous of people with artistic talent."

"Well, I'm not great at art stuff, either," I say. "But I signed up for A and C. I figured it would be a nice way to relax during the day."

"For sure. And A and C. Listen to you! Already got the slang down."

Drat! Did I overplay my hand? "Well," I say. "I've gone to camp before. Just not this one." It spills out of my mouth without me thinking, but then I realize I'm a genius! This will cover for so many things.

"Yeah? What camp?"

"Oh, just a small Jewish camp in Ohio," I say. "Camp Shalom." It's the most generic Jewish camp name I can think of.

"My dad wanted to send me to a Jewish camp!" he says. "But I told him I really wanted this one. I showed him how the outdoors counselor is an Olympian and then he was okay with it."

"Why wouldn't he have been okay with it?"

"Just…he liked the Jewish camp better," Hudson says, turning away. "Here's the boathouse." He does a presenting motion at the boathouse, which is locked up and dark, the motorboat and canoes parked next to the dock that extends out in front of it. There are no lights on the other side of the river, just trees. It smells like fish and faintly of moss. Hudson points out the boats and talks about waterskiing and canoeing.

"But mostly people hang out on the porch." He points at the covered porch that juts out over the water. "It's great to just chill there, watch the water."

"Cool," I say, trying not to laugh. The porch is prime make-out territory.

"Over here in the woods is the adventure trail stuff," he says. "This is where I spend most of the day. Obstacle courses, hiking…it's awesome."

"I signed up for it, too," I say.

"Cool," he says, putting his hand on my shoulder. "Then I'll show you tomorrow. It's kind of dangerous at night."

We turn and walk away from the river, and Hudson points out more—the soccer field, which is also used for touch football, capture the flag. The farm, with the two pet goats and three chickens. The archery field, the kickball field,

the basketball court. And the drama cabin, which he points out but doesn't have anything to say about. I wish he knew how special it is. I'm not sure he's even been in it, aside from sitting in the audience for camp-wide stuff, like the end of summer show. Maybe he doesn't even go to that. He could go to the bathroom and then go hang out in the woods instead of sitting through the show every year. It would explain how he doesn't seem to recognize me at all, even after my pretty groundbreaking portrayal of Domina in *A Funny Thing Happened on the Way to the Forum*.

"I'm excited for the show," I say out loud, then wince. I am, and I want him to be, too, but we are FAR too early in the plan to change him into a musical theater lover. "I mean, so many of my bunkmates are in it."

"Yeah. It's usually fun, I guess? I feel like it's so not my thing and it just goes over my head," he says. Which is better than I'd hoped—although that means he doesn't sneak out, and he DID see my Domina last year and I'm just going to take it as a compliment on how into my characters I get that he doesn't know Del is played by the same future Tony winner. "I guess I just don't get spending all your time on the show. You can't switch out if you don't like it, and it takes so much time every day there's like no time for anything else. I just think there are better things to do."

I feel my blood get hot and I look away, worried I might be turning red. Better things to do? I'm aghast at the idea. Musical theater is joy. It's expressing stories and song and

dance and a whole community. It's connecting with people—
your castmates, the audience—and playing, and getting to
see the same scene done dozens of different ways until you
find a truth in it you can express. That sounds so pretentious. But it's true. I get to be a version of myself that feels
real every time I act and sing and dance, and here it's queer,
unrestrained by gender or sexuality or any of that nonsense.
Here you get to find out more about yourself in every scene.

But I can't say that. That would give me away. And
besides—he's right. There is something better, otherwise
I would still be doing theater this summer. The something
better is him.

"Yeah," I say, instead of disagreeing. "I see what you
mean." He nods. I nod.

"So, anyway, that's the tour," he says. "You want to head
over to the talent show?"

"Absolutely."

"You have your talent ready?" he asks.

For a moment, I'm actually caught off guard, and panic
seethes through me like the fizz of a shaken soda bottle as
you open it. Did I miss something? It's always the counselors'
talent show first night. Then I get it, he's teasing me. The
new kid.

"What?" I say. "Do I need one?"

He laughs, and takes my hand as we walk toward the
drama cabin. And there aren't even any stairs around this
time. "I'm kidding. First night the counselors put one on.

Camper talent show is usually a few weeks in. And strictly optional. You have any talents?"

My cabin usually puts on a big musical number from a show we're not doing, but I guess I'll have to sit that out this summer. "Not really," I say. "You?"

"Nothing they'd let me do onstage," he says. I can feel his smile in the dark. "But I'd be happy to show you sometime in private."

I wait a beat too long before I say, "Sometime, maybe, in the future."

"Sounds like a plan. Oh, I should warn you, though. The counselor talent show...it can be kind of a lot? Like, it's awesome, sure, yay gay pride, but just...be prepared."

"Okay," I say, trying not to smile. I know exactly what he means. The counselor talent show is one of my favorite events of the summer.

NINE

'm Diana Loan. And I've come to terms with that."

Mark winks, his purple eye shadow sparkling like amethyst under the stage lights, his burgundy-painted lips twisted up in a slight smile. Not Mark, I should say, but Diana, his drag persona. She's got black hair up in an oversized bun, studded with a few white flowers, and is wearing a long-sleeved red gown, showing off her padded curves. It's sequined in some places, and patterned with white flowers in others. Her makeup is painted for the cheap seats, and a pair of long earrings flash as she turns her head in the light and stalks back and forth on stage. The spotlight follows her. It would be impossible not to.

"Welcome, young queer people, to Camp Outland. For you first-timers, hello, I promise to go easy on you. And for you returning campers, well, I guess they didn't want you at

one of the good camps." The crowd chuckles. "Don't worry! We take anyone here, long as they're queer. Just look at Nurse Cosmo!" He points at Cosmo, who's sitting in the front row, grinning. "We let him work here and he's been dead for seven years." Everyone, Cosmo included, laughs, even though she's told the same joke about him since I've been coming here. There's just something about her delivery. Mark might be high-strung, but Diana is cool and confident.

"I'm only kidding," Diana says, waving at Cosmo. "Cosmo is a piece of living queer history. Actually at Stonewall during the riots. He was in a crowd of people who fought the police for our rights. And it made such an impact on him—being right up against all those warriors. You know how some people don't wash their hands after meeting a celebrity they admire? Well, Cosmo hasn't bathed since Stonewall. You can really smell the history on him." That's a new one, and everyone, including me, laughs. Hudson laughs, too, I'm happy to see. I was a little worried after he said it was a lot that it meant he never enjoyed this drag show. And that would be crazy. I don't mind the masc-only thing, but if you can't enjoy a drag queen, you're probably a soulless monster. We're sitting to the left in the back—we were a little late. But I can see George and Ashleigh a few rows in front of us. They glance back once at us, and see us holding hands. George looks impressed. Ashleigh rolls her eyes.

"So, Joan is pointing at her watch, which means 'move it along, Diana,'" Diana continues. "Honestly, Joan always seems

in a hurry to get to the next thing and the next and the next. I think if she had it her way, the summer would be over tomorrow at noon. No, no, we owe Joan a lot. She built this place, keeps it running, so a big round of applause for Joan." Everyone starts to clap and Diana immediately says, "Stop," into her mic. "We have to move it along. So, to open tonight's talent show, we have..." She pulls a list out of her sleeve and checks it. "Oh...all right. I'm sorry about this, but it seems Marguerite from the arts and crafts cabin is going to be singing an original song for us. Everyone, round of applause for Marguerite!"

Diana exits, stage right, as music pipes in over the sound system and Marguerite comes on and does what it essentially an imitation of Björk, something she seems blissfully unaware of. The show continues, Diana introducing each counselor's act—Tina and Lisa, who drive the motorboat, do a decent cover of a Tegan and Sara song; Crystal does a tap number; Rebecca, who runs the canoeing trips, does a cover of an Indigo Girls song (she has a long-standing rivalry with Tina and Lisa); Karl, the German twink who runs the farm and usually is in overalls, comes out in sequined short shorts and a crop top to dance to a Years & Years song; and various other counselors do magic tricks, acrobatics, sing, dance, and are celebratorily, unashamedly queer. Some of the audience even starts dancing for some of the musical numbers. It's like being at a dozen gay clubs in one night—or what I imagine gay clubs are like, having never been to one (not many to choose from in suburban Ohio, and with no one to drive me

to the ones in Cleveland). Hudson even stands and pulls me up to dance when Pablo, one of the tennis counselors, shows off a ten-minute DJ mix of "the history of Madonna." Hudson puts his hand on my waist and we sway together before I realize that I stupidly never practiced dancing masc, and that I'm shimmying my hips much more than Hudson is. I try to imitate him, a sort of gentle sway side to side, but it feels stiff and awkward, and soon we're out of synch. He laughs and leans forward as a remix of "What It Feels Like for a Girl" plays in the background.

"Not much of a dancer?" he asks.

I bite back a rude response about how I'm actually one of the best dancers at camp, and it's just trying to match his lack of style that's holding me back. This is part of the deal—I can be a bad dancer for Hudson.

"Never danced with a boy before," I say. That's true. Oh my god—that's true! I'm dancing with a boy! Hudson has his hand on my waist and he's bringing me closer. Our stomachs are touching and I have to tilt slightly so he doesn't feel my hard-on pressing against him.

"Here," he says, putting his other hand on my waist. "Just sway to the beat. Put your hands on me."

So I do. I put my hands on his shoulders, resisting the urge to wrap them around his neck, and we sway like ten-year-olds imitating adults at a wedding until we reach the end of "I Rise," and one of the chefs comes on to juggle. But when we sit back down, Hudson puts his hand on my leg and

squeezes, and I glance over at George, who wiggles his eyebrows at me. Everything is going so well.

The evening always closes with Diana doing an outrageous lip-synch to a song from the show that Mark has chosen for us every year, and this year, she does a sultry version of "Honestly Sincere." Usually she comes down into the audience and sits in Joan's lap, or flirts with Cosmo, but this year, she makes a beeline to me, wiggling her padded butt between the seats until she's right in front of me, and, singing into the mic, leans forward and brushes my hair back behind my ears—or would, if I hadn't cut it all off.

" 'Write this down now,' " she sings at me. " 'You gotta be sincere, honestly sincere!' " And then she moves back into the aisle, still singing.

Well, Mark was never one for subtlety.

But I look over at Hudson, who grins at me, thrilled I was chosen, and I don't care what Diana was singing at me. I just feel happy. *Sincerely* happy.

After Diana closes the talent show to a standing ovation, we all pour out into the night, heading carefully back up the stairs to our cabins.

"So, that rocked, right?" Hudson asks me. We're not holding hands as we walk up the stairs, but we're in the middle of a crowd, so that would probably make things harder.

"It was amazing," I say.

"That Madonna mix was so good," he says. "I don't know anything about DJing but it just, like, rocked, right?"

"Yeah, and Diana nailed that lip-synch," I say. "Mark is going to be on top of the world tonight."

"Like, for me, drag isn't something I'd seek out," he says. "But I like it once a year. Sometimes, though, I feel like the normal one in there, but like, in a good way."

"Normal?" I ask.

"Like, to the outside world," he says. "Being queer is normal, of course, but then there's other stuff, like drag queens and musicals that I feel like . . ." He pauses. "I sometimes feel like I'm sort of split down the middle—like there's normal world and there's gay world, and here is the only time I get to experience gay world, and I love it—but I also feel like maybe I don't fit in it? And I wish it were more like my kind of gay world? I don't know, I'm not making sense."

"No," I say. "I think I know what you mean. We're definitely here in gay world now, and it can be hard to accept that this is your world—the one you belong in. Straight world—not normal world—doesn't want you. But here you can be anything you want and no one will care."

"I don't think straight world doesn't want me." He laughs. "I mean, we have to live in it, and I feel comfortable there, mostly."

"Well, yeah. But you should feel comfortable here, too."

"I do. I just don't want to be a drag queen, is what I'm saying."

"I don't think anyone is saying you have to be," I say, my turn to laugh. "Especially not with those shoulders."

He gives me a funny look, then laughs, too. We reach the top of the steps and the crowd of campers around us floods out, heading toward their cabins.

"You're really smart about this for someone who's new," he says.

"I thought about it a lot," I say, not exactly a lie. I have thought about it. The first time I put on nail polish outside of camp, I thought to myself, *This is another reason for assholes to be assholes in my direction*, and then I thought, *They're going to do that anyway, you may as well feel a little joy every time you catch your nails sparkling in the light*. And I thought about the boy at camp who'd told me I was special in the dark, and how I felt like I could be. But that's not a story to tell Hudson. Not a Del story.

"Yeah," he says. "Come over here, I want to show you something."

He takes my hand and leads me to the side of the meeting hall, in the shadows.

"What?" I ask.

"Was this a good first date?" His face is half in shadow, his cheekbones sharp in the light, his eyes bright.

"Yeah," I say. "Really good."

"Good," he says. He turns a little so I'm leaning against the side of the meeting hall to look at him now, and then before I realize it's happening, he leans forward and kisses me. I always thought his kisses would be kind of rough, honestly, almost unpracticed—a stupid thought, considering his

history, I know, but his energy is so strong, I thought his kiss would be like a punch. It's not, though. It's soft, but still direct, his tongue carefully opening my mouth as his arms wrap around me. He leans his body into mine and I don't mind he can feel my hard-on, 'cause I can feel his, too. His hands float down to my lower back, pulling me even closer. I know I should be pushing him off—this is more than just a kiss now; this is bordering on making out, and that's too far, that's playboy behavior, that's going to make me just another two-week conquest, but also it's happening and it feels so good. Breath-catchingly good. Singing a solo good. Standing ovation good.

But I call upon the strength within me and I pull away when we pause to breathe.

"Not so fast, now," I say. "Or I'll start to think you have more in common with that Hal guy than you let on."

He looks a little shocked for a moment, and I'm worried I screwed it up, but then he grins.

"Right," he says. "Slow. Sorry. You just...you're a really good kisser."

"You too," I say. I'm still leaning against the wall. My knees are too weak to support me. I didn't think that was an actual thing—weak in the knees—but here I am, so I guess it is.

"That's how a good date should end," he says. "Right? That was okay?"

"Yeah," I say. I want to grab him again. I want to feel him pushing up against me again. I want to wrap my legs

around him and have him hold me up as we keep making out and pushing against each other and—

"So, want me to walk you to your cabin?" he asks.

"Sure," I say. He takes my hand and my knees don't give out as I stand and we walk in silence to my cabin door, where I turn. I can feel my bunkmates watching from the windows.

"Well," he says. "Good night. See you tomorrow."

"See you tomorrow," I say. And he lets go of my hand and walks toward his cabin, glancing back once to find me still watching him. Then I go inside.

"This should not be working as well as it is," George says, leaning against the wall next to the door so he's the first thing I see when I walk in. "It's like some sort of disgusting meet-cute. If you somehow got a dog together before the end of the summer, I wouldn't be surprised."

"Isn't it perfect?" I ask, grinning.

He rolls his eyes but can't help smiling back. "I guess your ridiculous plan really is getting you everything you want. Maybe I should come up with ridiculous plans. Ashleigh, we need ridiculous plans."

Ashleigh is on her bed, going over what looks like a tech manual for lighting equipment. "For what?" she asks.

"I don't know," George says. "What do you want?"

"I want to be stage manager this year," she says, sighing. "But that's not going to happen. It'll be someone from cabin eight, same as always." Cabin eight is where most of the theater tech kids are. Ashleigh only bunks in seven with

us, where the talent is, because of how close we are. "I guess there's the whole falling-for-a-not-straight-girl thing. That's a goal."

"Okay, so…what's a ridiculous plan for that?" George asks. Ashleigh shrugs. George turns to me.

"I don't know," I say, walking over to my bed. "I think it's too vague. Ridiculous only works for really specific stuff. You could try drugging the water in cabin eight, though. Nothing deadly, just, like, make them all so dizzy, they can't read the cues in the script. Then you're stage manager by default."

"I don't want it by default," Ashleigh says. "I'll be happy if I'm just in charge of the lights this year."

"Maybe we need to dream bigger," George says. "I want ALL the parts in the show."

"Over my dead body," says Paz, from the bunk above George's. "I'm going to be a kick-ass Rose. You really want to sing 'Spanish Rose'?"

"A fair point. I want all the parts except Rose, which can be played by Paz."

"I'll still steal the show," Paz says. We all laugh.

The door to the cabin opens and Mark comes in, still in his Diana dress and makeup, but holding his wig. The cabin bursts into applause. Mark bows a few times.

"Thank you, thank you, I think it was a good show tonight."

"Better every year," Crystal says from the wall she's been leaning against, talking to some other campers.

"Help me out of this thing, will you?" he asks, and Crystal runs forward to unzip his dress. "I hope you all had fun. But auditions are tomorrow, so you'd better rest up. Well." He turns a withering Diana look at me. "Auditions are for most of you."

"I wish I could do both," I tell him.

He waddles over, holding up his now unzipped dress with one hand, and sits on my bed. "I just hope the summer doesn't end up being a disappointment for you. You can't join the cast mid-rehearsals, remember. Maybe I could find a place for you on tech, but there's choreography and harmonies."

"I know," I tell him. "I just...haven't you ever done anything crazy for love?"

"So many things," he says, leaning back. The front of his dress falls forward. "There was this one guy, we were doing the chorus of *Funny Face* on a cruise out of Miami. He was beautiful, had a huge—" Crystal clears her throat and he stops, looks at me and the other campers who are listening. "Personality. *Real* big. But he also had a boyfriend—but the boyfriend wasn't on the cruise. So I told him I knew his boyfriend, and that he wouldn't mind if I understudied the role, so to speak. Insane. Got some very angry phone calls when that cruise disembarked. I deserved them, too. I can't work Miami anymore. That's the level of stupid I think this is at."

"But did you love him? Or was it just lust?"

"What's the difference when you're twenty-three?" he

asks. "Or sixteen. Look, I don't want to keep having this conversation with you. Lie, remake yourself, whatever. But just make sure you're really happy, and it's not just that you're super unhappy but you finally got what you wanted so now you have to be happy otherwise what was it all for? That's a classic musical theater plot, and I just won't have one of my actors—even if he is...on sabbatical—play that part in real life. This isn't *Follies*."

"Or *Merrily*," Crystal says.

"Any Sondheim." Mark stands, the dress falling almost to his waist now. "Just be happy, Randall," he says. "You only get four weeks a year. Don't waste them."

I almost laugh. "I won't. I have a plan. And I'm ahead of schedule. I didn't think Hudson would kiss me until the end of the week."

"Kiss?" George nearly shouts.

Ashleigh's head drops over the side of the bed, staring at me. "You didn't mention a kiss."

"There may have been some lip-to-lip contact," I say, looking coy.

"This is not my business," Mark says, going into his room.

"But it's ours!" George says, now staring at me from his bed, stomach down, head propped up on his hands, feet in the air. "Who kissed whom?"

"He kissed me," I say.

"Where?"

"Against the side of the meeting hall."

"When?"

"Just now, after the talent show," I say, laughing at his questions. "It's no big deal."

"Isn't it?" Ashleigh asks. Her head is gone, so she's just a voice above me. "I mean, to you, anyway."

"It was a real kiss. Tongue and everything."

"Hands?" George asks.

"No hands in my mouth, no," I say, confused.

"I mean where were his hands, darling?"

"Oh! Lower back."

"No ass squeeze," George says. "A gentleman."

"Or a playboy who knows the right moves," Ashleigh says. "He kissed you on the first date. Even you said you're ahead of schedule. I thought the point was not to be one of his two-week flings."

"It's fine," I say. "It's going perfectly. I'm holding back enough. He can have my mouth, but not my . . ."

"Darling, don't finish that sentence. Everything about it is wildly inappropriate."

"Yeah," I say, regretting it.

"Was it a good kiss?" he asks.

"It was," I say, trying not to sigh and failing.

"Did he pin the pin on?" Paz asks from her bunk, quoting a *Bye Bye Birdie* lyric. "Or was he too shy?"

"No pins," I say. "We're not going steady . . . yet."

"At least not for good," Ashleigh says.

"What's the story, Morning Glory?" George sings, continuing the song.

"What's the word?" Montgomery responds from across the cabin. I bury my face in my pillow.

"Hummingbird!" Paz responds. And within ten seconds the entire bunk is singing "The Telephone Hour" from *Bye Bye Birdie*, all of them on their beds, miming telephones and doing stylized dance-in-place movements. Mark peeks out, now wearing pajamas, and nods approvingly.

"More head tossing," he says to Jen. "Kick more, Jordan!" He goes around directing as everyone sings. When they finish, he applauds. "Very good start. Now save your voices. Auditions are tomorrow. Lights-out in twenty."

He goes back into his room, nodding to himself.

"It's going to be such a good show this year," George says, standing. "I'm sad you won't be in it, darling." He grabs his toothbrush from his kit and goes into the bathroom. Honestly, I'm sad I won't be in it, too. But this is worth it. It *has* to be worth it.

Which means it *has* to work.

"Going steady for good!" one of my bunkmates sings from the bathroom.

TEN

FOUR SUMMERS AGO

'm woken by crying. It's gentle, almost haunting, and at first I'm worried that maybe there was some truth to what that older camper said about the ghost on our first night, but then I shake my head. Ghost stories are part of camp. Ghosts are not. Though if they were to haunt a queer camp, they'd have to be fabulous, so maybe that would be pretty cool, actually. I sit up in the darkness. The lights are out in the counselors' room, and there's no moon, so it's really pitch-black. I listen.

Yeah, definitely crying, slightly muffled. From right under me.

I'm on the top bunk because I'd never had a bunk bed before and grabbed the first top I could see. Bed, that is. And it's fun literally climbing into bed. Under me is another new

camper, a cute boy named Hudson who everyone is already crushing on. I carefully climb out of bed. It's definitely Hudson crying. I kneel by where I think his head is and I whisper.

"Hudson, are you okay?"

He keeps crying, softly. I reach out and carefully try to touch his arm. I think I graze his cheek instead and pull my hand back quickly. The crying stops for a second.

"Hello?" he asks in a whisper.

"You were crying," I whisper back. "Are you okay?"

He sniffs, the crying apparently over now that he's awake. "Sorry. I was dreaming."

"About what?" I ask, leaning against the leg of the bed.

"It's not important."

"I just want you to feel better," I say. And I do. Because these are the first queer people I've ever met and I want us all to feel better. Better than other people make us feel. I want to be his friend. I want to be everyone's friend. "If you talk about it, you might feel better."

He sniffs again, and I think for a moment he's fallen back asleep.

"It was my grandma," he says. "I dreamed she was back, but in the dream I remembered she wasn't, and..." He sniffs. I think he's crying again. Stupid Randy, making it worse.

"She died?" I ask.

"Yeah," he whispers. "Just before I came here."

"What was your favorite thing about her?" I ask.

"What?"

"It's what my mom asked me when my grandma died. She said if you hold on to your favorite memory of her, it means they're still with you."

"Oh." I'm sure he's crying again now. I hear his hand wipe his cheek. "She was . . . really cool. She sent me here."

"Really?" I ask. "I never even came out to my grandparents."

"She was the first person I told. She gave me this big hug and told me I should always be myself and be proud of who I was."

"That's a good memory."

"Yeah." He sniffs again. "She wanted me to come here so I had friends like me."

"Well, now you do," I say, and I reach up and put my hand on the edge of his mattress. He must feel it, because he puts his hand lightly over mine.

"Thanks," he says. "You won't tell anyone I was crying, right?"

"Not if you don't want me to," I say.

"I just really miss her."

"I know."

The darkness seems to pulse for a second, and he sighs.

"I just wish I could be better at this," he says.

"Better at what?" I ask.

"I don't know . . . all of it. Being gay."

"I don't think there's a better way to be gay," I say. That's what Mark, the drama counselor, had told us all during

auditions last week. That the show was going to be very gay, but that didn't mean what we thought it meant, that it just meant it was going to be very proud. That there was no better gay. I'm not sure I understood, but it feels like something worth repeating now.

"I don't know," Hudson says.

"I think we just get to be us. We don't have to worry about the outside where we need to hide who we are so people don't bully us. That's all we have to do to be good at being gay."

"Yeah," he says. "I like that." We sit in silence for a moment. "Hey... will you do me a weird favor?"

"What?"

"Will you rub my back for a few minutes? My mom always used to do it to help me sleep."

I smile in the dark. "Sure," I say.

"You're right, you know," he says as he turns onto his stomach. "We can be anyone we want. Not just here, even. My grandma would have wanted that for me. To be... better."

He takes a deep breath, and I feel his hand reaching blindly in the dark as it smacks my forearm. He holds on to it and then runs it down to my wrist, making goose bumps rise like the bubbles in seltzer. He finds my hand and grabs it, squeezing. I squeeze back.

"Thank you," he says. "You're really special." His voice is so soft, I can barely hear him, but suddenly, I can feel stars exploding inside me.

I rub his back softly for a few minutes until his breathing turns deeper, and then I get back into bed. I realize he probably doesn't even know it was me. If he's like my dad, he won't even remember it in the morning. But that doesn't matter.

I close my eyes and try to go to sleep, but it feels like a galaxy is forming inside me, and it's morning before I know it.

"Hey, you okay?" I ask, hanging my head over the edge of the bed to look at Hudson.

"Why?" he asks. "Did I snore?"

He doesn't remember. "Just talking a little in your sleep."

"Oh..." He rubs his eyes. "I don't remember. I think it was good dreams, though."

I smile. "I'm glad," I say. He looks at me funny, and I pull my head back up, staring at the ceiling. He had good dreams, because of me. He said I was special. And he's right—it's not just about being ourselves, about being who we can't be out in the rest of the world. It's about being who we want to be.

One of my new friends from drama, George, was wearing some cool nail polish yesterday. I liked it. Maybe today I'll ask him to do my nails. I think I'd like that. I think that's what I want. I like the way shimmery nails make it look like you're magic under the skin. Like you're filled with stars.

Hudson gets up and walks over to the bathroom, his hair adorably disheveled. I have a sudden memory of the way it felt when he squeezed my hand last night, and I think about how, if my nails had been painted, they might have sparkled

in the dark. I think he would have liked that. I know I would have—our fingers linked together, glitter winking out of every other nail. How it almost was like that anyway, because he knew I was special—he knew I had stars under my skin already, even in the dark. Even not knowing who I was.

I like this camp. I like deciding to be someone different. Someone special. I climb down from my bunk and go get ready for the day.

ELEVEN

Normally, I'd be auditioning today. No one auditions for specific parts (though I'm sure George is campaigning hard for Kim), but everyone gets up and sings a solo of their own choosing, and then Crystal does a few rounds of choreography to see who can move like they want. Then there's like a half hour where everyone hangs out outside, resting after the dancing, or reviewing the scripts. Then come call-backs. Singing songs from the show, people dancing together, acting together until lunch. Then, later that day, Mark and Crystal hang the cast list in the cabins of people who tried out.

It's a fun day. Stressful, but fun. Hearing everyone sing, dancing together, going over parts and practicing. It could be terrible, I know, with everyone backstabbing and saying

nasty things to psych each other out, but it's never like that. Everyone just wants the show to be great. I don't know if that's because it's a queer camp and we're all excited, or because Mark and Crystal don't tolerate meanness, or if it's just some magic summer thing, but auditions are always fun here.

But I'm not auditioning today. Well, kind of.

"First thing we're going to do is one run of the obstacle course each," Connie says. We're all lined up in front of her, like army recruits or something, but Connie wasn't in the military. She's a former Olympian. Track. Two silver medals, one bronze. She's the most famous person who works at the camp, which is probably why she's on all the promotional material and doesn't have to live here for the summer, like the other counselors. She drives in. She's tall, narrow, with dark skin and long, straight black hair. If she hadn't come out as trans, she might have had a career as a great coach. If there wasn't a more famous trans Olympian, she might have gotten a TV deal, or her book would have sold better. Being black probably makes the world overlook her, too. But she seems to like it here. She's a gym teacher during the rest of the year. She likes working with kids.

At least, I think she does. She's hard to read. She looks us each over, appraising. She raises one eyebrow when she comes to me, and one corner of her lip twitches up. Is it funny I'm here? I mean honestly, yes, it's hilarious, but also, no it isn't. I can do this. It's just an obstacle course. Hop through some

tires, crawl under a net, run up a steep ramp, get across a rope ladder suspended between trees, then go down the slide, hop from rock to rock over the small (but waist-deep and freezing cold) stream, get across the monkey bars and the wire-walk, dive through a tire swing into a sand pit, which you then need to get across for the big finale: the Peanut Butter Pit, a rope swing that hangs over a deep pit. Swing across that, and you've made it to the end. The trouble with the rope swing is it stays perfectly still, hanging over the pit—it's not waiting for you to grab it. You have to jump for it.

So it's just that. Sure, it's hard. But so is hitting the high note in "That Dirty Old Man," and I did that last year.

"If you fall or fail, don't worry about it. Just get back up and keep going. If you want to skip one of the obstacles completely, that's all right, too, just run around it. No judgments. I just want to see where you're all at. But by the end of the summer, you're all going to be running this, easy." A few of the new campers turn pale at that. I probably do, too.

"The wire-walk is new," Hudson whispers to me, excited. Our shoulders are touching and I'm so aware of his body, I feel dizzy. "That's going to take some crazy balance." I'm doomed.

"I'm more worried about diving through the tire," I whisper back.

"There's a mat under the sand. You can't hurt yourself."

"That almost sounds like a challenge. Which, to be clear, I will not be rising to."

Hudson laughs and Connie glances over at us, that eyebrow raising again.

"Don't worry," she says. "We're not just going to be doing this. We'll go for hikes, climb trees, and learn how to build tents and start fires. All the good woodsy stuff. But the obstacle course is a challenge. And I want to show you that you're all up for a challenge—'cause life is going to throw them at you. And maybe swinging across that pit at the end isn't going to make some asshole stop calling you names, but it is going to make you feel really good, I promise. So, who wants to go first?"

Hudson and a few others raise their hands, and she starts sending us through, one by one. We all watch, but it's like auditions—this isn't a competition. I'm rooting for each and every camper. Hudson is the fifth up and watching him move makes my whole body shiver a little. He's in low-slung beige shorts and a blue T-shirt that isn't tight but rides up a lot, showing off his stomach and hips. Watching him climb the ramp, then cross the rope ladder, I can see the muscles in his arms working. His calves flex as he jumps from stone to stone. He is the most perfect human specimen I have ever seen.

And I kissed him last night.

No, he kissed me.

What is even happening?

"Randy," Connie says, and I realize it's the second time she's saying it. "You sure you want to do this?"

"It's Del," I tell her. Luckily, Hudson is on the other side of the obstacle course now, so he can't hear. "I go by Del now."

She nods. "Okay, Del. You're up."

I couldn't train for this in Ohio. I lifted weights and ran track, but the only thing we had at school that's on the obstacle course is the tire hops—which are first. I get through them easily, and quickly—there's a pattern to it, like dancing. Crawling under the net isn't hard, either—just use your body to slither, like a snake—that's something Crystal makes us do to warm up sometimes. But then comes the ramp, and my training for that was running up the steepest hill I could find—which in Ohio was maybe forty degrees. I looked at the physics of it, though, and it's not that difficult. Not like Donald O'Connor running up the walls in *Singing in the Rain*. Just a really steep hill. I can do this, I tell myself as I hop up after the net. Just charge.

So I charge, and it works. I grab on to the top to pull myself the rest of the way, which isn't great—Hudson didn't need to—but it's allowed. The rope ladder isn't so bad, either, just crawl across a swinging rope ladder slowly and carefully. I've helped move lights in the theater at school, and it's kind of like that, I decide, as it rocks back and forth under me. Scary, sure, but doable. The slide is just a slide, and hopping from rock to rock isn't actually that hard as long as the stream isn't flooding over them, and it's not today. I'm shocked by how well it's going, honestly.

The monkey bars I should have practiced. There's a park near me with them, but they're for little kids and I felt silly going there. I figured if kids could do it, so could I. What I didn't figure was that it burns! I hang in place from one arm and stretch out the other for the next bar, my own weight heavy and pulling painfully on my arm. I'm sweating, too, so I try to go quickly, or else my hands will slip. One kid before me failed the monkey bars, so it's not the end of the world, but I don't want Hudson to think I'm the second-worst one here.

Maybe it IS a competition. But just for me. Win the course, win Hudson. In fact, was the kid who fell one of his exes? How many of them are here? I tried to never pay much attention—George said it made me mopey—so I only half know their faces, like blurry people in the background of a photo of Hudson. I think the guy who fell was one of his conquests. And maybe the one who went first and got through everything but the Peanut Butter Pit.

It goes slowly, but I make it across the bars, and I can feel my shirt sticking to my back with sweat now. If I still had my old, longer hair, it would be plastered across my fore-head. When I drop from the monkey bars, my hands clench closed involuntarily, and my palms feel like they're burning. But I have no time to check. Next is the wire-walk—a wire tightrope, but only a foot off the ground. I didn't prepare for it at all because it wasn't here last summer. But I pull myself up onto it by the tree it's tied to, and focus. The good news

is, no one has done this one yet. Everyone has fallen, only Hudson kept hopping back on where he fell, taking another step and then falling again. Everyone gave up after their first or second fall.

But actually, it's not that hard. It's not easy, don't get me wrong. The wire flexes and bounces under me and I wish I were barefoot so I could grip it, but walking a perfectly straight line is something we need to do for chorus choreography. Sway too far to the left or right, and you'll whack the person next to you with your jazz hands. So I do what I do when dancing, and I focus not on my feet, but the tree at the other end of the wire. I stretch my arms out for balance, and then, not too slowly, I walk.

I make it halfway before I fall, farther than anyone else. But I don't land on my feet, like they all had. Instead, I tumble, landing on all fours. That's...not good. I glance up, but Hudson isn't laughing. He's cheering me on.

"Come on, Del! Get up! You can do it!" I love him.

I give the wire a look from the ground, then push myself up and move on. I already proved enough. The tire hoop is next—suspended horizontally, four thick ropes holding it in place. This is about tumbling, I remind myself. You just have to jump through the hoop. Then land in a somersault, and ideally roll to your feet and keep moving.

I leap, and my stomach slams into the tire. I didn't leap high enough. I hear someone let out an "oof" from the side-lines, but it doesn't actually hurt much. It's rubber. But that

sound—someone thinking I've screwed up, because I have—that makes me feel like an idiot. That hurt. That floods me with stupid feelings of "Why are you doing this?" and "This will never work when Hudson sees how not-masc you are" and "Don't you wish you were auditioning now?" I feel my skin burning bright red. I hope it wasn't Hudson, but I can't see and I need to focus on finishing, but I'm half through the tire, arms in front of me like Superman, feet swinging just off the ground. I grab the bottom of the tire and pull myself through that way, landing inelegantly on my back in the sand, which smells like feet.

I stare up at the sun through the trees for a moment. Ever notice how trees against the sun looks like the Milky Way? George and I like doing this after auditions—lying in the shade, staring up and blurring our eyes just enough that the light between the trees becomes huge rivers of stars, and the leaves become empty black. Day into night, back into day again.

"You can do it, Del!" someone shouts. Hudson.

I push myself up.

There's only one thing left: the Peanut Butter Pit. Why peanut butter? I almost ask it out loud. The rope is in the middle of the pit, far out of reach. I back up and take a running leap. I make it pretty far, too. My hands scrape the rope as I fall into the pit. Luckily, there's a mat down here, too. And this I don't feel bad about. Only Hudson has made it so far.

I climb out of the pit at the other end, and Hudson imme-diately gives me a hug and every bit of pain in me evaporates. My hands go from being on fire to…well, still being on fire, but in their desire to pull him into me. My body, which ached a moment ago, feels fine now. My muscles go from stiff to soft…except for that one part of me that goes the opposite. He smells like earth and sweat, which I know makes it sound like I have some sort of fetish, but I think it's just his sweat. His sweat smells good. Sweet and dark, and a little salty. I wish I could bottle it or make it a fancy scented candle to keep in my room and only burn on special occasions.

Who am I kidding? I'd have it burning 24/7.

"You did really great," Hudson says. Over his shoulder, I see the other campers who have gone staring at me. One of the guys, one of Hudson's exes, I think, smirks and looks away. I hold him a little tighter.

"I screwed up the tire, like I said I would."

"But you did well on the new wire. That thing is impos-sible, too. How'd you make it so far?" He lets go of me, but keeps one hand loosely around my waist, resting on my hip. It's like all the nerve endings in my body have migrated to that hip and are sending lightning bolts to my brain, and it takes a moment for me to realize he's asked a question.

"I focused on the end of it, not my feet," I tell him.

"Smart," he says. "I'm going to try that next time. Oh, Brad's up."

Brad messes up on the wire-walk, too, but he's the second

person to handle the Peanut Butter Pit. When he lands, he high-fives Hudson.

"That tightrope is a bitch," he says.

"Del handled it pretty well, though," Hudson says, pulling me a bit closer. I have a sudden urge to giggle, but restrain myself.

"Yeah." Brad nods, looking at me. "You've got great balance."

"Thanks," I say, smiling and desperately hoping he's not going to give me away. George said not to worry about it, and I trust George, but maybe George shouldn't trust Brad.

"From dancing?" Brad asks. I do my best confused face as my mind empties of replies.

"Ha," Hudson says. "Nah. We were dancing last night, and he's...not a dancer. No offense, babe."

BABE. He called me babe and now my mind is blank again. I'm just a blow-up doll here, as these two men talk about me, shoving me back and forth between delight and fear.

"No?" Brad laughs. "That's funny."

"I'm awkward," I finally say, though I have no idea why I decided to say it, or why I've said it in such a high voice.

"Nah, just a little stiff," Hudson says. "It's 'cause you're new. You'll loosen up."

I laugh, a little forced, and swallow; my throat is dry.

"At least you didn't say you'd loosen him up," Brad says, rolling his eyes. "Don't let him use lines on you, Del. He might seem smooth, but he's just as awkward as you, underneath."

"Yeah?" I ask.

"I don't think either of us are awkward," Hudson says.

"Mmm." Brad nods, looking unconvinced. "I was wondering, though, Del...is George single? He have a guy back home or anything?"

"Who's George?" Hudson asks.

"My friend," I say, a little annoyed he doesn't remember. "In my cabin, Middle Eastern, wears nail polish all the time, and sometimes eye shadow?"

"Right," Hudson says, then turns to Brad. "Really? Nail polish and eye shadow?"

"And a hairy chest, and I'm guessing a hairy ass," Brad says, wiggling his eyebrows. "And he's funny. But..." He turns back to me. "Is he single?"

"Yeah," I say. "He's single."

"Cool," Brad says, and nods a few times to himself.

"All right!" Connie shouts, walking over to us. The last of us have run the course, and she's carrying a cooler of water bottles. We each eagerly grab some. The water feels almost as good going down my throat as Hudson. His hug, I mean. "You all did well. Looks like everyone had trouble with the wire-walk, though. Balance is important! Balance is what helps with every activity—hiking, sports, dancing, getting things off high shelves. So let's go work on that. Everyone gather around and spot."

We all head toward the wire-walk and stand on either side of it. Our water bottles are empty and we throw them

back in the cooler, then put our hands out, like walls for people to lean on as they try to cross the wire.

"Now," Connie says. "I put this in because even though yes, the obstacle course is a race, and yes, I will start timing you next time we do it, you still need to be patient. So every step you take needs to be careful, and you need to find your balance before you take your next one. Del, you did pretty well at it, you want to try again?"

"Sure," I say, not feeling like I have much of a choice. I pull myself up onto the wire again and find my balance, like I would before a high kick, and I take a step, focusing on the end of the wire. I go slowly. I slip once, but someone's hand catches me, and pushes me back upright.

"Thanks," I say, without looking at them. Then I keep walking. When I make it to the end, everyone claps, Connie included.

"Well done," Connie says. "Your breathing before each step, and how you lifted your leg from the hip, not the knee, was very good."

"Thanks," I say, suddenly feeling very embarrassed. "And thank you, whoever caught me."

"That was me," says the guy who smirked at me before. Maybe he's not so bad.

"Thanks," I say.

"That's what we do for each other," he says.

"Okay," Connie says. "Next up . . . Brad, how about you?"

"Aw, come on, I barely tried this one," Brad says.

"Exactly," Connie says. "Up you go."

I take my place spotting and Brad gets up, trying to find his balance. He looks down at his feet and takes a step, almost falling, but is caught by a few of the other campers.

"Look ahead," I say. "To the end of the wire."

Brad raises his head and takes another step, walking carefully across the wire. He stumbles a few more times, but never falls completely off when people catch him. When he gets to the end, he looks very relieved. We all applaud again.

"It's harder for those of us who are taller," Connie tells him. "Find that center of gravity." Brad nods. "And nice advice, Del."

"Thanks," I say, and I put my hands out to spot the next person.

"Jane, you're up next."

So I screwed up the tire...but Hudson still likes me, and now maybe Connie does, too? Maybe this plan isn't just going to work, it's going to earn me respect. Maybe all these jocks are going to become my friends. Wouldn't that be a laugh?

TWELVE

After the outdoors elective, we have instructional pool time, where we're tested on our swimming and put into classes—sadly, I'm not with Hudson. And then it's lunch. Hudson and I walk in together—not holding hands, but closer than two friends would walk—and I spot George and Ashleigh right away and head toward them.

"Babe, you don't want to sit with everyone from the obstacle course?" Hudson asks.

"They had auditions today," I tell him. "I want to know how they went."

"Okay, sounds important," he says, especially when Brad walks by us, heading right for George. He laughs. "I swear, Brad doesn't get crushes often, but when he does, it's like he doesn't know what to do with himself. He goes total puppy dog."

"That's cute, though," I say, watching Brad sit next to George. George grins at him.

"I guess we're going kind of puppy dog with each other, too," Hudson says. He takes my hand, and I grin as I sit down across from George and next to Ashleigh.

"So?" I ask. "How'd they go?"

"I sang 'Let Me Be Your Star,' from the fictional musical *Bombshell* from the hit TV show *Smash*, and I knocked it out of the park," George says.

"He really did," Ashleigh says. "People applauded."

"I'm worried he's going to get Rose after all," Paz says, from the other side of Ashleigh. That's interesting, them sitting so close. Paz is cool, she's a friend, but first the bunk over George and now sitting with us...I look at them, then look at George, who shrugs slightly.

"I just want Kim," George says. "But I don't know how well I did at the dancing. And she is a dance role."

Hudson leans into me. "Dance role?" he asks.

"A character with a lot of dancing," I say. "I mean, most roles dance some, but Kim has a dance solo in one song and usually dances in other parts..."

"You know the musical?" he asks.

"Darling, it's a classic," George interjects. "There's a movie, mostly the same aside from the stupid thing with the turtle. Netflix it when you get home."

"Um, okay," Hudson says, looking at me confused.

"It's a good movie," I tell him, but without too much enthusiasm, remembering that musicals aren't his thing.

"Sure." He narrows his eyes at me, but I can't tell what it means.

"I bet you're a great dancer," Brad says to George.

"I know how to use my body," George says, batting his eyelashes. Then he frowns. "But that's not the same thing. I screwed up some of the steps."

"Hey," I say. "Don't go over it in your head. It's done. And you said yourself you sang great. Mark knows what you can do."

"Yeah," George says, nodding. "Thank you, darling. I feel better."

"How about you?" I ask Ashleigh.

"They put in some new lights. Mark showed all the techies some design schemes, and it looks fun this year. I think I'll probably be the ASM on the lights again. We'll see."

"You always run an amazing lighting set," Paz says.

Ashleigh turns to me, away from Paz, so Paz can't see. She widens her eyes. I smile and nod. She frowns, anxious.

"So, I feel like you guys are old friends," Hudson says to me. "Not like you're a new kid."

Everyone is silent for a moment.

"Ah," I say. "Well…" I can feel my brain spinning through lies, trying to figure out the best way to distract him from this idea. Do I just kiss him? That works in movies. I'd like that.

"We are," George says before I can try my plan. "We met online. I told him about this camp."

"Oh," Hudson says. "In one of those, like, coming out support groups?"

"Yeah," I say, grateful to George for being as good an improv-er as I am. "George has really helped me."

"Well, I'm glad." Hudson grins, then goes to fist-bump George. "Good mentoring, dude."

George looks at his fist suspiciously, then pats it like a wet dog.

"I'm a delight, darling," George says.

The platters of food start passing around and we each take heaps of the pasta with canned tomato sauce and powdered cheese and eat hungrily. After my workout this morning, I'm starving. As we eat, we break off into little couple pairs—Brad and George flirt, though George keeps him at arm's length. Paz talks to Ashleigh, who seems horrified anyone would want to talk to her. And Hudson talks to me. About the obstacle course, mainly, about how to get through the tire dive—it's about your knees, apparently—and the Peanut Butter Pit—which is about your knees, too, but also about trying to grab the rope earlier than you think you'll need to. I nod and tell him how the obstacle course was for me, and the whole time, our thighs are pressing together and he's smiling at me, and this is everything I've wanted every summer to be for the past four years.

After lunch, he gives me a kiss on the cheek before

heading off to archery and I go to A&C. I stand there, outside the dining hall, just smiling as he walks away, not even staring at his ass, just feeling where he kissed me. Then remembering how he kissed me last night. Then wanting to kiss him like that again.

"Darling, you look like a deer in the headlights," George says, walking past me toward the A&C cabin. I follow him.

"Seriously," Ashleigh says. "You're getting everything you want, you're practically boyfriends already. Stop acting so surprised he's into you. You made yourself into his ideal."

"I've always been his ideal," I say, following them. "Just...now he'll notice, because I ran the obstacle course this morning. Same Randy, new hobbies."

"Mmm," Ashleigh says.

"You should talk," I say as George pulls open the screen door to the A&C cabin with a creak. "Paz wants to get to know you—the way you said you were going to—and you're freaking out."

"I talked to her." Ashleigh rolls her eyes as we sit down at the circular table in the middle of the cabin. It's a big table, taking up most of the cabin, but the walls are covered in cubbies, filled with craft supplies—sequins, construction paper, string, glitter, cardboard, pom-poms, paints...everywhere you look, there's something.

"So?" George asks her. "You talked to her....Any... feelings?"

"It was, like, two conversations. She's cool. I don't know."

"Okay," George says, then turns to me. "Now, tell us about this obstacle course. Did it end in Hudson's pants?"

I laugh. "No. It was awful...but kind of cool? I did really well on the wire-walk—it's new, like a tightrope—and Connie thought I did okay. Missed the Peanut Butter Pit, though."

"Oh please, only like five people at this camp can make that," George says. "But your ruse didn't collapse? Hudson believes you enjoyed yourself?"

"I kind of did." I shrug and smile.

"More than being in the show?" Ashleigh asks.

I frown, feeling suddenly very heavy. "No. But Hudson put his hand around my waist, and he left it there."

"Marking his territory," George says, impressed. "Not bad."

"And he called me babe!"

"The straightest of all pet names, of course."

"Okay!" Marguerite says, entering the cabin in a sudden burst. Other campers are sitting around the table with us now, some I know, some new, but none from the obstacle course, thankfully, and we all look expectantly at Marguerite. Most of the counselors wear T-shirts and shorts, but not Marguerite. She's in a red dress with large white polka dots, and since last night, she's braided some red beads into her short brown bob. "Today, we're going to make what are traditionally called God's Eyes. But what is God, really? Do you believe in her? I want you to use sticks and yarn to think about the way the world watches us—especially those of us

who identify as queer. Who is watching you? Is it out of protection? Or is it the cruel eye of the patriarchy?" She clasps her hands together, as if praying. "And do you watch back?" She smiles, then nods. "Go, find two sticks, about the size of your forearm, and pick out some yarn from the cubbies. You can use things besides yarn, too, if you want. Or you could use white yarn, and we could dye it with flowers!" She claps her hands. "Think about it."

She steps aside from the door, leaving us to go outside to look for sticks.

"It's cool that I'm better at all this outdoors stuff than I thought I would be, though," I say as we walk into the woods. "It's like Hudson said when he captained color wars—we can do whatever we want, if we try."

"I don't know if he means it that way," Ashleigh says, leaping up and pulling a thin twig off a branch. "Think Marguerite would be okay with a smaller God's Eye?"

"Sweetie, just tell her you think God has small eyes, which is why she can't see all the suffering in the world," I say. "She'll eat that up."

"Cool," Ashleigh says. She grins at me.

We gather our sticks, and back inside, Marguerite shows off her own God's Eye, which she calls "Panopticon" and is made of knitted wires and extension cords around sticks. We start working on our own God's Eyes as Marguerite walks the room, nodding and giving us tips.

"Thanks for that save at lunch," I tell George as I weave

glittery pink yarn around the two birch sticks I have. "Pen pals. Smart."

"Now we don't have to pretend not to be friends," George says.

"I was never going to do that," I say.

"No?" Ashleigh asks. "What if he wants you to sit with his friends at lunch tomorrow?"

"I can sit away from you guys every now and then," I say. "It's only fair we sit with each other's friends. Maybe we can join the groups. Brad likes you, George."

George sighs. "He does, doesn't he?"

"So?" I ask.

"So, he's cute. I don't know what I want. I was thinking the summer would be relaxing, that you would have enough romantic shenanigans for both of us. I just want something simple. Easy. And I don't know if Brad is it."

"Why not?" I ask.

"Different worlds. I'm not going to strip my nail polish off for him, like you did."

"Maybe he likes your nail polish," I say. "When Hudson asked about it, he said you were hot, and you made him laugh, and he didn't care about your makeup routine."

George smiles as he weaves some purple string around his sticks. "Did he?"

"Yeah," I say.

"He said he liked George's nail polish?" Ashleigh asks. "How did that come up?"

"Oh," I say, and suddenly my throat feels dry. I stare down at the sticks. "Just, Hudson thought it was funny that Brad would be into someone who wears nail polish."

"Mmmm," Ashleigh says. "This is the guy who you think will like you for who you are by the end of the summer?"

"It's only day two," I say, maybe a little too loudly. "We have to get to know each other first."

"Okay, okay," Ashleigh says. "Sorry."

"Just...it'll work," I say. "I really like him. He really likes me. We just have to talk more." I pause. "And maybe kiss more."

George laughs. "Magic lips, with lipstick that spreads the power of femme to even the butchiest among us!"

"Funny," I say, trying to sound dry, but I'm laughing, and so is Ashleigh.

"But darling, your plan is working. I'm so impressed. So is most of the camp."

"Most of the camp?" I ask.

"You think your makeover went unnoticed?" Ashleigh asks. "Do you know how many guys have asked me if you're single? And how many girls asked if you're okay?"

I laugh. "No way."

"Oh, darling, very yes. We've initiated a whisper campaign to make sure no one interferes, though."

"So everyone thinks I was hit on the head?" I ask, horrified.

"No...they know something closer to the truth than

Brad." George suddenly focuses on his yarn and sticks. "Sorry, but there were a lot of questions. But everyone is sworn to secrecy, I promise."

"And these are just the people who really recognized you," Ashleigh says.

"Oooookay," I say, taking a deep breath and looking at the center of my God's Eye, which makes me very dizzy. "Everyone knows my plan, sort of, then." Part of me is nervous—that means anyone could tell Hudson. But no one has, yet. And then part of me warms up a little. It's like I'm the star of a show everyone is watching. Better not mess up my lines, then.

"There's a betting pool over if you'll pull it off," Ashleigh adds.

"What?"

"Darling, she's kidding."

"George bet two packs of Junior Mints on you messing it up."

"I did not. She's making that up." George's eyes are wide with horror.

I look at Ashleigh. She's stone-faced, weaving her thin string over the sticks. We're silent for a minute and then she cracks a smile.

I laugh.

"That was so mean," George says, throwing a ball of yarn at Ashleigh, who laughs and throws it back.

"Art shouldn't be violent," Marguerite says calmly but

loudly. We all turn our attention back to our God's Eyes in silence for a moment.

"So what's the plan, anyway?" George asks in a low voice. "If you're already holding each other's hands and kissing?"

"Boyfriends next," I say definitively. "Then we talk more—get to really know each other. Parents, music, coming out. Everything. Then maybe more kissing. No sex, though. Not yet. Soon, though. Soon."

"You really want to get naked with him, don't you?" Ashleigh asks.

"So badly," I say.

"Four years of built-up sexual desire," George says. "Darling, I'd be impressed if you make it past tomorrow."

"Better grab some condoms from Cosmo tonight," Ashleigh says, smirking.

"And lube," George says. "More than you think you need, if you want to do anal. And clean up beforehand. In the shower, you know?"

"Unless you want to top," Ashleigh says. "Does he bottom, though?"

"He made a joke about being vers," I say. "I don't know. I'm up for anything."

Ashleigh rolls her eyes. "No erection puns, please."

I chuckle. "Whatever we do, it'll be next Wednesday. Not tomorrow." I realize my voice has become regular volume again and Marguerite is staring at me.

"What does a God's Eye see, Del?" she asks. "And what does your counselor hear that she really doesn't want to?"

"Sorry," I say.

We spend the rest of the period making our God's Eyes. George's is purple and red with bright pink sequins dotting it like stars. Mine is pink and blue, but with the glittery yarn, and Ashleigh's is tiny, made with thin string for bracelets, in every available color. Marguerite compliments our work before hanging them all from the ceiling at different heights, some low enough for her to hit her head on. "See you tomorrow," she says. "We'll be dyeing silk scarves with plants!"

After A&C, I have sports as George and Ashleigh head to the boathouse for their nature elective.

I show up just as Ryan, the sports counselor, is blowing his whistle and barely have time to say hi to Hudson before we're divided into opposite teams.

"Capture the flag, boys! And girls! And non-binary folks!" Ryan says, handing out bandannas in red and blue for us to wear to show what team we're on. Ryan thinks his baby face lets him get away with trying to be "cool" and "on our level." It's tragic. "Camp classic. You all know the rules?" He doesn't wait for anyone to answer. "Good. Let's play!" He blows the whistle again, and I scramble away from him, wondering where the border is. I watch the other campers, clearly used to Ryan's rules, and figure out it's the center of the soccer field we're on. Hudson stands on the other side of it, smirking at me, far too sexy.

"Hey," he says. "So, you gonna try stealing my flag, babe?"

I walk up to the border. "With the way you're watching me, I'm not brainless enough to try now," I say.

"But if you come over here, I can tackle you," he says, winking.

"If you want to get physical, why don't you come over to my side?" I ask. Flirting is getting easier. Maybe because, like Ashleigh said, I know he's into me, so it's not like I'm risking anything.

"It's hot," he says, and starts peeling off his shirt. His bandanna is hanging from his waist, and I try to stare at it, instead of the way his shirt peels away from his abs like it was vacuum sealed. I'm definitely licking my lips and doing that cartoonish loud swallow. He has just a little hair on his chest, and his chest and arms are defined, but still soft looking. They'd be nice to push up against.

"That's cheating," I say, when his shirt is off.

"What?"

"Causing a distraction."

"That's not a distraction," he says with a grin. "This is," he says at the exact same moment he tosses his shirt at me, covering my face as he runs by me. I laugh, but it works. I take the shirt off my face, trying not to obviously inhale his sweat, and drop it on the ground before taking off after him, but he has too big a lead. Then one of my teammates—a girl from the obstacle course—comes at him and Hudson

swerves. I take a sharp turn and gain a little ground. He looks back once, both me and my teammate chasing him now, and smiles, before veering to the left, toward where our flag is lying unceremoniously in the goalie net. But even once he has the flag, he has to get it back to his side, so I go wide, anticipating where he'll have to run once he has it.

And I'm right—he grabs the flag off the ground in one swoop and turns, heading now right for me. He sees me and tries to turn, but I pounce and tackle him. He falls backward, with me on top of him.

"Ooof," he says. "Rough."

"You said there'd be tackling," I say with a shrug, sitting up so I'm straddling him, and plucking the flag from his hand. "Isn't this how the game works?" I should get up. But I don't. Hudson puts his hands on my thighs, his fingers creeping just up inside my shorts, and I can feel his body press upward between my legs.

Then Ryan whistles. "Save that for your private time, boys," he shouts at us. "And this is a touch game. No need for tackling, Kapplehoff."

"Sorry," I say, blushing furiously as I get off Hudson. A few of the other campers are staring at us.

"I need some water," I tell Hudson. "You're in jail." I point to where caught campers are waiting for a teammate to free them.

"Yes, sir," he says with a smile. "So, where's my shirt?"

"Back over there. You can come get it later."

"I will," he says, walking to the jail. I walk off the field and go over to the nearest water fountain, where I let the water spray on my face before actually drinking. I was ready to pull down his shorts right there. No wonder he always gets laid by the end of the first week. I shake my head. I can't do that. I can't be just another conquest. I didn't give up the show for a lay, no matter how pretty he is. I gave it up for love. And that means no sex. For...at least two weeks? That seems a long time. Maybe ten days. That sounds fair.

I know I should be more nervous about losing my virginity, too, but if I'm losing it to Hudson, I don't feel nervous at all. It feels right.

Once my face has cooled down, I head back to the field, where Hudson waves at me from the other side, having apparently already escaped. I smile back.

Eventually, our side wins, but it's by the end of the period, and there aren't any more tackles, sadly. After that, Hudson and I head to the free swim, where we can just swim and play in the pool, and don't have to take lessons. The water feels amazing after running around all day. Hudson and I lean against the wall, holding hands under the water.

"So, you have a fun day, babe?" Hudson asks.

"Yeah," I tell him.

"Awesome. I'm glad. And after this, we have some free time until dinner, if you wanted to hang out or something."

"Yeah," I say as George and Ashleigh hop into the pool next to us. "I'd like that."

"Awesome," Hudson says again, nodding.

"Oh, hey," Ashleigh says, looking at the other side of the pool, "Janice is on duty."

"And you're not going to talk to her," George says as Ashleigh waves at Janice. Janice waves back.

"Hey, Paz," I say, spotting her walking by us. "Come get in."

"Okay," Paz says. She hops in. She's in a black one-piece with a low neckline. She smiles at Ashleigh. "What's up?"

"We didn't ask you how you thought your audition went," George says, stepping around Ashleigh, so she's closer to Paz.

"Oh." Paz nods, her shaved head gleaming. "I mean, I think it was okay. You heard. 'Big Spender' from *Sweet Charity*. Maybe a little on the nose, but I think I did it well."

"You did," Ashleigh says, after George elbows her. "You sang really well. If they don't cast you as Rose, it'll be, like, the worst decision."

"Thanks." Paz grins, and Ashleigh smiles back, not even paying attention to Janice anymore.

George nods at me.

"So, what's that about?" Hudson asks.

I swim away a little, Hudson following. "Ashleigh has a thing for one of the straight lifeguards. We're trying to redirect her affections somewhere they'll find more ground."

"Oh," Hudson says. "That's cool. Crushes on straight people are the worst. Like...I get it. I've had a lot. But I think

that's 'cause there's just more of them, you know? I don't get crushes on straight guys here."

"I don't think I've ever had a crush on a straight guy," I say, considering it. "Except for celebrities."

"Oh yeah? What are your celebrity crushes?"

"You first."

"I asked first."

"Fine... Taron Egerton," I say. I don't mention it's from seeing him in *Rocketman* with the makeup and amazing sequin jumpsuits.

"Okay," Hudson says, nodding. "Respectable choice. Little short, but cute."

"Yours?"

"Oh man. Chris Evans probably."

"Kinda basic, but understandable," I say.

"Basic?" Hudson laughs, then splashes me. "This from the guy who chose the little white dude. At least my guy sometimes wears a beard."

"Yeah, but it's not exactly original. His ass is a meme."

"So my opinion is shared by many," Hudson says with a shrug. "That just means it's a respectable choice."

I laugh. "Okay. Well, if Chris Evans ever shows up at camp, I'll make sure you don't know about it."

"Oh, what? You trying to land me?" he asks, smiling as he swims a little away from me.

"I feel like I'm doing a good job," I say, chasing.

"Maybe," he says, wiggling his eyebrows. "Maybe I really liked being tackled before."

"Yeah, I felt that."

He grins, and maybe even blushes slightly before diving underwater. Next thing I know, his arms are around my waist, and he pulls me under. I open my eyes to the chlorine-blue world of feet and bubbles and Hudson holding me close to him. I know he just pulled me under, but I'm not worried. When he kisses me, his breath is warm in mine, and the water between our lips tastes of chemicals. Then we both pop back from underwater.

"Did you two just kiss underwater?" Ashleigh asks. We're right by them again. "Gross."

I laugh and look away, and Hudson throws his arm around my waist again. "I don't think he's gross," he says.

Ashleigh rolls her eyes, and George raises an eyebrow at me.

"Oh no," I say, suddenly realizing it. "We're that couple."

Hudson turns slowly to me. "Couple?" he asks.

I feel myself turning bright red. I did just say couple. Well, that was stupid. I mean, was it, though? We're kissing and holding hands, right? But no, that's wrong. We're just kissing and holding hands. Couple is not a thing we've discussed. Except in my head, for the past four years, where I imagine him getting down on one knee and asking to be my boyfriend and everything is perfect, and later maybe we have a house in New York and I'm a Broadway star and I think maybe we

have a cat and a dog, 'cause I like them both. George kicks my knee under the water, and I remember what just happened and my mouth is dry again.

"I didn't mean, like, couple couple," I say. "I just mean, like, that couple of guys who are engaging in PDA that makes everyone around them roll their eyes."

Hudson laughs. "Okay. We're that couple, then, yeah, maybe a little."

"Maybe a little more than anyone wants," Ashleigh says. Paz covers her mouth as she snorts a laugh.

"So who do we think is going to be Birdie?" George asks, trying to defuse the situation. "Jen?"

"I think Jen is going to be Albert," Paz says. "I think Montgomery for Birdie—or you?"

"Me? Darling, I don't have that sort of swagger."

"That's why I like it," Paz says. "Birdie with a fan, Birdie as a drag show."

George tilts his head, considering.

"Is that how it is in the movie?" Hudson asks, confused.

"More Elvis," I say.

"Technically, Conway Twitty was the original inspiration," George says. "But yes, it reads as very Elvis. Which is sort of a drag show itself."

"How is Elvis drag?" Hudson asks, looking like he wants to roll his eyes.

"Performative masculinity," Paz says. "Exaggerated ideas of what maleness is..." She looks at Hudson, whose brow

is furrowed. "Acting butch to make fun of what masculinity is."

"I thought Elvis was just...like that?" he says.

"I think we all act a little," I say.

George raises an eyebrow at me.

"Well...okay," Hudson says, his voice getting hard. "But, like, being butch isn't drag. It's just being...like what you want to be."

"I think it has to do with how exaggerated it is. Or who it's for," Paz says. "At least, that's what we talked about in my women's studies class this year."

"I don't get it. I feel like drag and stuff like that is what straight people think gay people are, not what straight people think other straight people are."

"I don't think sexuality has to do with it, necessarily," Paz says.

"I think what straight people think queer people are shouldn't matter," Ashleigh says.

Paz barks a laugh. "True."

"Well, maybe not here," Hudson says. "But out in the regular world..." He frowns, then spots Brad across the pool. "I'm gonna go say hi to Brad," he says to me, giving me a quick kiss on the cheek before swimming away.

I frown. Did the conversation drive him off? I turn back to the three of them, who are staring at me, waiting for a reaction. I feel...angry? I shouldn't, I know. They were just saying stuff, but it felt like they were fighting with him

at the end. Or maybe he was fighting with them—or was about to?

"You sure this plan is going to work?" Ashleigh asks.

"Maybe if we don't try to thrust gender theory on him on day two," I say, crossing my arms.

"Sorry," Paz says. "I know what the plan is, but I don't know the rules."

"You don't need to apologize," Ashleigh says.

I sigh and lean against the side of the pool, slinking down. "He'll come around. We just need to ease him into it. This was good. We gave him some ideas. Ease him into it."

"Are you talking to us, or yourself?" George asks.

"Both?"

I look across the pool to the deep end, where Brad and Hudson are splashing each other.

"If it makes you feel better," Paz says, "it's all nonsense, right? Butch, femme, masc, whatever...it's meaningless."

"Not to him," I say, watching Hudson.

THIRTEEN

George, Ashleigh, and Paz get out of the pool early when they spot Mark walking from the drama cabin back to the cabins up the stairs, clipboard in hand. I swim over to Hudson, and we spend the rest of the swim period splashing each other, the conversation that maybe upset him forgotten. We even kiss underwater one more time.

When the lifeguard blows the whistle, signaling the end of pool time, Hudson hoists himself out of the water next to me. We grab our towels and walk up the stairs to our cabins.

"So...," he says. "Want to hang out after dinner? Before Joan's class tonight?"

"Sure," I say, smiling. Good. Everything is still going according to plan.

"Cool," he says. "I'll see you at dinner?"

"Yeah," I say, grinning.

"Awesome," he says. At the top of the stairs, he looks around quickly, then kisses me on the lips, pulling me tight against him by the waist. I feel my mouth start to open, dying to go further, to pull off my clammy swimsuit, to pull him close, but before I can even think about any of that, he pulls away. "I'll meet you at your cabin. We can walk to dinner together."

I know I'm still grinning like a moron as I walk into my cabin. The casting sheet is hanging where it always is, next to Mark's room, and I see it before I see anything else. I even instinctively start walking toward it, wondering what I got, what my role is—maybe I'm Birdie!—before I remember I'm not on it, and turn away. George is stretched out on his bed, Paz and Ashleigh sitting on the end of it in what space he hasn't taken over.

"So?" I ask.

"I have sad news," George says, suddenly snapping open a bright pink fan and fanning himself with it. "Let them go first." He leans back dramatically onto his pillows, still fanning himself. "I'll need time to tell my tale of woe."

"Okay," I say, worried. He clearly didn't get Kim. "So..." I turn to Ashleigh.

"I'm stage manager!" she practically squeals, a huge smile of delight opening across her face. Delight does not come

often to Ashleigh's face, and it looks uncertain on her, nervous. I wrap her in a hug, lifting her up from the bed and into the air. "I didn't think I would. But Mark says he trusts me, and we're talking the designs he wants to implement, and I might get to make some changes if I want, and I'm just so excited."

"That's amazing," I say. "Congrats."

"I'm going to boss all those cabin eight kids around so hard."

I laugh. "I bet." I turn to Paz. "And you got Rose?"

"Of course," Paz says, brushing her shoulder. "Mark says we can even try to throw some Portuguese in, really bring some of my Afro-Brazilian-American Girl Magic to the role."

"But...," I say, turning back to George. "No Kim?"

"No," George says, still fanning himself, pouting. "He went with Montgomery, though I think casting the tall redhead is a little OBVIOUS." He shouts the last word in the direction of Mark's closed door. "I'm Harry. The dad."

I sit down next to George in what little room is left and lay my hand on his shoulder. "Maybe it's an excuse for people to call you Daddy?" I ask.

He frowns. "You're the third person to make that joke," he says, his eyes darting to Ashleigh and Paz. "It didn't make me feel better the first or second time, either."

"It's not a bad role," I say. "Lots of comedy. Two songs."

"I know, I know." George sighs. "I shouldn't be complaining. It's a nice part. Just...not the part I wanted."

"You can complain to us. We're your friends," I say. "That's what we're for."

"I just...wanted to be the ingenue, you know? Here is the only place I even have a chance at playing that, and I know I'm...this big hairy guy now. I knew it was a long shot. I just wanted to try it this year, because I feel like I'll never have the chance again. I wanted to try it. To play with that—get to bat my eyelashes and do the big innocent eyes for laughs. I think I'd be good at that."

"You would be amazing at it. And you'll get a shot, I promise," I say, squeezing his shoulder. "When we're in college, in the summer, we'll create a touring theater company, and you can be any ingenue you want. Sandy in *Grease*? Cinderella?"

"Promise?" he asks. "You're still going to be doing theater even if your butch boyfriend doesn't approve?"

"He'll approve," I say. "And yes, I promise."

George stops fanning himself, and I realize he'd been drying his eyes, fanning them to keep them from getting too teary.

"Hug?" I ask. He nods, and sits up and hugs me. After a moment, Ashleigh wraps her arms around us, too. And then Paz, which is new, but okay. Then Jen from across the bunk, and Caroline, and everyone else—a big group hug around George. I laugh.

"Okay, darlings, stop it," George says, pushing us off and snapping open his fan again. "I'm fine. And we are all going to be amazing in this show. Especially you, Montgomery," George says, pointing his fan. Everyone smiles and returns to their beds. I sit across from George, Ashleigh's feet dangling down in front of me.

"So what's the rest of the cast? Who got Birdie?"

"Jordan," George says, nodding across the cabin, at Jordan, who's talking to Jen. "Non-binary Birdie. Mark says we'll be using 'they' pronouns for Birdie and that Birdie will be a 'Ziggy Stardust type pansexual genderfluid object of lust.'"

"That's pretty cool," I say.

"Jen got Albert. That new guy, Lyle, got Hugo. Mattie got Mae, though honestly, I was sort of hoping Mark would do that role as Diana. But Mattie will be good."

"Oh yeah," I say. "That's a great cast."

"It would be better if you were in it," George says. "I bet you would have gotten Mae if you'd tried out, and we could sing 'Kids' together."

I smile, imagining it for a minute: George and I onstage, maybe George in suspenders and a cardigan, me in a fur-collared coat, back to back, complaining about the youths today. It would be fun—George and I haven't gotten to play together much onstage. Domina didn't interact with Hysterium much in *Funny Thing*, and before that we were both in the chorus. We play in exercises, of course, but never onstage. And we'd be so good together.

I feel a lump in my stomach sort of like nausea and also getting punched. I wish I were in this show. I wish I were onstage, singing my heart out with George. I want it so badly that I almost want to rush up to Hudson and tell him the truth now so I can have him and the show this summer. But that's not the plan, and the plan is in place because it's what will work. Telling Hudson I'm a crazy stalker before the week is up probably won't.

Mark's door opens and he steps into the cabin. "Everyone feeling okay about the casting now?" he asks. His eyes linger on George. Everyone nods. "I was sad not to write your name on that cast list, Del," he says to me. "But I was on the phone with my therapist for an hour last night, and he says I have to let other people make their own mistakes. I mean, decisions."

"Sure," I say, trying to smile, but I can't. Maybe it was a mistake. "It's fine."

Mark looks at me a moment, pursing his lips, before looking up at the whole cabin. "We only have a few weeks to do this, people, and you know your parts, so start learning your lines, your notes, your dance moves. I expect you to come by after dinner to rehearse, too, and use all your free time to make this the show I know it can be. Everyone excited?"

Everyone shouts yes, in unison.

"I better shower off this chlorine," I say, and go to the

bathroom to wash while they talk about the show. I can hear laughing and a little singing as I rinse my face. I try to wash away the regret, too. I knew this would happen, I should have prepared myself. It's really hitting me—I'm not in the show this summer. And I'm going to miss it. But this was part of the plan. This is to get Hudson. This has got to be worth it.

I dry off and get dressed, and by then, Mark has put on the album of *Bye Bye Birdie* and the overture is playing loudly, my bunkmates singing snatches of lyrics that go with the melodies as they pop up. Some of them dance. They're all so happy. And I'm happy for them. Just a little sad for myself.

"Um, hi?" I look over at the front screen door to see Hudson walking in. He stares at the cabin filled with campers singing and dancing, and his expression is so confused and cute, but then he spots me and he breaks into a big smile and never mind, I think. It's all worth it. And I know that sounds so dumb, but then he reaches out his hand and I wave good-bye to everyone like we're not all about to walk to the same place, and Hudson and I walk down the stairs together, just holding hands, like we've been gone for so long when it was maybe half an hour and yet in that half an hour, he missed me. He missed ME. He might finally start to feel about me the way I've felt about him for four years and who cares if I can't be in the show one summer just for that.

"So, your cabin is crazy," he says as we walk.

A swarm of tiny bugs flies by and I laugh and dodge them. "I know, they're great."

"Are you going to be able to sleep? Will they let you?"

"Of course, they have to rest their voices. And Mark is strict about them getting enough sleep."

He laughs. "Okay, so I guess you don't want to sneak into my cabin for some shut-eye, then?"

I feel a spark jolt through me at the suggestion. "I don't think we'd get much sleep that way."

He laughs again as we go into the dining hall. "We can sit with my friends tonight, right? They're mostly from the obstacle course."

"Sure," I say. "We can all sit together, maybe. I know Brad would probably appreciate sitting next to George again."

He rolls his eyes. "I still don't get that, but yeah, okay."

We find a seat with his friends and when George and Ashleigh come in, they sit next to me, blending our groups together—at least spatially. Brad and I are the only two who really talk to the theater kids and the jocks. No, that's wrong. I'm a theater kid, and Hudson talks to me, so it's only Hudson and Brad. Or I guess it's me? I guess it depends who's asking. But I try to talk to Hudson's friends, too. There's the one named Drew who I think might be his ex, but spotted me on the wire, and Sam, the girl who chased him with me during

capture the flag. They seem cool. They talk about sports that I don't pay attention to, and training routines, which I can talk about but find boring. They're nice. I can hold a conversation with them. Hudson seems to like them, and he wants me to like them, so I try. And it's fine. But it's not like talking to George and Ashleigh. But why would it be? They've been my friends for years. It's easy with them. It's normal for it to be harder with new people.

Besides, they don't need to be my best friends, I remind myself. Just friendly. And we are. So it's fine, and by the time dinner is over, Hudson seems happy. We've blended our groups enough that Hudson and I can sit, thighs pressed together, and still talk to our friends. Which I think is all he wanted.

After dinner, my friends go off to the drama cabin to rehearse some more, and Hudson takes me by the hand and leads me to the boathouse porch. We're the first ones there, and no one else tries to follow us in, though we can hear people walking by below us. The porch has a love seat that faces the water but is out of sight from anyone walking by because of how far back it is, and we sit down there, holding hands.

"So," I say after listening to the water for a while. "About that 'couple' thing I said during pool time..."

"Don't worry about it, babe," he says, leaning his head on my shoulder. "I mean, between last night, and the obstacle course, and capture the flag, and two dinners, and all the time

in the pool...this must be like date five by now. Totally normal to call us a couple."

"Oh?" I ask. "You saying you want to be my boyfriend?"

"Maybe," he says, lifting his head and grinning at me. He kisses me softly on the lips. "What benefits would I get as your boyfriend?" He kisses me again, deeper, our tongues coming out, his hands around my waist, pulling me on top of him.

He must do this every summer, he's so good at it. Five dates in one day, making out, me already crouching over his lap.

"So we can be boyfriends," he says. "We're ready for that, right? I mean, really, we haven't done enough making out, considering we're on date five. I mean, that's a good date to get naked on, right?" His hand slips up my shorts—farther than it's ever been, and I gasp as he finds my briefs. His thumb slips under those and touches my hip bone. I never realized before what a pleasure center the hip bone is, but it's like he just pressed a button and I'm flooded with joy and lust and color—pink, mostly—and I can feel my eyes rolling back in my head. He pulls me forward and kisses my neck, his other hand roaming up the front of my shirt. I want to be naked with him so badly. I've wanted it for years. I want to do everything with him, but this is too easy, too smooth. This is Hal, and I want Hudson. I take a deep breath and roll off him so I'm sitting next to him again.

"That's all true," I say, looking into his eyes. They're gray with flecks of blue, and in the light of just the one bulb over the porch, they glow. "It is like five dates, and I really like you."

"I like you, too," he says, grinning and putting his hand on my leg, creeping it up my thigh again. "I've actually never felt so connected to someone so quickly."

Every part of me wants to believe that's true. And maybe it is. I'm sure it is. That's why my plan will work. Because we have this connection—one that goes through Del, and gets right to Randy—I know we do. But I don't know if he really believes it yet, or it's just a line from Hal. So I put my hand over his, interlacing our fingers and stopping its roaming.

"But we also would have talked more. Gotten to know each other," I say.

"Okay," he says, squeezing my hand. "So...what do you want to know?"

"I don't know...about parents, coming out, your favorite movies or music?"

He nods, thinking about it. "Let's start with those last two, then. I really like the John Wick movies, and before we got here, I was listening to a lot of the new Walk the Moon album. You?"

"Oh," I say, surprised, for some reason, that he's so willing to just talk. And a little disappointed. I was hoping

he'd push for more making out. Also, I don't know Walk the Moon, and I'm concerned I will be tested now. "Well, I..." Damn. My favorite movies are all musicals, my favorite music is all show tunes...But I don't want to lie, either. "Do you know Audra McDonald?" I ask.

He shakes his head. "She a pop singer?"

"She does a lot of genres," I say. Not lying.

"See, the thing that sucks about camp is no phones. I can't look her up to play some. At the end of the summer, when you have your phone back, you'll play her for me?"

I grin. He just said end of the summer. Like we'll still be together at the end of the summer. Everything is working.

"Yeah," I say. "So now you come up with a question."

He smiles and squeezes my hand in his. "Okay...what do you want to be when you grow up?"

The words *an actor* almost come dancing out of my mouth from sheer muscle memory of that being the answer I've given to this question since I was six. I laugh instead, to give myself time. What does Del want to be? I shouldn't say athlete. I shouldn't lie that much.

"I'm not sure," I say instead. "I think..." Don't lie too much. "I want to tell stories."

"Like a writer?"

"No, I don't think I'm good enough at writing for that. I like to read, but...I don't know. I'm hoping I'll figure it out later."

He nods. "I get that. And I like to read, too! My favorite

148

book is *Shoeless Joe*. It's like . . . older than I am. By a lot. But my dad gave it to me when I was little and I just loved it."

"What's it about?"

"Baseball . . . America. The way sports can sort of live on, I guess? Or players can, and plays and games?"

"That's cool." I grin. Sports can live on the way good theater does, I think but don't say. "I think my favorite book is probably *Finishing the Hat*. It's an autobiography by Stephen Sondheim."

"Who's that?"

I do my best acting to date by not slapping him. He'll learn, I remind myself. I'll teach him.

"He's a storyteller," I say, though that's barely scratching the surface. "But you never answered your own question—what do you want to do after school?"

"So, I don't know exactly," he says with a shrug. "I want to try to be an Olympian, maybe, like Connie was. Track and field. But I know that's a long shot, and I know it wouldn't be, like, a career. But maybe I could coach after or be a trainer in a gym? I know it doesn't sound like much, but I like encouraging people."

I nod. That sounds perfect for him. "Like when you encouraged me on the obstacle course," I say.

"Yeah." He grins. "I like doing stuff like that. I like helping people . . . be better. Making people feel like they can do stuff. And I like being physical. So training, coaching . . . I think I'd like that."

"Well," I say, "since you answered some questions, I think maybe we can get a little more physical ourselves now." I lean closer to him.

"Oh yeah?" He does that thing where he smiles and the tip of his tongue finds the space between his teeth.

"You said we had to do more of both, right?"

"Okay," he says, wrapping his arm around my waist, his finger sliding under my shirt. "A kiss per question."

"We'll work out the exchange rate," I say, leaning in.

FOURTEEN

We're late to the meeting hall for Joan's queer history lesson. Not just a few minutes, either, but ten minutes, and she's already showing a PowerPoint presentation. But at least I feel like we're bonding a little more. Yes, we did more kissing and question asking, but we kept our pants on (though not our shirts) and we did talk some. His mom's name is Lois, and she's a real estate broker, and his dad is Sam, a foreman. His mom's parents both came over from Korea when they were kids and met and got married here; his dad's great-grandparents fled pogroms in the Ukraine. He has a dog named Rufus. His favorite TV show, when he's not watching "the game" (I didn't ask what sport this meant, so possibly it means all of them?), is *The Simpsons*. I didn't have to lie about anything—I told him I liked watching old

Parks and Rec episodes on Netflix, and that seemed butch enough, and I definitely didn't make up parents or anything. So all still on track—but with bonus make-out sessions! And I think we're boyfriends now? We never clarified that point, but it feels like we were agreeing to it. I should have asked about that and done less kissing.

And also paid attention to the time. Joan sighs as we sneak in and take a seat in the back.

"As I was saying." She clicks something and the screen behind her, the only light in the otherwise dark amphitheater of a cabin, changes to show people in suits and dressed from the 1950s or maybe 1960s. It's a black-and-white photo and everyone is well dressed, wearing sunglasses, and holding up signs that say things like HOMOSEXUALS ARE AMERICAN CITIZENS TOO and GOVERNMENT POLICY CREATES SECURITY RISKS.

"These are from the first gay protest outside the White House, in 1965. The papers didn't cover it. No one paid attention. But there were queer rights organizations before Stonewall. The one that organized this protest was called the Mattachine Society. They were founded in the early fifties, so don't let anyone tell you we haven't been trying to get equal rights for very long, or that we're a new thing." She clicks and the PowerPoint cycles through more faces, and she talks about the history of the groups. My first year, I thought the history lessons felt a little out of place for a summer camp, but I've come to like them. I wish Mark gave them, instead

of Joan, so they'd have a bit more flair, but Joan cares about this stuff, and she finds interesting little details—like today's lecture. The Mattachine Society (which started as all men) and the Daughters of Bilitis, their sister organization, two "homophile" organizations, as they called themselves, that tried to campaign for queer rights with sip-ins, where they went to bars and asked for drinks and told the bartender they were queer—which, legally, meant they couldn't even drink back then. They very politely would drink, and leave.

"The idea was that they would show everyone that queer people were normal and respectable, not terrifying sexual perverts like the newspapers often made them out to be. And to that end, they trained themselves to be 'normal'— there's one story of a meeting at the Daughters of Bilitis where a woman who had previously had a short haircut and dressed in jeans and a leather jacket showed up in a dress and walked in heels, and everyone applauded, so happy they'd changed her."

I swallow and look at Hudson, who's watching the screen. The light makes his skin pale. He nods slightly.

Joan continues her lecture, telling us all about pre-Stonewall gay liberation movements of the fifties and sixties. When she finishes, she takes questions, and Ashleigh raises her hand.

"Was she happy, though?" she asks. "The woman who changed from jeans to dresses?"

"I don't know," Joan says. "Probably she was harassed by

153

police less, and fit in the straight society more, which would have made life a lot easier, and probably a lot safer from harassment and violence. But safer and happier don't always go hand in hand. It's a choice that a lot of us have to make—when to come out, who to come out to. You've all thought about it, I'm sure. As for her dress…I imagine it might have felt like a costume. You're all at that age where you're trying on identities anyway, so I don't know if you understand what it's like to be told there's a right and wrong way to be queer, and the right way looks just like being straight, yet probably some of you do."

"But there is no difference," someone in front says. "That's the whole point of what we're fighting for—equal treatment because we're all the same."

Joan nods. "Well, we're all people, deserving of respect and equal treatment. But straight people aren't all identical. Some straight women do wear jeans." The crowd chuckles. This is the closest Joan has ever gotten to a joke. "But it's different for a lesbian to wear jeans than it is for a straight woman. So maybe the equality we're fighting for isn't just marriage or the ability to not be fired from our jobs for being queer—which is still perfectly legal in over twenty-five states, by the way—but the ability to be whoever we want, jeans, skirts, makeup, heels, beards, whatever, and still be treated like anyone else."

"Is it possible the woman in jeans was trans?" asks someone else.

"Sure." Joan nods. "Again, I don't know. But I'd imagine that a lot of this idea of 'fitting in' hurt trans people who at the time identified as gay or lesbian because they didn't have the language for it. Of course, trans people existed before Stonewall, too, but the terminology was different...and the subject of next week's lesson, I think, since we're out of time now."

Joan flicks the lights on, causing momentary blindness in everyone as they flinch and wait for their eyes to readjust.

"Have a good night!" she calls out as we start to leave the cabin. "Sweet dreams."

Hudson and I walk out together, hand in hand. I feel like I should ask him about what he thought of the lesson, but I'm also afraid of his answer. I don't want him to say he thinks it was good that the woman could walk in heels. I don't think he will. He's not a bad guy. But I also don't know. I've never thought to ask why he only likes masc guys. George says it's a preference, like having a thing for blonds, or like Brad's love of body hair. A fetish, kind of. And that's okay. It's normal to have things you're into. But hearing about the way they treated that woman made me wonder if he would have clapped for her, too. 'Cause there's a difference between being into something in a person and thinking a certain type of people are better.

"So," he says, when we stop at my cabin. "I'll see you tomorrow, right?"

"Yeah," I say.

"I had a really good time tonight. It was a good fifth date."

I laugh. "Yeah. It was really good. I'm looking forward to dates six, seven, eight, and...nine? Tomorrow."

"Nine. That's awfully presumptuous." He smiles at me, leaning back against the wall of my cabin.

"You're right, I'm sorry. Want to hang out again tomorrow night, after dinner?" I ask.

"Yes," he says, smiling so widely, I swear his teeth are glowing. I lean forward and kiss him, and he wraps his arms around me, pulling me closer, his hands straying up the back of my shirt.

"Oh my god, are you two boyfriends yet?" Ashleigh asks, suddenly beside us. Hudson pulls back, looking a little sheepish.

"Yes," I say. "I was giving my boyfriend a good-night kiss," I say, raising my chin a little. Ashleigh rolls her eyes.

"That was more than one kiss," George says. He's next to her, fanning himself with a different fan, this one rainbow. "But if you want to keep going, I'm sure your audience wouldn't mind." He gestures with his fan at the campers walking around us, several of whom are staring at us. I feel my cheeks turning bright red and hope it's dark enough it doesn't show.

"Okay," I say, turning to Hudson. "Good night."

"Good night, babe," he says, pecking me on the cheek before he walks away.

"You two have got to get it under control," Ashleigh says as we walk into the cabin. "You're going to end up screwing in front of the flagpole with everyone watching. Unless that's your thing? No judgment if you're an exhibitionist, but you should probably find some consenting voyeurs."

"I'm not an exhibitionist," I say, maybe louder than I should, as a few of our bunkmates turn to look at me. I flop down on my bed. "And I don't think he is."

"It wasn't on his dating profile," George says, slipping his shoes off and taking out his nightgown. He slips it over his clothes and with a few quick movements removes his T-shirt and shorts from underneath.

"Yeah," I say. "What did it say, do you remember? Just, like, masc4masc, or . . . was it . . . worse than that?"

"Having doubts about your dream man?" Ashleigh asks.

"Just . . . after tonight's lecture. I thought it was a preference, but . . ."

"It didn't say 'no fats, no femmes, no blacks,' if that's what you're worried about," George says. "It was something like 'masculine guy seeking the same.'"

"Okay. So it's just a preference," I say.

"If it said *no* something, that would be bad," Ashleigh says, getting out her toothbrush. "That's exclusionary. Like, 'no fatties' is bad, but 'prefers fit women' is okay, I think?"

"Feels like a fine line," Paz says, hopping into her bunk. "What if it said they like 'white guys'? That's not far from 'whites only.'"

157

"Yeah," Ashleigh says. "You're right, sorry."

"But what about, like, guys into body hair?" I ask. "That's not bad, right?"

"Historically, people with body hair haven't had to use separate water fountains," Paz says dryly.

"Right," I say. "Sorry."

"When I see a profile that says they prefer skinny twinks," George says, "I know I won't ever stand a chance with that guy. But when it says 'no Middle Eastern guys,' then it feels like I'm being rejected for who I am, my identity. Hairy isn't such a huge part of my self-worth. But being Middle Eastern, being Jewish? That's about me. And saying you're rejecting all that preemptively because it doesn't get you hard? That's racist. Your dick is racist, and so are you, and you really shouldn't be putting that online. It's tacky."

Paz laughs. "Yeah, what he said."

"Okay," I say. "But that's not about masc or femme. That's behavior. That's mutable. I mean, I changed, right? Like the woman putting on heels. So...it's not bad, right? Like...would Hudson have applauded when that woman walked in heels? Or would he have said it's better to be herself, even if I—the lesbian version of Hudson, I guess?—am not into her in a leather jacket and jeans?"

"You mean if you were here, where it was safe to wear the jeans and not get harassed for it?" Paz asks.

"What he means," Ashleigh says, "is would he think it was okay you went butch for him, because that means it'll be

okay when you drop it later." She turns to me. "But we don't know him as well as you do." She sticks her toothbrush in her mouth and starts to brush. "You ashk him."

"What do you think?" George asks.

"I think...," I say. "I think it's just a preference. I think he'd tell that woman to be herself, because being herself has nothing to do with attracting femme-only women or something."

"So you think he'd tell you to be yourself," George says.

"Only if I was willing to give him up," I say quickly. Maybe defensively. "And I'm not. But he wouldn't think putting on the dress made her a better person. Just more attractive to people who like girls in dresses. And there's nothing wrong with that, right?"

"I mean, we could say you should be attracted to a person's character, not their wardrobe," Paz says.

"Oh please," George says. "I judge men entirely by the contents of their closets. And their drawers," he adds, wiggling his eyebrows.

I snort a laugh and stand up and take my toiletries into the bathroom. I brush my teeth and wash my face and stare in the mirror for a moment after, my face wet. I look different from last year. I look like what Hudson is attracted to. That was the point. I put on heels for him. And it's worth it. Tonight definitely showed me that—he's kind and fun, and I want to keep kissing him forever. It's just a preference, him liking this me, and not the chubby, long-haired Randy with flowers in

his hair and lace on his shorts. After all, he likes me. Not just my face, body, wardrobe. We've talked. He thinks I'm special, that we have a connection. And if a haircut was what it took to show him that, then it's worth it. And once he sees it, he won't mind if my hair grows back or if I love musicals or paint my nails. Heels or jeans, maybe Paz is right. It's about falling in love with a person—preferences are just things that make us think we're more or less likely to fall in love because of what our dicks react to at first. So I made his dick hard. Now we can fall in love. And love is more important. And I'm falling wildly in love with Hudson.

The next day goes by like the last one: We hike instead of doing the obstacle course, Hudson and I holding hands when we can, we eat lunch together, and I hear about rehearsals from Ashleigh and George during A&C (George has already mastered his song and is having fun with it, Ashleigh made suggestions about changing the lighting scheme that Mark liked, and apparently Crystal's choreography is panic-inducingly ambitious this year), and then we play kickball during sports. Then we all swim together, Hudson wrapping his arms around me and putting his head on my shoulder to talk to Brad in the pool. Then Hudson and I steal some time at the boathouse to make out, our hair still wet and smelling of chlorine, before running back to our cabins to change and head down to dinner, which we eat thigh to thigh before it's time for that night's

activity: a campfire by the flagpole where we all take turns telling ghost stories and making s'mores. I sit on a log, and Hudson sits in front of me, and I wrap my arms around him like he did to me in the pool, and I feel warm and happy.

True, I am ready to get naked with him already. And I know he is, too. But that's not part of the plan. So we stick to making out—though we're learning to hide it better, to avoid the eye-rolling from other campers.

The day after that, at the boathouse, his hands slip down the back of my swim trunks as I straddle him, and I feel his hands squeeze my bare ass for the first time. The day after that, lying down on the love seat, I feel our erections press against each other, instead of just our legs, for the first time. Every new thing our bodies do brings with it a heady lightness in my body, like I'm being thrown out of my own body because it's so crazy it's happening—really happening. Hudson Aaronson-Lim is my boyfriend. Hudson Aaronson-Lim is falling in love with me. This is better than a musical. A musical is just pretend. This is real.

Except that I'm not. Which I remember the next night, after dinner, when he turns to me, our hands interwoven as we walk out of the dining hall, and asks, "So what do you want to do?"

"Me?" I ask. "I don't know. What do you like doing?"

"Oh, come on, you've been here a week, you're not new anymore. You pick the date-night activity."

I smile on the outside, but inside I am feeling the sheer panic of being onstage when a spotlight pops on and you've

forgotten the opening lyrics. I was not prepared for this—he's supposed to be the one showing me the ropes, doing butch stuff. I know what I'd want to do—go hang out at the drama cabin and maybe paint each other's nails, but that is definitely not what he'd want to do, and not what Del would want to do. What do butch guys do on dates, anyway? It's been mostly wandering around camp and him showing me stuff, then going to the boathouse to make out so far, and I've been enjoying that quite a bit, especially the latter part. I suppose I can't just say "Let's go right to the boathouse," though. Or "Let's go watch sports," 'cause there's no TV, and there's not even a game going at the kickball field.

"So?" he asks.

"I was looking to see if there was a game." I nod at the kickball field.

"Nah, let's keep it just us," he says.

Right. Sexy butch date. Intimate butch date. I go through the sporty camp things to do that aren't team related—archery, hiking, tennis. TENNIS.

"How about I show you how to play tennis?" I say. This could be terrible, of course. He said he was bad at tennis, and I've gotten okay at it, but I suspect his definition of *bad* and mine of *okay* might be on completely different scales. "We can work on your serve."

He grins. "Okay."

We walk over to the tennis court, me going over serving form in my head. He gets out the tennis equipment.

The court is empty, so we stand next to each other on one end, Hudson looking at me expectantly in the light from the lampposts around the court.

"Right," I say. "So...this is, um, a..." And the name for the long stick with the round bit with the grid of wire or string or something is completely gone. I shake it like I'm doing jazz hands, like it's all very exciting.

"Racket?" Hudson asks, raising an eyebrow.

"Yes. That. And this is a ball!" I bounce the tennis ball on the court and it flies upward at an odd angle before I can catch it, rolling away to the other side of the court. Hudson eyes it suspiciously.

"I thought you said you were good at this," he says.

"Well...I don't know about good," I say. "I mean, I can hit the ball with the..." I swallow. "Racket." Phew. "Sometimes."

Hudson laughs. "Are you messing with me?" he asks, stepping closer and putting his hands on my hips, his thumbs finding the space between my skin and my clothes, just under the waistband, and gliding back and forth.

I look down at his hands and my mind is blank. Well, not blank. It's just been invaded by one thing. And it isn't tennis.

"Maybe we should just go to the boathouse," I say, my voice breathy.

He laughs, stepping back. "Uh-uh. You're showing me how to improve my serve. Come on." He takes a ball, throws

it into the air, and slams it—right into the net. "See? I always do that."

"Okay," I say, stepping behind him and letting my hands run over his shoulders. He presses his back into me, his whole body warm, my body warm. I have a sudden urge to just start nibbling on his ear, to lick down his neck, to keep going, taking his shirt and pants off so I can have him right there on the tennis court.

But no. I have to hold back! I won't be a two-week conquest! He's not going to be Hal for me.

"So, do you like tennis?" I ask, adjusting his shoulders and the way he holds the racket. "Do you play much?" Turn the conversation less sexy. Then I won't be as quick to give in. Get to know him, get him to fall for me. That's the plan.

"I don't know. I think I like stuff where I'm really competing with myself more," he says. "That's why I like the obstacle course. I actually really love track and field. I'm on the varsity team."

"Yeah?" I say, impressed, as though I don't already know this. I try to bend his arm for a volley, keeping it raised. His skin is so warm, it's intoxicating. I pull my hand back.

"Yeah. So tennis always seemed less my thing. How about you? Why did you get into it?"

"They have dogs that retrieve the balls," I say without thinking.

He laughs and turns to look at me. "What?"

"There are these videos online, they train dogs to retrieve

the balls when they go out of bounds," I say. It's the truth. It was my second-favorite discovery when googling sports, after some of the really fun uniforms they have out there. Well, third-favorite, if you count the men in the uniforms. Fourth-favorite if you count the men out of the uniforms. But a top five, for sure.

"So you're into tennis 'cause of the dogs?"

I shrug. "I mean...sort of?" *I'm into tennis because I wanted a sport because I'm into you!* I almost tell him, but that would give it all away. "I like the way you have to watch, I think," I say, trying to come up with something. "You have to read your opponent, find out what they want to do, and then give them a variation on that—something where they think they know what's happening, but then it goes all sideways." There—that's kind of like theater, like how actors play. That's true. That's Randy...through a Del filter.

"So you like competing against people," he says.

"I guess." I shrug.

"That's cool. I think they're both good ways of improving yourself, you know. Making yourself better."

I nod. "That's why you got into sports?"

"I mean...sort of," he says, stretching his arms up and looking at the sky. "So, I always liked running around and stuff. I was always an active kid. And my dad loves sports— they were always on. Not just baseball and football, but like track meets, the Olympics, snowboarding. And he was always trying to get me into them, too, and I had all this energy,

so, like, being in Little League was fun, sure, but it also was something to do and my dad would always cheer from the stands—'That's my boy' kinda crap, y'know?"

"Yeah." I nod.

"So I just did it. But I never loved Little League like I do track. Baseball, you have a team, other guys you have to rely on to throw you the ball..."

There's a long pause as I can sense him swallowing something.

"They don't like a queer kid on their team?" I ask.

He shrugs. "Kinda. I mean, they never called me a fag or anything, but...they used that word a lot."

I shake my head. "I don't like that word."

"Yeah," he says, looking up again so I can't read his face. "Me neither." His voice is weird, a little cold. But then he looks back at me, all charming smile. "Did you have trouble when you came out?"

I shrug. "I mean, some. Mostly people just ignore me."

"You said that before, and I still can't imagine it," he says, his eyes running up and down me.

I blush. "Well, I'm quiet at school. I mean, I'm out to some people, and I don't lie when people ask, but...people figured it out. Not much changed, though. No one was careful to stop using *gay* as a bad word or anything. Once someone wrote *fag* on my locker. My parents got so mad, stormed the principal's office. They found out who did it and suspended him. Since then, mostly they leave me alone. Dirty

looks, laughing...as long as I don't stare at anyone, keep my head down, though..."

"Wow, that's cool your parents were so...good."

"Your parents aren't?"

"Well, there was that thing with a swim class once. None of the other guys, a lot of them from the baseball team, would get in the pool, said they'd catch my gay, didn't want me staring at them or copping a feel underwater, stuff like that. This is when I wasn't really out yet. Like, I knew, and someone had caught me looking at pictures of Instagram thirst traps on my phone in study hall, so everyone else kind of knew, but no one was talking about it to me. Until this swim class. And then everyone knew. I could have denied it, I guess, but I didn't. I told them I was just going to swim alone, then, get my gay all over the water as I practiced for the swim race at the end of the semester. That was my coming out to the school. Kinda like yours. Oh, but I came in first place in the race."

"And your parents didn't care? Were you out to them?"

"Yeah, I was. But they just asked me what I'd done to get those guys' attention. Told me not to flaunt my sexuality."

"They blamed you." I feel myself glaring at shadows behind him that could be his parents.

"Not blamed," Hudson says quickly. "I mean, they're not bad people, just..." He sighs. "They're parents. They want to protect me."

"Yeah."

"Anyway, that's part of why I run alone. Challenge myself. Make myself better. No one to let you down with homophobia if you run alone. And they don't get to win as many games as they would if I were on the baseball team."

"Serves them right," I say.

"Yeah. And speaking of serves... aren't you going to help me with mine?" He turns around, sticking his ass out at me. "Is this the right form?"

I step up behind him and reach around, taking his arm and pull him back a little, our bodies flush. He feels so good against me. He smells so good.

He pushes his ass into me. I grab his hips and push back. He takes in a sharp breath, lets out a soft half moan.

"That doesn't feel like the right place to hold your racket," he says, and I laugh and step back. What were we doing? Serving, right. Tennis serving, not serving looks or anything. 'Cause we're masc.

Actually, I am good at serving, I remember. It's a dance move, hands over the head, then bring them down, but wrist at an angle, like when you want to show jazz hands to the audience.

"It's all in the wrist," I tell him, reaching around and taking his wrist in my hand. I lean my head on his shoulder and lower my voice as I shape his arms. "You want to keep your wrist higher, so the angle isn't so severe, like this," I say. Our bodies are pressed together, and he keeps pushing further back into me.

"Okay," he says. We both stand there for a moment, interlocked, before I take a step back.

"So try," I say.

He serves, this time whisking the ball over the net. "I did it!" he says. He takes another ball from the ground and serves again, and again gets it over the net. "Wow. Babe. That... actually really helped." He turns around, smiles at me. "I thought you just suggested it so you could wrap your arms around me."

"Can I not do that without a tennis lesson?" I ask.

He smiles, stepping toward me. "You can do whatever you want," he says in a low voice, before kissing me. His arms wrap around me, and our tongues find each other. He bites my lips slightly—new, but surprisingly enjoyable. I gasp and he moves away from my lips to my ear.

"Want to go to the boathouse?" he asks in a whisper.

"Absolutely."

On Friday, we run the obstacle course again, and I make it through the tire swing, and even grab on to the rope swing over the Peanut Butter Pit—though I don't make it across. Hudson says I did a good job, though, and kisses me on the cheek. I've been trying to get myself ready for today. The end of the first week, the time when Hudson usually invites his boyfriends to the Peanut Butter Pit after dark, where they finally get naked, and I would love to finally get naked with

him, but I know I have to say no. I have to show him I'm more than just a fling. And I have a plan figured out. When he asks me if I'm ready, I'm going to say I want to talk more first—and then ask him about the most unerotic thing I can think of—coming out to his parents.

"Hey, Del?" Brad taps me on the shoulder as we watch the other campers run the obstacle course. "Can I talk to you for a second?"

"Sure," I say. Is this where he warns me what Hudson means when he invites me here tonight? Tells me to bring condoms? That would be quite a system, but it wouldn't surprise me.

He pulls me away from Hudson, who shrugs and goes back to watching the other campers.

"What's up?" I ask Brad, when we're out of earshot of everyone else. Has he finally figured out I didn't bump my head?

"It's about George," he says.

"What?" For a moment, panic floods me like cold water. Did I miss something with George? Is he angry at me? Did he lose his voice? "What's wrong with George?"

"Nothing." Brad grins. "At least...I don't think anything. But I feel like we've been flirting now for a week, and he's funny, but he's not like...I don't know if he's really into me. I mean, look at you and Hudson—you guys have been boyfriends for the entire time he and I have just been flirting. Is he really into me? Or should I give up on this?"

"I know he thinks you're cute," I say carefully. No one has ever come to me for romantic advice before. But I guess having a boyfriend makes you an expert. Especially when you came up with a plan to get him. "George wants something easy," I say. That's what George had said.

"I can be easy," Brad says, smiling.

"Not like that," I say. "He just...he wants someone he can be himself around, and I think he's worried that you'd want him to..."

"Be someone completely different?" Brad raises an eyebrow at me, and puts his hands on his hips. "Wonder where he got that idea."

"So you know it wasn't a bump on the head," I say. I take a deep breath. He hasn't told Hudson yet, so that's good.

"I'm not an idiot. And hey, you do what you want. I thought you were cool before. You killed that song last year, what was it? 'Dirty Old Man'?"

"Yeah?" I find myself smiling, remembering it.

"But if this is the new you, that's cool, too. As long as you're not doing it to mess with my friend."

"No," I say quickly. "No. I just wanted him to notice me."

"Well...you got that. Now how do I get George to notice me?"

"You won't tell Hudson?" That would throw everything off. He likes me now, he's into me, and maybe he could even see me under the glittery trappings if he knew, but it would be too much, too sudden. I need to make him love me first.

"I'm not blackmailing you," Brad says, looking annoyed. "I'm asking. If you don't want to tell me, that's fine. I get it."

"No." I shake my head. "Sorry. George thinks you're cool, and cute, and I think you just need to show him you like him for him, and you don't care if he wears makeup or has an extensive fan collection. Or just tell him that. Ask him out. Stop flirting, and make a move. Make it easy for him."

Brad nods. "Okay," he says. "Thanks, man." He goes in for a hug, and I hug him back. "And for what it's worth, Hudson really likes you. But maybe he's the one person at camp who really has a right to know who you used to be?"

"He will," I say. "Once I know I'm not just one of his two-week romances. Once we're . . ." I let the sentence fade.

"Oh." Brad nods. "Playing for keeps. Okay. Good luck."

"Thanks. And there's no real difference, you know. Between Randy and Del. I'm still me."

Brad looks me up and down before nodding. "I get what you mean, but if you really want Hudson . . . if you want him to fall for you—for Randy—then you have to tell him, right? Because if there's really no difference, he won't mind."

"Right," I say. Which is true. Except . . . not yet. Playing for keeps, like Brad just said. And that means winning first, getting Hudson to fall. Then it won't matter. Then he'll have seen me—the most important parts of me—and the other stuff, theater, glitter, sports—all of that will be unimportant and he'll love me with nail polish or without. I'll tell him,

and he'll laugh and say, "None of that matters. I know *you*. And you're special."

If I tell him too soon, though, he'll tell me I'm a liar and never want to speak to me again. So I have to go slow.

"Thanks," I say to Brad.

Brad runs back toward the group and I follow slowly. Hudson turns to me and grins, extending his hand for me to take when I'm close.

"So, what was that about?" he asks quietly.

"He just wanted some advice."

"Advice? On what?"

"Loooooove, obviously. From me, the loooooove expert."

"You're such a nerd, babe." He laughs, resting his head on my shoulder.

"A love nerd."

"So he's still into George?"

"Yeah."

"What did you tell him?"

"To tell George he's not just flirting, that he really likes him."

He lifts his head up and looks at me. "You think they'll really work?"

"Sure."

"They're so different."

"So what? We're not the same."

"We're more similar than them."

I shrug. "I don't know."

"Please don't start wearing nail polish," he says, and it's like a sudden punch to the throat.

"Why not?" I ask, my voice coarse.

"I dunno. I just...like you like you are. A regular guy."

"Would nail polish really make a difference?" I try not to make it sound like begging. I know it's early in the plan, but this has to work. All of it, including turning back into Randy. And it will, I tell myself, closing my eyes for a moment. It will, it will, it will....

"Nah," he says, leaning his head on my shoulder again. I sigh, relieved. "I don't know. It's not like you're going to start wearing it, right?"

"Right," I say, watching one of the first-year kids leap for the rope over the Peanut Butter Pit and miss. Not yet, anyway.

FIFTEEN

Honestly, I'm a little offended," I tell George and Ashleigh that night after a camp-wide scavenger hunt, where cabins were teams, so I wasn't with Hudson, sadly. "Isn't the first Friday when he normally asks a guy to go to the Peanut Butter Pit with him?"

"But you said you wanted to take it slow," Ashleigh says.

"Well, yeah," I say.

"Darling, your plan is working. He's treating you like a real boyfriend, not a fling. You said you wanted to wait until week two, right?" George lies on his stomach, painting his nails a new color he found over the year. It's called Unicorn Trampocalypse, and it's prismatic glitter with pink, purple, and navy, and I have never wanted anything on my fingers so badly. He already promised he'd paint mine with it when I start wearing it again.

"Maybe ten days."

"Isn't that closer to his schedule?" Ashleigh asks. "His usual one?"

George snorts. "Getting a little tired of waiting?"

"Yes," I say, leaning back. "Really tired of waiting."

"Well, the next step in your plan is love, not sex, so you'd better take the scenic route as you get into his pants. Can you do my right hand?"

"Sure," I say, moving to his bed and taking the nail polish from him. I carefully fill in the nails on each of his spread fingers, watching the polish sparkle in the light. I look at my own hands—unpainted nails, skin rubbed raw from rocks and the rope swing. I'm a little proud of it, of how well I've adapted to this role, and how well I'm playing it. But I do wish I could sparkle again like Unicorn Trampocalypse.

"Besides, we don't know for sure it's Friday," George says. "Maybe it's tomorrow. Maybe he sneaks into your cabin tonight to whisk you away."

"Yeah," I say, moving on to his next nail. "You're right. I'm being silly."

"You're being horny," Ashleigh says.

"Who's horny?" Paz asks, coming back from having brushed her teeth in the bathroom and launching herself into her bunk, then immediately wincing.

"No one," I say at the exact same time as Ashleigh and George say, "Randy."

"There's a terrible pun there," Paz says, rubbing her shoulder.

"Which thankfully no one has made yet," I respond, my voice arch as I paint the last of George's nails.

"What's wrong with your shoulder?" Ashleigh asks Paz.

"I fell during the choreography for 'Shriners' Ballet' today. Crystal has me literally jumping over two of the Shriners' outstretched arms to be caught by another. He didn't catch me very well today."

"Ouch."

"I mean, I'm happy the dance isn't a bunch of dumb sex jokes, and now it's more about me beating them up, though. And at least I don't have to run up a wall, like Jordan does during 'Honestly Sincere.' I think Crystal was high when she came up with the dancing this year."

"I'm actually sort of happy I didn't get Kim," George says softly. "Montgomery has to walk along the edge of a raised bedframe at one point. It's like an inch wide. While singing."

"It's more Cirque du Soliel than musical theater, honestly," Paz adds.

"Sounds like the obstacle course," I say with a laugh. "Sweetie, this is going to be at least two coats." I point at George's nails with the polish brush.

"I know. It's quick drying, though. We have at least ten minutes before lights-out." We both blow on his nails to get them to dry faster. "What are you doing tomorrow, since

you don't have rehearsals all day like us?" Weekends are mostly free time. Counselors are around, so we can drop into the A&C cabin or get in line for waterskiing at the lake, but there's nothing scheduled, no planned stuff.

"Hudson wants to go on a hike, just the two of us."

"See, so that's when he'll probably ask. A lovely hike, he kisses you, he says he wants to see you again tonight, in private, and so on. I'm sure he has this down to an art."

"Probably," I say. George takes the nail polish back and does his left hand. "Yeah, you're probably right. And then I'll say no, and ask him deep personal questions so we connect even more."

"Sure," George says. "Sounds like a plan." He carefully finishes off the last of his left nails, then hands the nail polish back to me and spreads out his right hand again. I start painting. "You know, I have a date, too. Brad is going to come hang out at the drama cabin, and when rehearsals are over, we might go hang out at the boathouse or something."

"Oh?" I ask. "Finally giving him a shot?"

"It's funny, it's like he knew exactly what to say." I focus on carefully spreading the polish of George's nails, but I can feel his stare.

"I didn't coach him. He just asked why you seemed shy about taking it to the next level, and I told him. Should I not have?" I look up. "I'm sorry."

"Darling, no, it's fine. I had to make a decision about that

sooner or later, and when he told me he liked me—the whole package, not just the body hair—that helped a lot. He seemed to mean it."

"He did," I say, going back to his nails. "He says you make him laugh."

"Darling, I make everybody laugh."

"Eh," Ashleigh says from above my bunk. "You're okay."

"Thanks," George says. "I think so."

"So you're like a love guru now," Paz says from above us. "Randy with the romance plan."

"I mean...maybe a little. My plan is working, right? So I must know something."

"Darling, you know one thing. Don't get ahead of yourself."

"Yeah, Paz, don't say stuff like that, it'll go right to his head."

"Randy, the romance king," I say, handing the nail polish back to George. "Has a nice ring to it."

"If my nails weren't wet, I'd hit you with a pillow."

"Mine aren't," Ashleigh says, hopping off her bunk, grabbing my pillow, and knocking me on the head with it in one swoop.

"I'm kidding, I'm kidding," I say, blocking her with my arm. "I'm no romance king."

"Good," she says, throwing my pillow back and looking at George's nails. "That's a cool color."

"You want some?" George asks.

"Nah. It'll get chipped while I'm playing with the light rigs. Don't waste it unless your folks are sending you more."

"Maybe not this color, but they'd better be sending more nail polish," George says. "I only brought two bottles."

Paz dips her head down over the top of the bed and looks. "Oh, it is pretty."

"You want?" George asks.

"If you're offering…" Paz hops down from the bed and stands next to Ashleigh—much closer than she needs to. Ashleigh glances at her, nervously, then gets back into her own bunk.

"Sit," George says, patting the space next to him. Paz sits next to him and stares up at where Ashleigh is, like she's trying to look through the bed. "Spread your hands," George says. "We might only have time for one coat before lights-out, though."

"That's okay," Paz says.

George starts to paint her nails and I stand up, stretching as an excuse to stare at Ashleigh, who is frowning, and flipping through a comic without really reading it. I raise my eyebrow at her, not wanting to ask what's going on with Paz while Paz is sitting right below us. She looks at me and shrugs. Well, that doesn't clear anything up.

"Lights-out in five," Mark says, coming out of his room in pajamas. "So you'd better have brushed your teeth. Remember, plaque can lead to throat infections, and I won't have any

of you taking time off to rest your voices just because you couldn't be bothered to have good dental hygiene. Plus we want those teeth to sparkle under the lights."

"Are you really giving us a lecture on brushing our teeth?" Montgomery asks. "We're not seven."

"You all look seven to me," Mark says. "Everyone under thirty looks seven to me. My therapist says it's because of my anxiety over aging, but I think it's just my brain protecting itself from getting emotionally invested in children."

"Oh, sweetie, you mean you're not invested in us?" I ask.

"If I were emotionally invested in you, Randall Kapplehoff, I would cry myself to sleep every night until your hair grew back and you started dressing well again."

"You have been crying a lot," Crystal calls from inside the room.

"Be quiet, Crystal."

The entire cabin giggles.

"Laugh all you want," Mark says. "Lights-out in five."

I lie down in my bed as George finishes the first coat of Paz's nails.

"You want another layer on yours?" I ask him.

"Nah," he says. "It can wait until tomorrow. He closes the bottle up and puts it in his cubby. "Besides, I want to save some for when you can wear it again. It'll be your un-mascing nail polish."

"Oh my god, why have we not been calling it that all the time?" Ashleigh asks. "The Grand Un-Masc-ing. And right

now, you're masc-ed." She pauses. "And you want to go to a masc-ed ball. Or two."

"Gross, no, be quiet," I say, but everyone is already laughing and I start laughing, too. A minute later, Mark shuts out the lights, but we all continue to giggle quietly in the dark.

SIXTEEN

want to show you the best view in camp," Hudson says, taking me by the hand and leading me into the woods.

"Okay," I say. "How much of a hike is this?"

"It's not too bad, promise. You have bug spray on, right?"

"Yeah."

"Good."

He leads the way, and honestly, I have no idea where we're going. I've always stayed out of the woods in past years, except during color wars, when we have the nighttime Spy Wars—the two teams split the whole camp up and each try to get as many people as possible to "safety" in the other team's territory (usually the boathouse and meeting hall) without getting spotted by anyone on the other team. We have flashlights, so sneaking across the camp in the open is

out of the question and usually people try to make it through the woods. George and I always joke it's a disaster waiting to happen, but no one's gone missing yet.

But just hiking around the woods in the day hasn't been anything I'd done before a few days ago, and then Connie had taken us on a pretty easy trail. Hudson is already leading me up something much steeper than that. And with much thicker woods. And bushes.

"Is this really a trail?" I ask.

"Kind of."

"Do you know where we're going?" I squeeze his hand.

"Yes."

"And how to get there?"

"Pretty sure."

I laugh. "How do you know it, then?"

"Connie took us there at the end of last summer, as a treat, and I just thought it was really special." He squeezes my hand back. "And you're really special. So I wanted to show it to you."

My heart melts a little when he says that, and any anxiety I have about walking deep into the woods with no trail and no idea where we're going fades.

"Then I guess we should find it," I say.

We have to break hands as the trail gets steeper and we pull ourselves over rocks. We both have backpacks, with water and some snacks—he'd told me to bring them—and we stop a few times just to drink. Sweat is pouring down our

faces, and there's a perpetual hum of insects. I'm pretty sure something is crawling up my leg at one point, but I just swat it away and keep walking. We chat a little about favorite old movies (his is *The Fugitive*, 'cause his mom loves it, mine is *Bringing Up Baby*, because of Katharine Hepburn, but I tell him 'cause it's funny), but we're panting and it's hard to talk too much.

It's been nearly an hour by the time Hudson says, "Okay, we're almost there." The sun is high above us, and even though we're shaded by the trees, I can feel my shirt sticking to my back with sweat.

But then the trees part a little and we come out into a glade on the top of a cliff. It's grassy and covered in daisies. A small brook runs through it to the edge of the cliff, where it turns into a thin waterfall off the edge. The air smells amazing here. Green and floral, like freedom and love.

"Wow," I say, in a half whisper.

Hudson takes my hand and walks me to the edge of the cliff, where we can see the camp below us. We're not actually as far up as I thought we'd be. I can still hear people calling to each other, and we can't see as far as the drama cabin, but we still feel far enough away that we're in our own little magical glade. Hudson drops his backpack on the grass and sits with his feet hanging over the edge, and I do the same, sitting next to him, then lie back on the grass. The bubbling of the faucet-thin waterfall makes a sweet sound. The trees shade us, and when I squint my eyes, they turn into galaxies.

It's just Hudson and I, alone in this most magical place he's brought me.

He leans back, putting his head on my chest, and I wrap my arm around his shoulder.

"Like it?" he asks.

"It's perfect," I say. "Thank you."

I look at him and reach my mouth down to kiss him, and in moments he's straddling me, his mouth pressed into mine, biting my lower lip a little. My hands are up his shorts and boxer briefs, grabbing his ass. He leans back, chewing on his lower lip, and peels off his shirt, then pulls mine off, and tosses them on the grass. Then he dives back down into me, kissing not just my lips but working his way down to my neck, and then my nipples. I've never felt a mouth on my chest before, and gasp at the way his tongue draws circles on me, then moves farther down, to my belly button. I run my hands through his hair, and then he unbuttons my fly.

Oh. He's moved on from the Peanut Butter Pit, I guess. Or I'm special enough he wanted someplace new for me.

He tugs my shorts off, leaving me in a pair of black briefs, my hard-on visibly straining against them, and he puts his mouth over it and I toss my head back, spilling out half-slurred words as a thousand new sensations sing into me like a chorus.

No. Not yet. Stop. This is exactly how I become another two-week fling.

"Wait," I say, so softly he doesn't hear me, his mouth now on my thighs. "Wait," I say again, and he looks up.

"I have condoms in my backpack," he says, then kisses my stomach.

"No," I say, practically pant, "it's…"

"Too much?"

"I'm sorry," I say, trying to scoot away from him even as I want him to keep doing what he's doing. I pull my shorts back over my underwear. He leans forward and kisses me on the mouth again.

"It's okay," he says, adjusting himself so he's lying next to me, propped on one elbow. "You told me you wanted to go slowly…I just…I should have checked before pulling your clothes off."

"I mean…I wanted you to. I'm just…I don't want to dive in too quickly."

"It's okay, babe. I get it." He leans forward and kisses me again, his tongue slipping into my mouth. Then he pulls away suddenly. "But maybe we should cool down for a bit." He laughs and grabs for his backpack, pulling a bottle of water from it and chugging it. Some of it flows out of his mouth and runs down his neck and chest, and I need to look away or I will be naked with my mouth on whatever part of him he wants in less time than the most frantic backstage costume change.

I had a plan for this, I remind myself. Something to kill

the sexual mood, improve the emotional one. To make us bond. Right. Coming out.

"Why don't we talk?" I ask.

"Yeah," he says, wiping his mouth. "That's a good idea." He comes over and sits next to me again. "What do you want to talk about?"

"Who did you come out to first?" I ask, maybe sounding a little too prepared.

"Oh. So, this conversation. I guess...well, it ain't sexy."

I laugh. "I mean, only if your coming out led immediately to something sexy."

He shakes his head, laughing too. "Yeah, no. So, I did know one guy who came out to his best friend, though, and then they had sex right there, in their basement. So it can be."

"Oh. Well, yeah...that's sexy. Not what happened to me, though."

"Or me. Apparently they never spoke again after that. He was really sad about it."

"Oh." I look out at the camp and scoot up so my legs are hanging off the edge again. Hudson scoots beside me and hands me the bottle of water. I drink from it deeply.

"So, can you go first?" he asks, leaning against me. "Since you brought it up and everything."

"Yeah." I smile and put the water down between us and wrap my arm over his shoulder. Thinking about this almost immediately dispels the lingering tingling in my body. "Sure.

It was my parents. It wasn't bad, actually. I mean, I'd always sort of known. Like, I feel like there was never a time I thought I was straight, just a time I didn't really think about sex, if that makes sense. And then, I was twelve, and people were talking about sex and crushes, and we had health class, and I guess I realized that this was something my parents needed to know. So at dinner, I just told them. I was like 'So you know, I'm gay,' and they stopped eating and looked at me for a while, and looked at each other, and then my mom nodded and said, 'Well...all right.' And I don't know what they talked about themselves, but, like, a week later, Dad asked if there were any girls in my class I wanted to take to the end of school dance. And I was so confused! 'Cause I'd told them. And so I looked him in the eye and said, 'You mean boys. I'm gay, remember?' and then, that night, Mom and Dad asked me a bunch of questions—how could I know? Wasn't I young? Did someone else tell me I was gay? And I guess I just answered them well enough that they said okay, and that was that."

"Wow," Hudson says, taking my hand and squeezing it. "That's pretty easy. But it's cool you were so direct, and, like...insistent, I guess?"

"I mean, my parents were pretty great about it. They read up on everything, Mom joined PFLAG and apparently went in with a lot of questions. But then they were on board. They love me, you know, and that means all of me. That's what Mom said a few weeks later when I asked if she and Dad were angry about it. They love me, all of me."

"That's kind of amazing."

I smile, because this is Randy he's talking about. Randy who was direct and insistent. This is working just like it should—he's getting to know the real me.

"Were your parents bad about it?" I ask him.

He takes a deep breath. "No," he says softly. "I mean. They weren't that cool. But they were fine. But I told my grandma first. We were really close. And she was one of the most amazing people I ever met. She came over from Korea when she was like five? Was a teenager in the sixties and seventies and just loved that style. Had one of those round, like, big hairstyles so long, it came back into style. I showed her a picture of Amy Winehouse once and she was thrilled. And she always wore, like, neon and glitter. She was never afraid to be loud and herself. She was always happy, and she could always make me laugh. Kind of like you."

"I'm like your grandma?" This is more "not sexy" than I was hoping for.

"You make me laugh, I mean." He nudged me hard with his shoulder. "You know what I meant." He takes a breath. "She died a few years ago." He looks out at the camp, his legs swinging over the side of the cliff.

"I'm sorry," I say. "If you don't want to talk about it..." Though we already have, only he doesn't recall it.

"No. I was just remembering. I've tried not to think about her for a while, but now...it feels good actually? She was just this amazing person. She watched me a lot after

school when I was little. I went to her house and we...would just hang out. Or we'd go to the movies. I remember once, and...I haven't thought about this in years. But once when I was really little, we went to see some movie, and it was kind of scary and I screamed at one point—I don't remember what it was. Teeth, I think? Like an animal? Anyway, I scream, and burrow myself in her arm, and some guy behind us leans forward—and this is an adult—and he says, 'Hey, don't be such a girl about it.' And my grandma, she just turns to him and says, 'Don't be an asshole about it,' and he snorted and leaned back, and she said to me, 'You scream whenever you want, baby.' She was so great."

I look at him and I can see his eyes are wet, like he's trying not to cry, so I clasp his shoulder tight and he leans against me, wiping one of his eyes.

"Sorry," he says. "I haven't talked about her in years."

"That's okay."

"When I was like ten, my parents said I could start going straight home instead of taking the bus to her house, and I saw her less. But when I was twelve, and I knew—like knew I was gay 'cause I just really wanted to kiss this guy in my grade. And I didn't want to kiss any girls. And I knew it was...not great to be gay. I knew people didn't like it. And this was on top of being like one of five Asian kids at school. Not a good combination for popularity. So, anyway, I snuck out of the house and walked a few miles—in Virginia heat— to my grandma's place. Just so I could tell her."

191

"She take it well?"

"Yeah. I mean, that's why I wanted to tell her, I think. I knew she'd love me no matter what."

I want to tell him, suddenly, about our first summer, talking about her in the dark. But I don't, of course, because it would give everything away.

"She gave me a big hug and said it didn't matter to her at all, and yes, it would matter to other people, but who cared about them? I cried so hard, and she hugged me for what seemed like an hour, but when she let go, I felt so much better. She said I should be proud of myself for knowing who I was and what I wanted, and to never let anyone tell me that anything about myself that made me happy was something to be ashamed of. I've tried to keep that in mind."

"That sounds great. So she was fine with it."

"Yeah. My folks weren't as cool....So she drives me home, and they didn't know where I was, so they're freaking out, and she sits us all down and tells them I have something to say, and I tell them, 'Mom, Dad, I'm gay.' And Mom says Grandma is putting ideas in my head, and Dad says I'm not and we can worry about it when I'm older, and that was it for a while."

"But they sent you here. They must believe you now, right?"

Hudson shifts uneasily in my arms, pulling away and lying down on the grass to look up at the trees. I lie back, too, but he's farther away now. "My grandma died a little

after that." He takes a deep breath. "A lot of stuff happened. We were all upset. But I told them about it again, and I'd found out about this camp with Grandma—she'd wanted me to go, so I could make queer friends, have fun. And I told my parents that, and I told them it was like her last wish for me. So...I came."

"That's really great, though," I say, taking his hand and lacing our fingers. "That she could still do that for you."

"Yeah." Hudson sniffs. I look over and he wipes his eyes with the back of his arm. He turns his face away from me. "Sorry, I shouldn't do this."

"Do what?"

"Crying. It's not...I don't like people seeing me cry."

"I don't mind," I say, turning my whole body toward him. I take him by the hip and turn him toward me, too. His face is a little wet from tears. "It's okay to have emotions."

"No, it isn't," he says with a half-hearted laugh. "You ever cry in front of other people? They will give you a hard time about it. I remember I got hit in the nose with a soccer ball once in middle school, and the guys on my team all yelled at me to stop and called me crybaby for the rest of the year. It was already hard enough to get them to realize I wasn't, like, a math nerd, and then I screwed it all up by making them think I was, like, a girl. That's sexist, I know, but that's just how guys talk about other guys who cry. So I don't do it."

"Well, you don't have to worry about that with me," I

say, wiping a new tear away from his face. "You can have whatever emotions you want around me. That's what boyfriends are for, right?" I squeeze his hand.

"I don't know. I've never cried in front of a boyfriend before."

"Well, you can cry in front of me. I don't mind. I'd rather you feel okay having emotions in front of me than hiding them or something."

"That's nice to say, but..." He brings his hands up and wipes away his tears, and leaves them there for too long, covering his face.

"Really," I say, pulling his hands down. His tears are mostly gone.

He smiles. "Okay."

"Your grandma sounds like she was amazing."

"She was."

We lie there in silence for a few minutes, staring at each other. The tears stop running down his face.

"Have you ever done the trees into stars thing?" I ask him.

"The what?"

"Here, turn onto your back and look up at the trees and the light coming through." We both shift onto our backs. "Now unfocus your eyes a little, and imagine that the leaves are actually the background. They're the darkness, and the light coming through is stars. Like full galaxies, not just

little winking ones far away. Like you're right under the Milky Way."

"I . . . oh," he says, gasping slightly. "I see."

We lie there, staring at full galaxies that don't exist, our hands intertwined, until Hudson sits up suddenly. "We're going to be late for lunch," he says.

"Oh, right." Attendance is required at all meals. Last summer someone slept through lunch on a Saturday and the whole camp had to go on a search for him. He ended up getting teased pretty mercilessly once he was found, and Joan was very angry.

We quickly put our shirts back on and start hiking back. Downhill goes faster than uphill, but we still go quickly enough that we're not talking, and still burst into the cafeteria five minutes late. The whole camp looks up at us. Joan glares. George, Ashleigh, Brad, and Paz all snicker.

We quickly take seats that, thankfully, George saved for us, and grab at the grilled cheeses going around before getting up and washing our hands.

"So . . . were you busy?" George asks.

"It was a hike," I say. "We lost track of time."

"I'm sure," George says seriously, nodding.

"How were rehearsals?"

"Good!" George says.

"George has already mastered his dance for 'Kids,'" Paz says. "I still can't leap high enough to get over the Shriners' arms."

"Crystal added a thing where Jen has to swing on monkey bars during 'Put on a Happy Face,'" Ashleigh says. "I think Crystal has finally lost her mind."

"It's going to be really cool looking, though," Paz says. "They're doing it in a playground, so there are slides and stuff that Jen is trying to get me to go on and I keep turning away. And Ashleigh can get some happy-face lights, which is going to be so cool. Mark said he'd thought of it but assumed it wasn't possible."

"I'm not sure it is," Ashleigh says quickly. "I'm still figuring out if I can get it just right."

"You will," Paz says.

"I watched part of it," Brad says. "The rehearsal. It's hard, man. I didn't realize, like, I've just always seen it at the end of the summer and it's like done and perfect. I didn't realize all the work that goes into it."

"You didn't see all of it, though," Paz says, her face radiating mischief.

"C'mon," Brad says.

"I caught them making out in one of the prop closets," Paz says to us, grinning.

"I had some free time between calls," George says with a shrug. "You were the one who walked in on us."

"I didn't know you'd be in there. Next time lock it, or put a sock on the doorknob or something."

"In the drama cabin?" I ask, a little scandalized.

"It was just kissing," George says. "No worse than what you do in front of our cabin every night."

"Okay," Brad says, looking very embarrassed. "I learned my lesson. We can move on."

George giggles and puts his hand on Brad's thigh.

"How was your hike?" George asks.

"Good," I say. "Hudson showed me a great view."

"I'll bet," Ashleigh says. I glare at her.

"You're all terrible," I say.

"No, it really was amazing," Hudson says. "We just talked. I . . ." He pauses. He looks at me, and then looks away suddenly, his brow furrowing. "It was great," he says, quieter.

I look at Hudson, but he focuses on his food. His thigh moves away from mine and I can feel my heart racing. Did I just do something wrong? Did he suddenly remember me, or something, like real me, not Del, from last summer? Something about the light, or my voice? Talking about his grandma?

I put my hand on his leg, and he doesn't pull away, but he doesn't lean into me, either. We all keep talking, and no one but me seems to notice that there's a sudden wall between me and Hudson, when just an hour ago we'd been closer than ever. After lunch, Hudson says he's going to go shower and write his parents and takes off, so I walk with George, Ashleigh, and Paz to the drama cabin.

"Was he acting weird?" I ask.

"Hudson?" Paz asks. "No more than usual."

"I feel like he got cold all of a sudden."

"Did you finally screw?" Ashleigh asks.

"No. Really. We just talked. We made out a little, but that was it."

"Maybe lunch didn't agree with him," George says. "But he seemed fine to me. I wouldn't worry about it. Your plan is still very much on track. You going to come watch rehearsals? We're going to learn the big group number for 'A Lot of Livin' to Do.' Crystal will probably have us literally making human pyramids and jumping off them.

"She did have me bring in some trampolines," Ashleigh says.

"Please tell me that's a joke," Paz says.

We walk in nervous silence long enough that Paz's eyes get huge with worry before Ashleigh cracks a smile.

"You are so mean," Paz says, shoving Ashleigh's shoulder. Ashleigh's smile gets bigger.

"You going to watch?" George asks me.

"Sure, for a bit."

I watch the rehearsals for a while, but it feels bittersweet. I love watching them. I love seeing the theater develop amid a bunch of falls and misplaced feet. I love hearing the half-singing that goes on in a dance rehearsal, and watching Crystal move her arms in ways that make no sense as she directs the choreography, or hearing her wacky names for moves—"Now bunny spin, hug yourself, worm wiggle, keep worm

wiggling as you hop to your next position, good...now exploding star! Great. Montgomery, your solo now, so you kick to the front of the pack, and cross kick, cross kick, hands on hips, wink...no, wink a little more angrily. This is about your rebellion, remember."

After an hour, they have the basics down, and it's going to be a cool dance number. Jordan's Birdie radiates some serious swagger, and Montgomery has the ingenue sex kitten thing down. George and Paz are in the background of this one, too—as different characters—just so the stage feels really full of dancers. And it is. The entire company just out there, working together, dancing and singing. I miss it so much. I wonder if they'd let me just get up there and dance with them. Only for rehearsals. Just so I could feel that again. I wouldn't have to be in the show—though that would feel even better.

Damn, I miss this. And now Hudson is being weird, and maybe the plan isn't going as well as I want, and I don't want to give up on Hudson, but...Maybe if I came back now, they'll let me be in the chorus. I'm a fast learner. I could pick up some steps. Or just work backstage, at the prop table or something. I'd rotate every other day with Hudson or at the drama cabin. I could tell him I was sick. Like rotating your heart back and forth between two bodies. That's what it would feel like, I think. Slingshotting my heart back and forth until it got vertigo. No. I need to find a way to get my heart into both of them at once. That's what the plan is for.

They finish "A Lot of Livin' to Do" and move on to the

"Shriners' Ballet," the cast rotating off stage, lights flickering on and off. Being back in the drama cabin feels like home. It smells like rubber and wood and the cigarettes Mark quit two years ago but still has one of on opening night. I want to press myself into the stage, and I almost wouldn't mind if it was right now, with everyone dancing on me.

Maybe the issue with Hudson is that we really bonded today. I got too close, and even with everything I've done, remaking myself, holding back, maybe he's just not able to connect with someone like that. Or maybe he just needs time, and I'm spiraling because I want everything to work with him, but I still miss this so much, it feels like I haven't been breathing until now.

"Well, well," Montgomery says, sitting behind me as I watch Paz and the Shriners onstage. "Look who dragged his ass back to the theater."

"You were so good up there," I tell him, turning around. "You nailed it, really."

"Of course I did," Montgomery says, trying to act cool, but I can tell he's pleased with the compliment. "But what are you doing here? Shouldn't you be off pretending to be butch for your butch boyfriend?"

"He's writing his parents," I say. "And I missed you all."

"Really?" Jordan asks, sitting next to Montgomery.

"You were amazing, Jordan," I say. "You radiate that David Bowie vibe that Mark wants."

"Aww, thanks," they say, swatting at my shoulder.

"I still don't get why you're here," Montgomery says. "Won't it blow your cover? Aren't you above us now that you've ascended to the heights of masculine masturbatory fantasy?"

Jordan snickers.

"Oh please," I say. "Hudson knows I'm friends with you. Don't be a—"

"Drama queen?" Montgomery interrupts. "Like you used to be?"

"That's not what I was going to say." I roll my eyes. "And I'm still a drama queen. The whole camp is my theater."

"That's true." Jordan nods. "He is putting on quite a show."

"I've never been a fan of one-man shows," Montgomery says with a sigh. "They always seem so self-involved."

I laugh. "Are you really mad at me?" I ask. "Just for not being in the show?"

"I don't know yet," Montgomery says, crossing his arms. "And it's about more than the show."

"Montgomery," Mark shouts from the front of the theater. "Where are you? We need you for 'What Did I Ever See in Him?'"

"Coming," Montgomery calls, standing and walking to the front of the theater.

"He just feels like you abandoned us for a hot guy," Jordan says.

I nod. I can see their point. "Not just any hot guy,

though," I say. They have to understand that. They've known how I've felt about Hudson for years.

"Look, I love a rom-com, and you are making. It. Happen." They snap between each word. "Which is super impressive. But no one likes being a background extra in someone else's show. Is this the first time you've even been in the drama cabin this summer?"

"No, I was here for the talent show."

"Okay, first time you've been here for you?"

"I mean...I've been busy." I look down. I feel like I'm being grilled in a police station.

"I get it." They stand up. "But you can't act like nothing has changed, either."

"I'm still with you at night. I dance in the morning."

"My dad had this really big job when I was a baby," Jordan says. "Left for work before I was up, home after dinner. I was just starting to talk. Knew the word *dada*, though. Then I forgot it. My mom made him quit, take a job that had him home enough I knew who he was." They shrug. "Anyway, that's just a fun story my mom likes to tell me. I gotta go get measured for a costume. Good seeing you!"

They smile and walk off. I get what they mean, and what Montgomery is mad about, but it'll all be fine soon. Either Hudson's about to dump me anyway, and that's why he's acting funny, or in a few weeks I'll be able to tell him the truth. And then everything will go back to how it was.

I watch the rehearsals until I'm just up there, with them,

in spirit. George comes out once to say hi, but Mark quickly makes him run backstage for a costume fitting. Ashleigh sits next to me sometimes, making notes, asking me if I think a scene needs a follow spot or not, and then she vanishes again and the lights go a little bluer and she comes back and asks if the stage feels more "suburban" now, and I say yes to everything, because I think that's what she wants.

When Mark dismisses everyone, we go back up to the cabin together and change into our swimsuits and then go back down to the pool, where Hudson is nowhere to be seen. I feel sad in a way I haven't since camp started and Hudson said hi. I feel like I'm missing something I love, and without Hudson next to me, kissing me, resting his hand on my hip, I'm forgetting why I did it in the first place.

We only have ten minutes in the pool before they kick us out to get ready for dinner, and we make the most of it, cooling off in the water.

"You seem sad," George says, toweling himself off as we walk back to our cabins. "I'm telling you, he's probably having stomach issues. Living in the bathroom."

"Or he's jerking off. If you two really did just talk, he's probably feeling frisky," Ashleigh says.

I grin. Hadn't thought of that. "Maybe. But it's more just watching all of you onstage. I'm sad I'm not up there."

"Oh, darling," George says, sad for me. He wraps one arm around me as we walk, hugging me. "You made your choice, though. And you're happy, right?"

"I just wish I could have both, I guess," I say.

"Next summer, right?" Ashleigh says.

"Yeah," I say.

At the cabin we all shower off before heading down to dinner, where Hudson sits down next to me, but I still feel a strange distance between us.

"You okay?" I ask in a low voice. "I didn't see you in the pool."

"Sorry," he says, squeezing my leg. "Fell asleep writing my parents a letter."

"Okay," I say.

"I'm kind of groggy." He offers me a half smile before turning back to the watery lasagna in front of us.

We talk about the show a little more, and practice our stories for tonight's scary story bonfire, and Hudson seems fine, just a little distant, and I want to know what's bothering him but don't want to be a nag, but I also wish if something was wrong he would just tell me so I could know what's happening. I want to fight for him, but I don't know how, because I don't know what's wrong.

I barely pay attention to the scary stories around the campfire that night, not even Ashleigh's, which is always the most horrifying. I feel like my life is scarier than any ghost or whatever right now. Hudson stands next to me, roasting a marshmallow and smiling and laughing, but he's not calling me babe or putting his hand on my hip like he usually does, so I know something is wrong and it's a pile of dirt in my

stomach. I want him so badly to just pull me close and to feel that electricity between us again, that desire to run off and kiss in the dark, but he's somber now. I've gone from rom-com to drama, and it's not cute.

When we say good night, I kiss him on the mouth, and he kisses me back, but it's not like last night, or any of the previous nights. It's soft. It's quiet.

After lights-out, I lie awake for a long time, wondering what I did wrong, and how to fix it, or if I can fix it, or if I should bother fixing it if not fixing it means I get to be in the show again. Does he know? If he does, and he didn't outright end it, that's good, but it feels like my plan is failing, and if it's failing, what am I even doing anymore trying, when I could go back to theater? Was Hudson worth it if this is all going to crash and burn tomorrow?

No. Of course Hudson was worth it. Is worth it. I just feel like suddenly, with Hudson being distant and not being in the show, I have nothing. Like it's all slipped through my hands like glitter. I stare at my hands in the dark. I miss my nail polish. I miss Hudson. And for the first time this summer, I don't have a plan for getting back either.

SEVENTEEN

Astrud Gilberto, 'Fly Me to the Moon,'" Mark announces by way of waking us up. "Technically it was written in the fifties, but Gilberto recorded it in 1964, the same year as Sinatra, though they'd both been performing it for a while. Of course, Sinatra's version became the famous one. People associated it with the Space Race. Couldn't do that with a Brazilian woman, I guess. I find her version to be much more romantic, and frankly, superior."

He presses PLAY as we all begin getting out of bed, barely having listened to his lecture. The music, though. The music is...amazing. I've heard the song before—Sinatra, I guess—but this version is flowing and rhythmic, and makes me think of posing in silky robes that flow out like wings. And apparently I'm not the only one. George is up, already making

wings with his nightgown, and everyone else is following him, throwing their sheets over their shoulders and using them as capes. I hold back for a moment, wanting to join but also knowing it doesn't fit the Del character. But I don't have to play Del here. Here I can be Randy. And besides, maybe Del was a failure. Maybe Del is about to get dumped. I grab my sheet and start dancing with the rest of them, the smooth music moving me and making me feel like some sixties starlet.

The screen door creaks open and I turn dramatically to see who it is. And there's Hudson, staring at me, confused.

"Hey," he says.

"Hey," I say, in my matching pajamas and with a sheet around my shoulders like a dressing gown. This is probably very bad, but I keep smiling.

"What are you doing?" he asks. Everyone around me is still dancing, but I can see Mark watching us with a raised eyebrow. I drop the sheet on my bed and walk to the door, then outside. Hudson follows.

"I was just dancing. We start the day with music," I say, hoping I sound nonchalant.

"Like that?" Hudson asks.

"Actually, that kind of dancing is great for flexibility," I say. "My soccer coach taught me some of those moves." He stares at me for a moment, and I can't tell if he buys it. Change the subject, Randy. "So why did you stop by so early?" I smile up at him. His hair is wet. He must have been up early and showered.

"I wanted to see you," he says, shrugging. He grins for a second but it falls. "You know, just because you share a bunk with them doesn't mean you have to act like them."

"Them?" I say.

"I mean…" He frowns and we walk around to the side of the cabin. I can still hear the music from inside. "Sorry, that sounded bad. I just mean, you know, you don't have to be a stereotype."

"Stereotype?" I ask, my body feeling chilly. Inside, the music stops. A new song comes on.

"Like, all girly and stuff. I know plenty of queer people do that, but…that's the thing everyone expects us to do, right?"

"I don't know," I say. "As opposed to what?"

"Showing people that you're more than just gay, you know?"

"I don't," I say, genuinely confused. "You're being weird."

"Sorry," he says. He takes both my hands in his. "I'm nervous."

"Why?" I ask. Is he about to break up with me? Is that why he'd been weird last night? What did I do wrong?

"So, I wanted to tell you something. And…I'm afraid of what you'll say."

"Okaaaay…," I say, clutching his hands now, not minding that my palms are sweating. "Now I'm nervous."

"So…" He takes a deep breath, looks up, looks back at

me. "So, okay. You know that first night? When we went to the tree?"

Oh.

"Yes," I say carefully.

"I lied." He lets it hang there, and I do my best performance of serious/concerned/confused because inside I am jumping up and down. He's telling me the truth? Already? This is going SO well.

"About what?" I ask, a slight, Oscar-worthy tremor in my voice.

"I...I am HAL. Hudson Aaronson-Lim. So, all those hearts on the tree, those were me and my previous boyfriends."

"Oh," I say, all stunned silence. "Why did you lie?"

"Because." He drops my hands and turns away. "I liked you, like a lot, right away. You are so hot, and I felt like we had a thing, like, immediately." He turns back, and I nod a little so he can keep going. "And you said you wanted it slow, and so, I guess I just wanted you to think I wasn't some...slut. I mean, like a romantic slut. I've had a lot of boyfriends. But they never last long. I always liked the...fun parts, but then that's all it was, and I would get bored, and, I mean, I liked them, we stayed friends, but I never clicked with them. And I was worried maybe that was me. 'Cause I really wanted to click with someone. And then you were there and I thought it could be you, but I didn't want to ruin my chances before they started, so..."

"You lied."

He nods. "I'm really sorry," he says, reaching for my hands again. I let him take them. "I know it was a terrible thing to do, but the thing is, the reason I'm telling you is that yesterday, on our hike, with any other guy, I would have just given you a few lines and then coaxed you into making out some more—hopefully sex. But with you, it was different. I told you about my grandma. I mean, I cried in front of you! That's crazy! I've never done that…and I thought I'd feel stupid after, like I'd shown you something I shouldn't have, and you were going to leave me. But I didn't. I felt…really happy. And at lunch, sitting next to you, I looked at you, and it was like I knew I could be my best self with you. Like… there were stars inside me, galaxies like the ones we saw in the leaves. And I realized you did all that for me, and, so, I just…couldn't stand that I was lying to you anymore. It felt gross." He takes a deep breath. "So…that's why I'm telling you. I'm sorry. But I also think I might be really…falling for you."

I let the silence hang for a moment, and look down at my feet.

"What do you think?" he asks. "Are you angry?"

I look up at him, now not hiding my grin or the giggles starting in me.

"You knew," he says, his mouth falling open in shock.

"I mean…" I shrug. "Ashleigh's laughing that night told me something was probably up."

"So she told you?"

"I asked. They didn't, like, offer it up," I say, raising an eyebrow before he gets mad at them.

"So, why did you keep...seeing me, then?"

"Like you said," I say, stepping forward and wrapping my arms around his waist. "I felt like there was a thing between us...and you're really hot." I kiss him.

"So we're good?" he asks. This would be the moment to tell him. He just told me about his secret identity, maybe it's time to unveil mine. I take a deep breath.

"We're great," I say. Not yet. It's not time yet, that's not the plan. It's too soon, I haven't shown him enough of Randy yet; it would ruin everything if I told him now. Stick to the plan.

"'Cause I just said a lot of things I've never said before."

"That's why we're great." I kiss him again. He puts his hands one the small of my back and pulls me into a hug.

"Your pajamas are really cute," he says softly.

"Thanks," I say.

Everything is good again. Better than.

"You want to come dance?" I ask. Maybe now I can start showing him more of Randy, not just Del.

He grimaces and shakes his head. "Not my scene. But I'll see you at breakfast." He kisses me again before going back to his cabin. I walk back into mine. New music is playing.

Mark raises an eyebrow at me. "Everything okay?"

"Everything is perfect," I tell him. I start dancing with

everyone else again, floating light as air as I brush my teeth and get dressed. Everything is better than perfect. I don't know why I felt so down last night.

At breakfast, Hudson and I are back to how we were, sitting close, a hum of something unnameable between us, like we're passing one heart back and forth faster than light so we can both use it. Maybe it's even better than before. I'm aware of every slight glance in my direction, how even when he smiles at a joke someone else told, he looks at me, so we can share the smile. We're our own little universe.

There's a big game of soccer that we join in for the morning, and after lunch, we go to the pool and spend the afternoon splashing each other and stealing underwater kisses. We talk, too, all day, when we can. About stupid stuff—comic book movies and hot actors, and books we have to read over the summer for school.

We duck out of the pool early and go to my cabin, where we make out on my bed until we hear voices about to come inside and quickly separate as Montgomery and Jordan walk in to me pulling my shirt back on. Montgomery stops in the doorway and puts his hand on his hip, staring at us.

"Don't stop on my account," he says. "I like to watch."

Jordan snorts a laugh and heads over to their bunk, ignoring me.

"I'm gonna go," Hudson says, eyeing Montgomery nervously before pecking me on the cheek and heading for the

door. Montgomery doesn't move, so Hudson slips past him. Montgomery turns to watch him go.

"Can you not scare him?" I ask.

"But I like watching him run away," Montgomery smirks.

"Really?"

"Oh, come on," Montgomery says, rolling his eyes and going over to his cubby. "You used to have a sense of humor."

"Used to?" I ask.

"Well, maybe you still do, but you're too busy sticking your tongue down Hudson's throat to say anything funny anymore."

"That's not fair."

"I know I'm being that bitch again," Montgomery says from his cubby, where he's toweling his hair dry. "But it's fair."

"What do you mean? I thought you weren't really mad at me."

"I said I wasn't sure yet. And then you spent all of today with him again. It just feels like there's *us*, the theater gays," Montgomery says, taking shampoo and conditioner down, "and there's *them*, the..." He waves a hand. "Jocks or whatever. And now you're one of them."

"C'mon, we're all queer. It's not like we're in *West Side Story*." I turn to Jordan. "It's a rom-com, right? I'm in a rom-com."

Jordan shrugs. "Sure! But I told you, no one likes being

an extra…and like Montgomery said, after we told you that…you just went right back to him. We went back to being extras in your life."

I sigh. I was never as close with either of them as with George and Ashleigh, but I've always thought of them as my friends. "I'm sorry," I say. "I'm just really happy. Can't you be happy for me?"

"Sure, fine, whatever," Montgomery says, heading for the bathroom. "I'm sorry I said anything, just relax." He doesn't even look at me before he leaves. I hear the shower turn on a moment later.

"I'm still your friend," I tell Jordan.

"I know," they say. "Don't worry, he's probably just jealous he's not getting any yet."

"Yeah," I say. "And you?"

"I'm happy for you," they say with a shrug. "Just maybe a little sad for me."

"We'll hang out tonight, then," I say.

"Cool." Jordan smiles, then goes into the bathroom with a change of clothes.

So maybe I'm a little caught up in Hudson. But that's because it's all part of a plan. And that means work. They understand. They just miss me is all.

I make it a point to sit with them at dinner (Hudson on my other side), asking them about their parts—Jordan is exhausted from the running up walls but loves their

costume, Montgomery was "born for this." Everything is much better afterward, I think.

That night is the camp-wide water-gun fight. We each have to wear white shirts and are given water guns and balloons and access to blue-colored water. If your shirt gets stained, you're a ghost, able to walk around and shout at people but not shoot anymore. Hudson and I make it pretty far before ghost Ashleigh leaps out of nowhere and Paz shoots us both. But we get her back by being ghosts who warn her targets early.

When Hudson kisses me good night, it's around the side of the cabin, so people can only see us if they're looking. We make out against the wall of the cabin and my hands slide up the back of his shirt and pull him closer to me. I want to consume him, I want to join with him and never stop feeling the heat of his body wrapped around mine, his hips against mine. We only stop when I hear Mark, in the cabin, say, "Ten minutes to lights-out."

"That's my cue," I say.

"Cue?"

"To exit," I say. Does he really not know what a cue is? Is that just a theater person word? It can't be just a theater person word.

"Oh, right." He frowns. "I didn't want to understand."

"Sorry," I say, kissing him once more before walking for the cabin door. "Good night."

"Good night," he says. I watch from the window as he

walks back to his cabin. I think I might even sigh. Thank god no one notices.

"Del, darling, could you be Randy for a minute and help me show Paz how to properly snap open a fan?" George asks from his bed.

"Crystal has me doing it a lot for 'Spanish Rose,'" Paz explains. "But she says I'm not doing it with the right oomph."

She demonstrates, wildly gesticulating while she opens her fan, which only opens about halfway. It's an American flag pattern on one side and the Pride flag on the other.

I sit down next to her and reach for George's fan. He hands it to me and immediately produces another from under his pillow.

"First off, sweetie, your hands should be farther down, like so." I show her. "And then don't try to move the fan with your arm. Think of it as throwing one side of it." I snap open the fan, put it in front of my nose and mouth, and flutter it alluringly while batting my eyelashes at her. That feels so good. I've missed that. "Now you try."

She tries again, getting the fan all the way open, but without the satisfying clacking noise a good, dramatic fan opening has.

"Better!" George says. "Don't worry, darling. I wasn't very good at it at first, either, but I knew I had to be able to do this for all my dramatic moments," he says, snapping his fan open, widening his eyes and fanning himself. "Randy taught me."

"You're still using your arm too much," I say. "It's in the wrist. Here, can I hold your arm?"

"Sure."

I hold her forearm steady so she can't move it. "Now try—just your wrist."

She tries moving her arm but can't, and the fan barely opens. I close it for her. She tries again, this time just with her wrist, and it flies open with a clatter.

"YES!" George says. "Now flutter and say something dramatic!"

I let go of Paz's arm and she makes her eyes huge, fanning herself. "I hope it's pizza for dinner tomorrow!" she announces in a voice so booming, Jordan looks over, raises their eyebrows, and says, "Yeah . . . wish it into the universe," nervously.

"A-plus delivery," George declares, "but we need to work on your content."

"I'm not an improv person," Paz says, defensive. "But no, I know that was bad."

"The fan was good, though!" I say. "Try again?"

She opens the fan again with an even faster snap, and says loudly, "I AM your mother!"

"Better," George says.

"Oh . . . you're doing a bit," Jordan says from their bed. "You should have said."

"I think you have the snap down," I say.

"Me too. Thanks, Randy. Del. Sorry."

"I'll answer to anything," I say, winking. "But I gotta brush my teeth," I add, noticing Mark staring at me and tapping his watch. I laugh as I grab my toothbrush and get ready for bed, managing to sit down just as Mark turns the lights off. It's been the perfect day. And as I go to sleep that night, I only feel a little guilty that Hudson has told me his truth and I haven't told him mine.

The next day we're back on our regular schedule and in Outdoor Adventure, and Connie has us practicing the Peanut Butter Pit. I actually manage to get across once, though only after a few tries. But I'm getting better. I can almost always at least grab the rope. Sometimes I grab it too low, and I need to get more momentum, but I tell myself I might need this one day—there are plenty of shows with swinging: *Peter Pan*, some versions of *Candide*. True, they have the rope waiting for them, but leaping isn't so bad.

When we're done, Hudson comes over to me and puts his hand around my waist, kissing me on the cheek even though I'm pouring sweat.

"So, babe, I was thinking," he says softly. "Maybe tonight, after curfew, you and I could come back here..."

"Oh?" I say.

"Del." Connie comes over and Hudson immediately goes quiet. "I want to talk to you for a second." She looks at Hudson. "Alone. You'll see him later, I'm sure."

"Later," Hudson says, giving me another kiss on the cheek before heading toward the pool.

I look up at Connie nervously. Why does she want to talk to me? "Am I in trouble?"

Connie smirks. "No. Come on, let's go somewhere quiet."

I follow her away from the obstacle course a little farther into the woods. When the sounds of the camp have faded slightly, she stops and turns to me.

"I've been really impressed with you this summer, Del."

"Oh. Thank you." What is happening?

"I'm not going to say I understand your makeover, or what your intentions were with it. I've heard things, but honestly, your life is your life, and your choices are your choices. But, because of those choices, this is the first summer I've spent real time with you, and I think you're a leader."

"Oh. Thank you," I repeat. Still no clue what's happening.

"You put in the work on the obstacle course. You help the others learn the parts of it they don't understand. You're encouraging, positive, helpful." She pauses and I'm waiting for her to say, "But you're not fooling anybody, go back to theater," or something. Instead, she says, "I think you'd make a great captain for the color wars."

"What?" Can you have no feeling in your body? Is that a thing? All your nerve endings shut down as you reboot with new information? 'Cause that's what's happening.

"The teams this year are Blue and Red. I think you'd be a great Blue team captain. We start on Friday. You'd have to spend some free time planning stuff—before dinner, usually. But your job would be to organize your team, decide which cabins are participating in which games, and generally be a cheerleader for everyone. Encourage them. Show them what a proud queer person can do. You up for that?"

"I . . ." Me. A color war captain. My body has rebooted and feelings come flooding in. Pride and shock and the realization that maybe, in some way, I've become Hudson. I can be to people what he was to me—outside of the sexy stuff, of course. I could make other queer kids feel like they can do anything. Like they can be the best versions of themselves, or at least find the best versions of themselves here at camp, and then go back to the world outside and unleash them. That's what Hudson always wants us to do.

I feel stars inside me exploding, making new stars. "You really want me?" I ask.

Connie nods.

"I'm honored. Thank you so much. Not just for this." I clutch my hands to my chest. "But for all you've taught me, that helped me become this. And of course, I need to thank Hudson, and my parents, and my friends George and Ashleigh, and even Mark, who gave me a hard time about this, but has always been an inspiration to me. I feel—"

"Okay," Connie interrupts flatly. "This isn't accepting a Tony. You want to be captain?"

"Yes!"

"Great. You and your other team captains and I will meet after pool time in cabin four, up the hill." I nod. Cabin four is one of the empty ones, and each team on color wars has four captains. "Don't let anyone see you, if you can help it. And no telling anyone. It has to be a surprise when we all come out."

I nod, waiting for more.

"That's it. See you then. Go to your next activity."

"Okay," I say, nodding. "Thank you again. It means so much to me that you would—"

"Del. Go."

I nod again and walk away. My heart is so light, it might fly out of my chest like a butterfly. I might join it. Maybe this whole summer wasn't just for Hudson. Maybe it was for Del, too. For the people Del can inspire. Del is a leader. Del is someone people look up to. A Stella Adler, but, like, for sports or something. Randy was never any of that. And it feels amazing to know I could be, well, like Hudson. That I could be up on a platform, and the people staring at me could feel inspired somehow. Could feel like they could do anything, just because of something I said. I bet I could use it for theater stuff, too. It'll give me gravitas. I could take on some serious roles—*Death of a Salesman*, starring Randy Kapplehoff! *Glengarry Glen Ross*! That would be something different for me. I always I assumed I'd end up in *Who's Afraid of Virginia Woolf?* someday, though.

I barely pay attention in swim class, and at lunch, when Hudson asks what Connie wanted, I just tell him she told me my form on the obstacle course was getting better, and that must be enough to account for my dazed look, because he doesn't ask anything else. I giggle more than I should at things that aren't that funny. The lightness continues all day, through making "friends from stones" in A&C to touch football in sports and through free swim, where I keep wanting to pick everyone up and spin them around, I feel so happy.

After swim, I tell Hudson I can't hang out because I need to write my parents, and he nods and says he doesn't mind, he has to do something, too. We walk up the hill and I leave him in front of my cabin, and then, when no one is looking, I walk over to cabin four and casually pull the door open and go inside.

There are several empty cabins on the hill—the camp is only a hundred or so campers, and the cabins hold a dozen each, so we don't need all twenty of them—but I've never been in an empty one before. There are no beds. Connie has brought a plastic folding table and five folding chairs and has set them up in the middle of the cabin, but I can see where she dragged them through the dust on the floor.

"That's two," Connie says. She's sitting at the head of the table. Next to her is a camper a year older than me, but whose name I don't remember. He's got unwashed black hair and a goatee, and is wearing a torn T-shirt that's too big on him and cargo shorts. "Del, you know Jimmy?"

"Sure," I say. "I've seen you around."

"Yeah, man," Jimmy says, extending a hand. "Jimmy Mendoza. Del, is it?"

"Yeah," I say, sitting opposite him.

It occurs to me suddenly that Hudson must be a captain, too. Sure, he was one last summer, but people can be captain twice in a row. That must be why he didn't mind my not spending time with him. He's going to be so surprised to see me when he comes in.

The door swings open, but it's not Hudson who enters. It's Charity Levine, from cabin eight. Charity is usually in charge of the costume department. She's in A&C almost all day long. Everything she wears she handmade, including, I'm assuming, her current outfit, an A-line summer dress in pink-and-white check, with lace at the square neckline and a matching pink ribbon choker. Her brown hair is parted down the center and falls in perfect glossy sheets to her shoulders. Seeing me, she smiles brightly.

"Randy," she says. "I was wondering where they'd hidden you away. Cabin four, I guess."

The thing with Charity is I can never tell if she's being mean or if her voice just sounds like that, so I don't know if that's a joke or an insult.

"Wait," Jimmy says. "Is it Randy or Del?"

"Del," I say to him, then turn to Charity. "It's Del now."

"Right." Charity nods and sits next to Jimmy, smiling at me in a way that again—is she friendly or a bitch? I try to

assume it's friendly, but something about her eyes makes it so hard to tell. "Sorry. The plan, the plan. Del, not Randy. It's very exciting. Is it going well?"

"Yeah," I say. "Haven't you heard me talking to George and Ashleigh in A and C?"

"Oh, I try not to eavesdrop. Especially not when people are talking about sex and relationships. I have no interest in those. I just focus on my crafting. And you." She turns to Jimmy. "Jimmy, right? Tom's boyfriend, but he was too old to come this year?"

"Yeah, it sucks," Jimmy says. "I miss him. And now I gotta get my T injections from Cosmo. I mean, I'd do them myself, but I can't stand looking at needles."

"I can do them," Charity says. "I'm great with needles."

"But, like, you mean sewing needles, right?"

"It's about sticking the pointy end in the right place either way, right?"

"I guess . . ."

"Charity, it's generous of you to offer," Connie says, "but I think Cosmo should be handling any injections at camp."

"Yeah," Jimmy says, looking relieved. Charity shrugs.

The door opens again, and Paz walks in. She looks at everyone, her eyebrows raising when she comes to me. It's not Hudson, but I'm still glad to see a friendly face. She sits down next to me.

"Hey," she says. "So, this is our crack team?"

"It is," Connie says, standing. "We are the Blue team.

You'll meet the captains of the Red team tomorrow so you can plan your big entrance together. For now I want to show you how the cabins will be divided and the schedule for the weekend so you can start planning which cabins should participate in which activities."

So no Hudson. I bet he's on the other team. I can't imagine he's not a captain. I hope he won't be jealous if he isn't. Maybe he'll be on my team, though, and I can be his captain, make him do some push-ups, maybe do a dance for me....

"So here are the teams," Connie says, her voice taking me out of my daydream. She hands out clipboards to each of us with a list of cabins and campers on our team, and then the schedule. Friday is the big opener, which starts with a game of capture the flag after dinner. Then on Saturday we have the egg race, swimming races, a pie-eating contest, a relay race through the obstacle course, and a kickball game. Sunday is queer trivia and a talent show before the final ceremony, where the judges add up the points we've earned in each challenge and present the award—which is a plaque that goes up in the dining hall for the rest of the summer, and bragging rights, mostly. I look over the list. Hudson's cabin is on the other team. Oh well.

"Oh, my cabin should do the pie-eating contest," Jimmy says. "We're, like, always hungry."

Connie raises an eyebrow at that. "Remember, you get points for team spirit, too. So you'll need to lead your team

in cheers and songs, especially when they're not the ones participating in the event. So start thinking of rhymes."

"True Blue," Charity says. "Don't be Blue, we're better than you. Kill Red dead."

"Let's try to keep away from violence," Connie says.

"Put Red to bed?" Charity tries.

"Good." Connie nods. "But let's look at the activities and make sure you get them so you can start figuring out which cabin to assign to which game...."

We spend some time going over everything, and trying new cheers ("We're Blue, we're Blue, guess what we're gonna do? You're Red, you're Red, we're putting you to bed" was my favorite, probably because I constructed it from Charity's slogans). By the time Connie tells us to meet back here tomorrow at the same time and sends us down to dinner, I'm even more excited, but also kind of nervous.

"This is wild," I tell Paz as we walk down to dinner. "Right?"

"Yeah," Paz says. "I think it'll be fun."

"Can I ask you something?"

"Sure."

"Does Charity hate me?"

Paz laughs. "Nah. She's like that with everybody. Super friendly, but with those intense eyes. And I think she's a little defensive here, because there's always one kid who tells her it's a queer camp, and being ace and aro isn't queer."

"What? It's literally in the acronym on the website."

"That's what I say, but some people are rude. Charity doesn't even report them, either. I do, though. Joan takes them aside for a special lesson on inclusivity as punishment."

"So you're close?" I ask. We're almost at the dining hall, but I decide it'll look normal walking in with Paz; no one will know we're captains.

"We bunked together our first year. She's cool, trust me. If she's freaking you out, or you think she's being mean, just tell her—she'll immediately apologize and try to make it up to you by crafting you something."

I laugh as I push the door to the dining hall open. "Okay. And Jimmy? He's in cabin nineteen?" Nineteen is the stoner cabin.

"Oh yeah," Paz says. We sit down with our friends, though Hudson only comes in a few minutes later. He grins at me and sits down.

"Wait," George says. "Why did you and Hudson enter separately? Did you not spend this time together? Did Andrew Lloyd Webber finally write a good musical?" His eyes go wide. I resist the urge to point out that *Dreamcoat* isn't bad.

"I had to write a letter to my parents," Hudson says.

"Yeah...," I say. "And I was checking on something at the obstacle course."

"I thought you were writing your parents, too?" Hudson asks.

"At the obstacle course," I say. "I wanted to try to draw the distance of the Peanut Butter Pit for them."

Hudson laughs, but George looks at me curiously, able to see right through my lies. Luckily, he doesn't say anything until after dinner, when he pulls me aside as we walk to the queer history lecture.

"I can't tell you," I say. "But it's good. And Hudson doesn't know."

"Darling, what on earth?"

"Let's just say I'm going to help make camp more... colorful."

George raises his eyebrows. "Well, how exciting. I look forward to your outfits. Having to resist making them into drag fantasy costumes around the color of...yellow?"

"Blue."

"Ah, a missed opportunity. You'd like swimming in blue glitter eye shadow, maybe blue lipstick. Now all you can do is some football player lines under your eyes."

"Yeah." I shake my head. "Think I could get away with it? Team spirit is kind of butch, right? Like all those guys who do the tacky full body paint at football games. Lipstick and eye shadow aren't a huge leap from that. I'll say it's all for team spirit."

He looks at me pityingly and pats me on the arm. "I'll doll it up enough for both of us."

I laugh. "You'd better. I'm going to miss the opportunity to wear a full blue sequin jumpsuit, with, like, pink stars all over it."

"Do you have that?" George asks, suddenly serious. "If

you have that, you need to get your parents to ship it to you priority."

"I don't, I don't. I was just making it up."

George sighs. "Too bad."

The queer history class picks up where the last one ended—discussing pre-Stonewall trans people and organizations. Joan shows us some clips of a female impersonator named Julian Eltinge, who was in Hollywood movies in the twenties, and Christine Jorgensen, who underwent sexual reassignment surgery in the fifties and then worked as a nightclub singer.

"Though it would be an overstatement to say trans people were accepted," Joan says, "they weren't invisible, and they weren't all persecuted for being who they were. Though some, like Lucy Hicks Anderson, definitely were."

Joan tells us about Lucy Hicks Anderson, arrested for marrying a man. She'd been raised as a girl since a young age—had convinced her parents and doctors that was the right course of action in the late 1800s—but was arrested for signing her marriage certificate. That she was black also made her an easier target for persecution. Then Joan goes on to various people who seemed to have more fluid gender. Many drag cabaret singers in the thirties, forties, and later, female impersonators who preferred to stay identified as women, and just men who wore dresses when they wanted to, or women who wore pants.

"We've been playing with gender and sex forever. The

idea that stepping outside your society-defined gender was somehow perverse, while it existed to a degree, didn't really get codified until women started trying to take equal power."

At the end of the lecture, I walk back to the cabins, holding Hudson's hand.

"So, when you meet my parents at the end of the summer," he says, and I feel a little thrill—I'm going to make it as his boyfriend until the end of the summer, he wants me to meet his parents!—"don't mention this lecture to them, okay?"

"Sure," I say, keeping my tone cool. "Why not?"

"Just . . . they're cool, like, mostly. I don't think they'd have a problem with trans people, maybe. But the more, like, gender-bendy stuff? They might not like that. When my dad gets really mad at me he tells me I should be ashamed of myself 'as a man.' I don't think they even know what non-binary is."

"Well, the title character in the musical is non-binary this year, so . . . they'll be introduced to it," I say.

"They are?" Hudson asks, a concerned look growing on his face and then turning to concentration. "Okay. I'll explain it in a letter. Or maybe we'll just skip the musical."

I stop walking, which he doesn't notice until his hand pulls on mine. Then he turns around, confused. "What?"

"You can't skip the musical," I say. "Our friends are in it. It means a lot to them."

"Yeah, but, my parents..."

"Will deal with it. This is important." I tug on his hand.

"They're your friends, really."

I cock my head, confused. "No, they're our friends. Brad is...dating George, maybe? Kissing at least. We have lunch with them every day."

"Well, yeah, but...you're closer with them."

"So?"

"So, look, it's just about my parents, babe. I don't want them to think they've sent me to camp where I'm going to turn all...different." A mosquito lands on his neck and he swats at it. The way he bends his neck slightly to the side is so strangely sexy.

"You've been coming here for years. They won't think that. Come on, you have to go to the show."

He grins at me. "Okay. I can't say no to you." I feel my body get warm all over and start walking again. "I'll try to explain it to them in a letter, so they have time to prepare."

"Prepare?"

"You know. Old people."

"Sure," I say. We're at my cabin, and we go around the side to kiss good night for a little while.

"This week, we should go by the drama cabin. So you can see what *our* friends are doing all day. So you can feel like they're *our* friends. Okay?"

He shrugs. "I mean, if you want."

"I do."

"Then sure," he says, kissing me lightly on the lips. "So, I'll see you tomorrow?" he says. I nod, and kiss him again. He pulls me closer by my ass, and I shiver as our bodies collide.

"Hey, wait," I say, suddenly remembering this morning, before I was made captain. "Did you want to talk to me about something? You said something about going to the obstacle course?"

"Oh," he says, as if remembering, too. Honestly, I'm a little offended he hasn't been thinking about it all day. "So, yeah...I thought maybe, if you wanted some alone time, we could sneak out after curfew...but now I don't know. I don't want to get in trouble."

That's never stopped him before. "Oh."

"I mean...I'd love some alone time with you, babe," he says, sliding his hand up my shirt. "But maybe this weekend?"

"Yeah," I say, leaning forward to kiss him again as his finger makes a crescent moon under my nipple. "This weekend would be good."

"You'll be ready?" he asks. "I mean...what I'm saying is—"

"Yes. I know what you're saying." Honestly, I'm ready now. He's opened up to me, he's actually said he's falling for me, and he's talking about the end of the summer. The plan is working. And besides, I want it. If he asked me to strip right here I'd probably do it, but two weeks was the original plan anyway, and now I have the color wars stuff eating up my time, so this'll be perfect. Sunday, after Blue wins.

232

He smiles, his tongue against the gap between his teeth at the corner of his mouth, a little gesture I've only noticed this summer and am already obsessed with. I think it means he's happy, but also turned on. It turns me on, anyway.

"Cool," he says, like I didn't just say I want him naked and against me in so many words.

"Cool," I say back to him.

"So, good night," he says.

"Good night."

I float into the cabin and get ready for bed, barely paying attention to everyone around me, and when I fall asleep, I dream of Hudson, in a blue sequin jumpsuit covered in pink stars.

EIGHTEEN

The next day goes quickly—a hike, hand in hand with Hudson, swimming, lunch, softball, more swimming. I love every moment with Hudson, but when I have to go to meet up with the other color war captains, I get excited about that, too. I'm the first one in cabin four after pool time. Connie comes in a moment after me, then Jimmy, Paz, and Charity, who's carrying perfectly folded squares of fabric tied with curled ribbons.

"I made us matching rompers!" she says, handing one out to each of us. I look at Paz, who shrugs. "I know you're doing this butch thing this summer, Del, so I did them in black-and-blue plaid. Pretty butch, right?" She grins. I nod. "I'm good at eyeing people's measurements, but let me know

if anything doesn't fit. Oh, and I put a little black lace down the front of mine. I can do that for any of yours, too."

"Cool," Jimmy says, taking off his shirt.

"Jimmy, I don't think here is—" Connie starts, but Jimmy has his shorts off before she can finish, and is pulling the romper up over his candy-cane-printed boxers. It's unbuttoned to the waist, and he makes no move to button it up, but it does fit him perfectly. Charity has a great eye. And she's right, it may be a romper, but I don't feel like I'm going to look too femme in it. Just shorts and a button-up shirt—as a one-piece.

"These are great, Charity," I say. "Thanks."

"Try it on and make sure it fits when you have a moment," she says.

"Thank you," Paz adds, looking hers over. "We'll be pretty cute, all of us in these at once."

"It'll be so cute," Charity agrees as the door opens behind her.

We turn to see the Red team captains. First is Ryan, the sports counselor, and following him are Sam, who was on my team in capture the flag, Brad, and Jasmine Khatri, who's a year older than me and spends most of her time waterskiing and canoeing, and is always the first in the audience to stand up during the musical and clap. Behind her is Hudson. I grin at him when he comes in and he smiles back.

"I knew it," he says. "You wouldn't be sketching the obstacle course for your parents."

"I thought it was a perfectly good lie," I say.

"All right," Connie says. "Let's all sit down."

There are more chairs and we all sit around the table, Hudson scooting his chair up to mine.

"First of all," Connie says, "I want to emphasize that this is a FRIENDLY competition. No pranking each other, no cabin raids, no chants about the other team dying or being hurt or crybabies or anything like that. This is about fun, and part of fun is good sportsmanship. As the captains, you have to demonstrate that, and if you see anyone being out of line, even if they're on your own team, call them out for it."

"Yeah, people," Ryan adds, "play nice."

"Now, let's plan the big entrance on Friday night. Usually we do this at the end of dinner. Some kind of sketch with the captains leading into a big reveal as you run around the room, cheering, getting people hyped up. Any ideas?"

"We should use Del and Hudson," Paz says.

"What?" I ask.

"You guys are the most public couple this summer. You should have a big fight or something, and be like, 'There's only one way to settle this—color wars!' and then the rest of us come running out and do our thing."

"We're not the most public couple," Hudson says. "What about Lillian and Daphne? Or Dave and Dimitry? They've been together for years."

"No, it's you," Jasmine says. "You guys are waaaay into the PDA."

Everyone around us nods and I stare at my feet to hide my blushing.

"I dunno," Hudson says.

"I'm okay with it," I say, turning to him. "Could be fun." And my only chance to do some acting this summer.

"Yeah?"

I turn back to the group. "But the fight has to be over something really dumb."

"How about food?" Sam suggests.

"Oh yeah," Paz says. "Pepperoni or sausage pizza or something."

"Not sausage," Connie says quickly. "Let's see if we can make it color associated. And I'm not sure what the menu will be."

"Bug juice," Jimmy says. "The powdered drink stuff. Can you make sure there's blue and red that night?"

"Yes, I think we can." Connie nods.

"So I say the blue is better? And Hudson says the red is better?" I ask.

"Yes," Paz says. "It works because they all taste the same. Like sugar."

I turn back to Hudson. "You okay with this? I don't want to pressure you into it."

Hudson shrugs. "I just don't know if I'll be good at it. I'm no actor."

"It'll be short. We can practice beforehand." I lay my hand on his thigh. "I think it'll be fun."

"Okay." He shrugs. "I mean, if my acting is bad, at least that's part of the joke, right?"

"Yeah," I say.

"So just start shouting 'Red,' 'Blue,' 'Red,' 'Blue,' and that'll be our cue to come rushing in," Paz says.

"Great," Connie says. "Then Ryan and I will announce the start of the games and how the teams are divided. Now let's go over the scheduling and make sure you all understand what the events are, and where you'll be leading the non-participants in cheers and songs."

We go over everything, figuring out cheering sections and when we march our teams from location to location. The Red team leaves after a while and we start trying to figure out which cabins to assign to which activities. We have five cabins in total, and five activities. We give Jimmy's cabin the pie eating, and Charity's cabin the egg race. We give cabin five, with mostly younger kids, the kickball game. But then there's just the swimming races and the obstacle course relay race, and cabins eighteen and seven. My cabin.

"Hudson's cabin is definitely going to be our competition for the obstacle course relay," Paz says. "They run that thing every week. I don't know how we can beat them."

"I do," I say, smiling. "We'll take them on. Cabin seven." I point to our cabin on the list.

"Are you sure?" Connie asks.

"Positive."

"All right," Connie says. "Then we have it all set. All we

need are some good cheers…and I was going to say some good blue outfits, but I think we have that covered," she says, looking at our rompers, mine still expertly folded and tied with ribbon.

"Did you want one, too?" Charity asks. "I can make one. What are you, six-two and three-quarters?"

"I…yes," Connie says. "But no need to make me anything. Focus on your fellow captains' outfits. I'm just your supervisor. But for now, we should get to dinner. See you all tomorrow to work on cheers."

We leave the cabin and head down to dinner, Paz walking next to me.

"Hey," she says. "Can I ask you something?"

"Sure."

"It's about Ashleigh."

"Okay."

"So, I know she's demi, but…I mean, we've been hanging out a lot. I think she's really funny, and really hot, but if she's not feeling it, that's okay. But is it that she won't feel anything for me in that way, or just that we haven't clicked enough yet?"

"Oh," I say. This is not easy like the George one. "Honestly, I don't know. I'm not demi. I have no idea what it's like, aside from how she explained it to me."

"How did she explain it to you?"

"Well, this was years ago, but she said that non-demi people can go to a movie and see a movie star and be turned

on by them and want to get with them. She doesn't do that. She doesn't feel anything for someone she doesn't know. A character in a movie, maybe, though usually not, 'cause she knows they're just a character. But for her to get turned on by a person, she has to know them."

Paz sighs. "So you really don't know?"

"Just ask her," I say. "Tell her you're into her, and you're hoping she's into you, or will be, but if she's not, you don't want to spend the summer pining over someone with no interest. She'll get that, trust me."

"That sounds so awkward."

"Yeah."

"Can you ask her for me?"

"No," I say quickly. "I mean, I can, but I wouldn't tell you unless she said she wanted me to tell you, and then it's just passing notes in class, right? Just ask her."

"Yeah." She sighs again. "Okay."

When we go into the dining hall, Hudson is already there and I run to take a seat before helping myself to the chicken nuggets going around.

"Hey," he says. "So, I'm a little nervous about...the thing we agreed to." He looks around and speaks softly.

"Don't worry about it. It'll be silly and fine. We can practice later, if you want."

"Yeah, if that's okay. I don't want anyone to think it's for real, either. I don't want anyone to think I'm mad at you, babe."

My heart melts a little, and I run my hand down his arm. He doesn't want anyone to think the fight is real! That's too adorable. I'm so, so lucky.

"I think if they do think it's real," I tell him, "they'll figure out it's not the moment everyone else comes running in in costume."

"Yeah." He squeezes my thigh. "And, so, you're cool with this? Being on opposite sides?"

"Sure." I dunk my nugget into some ketchup. "It's just a game."

"And you'll be cool when we kick your ass?" He grins and wiggles his eyebrows.

"You can try," I tell him, staying cool. "But I'll be fine if we lose. You'll be okay, too?"

"I mean, that's not going to happen, but yeah, I think I'll be okay."

"Confident man," I say, licking my lips.

"I have some experience."

"Maybe I'll give you some new ones."

"So, are we still talking about the thing...or a different thing? 'Cause I thought we said this weekend. I meant when the first thing is over, by the way."

"That's what I meant, too. And yeah, I think that'll be perfect timing."

His hand inches up my thigh, his fingers under my shorts.

"I don't know which thing I'm more excited about," he says.

"You don't? I'm a little offended."

"Okay," he says, leaning in so I can feel his breath on my neck. "I know."

I swallow.

He pulls his hand back. "So we can rehearse a little after dinner, before the night swim?"

"Perfect," I say, happy he's pulling back. I didn't want to be sporting this hard-on when I stood up after dinner. I make a point of asking for the blue juice, just to seed our act a little, and spend the rest of the night hearing about the rehearsals and planning our skit in my mind.

After dinner, as everyone goes up the hill to the cabins to change into swimsuits, I take Hudson aside behind my cabin to practice our performance. He picks it up quickly, not that there's much to it. I open with a comedic monologue on why blue juice is better than red, he disagrees, I disagree, he shouts *red*, I shout *blue*, repeat until people run in. It's simple. But his acting could use a little work.

"Be more forceful," I tell him. "Make me believe you really think red juice is better."

"Um...okay. The red JUICE is better."

"You don't need to emphasize the word *juice*."

"Right. So, you learned all this stuff from your bunkmates?" he asks, leaning on the wall next to me.

"From our friends, yes. Try it again."

"The RED juice is the best!"

"Good. No, you're wrong, blue is clearly superior," I say, giving him my most heated look.

"So . . . you look kinda hot doing that."

"Doing what?" I say, smiling.

"Just, being so forceful."

"Oh. Well . . . the blue juice is better," I say, and grab the collar of his shirt and pull him toward me for a kiss.

"Is this part of the sketch?" Hudson asks in a whisper.

"Del!" Mark calls. "Come on! We're headed down and I have a cheap disposable underwater camera to give you, which Joan is going to mail away to get developed because no one uses these anymore except for underwater photos."

"I'd better go. But I think you have the sketch down."

"I never realized being on opposite sides could be sexy," Hudson says.

"Don't say that when I'm leaving. That's just mean." I grab him, and pull him in for another kiss before running back into the cabin, where Mark hands me a camera and I quickly change into my swimsuit. They give us the cameras every year for the night swim, even though the photos never come out. Mark says Joan wants a cool nighttime underwater shot for the website but is too cheap to hire a real photographer to get one.

At the pool, Joan, who is not in a swimsuit and will not go into the pool, loudly reminds everyone to wind the camera between shots before we all dive in. The sun is low, so most of

the light comes from the few lights set up around the pool and the underwater lights. Everyone dives under, snapping selfies or shots of their friends with bubbles coming out of their noses, hoping for a shot that isn't blurry. I take one of Hudson kissing me on the cheek above water, and one underwater. Neither of them will come out, but it's fun to do this couple-y thing, the taking of the selfie, the posing, the being willing to display it…if not on our phones, then maybe on our bunks when we get the prints, and at the end of the summer, we can download the photos with a code they send us.

So that's neat.

I spot George and Brad doing some cute, couple-y photos, too, and Paz and Ashleigh doing photos together, if not kissing ones. But Paz does put her arm around Ashleigh's waist, so maybe they've talked. I should check in on that.

After pool time, Hudson and I kiss good night, and in the cabin, I try on the romper Charity made me, which fits perfectly. And, which, when left unbuttoned most of the way, showing off my somewhat hairy chest and treasure trail, looks perhaps too sexy. I'll have to remember to unbutton it for Hudson.

"Darling, you look amazing. Where did you get that? If we had real cameras, I would take a photo of you for your dating profile right now."

"I don't need a dating profile anymore," I say, grinning and turning around from the bathroom mirror I've been

admiring myself in. "And from the looks of you and Brad, neither do you."

"Oh." George waves me off and starts brushing his teeth. "It's just a fwing."

I shrug. "Whatever. It's cute. I'm glad you're having fun."

"I'll have more fun when we can have some awone time." I laugh.

"What's funny?" Ashleigh asks, walking in. I look behind her—no Paz.

"George. But I want to know..." I lower my voice. "What's going on with you and Paz?"

"Oh." Ashleigh looks behind her at the bathroom door. "I don't know. She's nice."

"And?" George asks, foam dripping from his mouth.

Ashleigh shrugs. "I could be...maybe...thinking she's kind of hot."

"YESH!" George says, spitting foam everywhere, though thankfully not on my romper. He spits into the sink. "Good."

"But that doesn't mean she likes me," Ashleigh says, putting toothpaste on her own brush.

George and I roll our eyes at each other and I go back into one of the stalls to put on my pajamas.

"Of course she does," George says.

"She's friendly, I don't know," Ashleigh says.

"Just talk to her," I say. I don't want to betray Paz's

confidence, but if neither of them speak to each other all summer, it's going to be ridiculous.

"Maybe," Ashleigh says. I step out of the stall, changed. Ashleigh is brushing her teeth, and George shrugs at me. I go to put my romper away, and George walks with me.

"You never said where that came from," George says, nodding at the romper.

"Uh . . . someone made it for me. For a thing," I say.

"Oh." George nods. "Blue. Right. Good. I just got a package with blue nail polish and eye shadow. I'm set."

I smirk and get into bed, not wanting him to show me the makeup I won't be able to wear.

"Oh, and I think there's some glittery blue lipstick in the drama cabin. I bet Mark will let us use it."

"Probably," I say, getting under the covers.

"Sorry, sorry, I know, shouldn't talk about it. But I'll be prepared. I have a blue fan, too. I'm excited for the looks I'll be working."

I don't say anything, feeling sad about the two streaks of blue under my eyes being the closest I'll get to makeup of any kind this summer. The closest I get to expressing my real style. Maybe I can put some glitter on them. I can get away with that, right? And besides, what am I even worrying about? Hudson is falling for me. I could probably wear a full face and he'd be fine.

The next day, when I meet with the other captains, we finalize all our cheers and go over which cabins are on what games again. Everyone is still skeptical of my cabin taking on the obstacle course, until I explain my reasoning to them, and then everyone gets excited, like maybe we have a chance.

"You'll have to convince everyone, though," Paz says. "I mean, I'll help, but this is your idea, and theater kids are great at self-esteem when they know they're going to be good. But if they think they're going to come in second place . . . well . . . you know how we are."

"I think it'll be good," I say.

That night, the camp activity is stargazing. We've shut out all the lights in camp and are lying in the middle of the soccer field while Karl, the nature counselor, points out constellations and planets, his accent making it all sound very academic. Hudson and I lie in the grass holding hands.

"So, tomorrow, we're not meeting before dinner," I tell him. "Are you?"

"No. We have everything worked out, so we're not worrying about it again until Friday."

"So, maybe you want to visit my friends in the drama cabin? Mark is running rehearsals before dinner now."

"Oh," he says, as though he'd forgotten we were doing that. "Yeah, okay. We're just going to watch rehearsals?"

"And go backstage, maybe. It's chaos, but fun, relaxed chaos."

"Have you been already?"

"Yeah," I say. "They invited me." And I want to tell him how it felt like home and how I felt sad to be there, but not REALLY be there, but I can't, and holding all that back makes me cough suddenly, and feel like I've been hit in the throat.

"You okay?" he asks, turning onto his shoulder to look at me. I sit up and cough again and he pats me on the back.

"Yeah." I wipe away at a tear gathering in my eye. "Just swallowed funny."

We lie back down and look up at the stars. They're not as good as the imaginary stars you see when you look at trees. The stars you can make yourself see. Those are a flood, like diamonds spilled over black velvet in a heist movie. These are like pinpricks in black canvas, a Fresnel light shining through them. You can see each of them individually, and you can see how they run together.

"Each of them is really millions of kilometers away," Karl says.

"That's like miles," Joan says quickly.

"Ya," Karl says. "Millions of miles. And they're millions of kilo-miles from us, too."

"I like the stars you showed me better," Hudson says, taking my hand in his.

"Me too," I say as our fingers interlace.

NINETEEN

When we go into the drama cabin after pool time the next day, it's still perfect. The smell, the lights, the sounds of it—people dancing onstage, people murmuring in the audience, watching, people backstage trying to figure out cues, stage makeup, costume changes. We go in through the back, but I check the call sheet and see George is probably onstage, rehearsing one of his big numbers: "Hymn for a Sunday Evening." The Ed Sullivan number, performed as a kind of church choir hymn, hence the title.

"Come on." I take Hudson's hand. He's looking around at the chaos of backstage, kind of nervous. I'm thrilled he's getting to see it, though. This is part of the plan, the easing him in—although I guess backstage is never easing of any kind. But he's getting to see what Randy is into now. And

he's seeing that Del is into it, too. That Del is Randy . . . a least a little.

"What is all this?"

"It's backstage," I say. "You think people just wait calmly in lines to go on?"

"Yeah, I did."

I laugh, quietly, and pull him through the doors that lead to the audience. "Be quiet here, they're rehearsing."

Onstage, George and Mark are talking. George is in a big rainbow choir robe, along with the actors playing the rest of the family. In the audience, I see Brad waving at us. We go over and take the seats in front of him.

"You come here?" Hudson asks.

"Yeah, to watch George. It's pretty cool."

"That is a big crush you have," Hudson says.

"Right back at ya," Brad says.

Hudson snorts as Mark runs back to the audience. Montgomery and David, who plays Mrs. MacAfee, take the rainbow robe off George, revealing George's own T-shirt and shorts.

"They don't have his suit ready yet," Brad whispers.

"Okay," Mark calls from the audience. "Crystal?" Crystal, at the piano, gives the thumbs-up. "All right. Don't destroy that dream," he says, the last line before George's.

"Me, on *The Ed Sullivan Show*?" George says, turning to the audience, his face moving from astonished to a manically

pleased grin. Crystal starts playing the piano and George starts singing.

It's a hilarious performance. George is playing it not just like he's obsessed with Ed Sullivan, but like he wants to get in Ed Sullivan's pants. Like he's finally being given the opportunity Kim has been given—to kiss his celebrity crush. It's a smart, super queer, and amazing move, and reminds me again of how much I miss being in this show—being in Mark's vision of the show especially. George keeps singing as the rest of the family comes forward and places the rainbow robe around him, and George lets his hands trace down the front of the robe—zipping it closed, but also very sexy—as he sings. When he cries out "Ed, I love you!" at the close of the song, it feels romantic and sensual. David, playing George's character's wife, even looks at him, a little hurt, but shrugs, as if he understands, and maybe shares the crush. And George does it all perfectly. The notes, the face, the way he makes it funny, but also into an aching love song. He's brilliant. I stand up and applaud when he's finished. He spots me in the audience and waves.

"We're working here," Mark shouts at me—or us, rather, since Brad is standing and applauding, too. As he sits back down, he grabs the seat in front of him—the one next to Hudson, and Hudson does a double take. Even in the dim audience lighting, I can see why: Brad is wearing nail polish. Unicorn Trampocalypse.

"What is that?" Hudson asks, grabbing one of Brad's hands.

Brad pulls his hand away. "George put it on me. It's fun, right?"

"What?" Hudson asks. "I get you have a big crush, but you're going to let him change you like that?"

"Hudson," Brad says, "it's just nail polish. What's the matter?"

"It's not...that's not..."

Brad looks at me, asking for help, and I take Hudson's hand.

"It's just nail polish," I say.

"You too?" he says, and he looks at me like I've stabbed him in the back. The look I'm afraid he'll give me if he ever finds out the truth.

"Dude," Brad says. "What's going on? You're being an asshole."

"We're trying to rehearse here!" Mark yells at us from the stage. Hudson frowns and walks out into the aisle, heading for the exit. Brad crosses his arms and leans back in his seat. Onstage, George is staring at us, confused. I sigh and run after Hudson.

He pushes open the door to the cabin and walks outside. The day is bright.

"Hudson." I catch up to him. "What's wrong?"

He sighs and sits down on the grass. He starts pulling out blades of it. "I was being an asshole, wasn't I?"

"I mean, it seemed like a big reaction to a little nail polish."

"But what's after that? Eye shadow? Does he start carrying around a fan?"

"So what if he does?" *George does all that*, I don't say. Does he have a problem with George?

Hudson lies back on the grass, and I sit down next to him. We're silent for a while. Something is going on, and I can't tell what it is. Does he just really hate anything even mildly femme? Every summer he's been telling us our queerness made us powerful, that we could do anything we wanted. Every summer he's been making me feel like I really could. I could understand if it didn't turn him on, but I can't believe he really has a problem with men wearing makeup or using fans. That's not the Hudson I know.

"I just..." He looks at the trees over us, and I can tell he's unfocusing his eyes. I reach out and take his hand, and he squeezes mine. We sit there for a while, holding hands. "Remember I told you I stopped going to my grandma's after school for a while? It wasn't because my parents thought I was old enough to stay home alone. It was because my dad walked in on me doing my grandma's makeup."

"Oh," I say. I know I shouldn't smile right now, but I want to. Little Hudson, carefully applying lipstick to his grandma! It's so cute, right? But it's shocking, too. Not so masc after all, I guess. But I like that. I like that maybe he's more like me—the real me—than I knew.

"I know, it sounds weird."

"No," I say quickly. "I was thinking it was cute, actually."

Hudson refocuses his eyes and looks at me and smiles. "Yeah?"

"Yeah. But I don't get why that would make you angry at Brad for painting his nails."

Hudson frowns and looks back at the sky. "So, I used to watch her do her makeup in the mirror every day. And I thought it was, like, so pretty and so cool, so one day I asked her to show me how to do it. And she just taught me. Didn't even question it. So, then I start doing her makeup for her when I come over, and she let me play—crazy colors that don't go together, drawing butterflies, sports team logos. A lot of really awful stuff, not pretty, but some of it . . . Anyway, so I put some on me, too, sometimes, but Grandma always wiped it off really quickly.

"So, then one day, my dad got off a job early and he came to pick me up—he had a key, and he walked in on me putting purple eye shadow on Grandma. And he stared at me, like he was really shocked, and I didn't get it. Like at all. And even Grandma went kind of weird and immediately put the makeup away and got my backpack and sort of sent me away with Dad.

"I didn't get what was happening at all. I just knew something was . . . off? And then that night, Mom came into my bedroom and she said that makeup was for girls. And I said okay, because I kind of already knew that. I wasn't going

to wear lipstick. I just liked putting it on Grandma. And she said that meant I shouldn't do Grandma's makeup anymore. So then I sort of understood. And I asked why. And this was before I even knew I was queer, but Mom said that boys who do makeup are a different kind of boy. 'And those boys aren't what you are.'" He pauses and says the words not in his mom's voice, but solemnly, like a commandment. "And I didn't get it, but I got it, you know? It felt a little like she'd been yelling, but she hadn't. She was speaking in a soft voice and stroking my hair and she told me she loved me and tucked me in and I went to sleep. And so the next day, Dad said I could take the bus home and just hang out, and gave me a set of keys. Which seemed so cool! I didn't even put the two together—me being home alone meant me away from Grandma."

"Okay," I say. He's been just staring at the sky as he said it, and I'm doing my best to hold back tears for Little Hudson having this special thing he did with his grandma taken away from him. "But you know better now, right?"

"I mean...I get it, yeah. I know it's just makeup, and here, at camp, it's fine, right? But out in the world? My parents have met Brad. They know he's one of my best friends. I think they think we'll get married someday."

"Oh." I swallow, suddenly nervous and jealous and my body is shaking.

Hudson laughs. "Babe, don't worry. I am not his type. But, like, Brad is one of the reasons my parents let me keep

coming here, I think. Because there's another gay guy like me. Who doesn't have the makeup or the fans. And if he starts that, and he has makeup on or anything when my parents come to visit..."

"You're afraid if he changes, your parents will think this place will change you," I say. "And then they won't let you come back."

There's a long pause.

"Yes."

I lie down on the grass next to him. The sky has a slight haze in it as it gets later. It's not dark, just grayer, and when I unfocus my eyes, the fake stars aren't as blinding as they usually are. I try not to show the relief I'm feeling. He doesn't hate makeup and fans and femme—he's just afraid of his parents. He still thinks we can be whoever we want here...just not out there. Which is funny, because he always talks about being who we want out there. He's made me braver. But when it's your own parents, it's different, I guess.

"I get why it freaked you out," I say. "But also it's Brad's choice. And I don't think nail polish means he's changing. He's still Brad. Just like if you took all the makeup off George, he'd still be George." Just sadder George, I think. Although, isn't that sort of what I've done to myself? Am I sadder? I would be if I didn't have Hudson.

"I get that. I just...I saw it, and I thought of my grandma, and I thought of how I didn't get to see her as much, and then

I thought of my parents, and them seeing Brad, and them telling me next summer I should just stay home, and not seeing Brad again, or you... and it was like it all suddenly leaped into my head at once and I freaked out. But I was an asshole."

"Yeah," I say. "You kinda were. You should go apologize to Brad."

"I will." He laughs and turns onto his side, and I turn onto mine to look at him. He kisses me on the lips. "Thank you."

"For what?"

"Just for listening. I've never told anyone any of this before, but with you, it's like, when I say it, I can deal with it."

"That's what boyfriends are for, right?"

"No." He shakes his head. "Or if they are, I've never had a boyfriend before."

"Well, you haven't. That was Hal."

He smiles and kisses me again, deeper this time, his hands around my back pulling me into him. Then he rests his head on my shoulder, still squeezing me.

"I love you," he whispers.

My heart actually stops for a minute. I'm positive. I'm a medical marvel for one instant as every cell in my body freezes up, blood stops flowing, lungs stop breathing, brain stops... brain-ing. And then it all starts up again.

"I'm sorry if it's too soon to say that," he says.

"I love you, too," I say quickly. I don't add: *I've loved you for years*. Later, I'll tell him later, when I reveal everything to

him. He loves me. He said so. That's the part of the plan I never thought would work, really. The next part. The part that means now I CAN tell him, but he won't mind, because he loves me, and maybe I should tell him right now...but why ruin the moment? Right? It would ruin the moment. I'll tell him later. Not now.

I kiss him instead.

TWENTY

By the time color wars starts on Friday, I haven't told anyone about our I Love Yous. I wanted to keep it private,
hold it close, not to be shared for George and Ashleigh to
make fun of, even if it would be the friendly teasing, the
kind I deserve for getting what I want. At least for a little
while. But my moments alone with Hudson—holding hands
at dinner, kissing good night—feel so much more special
now. So much more intense. This isn't a summer fling. This
isn't just hormones. This is fate. This was meant to be. And
everything I've done, my crazy scheme, all of that was what
needed to happen for Hudson to finally love me the way I
love him.

Honestly, I'm pretty proud of myself. I made a plan,
and it was hard work, but I executed it. Sure, it's not quite

done—I still haven't gotten all the way naked with Hudson (at least outside my imagination in the showers sometimes), I still haven't told him the truth, or worn nail polish, or clacked a fan open in front of him, but I'll do those things soon. Sunday after color wars, we already have plans to find some alone time at the Peanut Butter Pit. And if that doesn't work, we signed up to share a tent on the canoe trip next weekend. Though the idea of waiting that long makes me kind of crazy. I'm willing to sneak out after curfew just to finally have sex with the man I love—and who loves me. Even if we get caught, it would be worth it.

Which makes the fake fight even more fun. I know he loves me, and he knows I love him, so when I tell him, in a louder-than-usual voice, that his choice of the red powdered fruit beverage is "disgusting. It tastes like candy that melted in someone's shoes," it's almost hot, the way he turns to me, nervous about the acting, but happy to be doing something with me—his boyfriend whom he loves.

"Oh please," he says. "Blue is the gross flavor. And it stains your tongue so you look like a corpse!"

"Nice improv," I whisper. He grins at me.

"Really? This is how we're doing this?" George asks, across the table from us.

"Better a blue tongue that those red lips!" I shout, going full drama now. "It looks like you have a harlot's disease. Red is the color of blood, but blue is the color of peace! Red is small, limited anger—blue is the endless sky! Throughout

time, red has always been the color of villainy, and blue the flag of heroes! Blue is clearly the superior juice!"

"Ha!" Hudson says, standing and knocking my glass down to the floor. Color me impressed—he's getting really into it. "Blue? Blue is the color of sadness. Blue is for people who can't appreciate red."

"You red-tongued monster!" I declare, standing up and then standing on the bench and pointing down at him. "Blue juice is better!"

"Red is!" he shouts, standing up on the bench next to me, his face close to mine.

"Blue!"

"Red!"

"Blue!" As I shout, Paz comes marching in with Charity and Jimmy behind her. They're all wearing the rompers, and wearing blue makeup on their faces (Jimmy and Paz like war paint, Charity more like she's doing a mermaid photoshoot for her Instagram). Paz is carrying a blue flag and raises it up, chanting "Blue" in unison with me as everyone around us rolls our eyes, aside from a few of the younger campers who either look confused or excited. Then the other Red captains march in with their flag—and much less well dressed— and Hudson and I get down and join our teams, me tearing off the faux T-shirt I'd been wearing over my romper for just this purpose (Charity is a FAST sewer, made it in a few hours). I love a good reveal.

We all march in place at the front of the dining hall,

shouting our colors at each other for what feels like far too long before Joan jumps up on a table and shouts, "Color wars!" without nearly the amount of passion as is required by the moment. Luckily, Mark is there and he gets up, and starts screaming, "Color wars!" jumping up and down, circling the room until everyone is also screaming, at least half-heartedly. A brave and powerful bit of acting from him, considering how much he hates color wars.

Joan puts her hand up and the room quiets, and she starts telling us which cabins are on which team, and everyone is forced to sit on the left or right side of the room for dessert—chocolate pudding with strawberries or blueberries, respectively. Connie addresses our side of the table, telling us which games each cabin will be playing for the Blue team.

"We're doing what?" Ashleigh asks when she hears we've been assigned the obstacle course.

"Trust me," I say. "We're going to beat them."

"Darling, did you hit your head? For real this time?" George asks.

I grin. "I'm telling you. I have a plan."

They lean in, and I tell them. They look skeptical, but nod.

"Maybe," Ashleigh says finally. "I mean...if nothing else, we'll surprise them."

"I really think we can win," I say.

"And Hudson won't mind if we do?" George asks.

"Nah." I wave him off. "It's just a game. Besides. He loves me." I couldn't keep it in anymore.

George's eyebrows shoot up. "Oh, does he now?"

"He does. He said so and everything."

"Wow." Ashleigh's eyes widen. "I'm genuinely impressed. You really tricked him into loving you."

I stare at her, not trying to hide how much what she said hurts. It wasn't a trick. It was a *plan*. And it worked. He *loves* me. Not just Del, but *me*, underneath it all.

"Ashleigh," George says, slapping at her hand. "Don't be mean."

"Sorry, that came out wrong."

"It wasn't a trick. He knows me," I say. It feels wrong in my mouth, though. "I'm going to tell him everything. After color wars. And he'll still love me."

"Of course he will, darling," George says, nodding. "Right, Ashleigh?"

"I hope so," Ashleigh says.

I frown. There's no need to hope. It'll work. Love doesn't just go away, right? I shake off this sudden jitteriness in my legs and go back to telling people about how I know we can beat the obstacle course.

The first color wars event is that night: the Spy Game. We're given little red or blue vests to wear and then the whole camp is divided down the middle, from the cabins to the river. Blue team starts at the meeting house and has to get to the boathouse, and Red team vice-versa, with the line

down the middle being at the tennis courts. While in enemy territory, if you're spotted by the opposite team, you go to jail. We're all given flashlights.

Paz takes control outside the meeting house, assigning some people to patrol and some to try to get to the other side. Then we begin. I honestly don't know how this game is allowed, it's so dangerous. A bunch of us sneaking around the woods with no one able to watch all of us? Seems like it's asking for trouble. But that might be what makes it more fun? Even previous summers, I've always loved trying to sneak across camp in the dark. And this summer, I feel like I'm extra prepared for it. I rub mud on my face and arms. I pull my black socks all the way up. And I take off into the woods behind the cabins.

The woods that extend around camp aren't so thick you can't find the camp again pretty easily just by looking for light. They do go pretty far out, but I think most of us are too scared of getting lost to get too deep. I have a few other campers with me: Montgomery, who I make wear a black hat to cover his red hair, and Jordan, who is prepared in a black ski mask and black pants and long-sleeved shirt under their blue vest. I'm supposed to lead them across the camp, though honestly, I feel like Jordan should be in charge. I tell them to keep low to the ground and move quietly. Getting down the hill is easy—the woods have a gentle slope, and besides, we're still on our side of the camp. But I don't want anyone to see us going into the woods.

"Last year," Jordan whispers, "they had people patrolling the woods by the border, but there's a stream there that looks like the one from the end of *Funny Face* that covers the sound of rustling bushes."

"You lead the way, then," I say.

"Okay," they say. "But keep up. I'm going to get there before Ashleigh this year, so help me."

Montgomery and I follow Jordan deeper into the woods, and sure enough, there's a small brook nearby. It murmurs loudly enough to create white noise. We walk along it, keeping low and in the bushes. A few times we spot beams of light, but they swing over us. I'm not sure how far we get, but soon we see two figures right in our way. Jordan holds up their hand, and Montgomery and I stop, hiding in the bushes.

"The teams are so unfair this year," says one of the figures. I think the voice is Drew's, from Outdoor Adventure. "I mean, we're going up against cabin seven for the obstacle course? Did you see that? Hudson laughed when he read it."

"Don't be an ass," says the other voice. Sam, from sports.

"I'm not being an ass. I'm just saying. They're not the most athletic bunch. They're theater kids. They'll win with the cheers and stuff, for sure, but that's not enough points to even make a dent."

"That doesn't mean you have to gloat. Let them try their best and have fun. That's what this is about. Fun." They're quiet for a minute. I try not to breathe too loudly.

"Think this'll break up Hudson and Del?"

"Jealous?"

"I mean, he's at the two-week point. That's when it usually ends. And Hudson will need someone to get together with for the last two weeks."

Jordan puts their hand on my wrist, and I realize I'm clenching my fists.

"He's not getting back together with you, Drew," Sam says, walking off. Drew follows her. "If you're horny, just hook up with Derrick. He's easy."

"Not as hot, though," Drew says, sounding resigned as he walks after her.

"Trouble in paradise?" Montgomery whispers to me. "If you're feeling lonely, you know..."

"Shhh," Jordan says.

I roll my eyes in the dark. Hudson and I are fine. Though I don't like that he laughed at my cabin taking his on in the obstacle course. If he did. Drew might have been lying.

We follow the stream through the woods until it hits the river. No one is patrolling here, but we see some flashlights swinging around in the distance, and we're out of bushes here, so we keep very low to the ground—Jordan slithers on their stomach. There are two Red team guards outside the door of the boathouse, though. Luckily, there's the porch. I boost Jordan up and they climb onto the porch. Then I lift Montgomery, and once he's up, he and Jordan extend their

arms. I jump and grab their arms and they lift me up onto the porch, where we collapse in a gasping pile.

I look out over the rest of the porch. Ashleigh is relaxing on one of the chairs. She turns to us and nods.

"S'up?"

"HOW?" Jordan asks, standing. "How did you beat us? I was timing us. We went fast along the safest possible route."

"That's your trouble right there," Ashleigh says, lying down in the chair and crossing her legs at the ankles. "Safest."

Jordan makes a noise like a growl and goes into the boathouse, where there are stickers to put on our vests, to prove we made it. Wearing those, we can walk freely to the jail and release everyone there, as long as we go back to our side with them, and give up our sticker in the process—giving up our win to free everyone so we can all try again. It's a risk, though—the team with the most people who've made it across wins. So giving up one person to try to bring more over is a gamble.

"You should wait half an hour so the jail is more full," Ashleigh calls.

"You're going to make them crazy, you know," I say to Ashleigh, sitting down next to her.

"Jordan is too careful. They'll beat me next year, though. Or I'll take them with me and show them how it's done."

"Now," Jordan says, appearing in the doorway.

"What?" Ashleigh says.

"You'll show me now," Jordan says.

"I'm waiting half an hour," Ashleigh says. "But then, sure, I'll show you. If you can handle it."

Jordan narrows their eyes and sits on the floor of the porch, cross-legged.

"I'm just staying here the rest of the night," Montgomery says, settling into one of the chairs.

"Hudson is one of the guards if you wanna go make out for half an hour," Ashleigh says to me.

"Or ask him why he laughed at our cabin being the one going against his on the obstacle course," Montgomery adds. I roll my eyes. No way Hudson did that.

"He did?" Ashleigh asks.

"If he did, and I don't think he did, it's out of context. It wasn't, 'They're ridiculous for trying to take us on,' it was, 'Ha! I know exactly how to defeat them!' But he's underestimating us," I say. "Only because we don't know the obstacle course, is all. That'll be our advantage."

"I still don't think we have a chance," Montgomery says. "I mean, they're like an army that does that course every day. Or did you choose us 'cause you wanted Hudson to win and feel big and strong?" He raises an eyebrow at me and purses his lips, mocking me.

"No," I say, crossing my arms. "I chose us 'cause we'll win. You just have to trust me."

"Trust you? You're not even in the show this year,"

Montgomery says. "You're barely in the cabin. All you do is make out with Hudson. We get it, you did it, yay you," he says flatly, doing unenthusiastic jazz hands. "But look at you—all butch and playing sports. Do you even care about the show this year? Do you care about anything besides Hudson? You want us to trust you, but I don't even know you."

It's like he's slapped me across the face, and my mouth hangs open, my eyes watering a little. I thought it was better with him and Jordan, after that one time they said I wasn't around enough...that one dinner we talked...and then they said it wasn't much, and I just...forgot about them. I haven't been a good friend, I realize.

"Of course you know him," Ashleigh says.

"We do," Jordan says. "But we haven't seen him much this summer. It just feels like you're not really part of the bunk anymore, Del."

"I'm sorry," I say softly. "I know I've been wrapped up in my relationship, but..."

"You can't say you're one of us and then not be," Montgomery says. "We've spent rehearsals together waiting for our cues, practicing dance moves, we've done the chorus together and had inside jokes and been part of...something. And now you're not. And then you swoop in and ask us to do this thing that you just KNOW we can do that none of us want to do, that we all know we're going to be awful at, and the person in front of me is like...I don't know him. I don't

trust him. And I don't want to embarrass myself in front of the camp so he can look good for his boyfriend."

Jordan nods. "It just doesn't feel like you're one of us."

"I still am," I promise them. "I'm just working on something else, too."

"Is that what they call it these days?" Montgomery asks, raising an eyebrow.

"Look." Ashleigh sits up and puts her hand on my shoulder. "I get it. You're still you. Del is a role. And you're still our friend. But it's hard to follow you into what looks like a losing situation for us—one that'll totally humiliate us—when you've only spent a fraction of the time with us this summer that you usually do. When we see Del more than Randy. That's all they're saying, I think." Jordan and Montgomery nod.

I look over at Ashleigh. Her, too? I thought out of everyone, she really understood what I was doing, what it meant to me. Maybe not approved, exactly, but was hopefully for me. Was supportive. But if I'm letting even her down...

"You don't look like Randy," Montgomery says, his hand waving up and down my body. "I only see Del."

I nod, slowly. Okay. Yes. I've let them down. I've spent too much time being Del, not enough being Randy. So they don't trust me.

But I can fix that. I just need another plan. And one comes to me almost immediately.

"Okay," I say. "I get it. But we're going to win tomorrow. I have a plan, and I'm going to show you I'm still one of you."

"In one day?" Montgomery asks.

I stand up.

"Going to your butch boyfriend now?"

"No," I say, giving him my sassiest smile. "I'm going to free the jail and then get ready for tomorrow." I grin. I have an idea.

I run out of the cabin, past Hudson, who waves at me. I run back to give him a peck on the cheek, then take off for the prison. There are only a few kids there, but I free them and run back to my side, looking for Charity. She usually plays guard.

I find her by the A&C cabin, shining a flashlight around. I'm out of breath from running when I stop in front of her, and have to bend over for a moment before I can talk.

"You all right, Del?"

"The A and C cabin is open?" I ask.

"Yeah, they don't lock it up in case we need glitter or something."

"Great. How fast can you sew?"

TWENTY-ONE

When we march toward the obstacle course the next day, we are feeling pumped. After some frantic sewing last night from Charity and a talk with my cabin, I decided to show them that not only was I still Randy at heart, but it was Randy, not Del, who was going to lead them to victory. So, that morning, after a rushed breakfast, we'd raided the costumes of the drama cabin and shared all our makeup, and made ourselves into a team.

Paz and Montgomery are practically matching, in sheer blue stockings, blue briefs, blue bras, and nothing else. George has a blue feather boa and fan. Jordan is in a blue sequined flapper dress. Even Ashleigh is wearing a blue tutu and has her hair pulled on top of her head and tied with a blue bow. We're all dragged out in our own way. Lipstick, glitter eye shadow,

and earrings, all in shades of blue, paint our faces in different ways. And I'm in the pièce de résistance: a blue sequined jumpsuit covered in pink satin stars, and on the back, like a sports jersey, the number 7 with a big lipstick kiss over it. I also have huge false eyelashes, blue glitter lipstick and eye shadow, and the jumpsuit is unbuttoned to my belly button.

I know this is a risk, but I don't think it's too big. Sure, after Hudson's freak-out about Brad's nail polish, maybe he won't love this. He won't think it's hot, like I know it is. But we talked about that, and we said I love you. He loves me! What's some makeup and sequins going to matter? Maybe he'll even kind of like it—I do look pretty hot—and this will be the way I can show him who I really am. And even if he doesn't like it, isn't turned on by it, then I can just say it's for team spirit. To bring us together, to win the competition. It's like those guys at football games who paint their bodies to match the team colors. He'll understand that. He has to understand that, right?

And besides, he loves me. So everything will be fine. You can't take that back over a jumpsuit and some makeup.

We march up to the front line, Mark trailing behind us with the boom box. The way Hudson's bunk looks at us, we may as well be walking in slow motion. Mouths drop, eyes go wide. The entire Red team cheering section goes quiet for a moment, cowed by our fabulousness.

Connie raises her eyebrow at me. I blow her a kiss. Joan seems unfazed.

"Take your places," she says, and goes to wait at the Peanut Butter Pit, the finish line. Me and my team take our places at each of the obstacles. I'm last—the Peanut Butter Pit. Right next to Hudson.

"What are you wearing?" he asks.

"My team needed a morale boost," I say. "This is it." I grin. He doesn't grin back. "I know it's a lot, but it made them feel good." And me too, I don't add.

"You look ridiculous."

I force a laugh, even if that feels like falling off the wirewalk. "Come on, I look pretty hot."

Hudson turns away from me, but before I can say anything else, Joan blows her whistle. The moment she does so, Mark hits PLAY on the boom box. A song from *Bye Bye Birdie* rings out over the course. The opening one from the movie, which technically isn't in the show, but felt right for the moment.

From where I'm standing, I can see each of the events. George is on the tires. George isn't the most elegant dancer, but he can land a step, and these are some of the simplest steps he's ever seen. He keeps pace with the Red team no problem.

He tags Jordan, who immediately is on the ground, crawling under the net at top speed, and then, at the end of it, running up the wall with practically zero effort. They've been running up walls in rehearsal all day, so I knew this wouldn't be a problem for them, just like I know Ashleigh, whom Jordan tags, will have no trouble walking over the

rope ladder and taking the slide down. We're in the lead by the time she lands and tags Daniel, who handles the rock hop as easily as any chorus boy would.

Jen is up next on the monkey bars. She's been doing this for the "Put on a Happy Face" routine, so she handles herself well, but not as well as Brad, who manages to catch up with her. When they land, we're neck and neck.

Luckily, next is the wire-walk, and Montgomery is our secret weapon. Jen tags him and he hops up and walks across it at a decent clip, not falling once. He does lose a few seconds with a fancy dismount, and a wink at his opponent, though, so when he tags Paz, she only has a slight lead. She'd been nervous about the tire dive, but I explained to her it wasn't any different from diving through the Shriners' arms for the "Shriners' Ballet," so she backs up, runs, and flies through the tire, landing in a somersault and rolling up to me with much more grace than I've managed all summer.

When she tags me, we're a little in the lead, but if I screw this up, we lose, end of story, no redos. I've gotten across a few times. But now it's all on me. Not just winning, but proving...something. To my cabinmates, to Hudson and his friends, to me, maybe? To show that Randy can do what Del can do. To show that maybe they're actually sort of the same person.

So I back up and I run and I leap for that rope and catch it, and even though I can feel Hudson swinging next to me, I jump and hit the ground like he's not there.

"Blue wins," Joan says with very little excitement. I leap in the air, and my team, seeing my reaction, starts screaming.

Hudson crosses his arms. "What was that?" he asks, staring at me.

"That was us winning," I say with a grin. "What do I get for winning?"

"Points," Joan says, still deadpan.

"I mean...," I say, walking up to Hudson and running my Unicorn Trampocalypse–nailed hands down his chest. "Do I get a kiss?"

"Not like that," he says. "I can't believe you won. With them. Looking like that. It's like you...it's like you spit in my face."

"What?" I ask, taking my hands off him. "It's just a game. We dressed like this for morale. It's just makeup, clothing. Your parents aren't here. Why does it matter?"

"Just..." He looks up at me, and I've never seen his face like this. He's angry. Really angry. I feel a thousand things at once. Hurt, that he'd be angry. Afraid, that my plan has failed, and now he doesn't love me anymore. Stupid, for ever putting this makeup on. Stupid again, for thinking he loved me enough not to care what I wore. And stupid a third time, for ever thinking this plan would work. That he would ever love *me*.

All the emotions are forming a chorus line in my chest for their big tap number, their feet working in perfect unison, and it's like one of those big routines you see in movies

from above, where they spiral and make different loops, mixing, mingling, but all putting their foot down at the same time, and stomping down into me.

He walks away into the woods, and I follow him. It's just like when Brad wore the nail polish, right? He just needs to talk it through. He LOVES me. He's not going to change that because I beat him in an obstacle course in sequins. What, he can't handle me winning and looking fabulous?

Or maybe it's just the looking fabulous. I don't know. He sits on a rock in the woods, hidden from everyone else by bushes. I sit down next to him.

"What's the matter?" I ask him again, more serious. I put my hand on his leg.

"I...look, if you'd won, it would have been embarrassing, 'cause this is my thing, the obstacle course, you know. But you did it in makeup and whatever you're wearing now."

"Sequin jumpsuit," I say quickly.

He sighs. "I just think that you're better than that."

"Better than what?" I ask.

He doesn't say anything, but I feel like I'm starting to understand, and now a new emotion joins the chorus in my chest. Anger.

"Every year," I say, "you tell us we can be better. You stand up and tell us that no matter what straight people think, we're just as good as them. We just showed you that." I take my hand off his leg. "I don't know why you get to be angry about it."

I go to get up, but he puts his hand on my leg, and I stay.

"I lied about my coming out," he says softly. "My parents. They didn't actually handle it that well. I mean, they seemed to, at the time, but later…right after my grandma died, I was in the mall with my mom. I don't remember why. And she was looking at makeup, and I was with her. And I found this eye shadow. Blue…" He looks up at me, but he's not smiling. "Sort of like what you're wearing now. I picked it out, and I showed it to my mother. I said, 'This was Grandma's favorite shade. Can I buy it?' Don't know why I asked permission. No, I do. Because I knew I shouldn't want it. Or, like, I wanted her to say it was okay to want it. Or something. And she took it from my hand and put it back in the little sliding tray it came from, and then she grabbed me by the wrist and pulled me around the corner, where it was empty, and then she pushed me up against the wall—not hard, but hard enough I can remember my head kind of knocking on the wall. And she held her hand against my chest, like she was pinning me there, and she said in this low whisper voice, 'I don't care what your sexuality is, but I won't have my son wearing makeup like a faggot.' And then she let go."

"That's awful," I say. I knew his parents weren't super comfortable with the queer thing, but calling your kid that word…that's something else.

"Her mom had just died. She was upset. And she apologized right away. I remember, I just stood there, and I felt like she'd carved my chest out, like I was just empty, and hollow,

and like, if I spoke, it would echo because of how there was nothing inside me, and she walked away, but then she turned around. Like, not even five steps, and she said, 'I'm sorry, I shouldn't have used that word. Come on, we're going to be late.'"

"That's all she apologized about?"

"And that night," Hudson says, not having heard me, "my dad came into my room, and he sat on my bed and he said he heard Mom had used a bad word, but she'd apologized, and he asked if I was okay. And I told him I thought I was, but it was also kind of shocking. And he said to me, 'Hudson, you need to understand. You're special. Your mom and I . . . we don't really get gay people. When you told us you were homosexual, we thought that maybe that was it—that you weren't really our son anymore. We worried. But we came to terms with it. It's not what we wanted for you . . . but it's fine. But, stuff like makeup, drag queens, dancing in their underwear on parade floats with feather boas and stuff isn't you. That's . . . being a freak. And it's weak willed of them, I think. I mean, that's what society tells them they're supposed to be—these fairies prancing around in their short shorts. But you're not like them. You're stronger than that. You look at society and say, "Yeah, I'm a homosexual, but I'm no sissy." I'm proud of that. I'm proud of you for being like that. And I think that's all your mom was saying. That we're proud of you. Okay?' And I said okay, and he left."

"But that's not okay," I say. "That's terrible."

"The thing is," Hudson says, taking his hand off my leg. "I liked that he said I was special. And...I think he's right."

The chorus line stops dancing for a moment, and then starts up again, but the orchestra is out of tune. Off tempo.

"Right how?" I ask.

"I think it's weak willed to be a stereotype. Being what everyone tells you you should be. I think being more...masculine, I guess, is strength. I think it's better."

"That's ridiculous," I say. "My team just kicked your ass in high femme."

"That's why it made me so mad," he says. "But...I know what you're going to say. That clothing doesn't matter. Makeup doesn't matter. And maybe here it doesn't. But back home? You know what would happen to me if I wore what you're wearing in my hometown? Or held hands with someone dressed like that?"

"I think if you hold hands with a boy, homophobic assholes won't care what that boy is wearing."

"Maybe. But maybe all they want is for us to be like them."

"Screw them for wanting that. You said we could be better. But being like them isn't better. We can do everything straight people can do, you're right, but what makes being queer special is we don't have to if we don't want to."

"I...don't know if I'm that brave," Hudson says. And when he says it, the dancing in my chest stops. The dancers are collapsed in a heap. My heart breaks for him.

I take his hand. I squeeze it. "Sweetie, you are."

"With you..." He looks down at our hands linked, my nail polish peeking out between his fingers. "How did you know?" he asks suddenly. The forest goes quiet. Not a bird is chirping.

"Know what?"

"What I've said every year? How I always say people can be better?"

Well. Jig is up. Now or never. Time for my big number. Deep breath, Randy. Like before your solo.

"Because you always said it to me. Every year," I say.

"What?"

I stand. Revealing monologues can't be given in a sitting position. I stand in front of him and I take both his hands and I try to look loving and sincere. This isn't part of the plan. I was going to ease him back into it. I was going to show him all the sides of me he hadn't seen yet and then tell him everything, when we were happy and in love. The jumpsuit was supposed to be safe, because it was a costume, a preview, but not something he would take so seriously. I don't know if he's still in love with me—I think so—but right now, we're not happy. Not like we've been before. And I haven't eased him into anything.

"My name is Randall Kapplehoff."

"I know," he says, looking confused.

"And this is my fifth year at Camp Outland."

He pulls his hands back. "What?"

"Every other year, I went by Randy," I say, walking a little away from him, then back. "I looked different, too. I had longer hair, I was chubbier. And I was in the show every year. I've always been a cabin seven kid. Last year, I was Domina in *A Funny Thing Happened on the Way to the Forum.*"

He looks up at me, brow furrowed, and I can see the recognition pass over his eyes. And then pain.

"Why?" he asks.

"For you." I step closer to him and kneel in front of him. "Every year, being around you, the way you talked to us—even if it was just a crowd during color wars—made me feel...special. Like stars inside me, galaxies. You said we could be anything, and I believed you, even if you didn't mean it the way I thought you did..." I pause, wondering for a moment as I say it if that means everything I loved was a lie, and I only really knew him, really fell in love with him this summer. "It made me feel like I could do anything. You made me feel that way. And...I wanted to do the same for you. I wanted to be with you. So I..."

He stands up and walks away, anxious footsteps, his back turned to me. "So you lied?" he asks.

"No," I say quickly, standing and going to him. "No. I changed my hair, my clothes, lost some weight, and I did different activities this summer. But I never lied. I just...didn't show you everything about me."

"You lied," he says again, not a question this time. His eyes are wide, looking at everything but me.

"No," I say. "Hudson. I'm still the same guy. I really liked the obstacle course. I like being color wars captain, I like sports and hiking...it surprised me that I liked them, but I do. I just also like musical theater and dancing and singing and wearing makeup and nail polish. And I love you." I reach out for both his hands but he pulls them away.

"So this," he says, pointing at my outfit, his hand moving up and down in disgust. "This is the real you."

"Yes," I say. "But it's still the same person you know and love."

"No." He shakes his head, backs away from me. "I don't know who this is. And you've been lying to me all summer. From the moment we met and I asked if you were new. Lying. Does anyone else know?"

I can feel the tears starting. They stream down my face as I nod. This isn't going to work. This was never going to work.

"Who else? Brad? People in my cabin? I mean...who doesn't know?"

"It doesn't matter," I say.

"Everyone has been laughing at me this whole summer? Tricked by...by some theater kid in makeup. Role of a lifetime, I guess."

He's crying too now, but he wipes it away with the back of his clenched fists.

"I'm still the same," I tell him, though I know it's pointless now. "I'm the guy you fell in love with."

"No." He shakes his head. "You're what my mom would call a faggot."

The word shoots out of him like a bullet and hits what was left of my heart, and just like that, it's gone. I don't feel sadness anymore. The waterfall ache of our relationship collapsing in front of me like a glacier refreezes. Everything freezes. I can see it on his face, too, how this instant is being etched into our brains, how neither of us can even breathe in it.

And then it ends.

And I walk away.

"Del, wait," he says, coming after me. "I didn't mean to use that word."

I turn around. "It's not about the word. You think I haven't been called that before? Heard it whispered about me by girls in the hall at school, or just hurled at me by guys on the street? Hell, Montgomery calls people faggot as a term of endearment sometimes. I know that word, Hudson. I know what it means, and I know what you meant when you said it. Even if you hadn't used that word, you would have found a way to say it. Because it's what you think, isn't it? We can be better. You said you meant it as be less of a stereotype. Act more like the straight people. You thought I was better. Just like you—special. I am special, Hudson. I am better. And I am a faggot."

"Del, I'm sorry, I was angry, I don't know who you are, and—"

"Yes, you do," I say, turning my back on him. "And my name is Randy."

🌲🌲🌲

I find Mark at the egg races, still playing the *Bye Bye Birdie* soundtrack.

"Where were you?" Mark asks. "Blue needs some cheer power. Oh, your makeup is running. Are you okay?"

"Can I come back to theater?" I ask. My voice sounds hollow, so I try to smile, make it seem better. "I know I can't audition. I'll work backstage, make sets, run the prop table, whatever. I just want to come back."

"Are you okay?" he repeats. He looks sad.

"Just...please, can I come back?"

He gives me a hug suddenly, arms wrapped so tight around me, and me crying blue makeup onto his shirt.

"Of course you can. You can always come back."

TWENTY-TWO

LAST SUMMER

The lights are so bright, I can feel myself sweat under the makeup and my toga the moment I set foot onstage. The audience's energy is eager, but not anxious. It's the top of act two, and it's been a good show so far, so they're willing to go along with what happens next.

And what happens next is my big number.

Mark and Crystal have crafted quite a dance for me, as if booming and holding the notes and the tongue-twisting lyrics weren't enough. The stage is an amphitheater, a coliseum, steps all around me as I walk onto the stage, look out at the audience, and sing.

The great thing about "That Dirty Old Man" is that it's a song I can go super dramatic on, and Mark has encouraged this. "Golden Age of Hollywood Elder-Diva," he said.

"Think Norma in *Sunset*, Davis in *All About Eve*." And so I've mastered the slight head tilt back, the wide eyes. I'm not in drag, but we put false eyelashes on me anyway, just to get that vibe. And now I have to keep it all while singing about the man I love—who is the worst, and I know it—and how he cheats on me, and how victimized I am, and how I don't know if I want to kill him or kiss him.

And while I sing, I'm walking up and down the steps of the amphitheater. Not walking. Dancing. And then giving poses. It's tricky. Singing is most important, then acting, then dancing, at least according to Mark, so if I miss a step, I shouldn't worry about it. But I don't want to miss a step.

And I don't. As the melody builds and I sing, I can feel the audience getting into it. I can feel them trying not to laugh for fear of interrupting, feel them hanging on my words, my faces, my steps. Up and down the steps, just like my character's relationship with his husband. Every new affair a challenge, every moment I keep loving him a downfall, and the only compromise anger. Funny anger, of course. The poses, the faces, the wide, high steps, the fluctuating between rage and lust. As I sing I can feel the audience laughing quietly, but also feeling for me. I can feel us having a conversation, playing with the idea of this character, and who he is and what he wants. How lonely he is. And we can all relate to that.

I finish by holding a high note, then a flourish and a bow, and then the applause. It hits me like a strong wave in the

ocean, almost knocking me over. And as the lights go out, I see Jasmine, in the crowd, stand while clapping. I smile, but Jasmine stands for everything. But then, shockingly, other people stand. Other campers. My parents. Other campers' parents. The whole audience, and I can feel tears prickling in my eyes as I clasp my hands together and bow, and blow some kisses—staying in character—before sweeping offstage.

"Listen to that applause!" George says, hugging me the moment I'm hidden from the audience.

"They were standing!" I say when he lets go of me. My voice is nearly a whisper.

"WHAT? A standing ovation?" George says, hugging me again. "Darling, that is amazing and you deserve it!"

"Shhhh," Mark says to us. "But that was fabulous, Randy. You should be proud. Now get ready for your next cue."

After final bows, the entire cast and crew is backstage hugging and laughing and crying. The most bittersweet thing about the show is it's the last day. After this, we go clean up, finish packing, have a late lunch with our parents, and then we all leave. Our proudest moment is also our good-bye.

But for the moments after the show, the happiness overwhelms the sadness. I hug George and Ashleigh and Paz and Montgomery and everyone else. When we're done celebrating, Mark and Crystal have us all hold hands in a circle on

the stage (the audience has cleared out by now) and Mark gives a little speech.

"Thank you all for being part of this show this year. We really created something special and amazing and I hope you all know that. My therapist says that theater is a way for us to play with different identities without losing who we are, to try things on, to let go and not care what people think. And maybe he's a little right, but he's also wrong. Because theater is who we are. Those identities aren't different costumes we try on—they're different facets of us, different bits of truth. And it takes bravery to show those truths to the outside world. So I am SO proud of you. All of you." He sniffs as tears start to run down his face, and Crystal lays her head on his shoulder. "For showing not just the vision I had, but yourselves. We are a family. A crazy, dramatic queer family. And I'm so glad we had this summer together and this show." He shakes his head, trying not to cry any more, and that makes me cry a little, too. "I will e-mail you all the video from the show. I know I won't see you all over the year, but I will be thinking of each and every one of you, and our show next year. Now...will the people whose last summer it is here please step into the middle of the circle?"

Five campers step into the middle of the circle, and Mark starts to name them, but just ends up bawling. Crystal takes over.

"You will always be part of this family," Crystal says. "You

will always have a place in this theater. And we will always e-mail you back or call or video chat or whatever if you need us. I know it'll hurt not to come back next summer, but you're going to go out there and have amazing queer theatrical lives. And next summer, you'll come back and sit in the audience and tell us afterward about everything you've done at college. We'll be proud of you forever. And we'll miss you, too."

"But not a lot because you can always, always e-mail," Mark says quickly.

The outer circle closes in on the leaving campers, a big group hug with more than a few of us crying. Then we break, and wipe our faces, and change into our normal clothes to go back out into the world.

Outside, my parents are waiting.

"Honey! You were amazing!" Mom says, running up to me and hugging me.

Dad slaps me on the back. "You were great, kiddo."

"Thanks," I say.

"Were you wearing fake eyelashes?" Dad asks. I nod. "Wild. Theater is so kooky."

I laugh, and my mom spots George and Ashleigh walking over with their parents, too.

"Hi, George, you were amazing," my mom says. "And Ashleigh, those lights were beautiful."

"Thank you, Mrs. Kapplehoff," they say almost in unison.

Their parents compliment me, too, and then we take a short walk around camp before heading to the cafeteria.

"Darling, I don't know how I'm supposed to go back to school after this," George says to me at lunch. "What a summer! And now, back to New York, where my high school will no doubt put on some perfectly straight version of some perfectly straight musical, and me and all the other kids will be fine in it, but not...transcendent. That's what today was. Transcendent."

"We'll have next summer," I say.

"That's true," George says, reaching out for my hand, which I take. Ashleigh looks over at us and we look at her until she sighs and lays her hand down on ours, too.

"It's not like we're not going to be texting all the time," she says. "But sure, next summer. It'll be amazing."

TWENTY-THREE

It's easy to slip back into theater. It's almost like I never left. Backstage jokes, learning cues, watching rehearsals from the audience. Everything feels natural. My nails are Unicorn Trampocalypse, my wardrobe has been rearranged into its most stylish version, and I have a fan in my pocket for when I get warm or need to make a STATEMENT. If I weren't just working backstage, it would be like the first two weeks of camp never happened.

Well, that and the pitying looks. And the strange heaviness in my stomach that I feel like I have to hide all the time.

No one knows exactly what happened. I told them it was over, and that I was coming back, and that was that. We played through the next day of color wars—Blue won, and I knew I felt proud of that, but I felt it the way you feel

something through a thick sweater. It never really touched my skin. But I performed proud and happy, and danced with my fellow captains onstage in our matching rompers. And then that was over, and I went to the drama cabin and everything just sort of slid back into what it had been before. What it was always supposed to be, if I hadn't been so stupid.

Hudson ignores me, just like I ignore him. I don't look at him the way you don't look at the sun. I'm always aware of where he is, just so I can avert my eyes.

"Do you want to talk about it?" George asks on Monday night as we're getting ready for bed.

"There's nothing to talk about," I say. "The plan failed. I told him the truth, and it turned out he wasn't who I thought he was, either."

"Okay, darling, but we're here, you know."

"Yeah, what George said," Ashleigh says. "I'm happy you're back in theater . . . but I hate that you're hurting."

"Not hurting," I say. Which is true. More numb than hurting. "I just feel stupid."

"Not stupid," George says. "A romantic, maybe. A dreamer."

"A theater kid," Ashleigh says.

"But never stupid," George finishes.

I smile, lying in my bed. "Thanks."

"Whatever you need," George says.

I'm really lucky. I shouldn't complain. So my dream guy ended up being just a dream. It was a long shot anyway, right?

Mark turns the lights out, and I can feel tears prick their way out of my eyes and I don't know why. I don't have anything to be sad about. Everything is back to the way it was.

So I don't feel like I'm filled with stars anymore. So what? Space is mostly just emptiness. Miles and kilometers between them.

I feel worse for Brad. Hudson and I splitting has led to the two groups splitting up at lunch, but he wants to sit with George, too. So he splits—breakfast and lunch with Hudson, dinner with George.

"Dinner is more romantic," he explains. George rolls his eyes, but smiles when Brad kisses him on the cheek. I look away. I'm not going to be that friend, the one who can't handle his friends being happy in a relationship because his just ended. Because if I did that, I'd be alone, with the way Ashleigh and Paz are holding hands all the time now. Ashleigh hasn't said anything, but on Tuesday, George spots them making out behind the drama cabin before rehearsal.

"Ashleigh had Paz against the wall and was practically doing a vampire impersonation," he whispers to me backstage right after spotting them. "If Paz vanishes mysteriously and then becomes a night person with a pale complexion, we'll know why." A few minutes later, they come back into the theater, a hickey already forming on Paz's neck.

"I guess they talked," I say, giggling and looking away.

I really am happy for her, and for George. I genuinely mean that, but for some reason, looking at them being happy is hard.

After they all go back backstage to get into costume, I go watch from the audience. Mark hasn't found anything for me to do yet. I'm watching Paz and Montgomery rehearse "One Boy" from the audience when Mark, sitting in the front, calls back to me.

"Randy—what did you think?"

"What?" I call back.

He waves me up and I walk to the front and sit next to him. "Congratulations," he says. "You're my new assistant director. Crystal and I decided we could use your input. So what did you think?"

What? I'm what now?

"Of the song?" I ask.

"Yes, of the song, Randy," he snaps. "Come on, keep up."

"Oh…" Deep breath. "Okay, so I think since the lyrics switch up a lot anyway, you can switch the genders every other verse. Guy, gal, boy, girl."

Mark nods. "Good. But the performances?"

I look up at Paz and Montgomery. I don't know if I want to critique them.

"I know they're your friends, but they want to do their best," Mark say. "Right?" Paz and Montgomery nod. "And we all know you have a bit of director in you. All you've been doing for the past two weeks is starring and directing in your own show. So…this is a song where they're talking about

how they love one person, how they want to settle down now. What's wrong with it?"

"It's too performative," I say, without thinking. "Sorry."

"No," Mark says. "Go on."

"They're looking out at the audience, like they're trying to prove their love, but when you feel that, I think it's more inside...you don't need to show it off, don't need to prove anything. They should look up more."

Mark scratches his chin. "I like it. Let's try it. Don't look at the audience this time. Look at the stars."

Crystal starts playing again, and this time it looks much more romantic if I do say so myself. When it's done, Mark is nodding.

"Good! I like it. Crystal, I want more movement, though. What do you think?"

Crystal stands and gives them some new steps and I turn to Mark as they work.

"Are you doing this because you feel sorry for me?" I ask.

Mark raises an eyebrow, then looks sad for a second, sorry for me—but not the way everyone else has been looking at me. He doesn't feel sorry for me for losing Hudson. He feels sorry for me for some other reason.

"I'm doing this, Randy, because you're a talent, and it might be too late to put you onstage, but I'm going to use your talent the best way I can. And that means your eye. This isn't a pity position. I want you working with the actors,

making sure they really convey feelings, like you just did. Got it?" I nod, and he smiles, putting his hand on my shoulder. "Of course, all final decisions are mine, though."

I laugh. "I wouldn't have it any other way."

I sit with Mark the rest of rehearsal and give a few notes. I might not be onstage, but I actually love helping in this way. Maybe this is my future. Randy Kapplehoff: Broadway director. Well...director/actor/dancer—Triple-Threat Randy, they could call me. I like a slash, I realize. I like how they add to your identity instead of replacing it full cloth. Just the thought of it makes me open my fan and cool myself off as I watch the rest of the show.

When rehearsal is over I go backstage, where George gives me a hug. I wave to Ashleigh, who is up in the stage manager's box behind the audience.

"Darling, you are so good! That note you gave me about the sneer during 'Kids'? It felt so much better after that."

"Yeah?" I ask. "You don't mind me giving you notes?"

"Not at all," Paz says, walking up to us. "Not when you do it so well."

Ashleigh creeps up behind Paz and puts her arms around her. "So Randy is a director now!" she says. "That fits."

I grin. "Thanks."

"I liked it, too," Montgomery calls from across the room. He walks toward me. "Very authoritative and butch. Hot. You know, since you and Hudson are done, maybe you and I..."

I turn away. The mention of Hudson feels like being pushed offstage.

"Really, Montgomery?" George asks. "There's shameless, and then there's you."

"Oh whatever. He's hot. Every boy at camp who isn't trying to screw Hudson is going to try to screw him now. I just want to throw my hat in the ring."

I swallow at the mention of other people screwing Hudson. Or I try to. My throat is too dry, though.

Montgomery walks by me, trailing his hand down my arm as he does so. "Think about it. You've seen how flexible I am."

He walks out the door, swaying his hips a little. Ashleigh, arms still around Paz, asks, "Are you okay?"

"I'm fine," I say, and walk toward the door out into the hot air of the summer. I squint against the light.

George and Ashleigh run out after me. I walk away from the cabin, but they follow, and I love them for it.

"For what it's worth," George says, "I don't think Hudson will be hooking up with anyone else this summer. Brad says he's...really confused. And heartbroken, Brad thinks, though Hudson won't admit it."

I feel a little ping inside me, like my heart is beating again after not for who knows how long. "Heartbroken?"

"I don't think that means he wants to get back together," George says quickly, and I nod. Of course not. Why would he? Why would I, after what he said? Why did my chest leap

at that thought? "But maybe you should try to talk to him? He keeps looking at you at lunch like he wants to, but you won't even look at him. . . . What did he do that's so awful?"

"It doesn't matter," I say. He said what he's been saying for the past four years, I just never understood. That he's better than me. Better than my friends. Because our makeup makes us queens. Because we're just weak-willed stereotypes.

"Darling, I only want you to be happy. And you don't seem happy."

"What do you mean?" I ask, putting on a perfect face of joy. "I'm happy."

"Randy, you're an amazing actor, but don't try that with me. You're unhappy. I heard you crying last night."

"We both did," Ashleigh says, sitting on the ground next to me.

"It'll pass." I let the happy face drop. "There's nothing to be sad about, really. He . . . wasn't who I thought he was."

"Okay," George says. "So who is he?"

"I don't want to . . ." I sit in the grass next to Ashleigh and lie back. George lies down next to me, and Ashleigh, too, all of us looking at the trees. "If I tell you what he said, you won't tell? I don't want people to hate him."

"Okay," George says carefully.

"Fine," Ashleigh says, sounding annoyed about it.

"He said that when he means 'better'—when he says every year that we can be better, better than straight people think we are, that he means less of a stereotype. He

thinks it's weak willed to wear makeup, or like musical theater. He thinks we're just..." I don't want to say the word. "...Queens," I say instead.

"He said that?" Ashleigh asks.

"Yeah."

"And what did you say?"

I stare up at the trees and try to make them stars, but trees are just trees. "I said that that was a terrible way to think. And he told me why he thought it...but said maybe he was wrong." I can feel an ant crawling on me and look down. He's marching carefully over my forearm. I let him keep walking.

George props himself up on one arm, staring at me. "Wait...so you changed his mind? You got masc-only Hudson to say he was wrong about masc being superior queerness? So what went wrong?"

"Wait..." I close my eyes. "Did you know Hudson thought like that?"

"I always guessed," Ashleigh says. "I mean...that's usually where masc4masc comes from, right? Masc is better. I don't want to date a woman, that's why I'm gay. Men are better and women are gross. I are manly and only suck on the manliest penises. Grrr."

George laughs and nods. "What she said."

I laugh and it feels good, like my heart is singing. "I wish you'd told me that's what he meant."

"Would you have believed us?"

I'm silent for long enough that we all know the answer is no.

"But I'm still confused, darling. You won him over, I thought. That was part of the plan. You got him to love you, and next you were going to get him to appreciate the finer things in life, like nail polish and Broadway, and then ease back into regular Randy before you told him."

"I . . . accidentally let something slip, and he asked about it, so I told him everything. The plan."

"Oh," George says. Ashleigh makes a tsking sound.

"And then it was like everything I'd just said was undone." I lower my voice, afraid to say it. "He called me a faggot. Not in the nice way."

"What?" George sits up. "I'll go kick his ass. Show him what a good manicure can do to that pretty face of his."

"If I get to him first there won't be anything left," Ashleigh says, already on her feet.

"No," I say, pulling them both back down by their arms. "No, don't do that. That's why I don't want to tell anyone."

"Fine," Ashleigh sighs.

"And really, he said his mom would call me a faggot. But . . . he was saying it, you know?"

"His whole family sounds messed up, then," Ashleigh says.

"Yeah, they are. I feel bad for him. They really made him hate himself, I think."

"That's all straight people ever make queer people do,"

301

Mark says suddenly as he steps into our sun, hovering over us. "You're late for lunch."

"Sorry," I say as we stand up. "Sorry. And you didn't hear all that, did you?"

"More than you wanted me to," Mark says. "George, Ashleigh, why don't you get to the dining hall? Randy and I need to talk about the show."

George and Ashleigh nod, and start walking away.

"You did a good job today," Mark says when they're out of earshot, walking slowly toward lunch. "I'm very proud."

"Thank you." I look down at my feet. "You won't tell anyone what you heard, right? I shouldn't even have told George and Ashleigh."

"You had to tell someone. You can't keep that sort of thing buried. My therapist would say trauma like that needs to be shared."

"It wasn't trauma," I say, rolling my eyes. "It was just a fight. He said something mean. I was the crazy one. Cutting my hair, treating this like a role."

"Don't do that," Mark says. "Don't say the thing that happened to you wasn't a big deal, or you deserved it. Someone you loved said something terrible to you. That's trauma."

"He said it because of what his parents have said to him for years, though."

"That's not an excuse," Mark says. "Terrible things happening to you are never an excuse to do them to someone

302

else. But maybe it's a reason to forgive him…if he's willing to apologize. And change."

"I don't know if I want to."

"Because then you'll still be in love with him and he'll still be mad at you for your playing out a rom-com for the entire camp without telling him?"

I sigh. "Yeah."

"Sounds like you need to apologize, too."

We're at the dining hall, and Mark pulls the door open so we can walk inside. It's crowded and I glance over at where Hudson has been sitting. He's staring right at me, and our eyes meet, and I feel a thousand things rise up inside me like a zombie horde clawing its way out of the graveyard. I'm hurt and angry and guilty and sad and still so in love with him. All I want to do is go to him and hold him, because I can see he's feeling his own zombie horde of emotions.

But I can't. So I look away instead, and the emotions quiet. Not gone. Just easier to ignore.

"What do you think of Paz's costume for 'Spanish Rose'?" Mark asks, not noticing the little war that was just fought inside me. "I feel like we should make it more Afro-Brazilian, but I don't know what that is, honestly."

"Ask Paz," I say. "She'll know."

"You do it," Mark says. "And then get Charity to do adjustments, if needed. I trust you."

"Thanks." I smile, but I feel Hudson's eyes on my back

and it's like everything else is quiet because of that. I smile and laugh through lunch, but it's all just acting again.

I talk to Paz about her costuming during lunch and take her suggestions to Charity during A&C. Charity, blissfully, does not give me the same pitying look the rest of the camp does. Instead, she wants to focus on the work, adding stripes of red-and-gold-patterned fabric and red feathers to Paz's dress for the number.

After A&C, I go back to the drama cabin instead of going to sports. Technically, it's not theater elective now, but everyone still comes and goes, doing optional dance rehearsals with Crystal, or blocking scenes with Mark. The second half of the summer is crunch time for the show, and everyone crams in as much rehearsal as they can to get it right. It's good to feel like I have a purpose. Every moment I'm working on the costume with Charity or watching scenes with Mark, I forget about Hudson. There's still a hollow part of me, a place that used to be filled with stars that I can feel like an ache, but I don't notice it as much when I have so many other things to focus on. So many new stars to add, like Mark nodding with approval when I tell him about the changes to Paz's costume, or Jordan saying, "Yes, I get that, I love that," when I suggest they think of "A Lot of Livin' to Do" as not just about going out and partying, but about going to the one queer club in this small town. It changes their whole performance, too,

from a dance number to a real scene, and Mark squeezes my shoulder and says, "I am so smart for making you an AD." Each moment like that is a star, and they start to fill me up.

When pool time comes around, Mark sends me out to go play in the water. "You need to relax after a long day," he says to me, and to all the other campers who are backstage. "Go swim."

Hopping into the pool, I realize how right he is, too. The water and sun feel amazing, and I don't even mind Brad and George flirtatiously splashing each other, or Ashleigh and Paz standing shoulder to shoulder against the wall. I don't even know where Hudson is anymore.

That's a lie. He's by the diving board. I don't look.

Instead I try to relax. I sink under the water and let it surround me, let myself float in a little cocoon where the rest of the world is far-off splashes. When I pop back up, George splashes me and I splash him back and soon all of us are chasing each other around the pool trying to splash each other.

We stop when Janice blows her whistle at us and shakes her head. I laugh and swim back toward the side of the pool with George. Paz and Brad keep chasing each other, with less splashing, and Ashleigh goes over to Janice.

"Should we worry about that?" George asks, looking at Ashleigh, popping out of the water onto the side of the pool like a mermaid to talk to Janice.

"Nah," I say. "She's got Paz now, right?"

"That doesn't mean the old crush is gone."

"She hasn't said anything about Janice in weeks." As I say it, I look over at them. Ashleigh laughs at something.

"I don't know, darling. This worries me."

"They can be friends, maybe."

"Like you and Hudson?"

"That's different," I say, my voice a little too quick and flat. "They're not exes. It's just a former crush."

"Former might be overstating it," George says as Ashleigh swims over to us.

"She hooked up with a girl," Ashleigh says in an excited whisper when she's next to us.

"What?" George asks, his voice monotone. He looks at me like I should have known better.

"Janice. She went to some party this weekend and she ended up making out with a girl, and she says it was cool! She might be bi!"

"Might?" I ask.

"Heteroflexible, three-beer queer," George says, "whatever. But none of them are relationship material, darling."

"Why not?" Ashleigh asks. "We click so well, and now she might want to make out a little, like I've always wanted. I should tell her, right? I should ask her to hang around when she's off duty and we can go somewhere private."

George and I exchange a worried look. "First," I say, "that would get her fired."

"How do you know that?" Ashleigh asks. "She's a lifeguard, not a counselor."

"Darling, don't you have Paz now?"

Ashleigh sighs and looks at her reflection in the water. "I like Paz. I do. Enough that I've been getting a little...friendlier with her."

"We know," George says with a smirk.

Ashleigh glares at him. "And she's pretty. And funny, and really smart. But Janice is..." She looks behind her at Janice. "She's the dream."

"But she's a real person, too," I say. "And when you meet one, the other goes away."

"Just because you and Hudson didn't work out—" Ashleigh starts, and I shake my head so violently, she stops.

"Yes," I say after a moment. "That's part of it. But, sweetie, I'm just saying. You don't know how it could go. You could give up Paz for her, and lose them both. That's what happened to me, with the musical, kind of. Do you want to risk that?"

"You did," Ashleigh says. "Wouldn't you do it again?"

I sigh.

"It's not the same," George says. "She will reject you, Ashleigh. She has to keep her job. And then you'll be awkward together. Just...keep being friends. And see where it is when she's not a lifeguard anymore. If you and Paz aren't together, I mean."

Ashleigh sighs. "I just..."

"I get it," I say. "She seems in reach. But George is right. You can't force it. You can wait a week and a half to talk to her about this, right?"

307

"But then she'll be here and I'll be back in Boston."

"Not so far, really," George says.

"Yeah, okay." She nods, looking sad. "And I shouldn't do that to Paz anyway. I should see where it goes. And she's a great kisser. I bet she's good with her mouth other places, too...." She smirks as George and I roll our eyes. "But I am going to invite Janice to the show."

"Oh yes." I nod. "Do that for sure."

Ashleigh takes off, swimming back to Janice. Across the pool, I see Paz watching, too. I frown a little in sympathy.

"You know, just because Hudson wasn't what you thought he'd be doesn't mean you can't have a dream guy," George says.

"I know," I say. "I just have no idea who that would be."

"Hudson in nail polish?" George asks.

I laugh. "Something like that."

It starts raining during dinner, so for the evening activity we all go to the meeting hall and Joan puts on *The Miseducation of Cameron Post* so we can all sob for a while. George and Brad sit on one side of me, and Ashleigh and Paz sit on the other, and sometimes I catch all of them giving these worried "Are we being too cute next to him?" looks to each other and me, but I just watch the movie and think about what was missing in the "Honestly Sincere" number today. I'm actually pretty impressed with how well I'm handling it all. I mean, sure,

I'm not happy, but I'm putting on a good show of it—I'm not spending the day in the infirmary bawling my eyes out over a broken heart, or being betrayed or anything.

I'm sad. But I'm happy, too.

After the movie it's still pouring outside, so we all run to our cabins, T-shirts lifted over our heads in a futile attempt to keep our hair dry (also—why? We're going in the pool tomorrow, right?), screaming and laughing as we get soaked anyway.

Except Hudson is standing at the door to my cabin. He's already soaked, his white T-shirt plastered to his body, hair falling over his forehead in rivers, eyes squinting against the fury of the raindrops. He waves, sheepish, when he sees me, and I know I can't just walk away, not when he's getting soaked, some romantic puppy dog gesture or preamble to a speech in the rain about how I "done him wrong" maybe? Some kind of monologue in the rain, surely. And I thought I was supposed to be the drama queen.

"What?" I ask him.

"Can we talk?"

"Not now. It's pouring."

"So maybe tomorrow?"

"I'm getting wet," I say, and then immediately flinch at the flirtiness of it. Nice job being cool and aloof, Randy. "I'm going inside."

"But—"

I don't let him finish, I just open the door to my cabin and

go in. I want to peek out the window, see if he's waiting, looking up at me, getting wetter and wetter, hoping I'll come back out, but I shouldn't, and besides, George is doing it for me.

"He's leaving," George says after a minute. "You didn't want to talk to him?"

"In this weather?"

"It would make quite the scene," George says.

"I've dealt with enough scenes today," I say. "I'm going to sleep."

George shrugs and I only glance out the window once as I'm getting ready for bed. Hudson isn't there. Why would he be?

I fall asleep to the sound of the rain on the roof. It has a rhythm to it, somewhere in between a heartbeat and the overture to a show.

TWENTY-FOUR

t rains all the next day, too, which is fine, because it gives us an excuse to spend all day in the drama cabin, working on scenes, costumes, dancing. We're having our first run-through of the entire show tomorrow: a full performance with costume changes and lighting cues and a million other things that can go deeply, horribly wrong. Two years ago, during the first run, a sandbag fell and almost literally killed a chorus boy. Not me. But that kid never came back to camp after that. Probably for the best. He was unlucky.

But I don't want any sandbags this year, and as few mistakes as possible, so I go around asking people what they need, and making a list, which I give to Mark, so we can practice all the bits that feel off. We spend the whole day

doing that, breaking only for lunch. It's busy and exciting and frustrating. And I don't think about Hudson even once.

Thursday morning, though, I realize I have to.

"This one is cheating a little," Mark says as he wakes us all up. "The song itself—'It's in His Kiss,' sometimes called 'The Shoop Shoop Song,' was released in 1963, first sung by Merry Clayton...but this cover is from 1990. It's Cher! How can I not use Cher? I won't apologize! In fact, I will say that Joan not letting me show *Mermaids* during movie night is a gay travesty!" He nods as if having made his point, and hits PLAY.

The music starts playing as we get out of bed, and it's impossible not to dance to. Or sing into a comb or hairbrush to. Or do little coordinated backup dances to, as George and I quickly start doing, tossing our heads and lip-synching to the backup singers. Montgomery takes it upon himself to lip-synch to Cher until Mark comes back out of his room and takes over. It doesn't take long for the entire cabin to have a dance routine worked out, a virtual music video, and it feels so good to be dancing and shooping and being myself, and not caring if Hudson is going to walk in and see me like this. George grabs our fans and when the song goes on to another (another Cher, definitely not from the 1960s, but we'll give Mark a break) we start voguing and catwalking down the cabin.

Mark hops in the shower, and when he comes out we're all still dancing.

"Get ready! Come on! Don't make me turn Cher off!"

He laughs as we all scramble to get dressed and brush our teeth. "And don't forget to pack up what you need for the canoe trip. We leave tomorrow."

The canoe trip. Right. Oh.

Oh no.

I turn to George, wide-eyed, no longer dancing. George is lost in the song, flapping his fan in one hand, brushing his teeth with another, still dancing to the music.

"Trade tents with me?" I ask him.

He turns to me, his eyes going wide. "Oh...," he says, toothpaste dripping from his open mouth. "Fuh."

I nod in agreement. "So you'll trade?"

He shakes his head and spits the toothpaste out. "Sorry, darling, but Brad is really excited for this. We haven't really had a chance to..." He wiggles his fingers. "Perform a duet. The kind with a climactic high note." He tilts his head. "Actually, he's a bass, so it won't be that high. But it'll be loud and long, so help me."

"Okay, but I can't share a tent with Hudson," I say.

"Sorry, darling, I feel for you, I do, but you'll survive a couple of nights of sleeping next to the boy. You can ignore him up close."

"Please?" I beg.

He gives me sad eyes. "Do you really need this? Because if I say yes, it'll break Brad's heart."

"I..."

"I'll talk to Brad about it," he says, but he looks sad. And

313

now I feel terrible. I should have remembered this earlier. What if this is what Hudson wanted to talk about the other night and I acted like it was some big weird emotional thing and did the cold walk away. I was the drama queen after all.

"Oh!" Mark says. "And I forgot to give these out last night." I pop my head back into the cabin and see Mark putting little packets of photos on each of our beds. "From pool night. Printed photos. There's a link where you can download them on the package, too."

As if today didn't have enough unpleasant reminders.

Mark throws a pack of photos on my bed and Ashleigh swiftly grabs it and puts it on hers.

When she sees me watching her she shakes her head. "You don't need those right now."

I nod. She's a good friend.

Hudson doesn't try to approach me at breakfast, so maybe he figured something out with the tents and George won't have to trade. Maybe Hudson found someone to trade with and I'll be in a tent with Sam or someone whom I wouldn't mind sharing with. Even a stranger. That would be fine.

Maybe he burned the photos of us from the pool.

I try not to think of any of it as I go into the drama cabin. I push aside guesses as to where Ashleigh could have hidden the photos—why do I want them anyway? I can see myself sobbing over them in bed, and I still want them. I shake my

head. I could ask Mark if he can make someone trade tents with me, but that would be stupid and childish and he would roll his eyes and tell me to deal with it. And he would be right. I shouldn't even have asked George. I can get through it. I don't want those photos. I can do without.

The first run-through goes really well. The show is Mark's best I've seen. It's gay and funny and campy and filled with real love in a way that shines above the source material—which was already one of the best musicals of all time. But Mark has made it his own. No, our own. Everyone does an amazing job. A few cues are missed, some costume changes go wrong, but nothing we can't work out. After lunch, Mark gives notes on everything and we run a few more scenes before he lets us go swim.

The moment I get into the pool, Brad is there, glaring.

"I am not giving up a night of eating that hairy ass just so you don't feel weird sharing a tent with Hudson," he says.

"Hi," I say. "That's a lot of information."

"Come on, Randy. Tell George he doesn't have to trade."

I know he's right. "Did Hudson find someone to trade with?"

Brad rolls his eyes, shakes his head. "You're so... You really need to talk to him. Just... don't trade, okay? I really want to—"

"You've already explained."

"Hey, don't kink-shame me."

"Sorry, you're right. I will... share the tent with Hudson. And I hope you have fun with George."

"Oh, I will. He is so my type and I cannot wait for him to have my legs in the air while he pounds—"

"You really like to share, don't you?"

"Sorry." Brad shrugs. "Just looking forward to it."

I laugh. "It's fine, but George is like my brother."

"Oh," he says, eyes wide. "Yeah, sorry. But thanks for being cool about it. And just...look, Hudson is upset, too, y'know? He's not a bad guy. You really kind of messed with his head, the way he sees the world. But...I think he needed it. But now he's feeling unbalanced and you left, and..." He leans against the side of the pool, next to me.

"I'm not going to help him," I say. "He doesn't want me to."

"Are you sure?"

"He said something—"

"He told me. And I told him that wasn't okay, even though he already knew. And he wants to apologize. For real. You should let him."

"Why?"

"Because you're not the one on the high ground, Del," he says, raising an eyebrow at the name. "You both screwed up."

I cross my arms. Maybe he's right, but I did what I did for love. Hudson can't say that. "So what good will talking about it do?"

"What will it hurt?"

"What will what hurt?" George asks, hopping into the water next to Brad.

316

"Apparently, Brad's ass will hurt after the pounding you'll be giving him—"

"Hey!" Brad says. "Come on, you just said I shouldn't talk about him that way 'cause he's like your brother."

"Oh, you absolutely shouldn't. But I'm going to tease you about it anyway. George, he has both nights of the canoe trip planned out. There's going to be twenty-three minutes of sixty-nineing—"

Brad splashes me as I laugh and swim away. They chase me, still splashing, until Ashleigh comes to my aid, cannon-balling in front of them, and then it becomes an all-out splash war until the lifeguard blows the whistle at us.

"So I don't have to trade with you?" George asks when we're sitting on the edge of the pool.

"No. I'll be fine. You should get to . . . see what Brad has planned."

"Oh, I intend to. What do you think you and Hudson will do?"

"I don't know. Maybe we'll try to talk. Maybe we'll just fight. Maybe we'll lie there in silence and sleep. Or maybe he swapped with someone at the last minute. But it's not the end of the world, and I shouldn't take something away from you just so I don't feel awkward."

"Thank you, darling. You know I'd trade if you need me to."

"I know. Thank you."

George hops back into the pool, and I watch him and Brad

dive underwater to sneak a kiss. I spot Hudson watching them, too, and then looking up at me. He tries to smile, but looks frightened. I look down at my nails. The nail polish I put on for color wars is chipped now. I should put on a new coat.

I dive into the pool.

Very few of us actually enjoy the canoe trip. It tends to be more busywork than fun. After lunch, we all go down to the boathouse and get in canoes and then we paddle upriver for about an hour to a small island where we set up tents and camp out for two nights before heading back. Rowing, fire building, tent-setting-upping, cooking (barely). It's more sur-vivalist than entertainment. Maybe Joan thinks it'll serve us well if ever have to run away and hide in the woods because we flee a conversion camp or because we escape a heterosex-ual society where conversion camps have become mandatory. Or maybe she just wants a weekend off—she doesn't come with us. Connie takes over as boss, leading us all in songs (Mark, begrudgingly, comes along, and Crystal plays guitar), showing us how to set up tents, dig firepits. Karl takes us for-aging in the woods for berries and mushrooms. We swim in the river. It's all VERY dirty. Not in the fun way. Well...the sharing tents without counselors certainly makes it dirty in the fun way, too. But only if you're sharing your tent with the right person, which I, obviously, will not be.

Connie says a weekend in the woods is what camp is all

about. I say the point of camp is to be able to be near enough to the woods to appreciate them, but not live in them.

"I do not like the look of those clouds," Ashleigh says as we row downriver. It's three to a canoe, so naturally George and Ashleigh and I are sharing one. George is at the back steering, and I'm at the front. I look up at the clouds she's talking about, and I don't like the look of them, either. They're thick and there's no end in sight.

"I thought we were done with rain," George says, swatting at a mosquito on his neck.

"I think we're following it," Ashleigh says. "It's the same rain."

We all groan in unison. We've only had one other summer when it rained on the canoe trip, but it made the whole thing that much worse. A ramshackle awning over the fire that means the smoke gets everywhere, and no hiking in the woods, foraging, or swimming. Just hiding out in your tents or getting blasted with smoke as Crystal has a coughing fit trying to sing the next verse of "The Rainbow Connection." At least that's how it was last time.

"Connie," I shout. She's in a canoe with some twelve-year-olds, practically handling the canoe alone, but within shouting distance. She's bringing up the back, while Rebecca, Tina, and Lisa try to race each other to the island up front.

"What's up, Del?" Connie shouts back, smiling at me. I realize I kind of missed her this past week. She was fun to hike with, encouraging with the obstacle course.

319

"It's Randy again," I say, realizing we haven't really spoken since I left her elective. "Are you worried about those clouds, too?" I ask, gesturing up with my chin.

She looks up and purses her lips. "It should be okay," she says. "Might be a little wet tonight, but we'll be good by morning." She nods while looking at the clouds, like making sure they've understood their orders. Weirdly, that makes me feel better.

"Well, there you have it," I say.

"I hope those silver medals made her psychic," Ashleigh says.

"Sweetie, if I were to trust anyone at this camp about the weather, it would be her. Or maybe Karl," I say, looking around and finding his canoe a little ahead of us. He's also looking at the sky. I look back at Connie, who is still staring at the clouds.

"Darling, I think they're worried, too."

TWENTY-FIVE

The storm breaks almost the exact moment we pull our canoe onto shore. Thankfully, it's not heavy at first, just a drizzle, but it quickly turns to real rain as the other campers pull their canoes up.

"A snake!" one of the young boys from Connie's canoe shrieks, hopping out of the water.

"Okay," Connie shouts to the group. "Get with your tent buddy, take one of the tents, and set it up. Karl, help me get a tarp up so we have somewhere to try to make a fire."

"Use Tina and Lisa," Karl says. "I'm going to collect firewood before it all gets soaked."

Connie nods and motions for Tina and Lisa to help her. They lift the tarp out of one of the canoes as the campers line up in front of Mark and Crystal, who are handing out tents.

"Del." I hear the voice call to me, and I don't want to turn, but I know I have to. Ashleigh and George give me pitying looks, then turn away. "Del, I have our tent."

Hudson runs up next to me, holding a tent. I turn and look at him. He's smiling. I want to smile, too, but then I remember everything and I can't.

"Okay," I say.

"Maybe over there?" he says, pointing a little out of the way.

"Sure," I say, without much enthusiasm. I follow him to the spot where he unfurls the tent and he starts putting pegs in the ground while I assemble the rods that hold it up.

"So, I'm glad you didn't switch," Hudson says. "I mean, I know you wanted to. But I'm glad you didn't. I was hoping we could talk."

I don't say anything. I work on getting the rods straight and then threading them through the tent itself. It's tricky, but Hudson pulls them through on the other end and we latch them into place.

"So you don't want to talk?" Hudson asks, sounding angry. "All that work you did, all those lies, and now you just want to drop it?"

"You lied, too, *Hal*," I say.

He nods, then sets the tent into the ground. "So, I thought about that. A lot, actually. But you knew I was lying. That must have been funny to you."

I don't say anything. The rain gets heavier. Hudson

stamps the pegs farther into the ground on one side, I hit them with a rock on the other.

"No?" he asks.

"No," I say. "I didn't think it was funny."

"Your friends were laughing."

Hudson unzips the tent and throws his backpack inside. I throw mine in, too, and then we both try to get in at the same time, bumping shoulders. I step back and motion for him to go first. He does.

It's not a bad tent, as tents go. Big enough for way more than just the two of us. Mesh panels for airflow, which Hudson starts zipping halfway up to keep the rain out. I roll out my sleeping bag, checking it's still dry. It is. Good thing I brought a fancy camping one this year, not my soft pink one.

I sigh and lie down on the sleeping bag. The rain is loud enough now I can't hear anything else.

"So, was it funny to you?" Hudson asks, rolling out his own sleeping bag on the other side of the tent.

"No." I shake my head. "It was sweet." I sigh and turn onto my side, away from him. "This is why I didn't want to share a tent. I don't want to fight. I get it, I was wrong, I lied or whatever, I tricked you. I'm terrible. I'm crazy. I get it. You're angry. Fine. Let's just not talk."

"We could do plenty without talking," he says, in a tone I hadn't expected to hear from him again and which immediately makes all the nerve endings in my body stand at attention.

I turn around to face him, and sit up. He's smiling,

naughty. "Oh," I say. "Is that what this is? Going to reward me for my successful masquerade with a nice tumble in the sleeping bags? Or is it an apology?"

He looks confused. "No, look, Del—sorry, Randy. That came out wrong."

"Let's just not talk," I say again, lying back down, away from him.

"Okay, everybody," I hear Connie shouting through the rain. "We need some help building the fire, if you want to come over here, under the tarp."

I wait to see if he'll go. If he does, I'll stay, but if he stays, I'll go. He doesn't move, but then we get up to leave at the same time.

"You want to help build the fire?" he asks, surprised. I narrow my eyes. We went on the same hikes, did the same activities with Connie, but now that he knows I'm a theater kid, it's like all I am to him is some nature-averse princess, and I would be an amazing princess, don't get me wrong—I rock a tiara—but I can do anything he can do and be a princess while doing it.

"What, you don't think I can?" I ask.

"No," he says quickly. "Come on, let's go help."

I follow him out into the rain, which is getting heavier by the minute. Soon it'll make the world invisible.

We trudge through the thankfully only slightly muddy ground to where we see a bright yellow tarp slung between the trees. It's big, but probably not big enough to cover

everyone sitting around a fire. The ground is sandy here, dotted with stones, but it looks like the tarp went up quickly enough that it's not soaked. Karl is in the center of the dry ground, putting stones around a shallow pit. A pile of dry and dry-ish wood is next to him. Other campers stand around, watching him, but it looks like most have stayed in their tents.

"We need more stones," he shouts. I run out into the rain, away from Hudson, looking for stones. My clothes are wet against me pretty quickly, my shoes start getting uncomfortably cold and squishy. The ground is mud, and I admit, I'm not being as careful as I should. The rain makes it hard to see, and I can feel the ground trying to suck my shoes up, so I lift them high and hard, marching...but then I put them down just as hard. Which might also just be because putting your foot down hard feels good when you're angry. And I'm angry. Angry at Hudson for what he said, angry at myself for my whole stupid plan, angry at the weather for raining, at the world for making us share a tent, and angry again at Hudson for his weird little flirting. What was that about?

And maybe I'm so caught up with how angry I am that I'm not careful, which is how I slip into the ditch.

It's not a big ditch, but it's a bit of a mudslide, and at the bottom, my ankle hitches on a root and I fall over it. I don't hear a pop or snap or anything, but in this rain, what could I hear? All I know is it hurts. A lot. Tears-mingling-with-rain a lot. I get myself into a sitting position and try to stand, but the ground is slippery and putting too much pressure on

my foot makes it send up big, blaring, painful alarms. So I'm stuck.

"Help!" I shout. I can't hear anything over the rain, though. I doubt anyone can hear me. I'm going to die in the rain in a ditch. Hudson will go back to our tent, I won't be there, and he'll think I've gone off to crowd into someone else's, or maybe he won't care at all, just be happy I'm gone, and no one will tell Connie I'm missing, and I'll sit here all night in the rain, sinking into the mud, dying of hypothermia. I can already feel myself shiver.

"Help!" I try again.

"Hello?" comes a voice through the rain.

"Yes! Hi! I tripped, please, can you help me get back to the main camp?" I shout out, trying to keep the rain out of my eyes to see who it is. "Be careful, it's a pit."

He comes closer and then gently climbs down into the pit.

It's Hudson. Because of course it is.

"Whoa," he says, looking at me. I'm covered in mud, I know. "What happened?"

"I slipped," I tell him, really wishing it were someone else. "Can you go get Connie?"

"Nah, come on." He kneels next to me in the mud and puts my arm around his shoulders.

"Just get Connie," I say, but he's standing, lifting me up. I lean on him as we walk, and he finds a gentle slope out of the pit. "Thanks," I say softly, angry now that he had to be a nice enough guy to save me.

"Of course," he says. "You okay?"

I try putting some weight on the bad ankle, now that we're out of the mud and the land is firmer. It doesn't feel so bad. Just a twinge now. A half-hearted "please don't," which I happily ignore as I take my arm off Hudson and walk back to camp.

"Randy, wait," he says. I can walk but not very quickly, so he keeps pace. "You'll fall again."

"Oh right, 'cause I'm just some fairy who can't even put one leg in front of the other unless it's a runway sashay, right?" I say.

"What? No. I just mean, you slipped the first time, so be careful."

"I can handle myself. I know you think I'm some limp-wristed, weak-willed stereotype, but I was on all those hikes you were." I'm not yelling. I'm talking loudly so he hears me over the rain.

"I know, Randy, I just mean...it's slippery."

"I'm fine." I walk ahead and he lingers a step behind me until we're back at camp, and then I sit down close to the fire.

Connie sees me covered in mud and comes up. "What happened?"

"I slipped."

"He twisted his ankle," Hudson says, standing behind me. "He couldn't get up."

"Okay, go get the first aid kit," she says to him. "And some towels to get this mud off you." Hudson runs over to

the Black Bag—infamous for holding endless condoms, dental dams, and lube (the counselors know what happens on these trips), as well as first aid kits, and being open all weekend, just left there for folks to use.

Connie has me lift my leg and puts it on a cooler to keep it up and then touches it in a few places. I wince, but only a little.

"Just a little turned, I think," she says as Hudson comes back with towels. He's wiping himself off, and when he sees a cut on my knee immediately starts wiping that off as well.

"Thanks," I say, trying not to sound friendly.

"Sure," he says, taking out a Band-Aid and slapping it over the cut.

"You'll be fine by morning," Connie says to me. "Just keep it up for a while. No more rock gathering, okay?

"And Hudson, help him back to the tent later, just in case, okay?"

"He doesn't have to—"

"Yeah," Hudson interrupts me. "Of course."

Connie goes back to the firepit, which is starting to liven up. Smoke is pouring out and getting stuck under the tarp, making my eyes prick a little.

"Thanks for helping," I say to Hudson.

He sits down next to me. "What did you think I was going to do? Just leave you?"

"I don't know."

"You really think I'd do that?" he asks.

I sigh. "No."

"Good."

We sit in silence for a moment.

"So, I'm going to go help with the fire. Don't head back to the tent without me, okay?"

He puts his hand on my shoulder, and for a second I think he's going to kiss me on the cheek, like he used to, and I can see in his eyes that he thinks of it, but he turns and heads toward the fire instead. I watch him build it up and think maybe I was being an ass. I mean, he was helping. I fell. It was human. It was the right thing to do.

But it doesn't mean anything, I remind myself. He was just being decent. And besides, I don't want it to mean anything. I want to go to sleep and not think about him anymore.

"We got hot dogs!" Connie shouts to the campers still huddled in their tents. "Hot dogs and s'mores. Come and roast yourself some dinner!"

People come out of their tents, shrieking as they try to cover themselves and dash under the tarp. More than a few slip in the mud. Everyone gathers around Connie, grabbing hot dogs and sticking them on the ends of sticks they've plucked from the woods before lining up to roast them over the fire. Mark and Crystal hand out buns and soon there's a decent line going as everyone roasts and eats. George and Ashleigh see me sitting and bring me a stick and then, when I tell them what happened, help me closer to the fire.

"So he came to your rescue?" Ashleigh asks, raising her eyebrows. "In the rain?"

"He heard me yelling. It was what anyone would have done."

"It's just very...Jane Austen?" Ashleigh says. "Heathcliff? Something."

"Darling," George says, gently telling her to stop.

"Sorry, right," she says. "It wasn't anything. Want me to roast a weenie for ya?"

"Yes, please."

George and Ashleigh act as my roasters, cooking my hot dogs and then marshmallows for s'mores, since there's nowhere to sit that's close enough to the fire.

Crystal gets out her guitar and tries to play some songs, but she's difficult to hear under the sound of the rain on the tarp.

"If I catch a cold from this," George says next to me, licking chocolate and marshmallow off his fingers, "I'm going to be deeply angry."

"Mark is handing out chewable vitamin C to everyone in the show." I nod at Mark, who's carefully going around, looking for his actors and crew and making them take chalky orange-flavored tablets (he got me first).

"Hey, Randy?" Hudson calls to me. "You ready to go back to the tent?"

"You're not going to stay up?"

"For what?"

I shrug and nod and let him help me up—though it barely hurts now. I grab a few bottles of water as we head back to

the tent. We're both totally soaked by the time we get inside and Hudson takes out a towel from his bag and starts drying himself and the tent where we've dripped. Then he takes off his shirt.

I swallow as I look at his damp naked skin and quickly turn away. Romance may be over between us, but lust definitely isn't, at least not on my side. He's still top-name-on-the-marquee gorgeous, his body still carved from some stone I don't know the name of. I pull my shirt off, too, and lay it flat in the corner to dry. I hear him unzip his shorts, the sound impossibly loud over the rain. I stare out the window, even though there's nothing I can see. There's some rustling behind me.

"You can turn around now."

I turn, and he's in his sleeping bag. In his corner of the tent, his shoes, shirt, shorts, and underwear are all laid out to dry.

"You could have turned around before, too."

I glare. "Why are you flirting?"

"What?"

"Before and that, what you just said. You're flirting."

"I don't know...we used to flirt before."

I put my hands on my hips and cock them to one side. "Yeah, but now I'm not your type, right?" I lift a hand and bend my wrist at him. "Now I'm just some faggot," I say, giving myself a lisp. "Some weak stereotype, right?"

He frowns. "No," he says. "And I'm sorry for what I said.

He sits up a little, his sleeping bag sliding around him to his stomach. Did he put on clean underwear? "Randy, I need you to know that. I am really so, so sorry for that."

I let my arms drop and I sigh. "I know. But you still said it."

"I was angry, embarrassed that everyone, the whole camp, knew everything and had known the whole time, and I. . . . I wanted to hurt you."

I sit down, my wet shorts making me cold. "I know."

"If you know that . . . why are you so angry? I'm not angry anymore. I . . . look, what you did is wild, no doubt about it. Over-the-top. Just . . . like from a movie or something. But . . . it was flattering, too. And the really out-there thing is that it worked. I really fell in love with you, Randy. I told you things I've never told anyone, not even Brad, and I feel closer to you than anyone else in my life."

Some water drips from my hair onto the tent. Hudson sighs and reaches for his towel, and as he leans forward, I can see down his lower back to the top of his ass—he is definitely not wearing underwear. He throws the towel at me.

"Dry off," he says. "Change out of those wet things. I won't look."

He turns around and I strip and use his towel to get myself dry. The towel smells like him—that electric deodorant and the faint maple smell. I try not to think about it as I get in my sleeping bag. I throw the towel back at him. It lands on his head.

"That means I can turn around?" he asks.

I grin, then make my face angry again. "Yeah."

He turns around so we're both facing each other on our sides, naked in our sleeping bags, a wide space between us. I hate it, but my body is tingling. Maybe I don't hate it.

"So why are you so angry?" Hudson asks.

I shrug. "You don't like me. That makes me angry."

His eyes get large, sort of sad. "Why do you think that?"

"Because of everything you said. Everything you are." I sit up and gesture up and down his body. "Masc4masc, straight-acting only, all that."

"I just thought that people like that were...stronger," he says. "And safer. I could never bring someone back to my parents who wasn't...different, like me. Not a stereotype in their eyes. I could never hold hands with him on the street. So I just...didn't even look at them. That was wrong, I know. You showed me that. I'm not better than you, Randy. I'm not better than George or anyone else in the show." He pauses. "If anything, I'm worse."

"Worse?"

"You guys are just being yourselves." He sits up again, then lies down, unable to get comfortable. "I...I'm a character just as much as Del was, maybe. I don't know. I don't feel like I'm acting most of the time, but then...when Brad put on that nail polish, I was so jealous."

"Jealous?"

"Yeah. It was a cool color."

"Unicorn Trampocalypse."

He laughs. "Is that the name?" He turns to look at the ceiling of the tent, on his back but out of his sleeping bag enough that his stomach is exposed. "I like it. I wish I could wear it. I wanted to, in that moment. I wanted to be . . . more like me? Not that I think all gay guys have to wear nail polish to be themselves or anything. But it reminded me of my grandma, and painting her nails, and her sometimes painting mine and how happy that made me. I really loved it. Picking out the color, holding it up to the light, seeing it on me. Not just nail polish, either. Lipstick, eye shadow. I had so much fun putting makeup on Grandma, and wearing it. And then she would wipe it all off before my parents got home and tell me not to tell them. She was protecting me. So then, when she died, I started protecting myself because of . . ."

"What your mom did."

He nods. "But I think Grandma wanted to send me here because here is a kind of protection. Here I can . . . be myself. Right?"

"Like you've always said: You can be anyone you want," I say. "I kind of proved that."

He laughs. "Yeah." He turns back to me. "So, I want you to know, and, like, you don't need to say anything back, but I just want you to know, that I thought about everything—everything you said and did and . . . you were right. I do know you, Randy. Maybe not all the parts of you—I don't know about your love of musical theater, or your real fashion sense

or anything like that. But I know the parts of you that make me laugh, that make me feel good about myself, that talk to me and make me feel special not because of what I'm not, but because of what I am. And, so . . . I still love all those parts."

I can feel my throat closing and force myself to take a deep breath through my nose. He reaches out his hand to me, but it doesn't close the distance, so he wriggles his sleeping bag closer, which makes us both laugh and then his hand is on my cheek and every part of me feels like it's filled with stars again.

"Wait," I say, pulling his hand off me.

"I want to know all the parts of you," he says. "I mean that. I want to hear all about the show and what you've been doing this week, I want to know about musical theater and clothes and . . . anything you want to talk to me about."

I smile. "Okay," I say. "But . . . I don't know you anymore."

"What?"

"Every summer, I've watched you, seen you inspire people—inspire me. You always made me feel like I can do anything . . . but it turns out what you meant was you thought I could be more . . . like you. And now, you're saying you want me to be me, but . . ."

"Randy," he says, looking straight into me, making new stars appear just with his eyes. "I do want you to be you. So, I know what I've said is . . . not, like, what you thought I meant. But . . . I like your version better. So . . . that's what I believe now." He shrugs. "You made me believe what you

thought I believed this whole time. You're special. I think maybe...we're special."

Stars are born from explosions, and a thousand stars are born in me as he pulls my face close to his and kisses me.

When we pause, I pull back. "You want..." I swallow. "I mean, are we just picking back up where we left off, like nothing happened?"

"We are...trying," he says, and kisses me again. "But there's something I want you to do to me."

"Okay," I say, my voice a little breathier than I mean for it to be.

He scoots back over to his stuff and goes into his bag and pulls something out, then comes back over to me and shows it to me—nail polish. It's a deep purple color with dark blue glitter.

"Paint my nails?" he asks a little loudly.

I laugh. "Where did you even get this?"

"You're welcome, darling!" I hear George's voice shout through the rain.

"They set up their tent near ours," Hudson says with a sheepish smile. "George said I could use the nail polish as long as I let him know when it was happening so he could take credit."

Brad's voice comes in loud for a moment, over the rain, "Now can we—" The rain gets heavy again, cutting them off. Hudson and I laugh.

"So, will you paint my nails?" Hudson asks.

I nod, shaking the bottle. Hudson spreads his hands in front of me. I've held those hands a hundred times, linked my fingers through his, but I've never really looked at them before. They're delicate, more than I thought. They could use some moisturizer—they're a little rough—but the fingers are slender and graceful, and his nails, though short, are smooth. I take the brush and carefully spread it over his nails, trying to leave an even coat.

"I love this color," Hudson says. "It's so . . ."

"Regal?" I say.

"Yeah. Exactly. I'm like a king wearing this."

I smile, focusing on painting carefully, not dripping onto his skin or the tent. I go slowly, even though part of me wants to rush. Part of me knows what will happen next, when his nails are dry and his newly colored hands run down my body. I'm ready for it. I want it.

But also, I think, finishing his first hand, maybe this is stupid. I said I wanted Hudson in nail polish, and I'm getting him, but what does that even mean? How can this work when he's just coming out of his shell and I've only shown him part of me? Is that enough? Is one week left of camp enough?

I finish his second hand and blow on his nails.

"Shake your hands so it dries and I can do a second coat if you want."

"Can I do yours?"

I show off my hands. My nails are cropped short, and

bright pink metallic polish dots every finger. "Just painted them last night. But you can paint over them, if you want."

He nods, happy. "It'll be a cool effect," he says, starting to paint. He's a natural, too. All those years practicing on his grandma must have taught him well. He glides the brush in quick, precise strokes. He finishes faster than I did.

"I haven't done that in so long," he says. "It felt...nice." He looks up. "Thank you. I'm glad it was you."

I smile and blow on my nails and shake them in the air, wishing they would dry faster. He leans forward and kisses me again on the lips, then the neck.

"Stop," I say, "my nails are still wet."

"So you'd better not touch me," he says. "But mine are dry...." He puts his hand on my chest, then runs it down my stomach, and then he pauses, waiting for me to say something. I don't, and his hands go farther down in my sleeping bag. I gasp as he starts stroking me. I'm already hard—I have been since the moment I heard him take off his shorts.

"This is okay?" he whispers. I nod and kiss him again, then stop to frantically blow on my nails. "Relax," he says. "They'll dry." He unzips my sleeping bag and starts kissing down my neck onto my stomach until his mouth finds what it's looking for and...oh.

First blow job. That's happening now.

I look down and just the sight of Hudson doing what he's doing is enough to almost make me involuntarily end it

prematurely, so I look away. I always thought it would be a bit like what I do in the shower when the cabin is empty, but it's very different from that. Much better. Should I do something, though? Do I put my hand on his head, or does that mean I want him to go deeper? I don't want him to do anything he doesn't want to do, so I carefully lay my hand on his head, like I'm patting a dog. No...this is not how it happens in porn. I grab his hair with both my hands.

"Ow," he says, stopping.

"Sorry."

He smiles and goes back to it. I let my hands rest in his hair and try to lie back and just enjoy it. And it feels...*amazing* is a cheap word for these sensations. I need some new word that makes me arch my back and makes my whole body feel like electricity is shooting through it—like my skeleton can feel things now.

I lose track of time, but also I'm aware of every moment of this. It's just that moments have no meaning, time wise, until I can feel that I need to stop him or else ask him if he's a spitter or a swallower.

"Wait," I say, panting. "I'm...not yet."

He lifts his mouth to mine and kisses me. "Your nails are probably dry by now," he says.

I laugh and touch one of them. Totally dry. I wrap my arms around him and kiss him, my body pushing against his sleeping bag, which I hastily unzip. He smiles and the space

between us closes, our bodies knitting together, legs between legs, arms wrapped around bodies, hands running up and down. I pull away, enjoying myself too much.

"Do you want to?" He looks down at his own body.

I nod. "I've never." What do I do? I know no teeth. But is it like a lollipop scenario, or more of an ice cream cone?

"Just do what you think you'd like," he says, maybe seeing my panic. Which sounds well and good, but I just experienced it for the first time, so how do I know exactly what I like?

I'm not super sure how to do this, so I just open my mouth as wide as I can and go as far as I can. I must look like a fish. So sexy, Randy. I'm surprised by the taste. I thought it would be dirt-tasting and with an uncomfortable smell, but it tastes and smells like the crook of his neck. I use my tongue and lips and I smile when I hear him moan. I'm doing it, and doing it well enough—my first time giving a blow job. I try a few things, twisting my mouth, using my hands, going as far down as I can, which results in a very unsexy coughing fit that I try to hide and makes us both laugh. He starts giving me instructions, and that makes it easier.

"Like that. Slower. Don't press your lips together so hard."

He runs his hands through my hair and I stop for a minute to take a breath.

"You all right?"

I nod. "Am I doing it right?"

"Yeah," Hudson laughs. "You're a natural."

340

What surprises me most is how much I enjoy it. Not just for his sounds of pleasure, but because I want this. You always hear about how hot getting a blow job is, but never hear how hot it is to give one.

"Okay, okay," he says, after not enough time, pulling me back up to him. We kiss.

"I want you in me," he says. My eyes widen a little. "If you want."

"Are you sure?" I ask. "I mean, I could..."

He grins. "You're new to this. Let's start this way. If you want. We don't have to—"

I nod, cutting him off. "Yes," I say quickly. I'm not saying no to that. I'm checking every box I can on the virginity score card tonight. Is that a sports metaphor? Maybe I'm still a little Del after all.

He turns back to his bag, letting me admire the perky slopes of his ass, and pulls out several packets of lube and a condom.

"You'll have to show me," I say.

"Okay," he says. "Let's start with your finger."

I hold out my hand, and he opens a packet of lube onto his hand and mine, then he reaches behind himself. I test the lube between my hands. It feels...silly. Almost like rubbing Jell-O between my hands. I giggle at it, then look up and see Hudson biting his lower lip, his eyes rolling back as he fingers himself. All thoughts of Jell-O and silliness vanish.

"Can I see?" I ask.

He smiles and turns onto his stomach so I can watch him lube everything up and push his own finger into himself. He sighs deeply. Then he pulls it out. "You," he says, reaching for my lubed hand. Carefully, I push my finger into him. He stops me after a minute, pulling my hand out. "More lube," he says.

I grab another packet and try to open it, but my hands are already lubed up and it slips out, flying up and hitting the roof of the tent, then falling back down. Hudson laughs and picks it up, opening it with his teeth, and then pouring it over my hands. He rolls back over and guides my finger into him, farther than before. When he gasps, I stop.

"No, it feels good. Keep going. Slowly." I keep pushing in and he cranes his neck up so I kiss him on the mouth as I push. "Now in and out," he gasps. I follow his instructions, moving my finger as he makes noises that make every part of me stand on end. At his instruction, I curl my finger slightly, and the noises grow louder. He grabs my face close to him, kissing me hungrily. "Two fingers now."

I swallow and pull my finger out, and add more lube from one of the open packets before going back in with two fingers. I'm so glad I cut my nails before re-painting them yesterday.

"Wait," he says, and I stop as he takes a deep breath. "Okay." I push again, slower. When both fingers are nearly in all the way he gasps again, throwing his head down into the built-in pillow of his sleeping bag.

"Should I stop?"

"No," he says, his voice low and throaty. "It feels so good," he says half into his pillow. He looks up at me, his face both hungry and looking a little drunk and pulls me in for a kiss again. He rotates slightly, so our bodies are pressing together, my hand wrapped around his waist. "I'm ready," he says after some more kissing. "I want you."

I nod and he tears the condom open, rolling it down on me, which is much more fun than when I've practiced putting on condoms myself, and then he opens two more packets of lube and pours them over it.

"I'll start on top," he says, "if that's okay?"

"Anything is okay," I say, words not working quite right, so I kiss him. He smiles into the kiss, almost laughing, and then shoves me, so I'm lying on my back, and kneels over me. He slowly lowers himself, grabbing my body and guiding me, easing me into him. At first, the tightness is so intense it almost hurts, and I wonder if I've done something wrong, but his breathing turns heavy and he smiles, openmouthed, turning his head to the ceiling.

"Oh yes," he says, and starts moving up and down on me. It feels astounding. Different from the blow job. And much better than by myself in the shower. But even better than how I feel is watching Hudson, hearing the sounds he makes as he moves up and down on top of me.

He leans forward, kissing me, and I grab his ass, squeezing it as our tongues mingle, our bodies combine, then he

throws his head back again, making more noises as I rock my hips gently up and down. He touches himself, his purple nail polish gleaming in the dim light. I love watching him; it's the sexiest thing I've ever seen. Here I am, finally having sex with Hudson, a man I've loved for years, who loves me, the real me, and it's like the world is applauding for me. Not like we're being watched—that's not something I'm into. I don't think. But it's like a standing ovation, but not from people, from the world itself. The world itself, the universe, the stars, all clapping for us, and saying, "What a wonderful end to a perfect love story."

"Want to try missionary?" Hudson asks. His hair is wet again, but now with sweat.

I grin. "Yeah."

TWENTY-SIX

ight pours in through the walls of the tent, kind of gray.
The rain has stopped, but it's stuffy. I'm naked, on my
sleeping bag, which is open and next to Hudson's, but Hudson is gone. The clothes he set drying are still there.

I take a deep breath. I'm not a virgin anymore. But I'm
also alone. I want to replay last night over and over, but Hudson not being here is worrying me. I go through my bag for
clean underwear and slip it on. Where did Hudson go? Is he
regretting what we did, what he said, off somewhere trying
to scrape away the nail polish? An image of him comes into
my mind, scraping his nails until they bleed or come off, and
I wince. If that's what he's doing, he's definitely done with
me. Or maybe it was just an act, a new smooth routine from
the Hal who carves his name in the tree every summer, a

new conquest. Or a new flavor to try, which he'll now throw in the trash.

The front of the tent unzips and I try to cover myself with my sleeping bag as Hudson pokes his head in.

"Oh, you put on underwear," he says, disappointed.

I smile. "I can take it off again." Did that just come out of my mouth? One night of passion and suddenly I'm a femme fatale in a made-for-TV movie. I am doing this all wrong.

He steps into the tent and kisses me. "Maybe in a bit," he says. "I grabbed us breakfast. Bagels and cream cheese." He hands me a cold bagel, a mini packet of cream cheese, and a plastic knife. The same thing they send on the canoe trip every year. "Oh, but maybe..." He reaches into his bag and throws me a mini bottle of hand sanitizer, which I use.

He takes off his shoes and sits on his sleeping bag. He has his own bagel, already half eaten, which he finishes, smiling at me as I try to spread the cream cheese on mine. I start eating and he pulls his shirt off, putting it back in his bag. Then he strips his shorts off, revealing blue boxer briefs.

"It's stuffy in here," he says. "It's warm."

I nod, eating my bagel and watching him.

"So, the rain stopped. We can probably do stuff today. Karl says there'll be a lot of mushrooms out."

"Probably," I say.

"So, do you want to talk about anything?" he asks, tilting his head at me.

"I just..."

"You're not a virgin." He grins.

"That's part of it." I laugh, and then take another bite of my bagel. "But...I mean. What are we now?"

"Oh." His eyes widen. "I thought we were boyfriends again. If that's okay. Is that what you want?"

Is it? It's what I've always wanted. And...I love him. I think I do, at least. It's hard, peeling back these layers of Hudson and finding out how he feels about gay men, about himself, about what his parents taught him to hate, and what his grandmother tried to teach him to love. He's not the simple dream guy I thought he was. He's not just someone who's going to make me feel good because he believes in the best of everyone. His beliefs are changing. I'm changing them. I cut my hair and figured out I like the obstacle course, though, so he changed me first.

I look at his nails. They need a second coat. I should have done that last night.

"Randy?" he asks. I realize I've been quiet for a while.

"I was just trying to figure it out," I say. "Who you are. Who you think I am."

"I don't know if we can ever really know everything about each other," he says. "But I'd like to try. And like I said last night...I know enough of you to love you."

I smile. "I know enough of you to love you, too," I say.

"So, boyfriends?"

"Yes. Now get over here, because, sweetie, those nails need another coat."

He grins and takes out the nail polish, shaking it as I eat, then gives me his hands, and I carefully paint each nail.

The entire day is spent swimming in the river or helping Karl find dry wood and mushrooms and berries (which no one eats without checking with him first, since three summers ago when one of the girls from cabin twelve spent the day vomiting). And just like I slipped easily back into theater, I slip easily back into Hudson.

Not like that.

But it's like the fights and the last week never happened. No, they happened, but we worked through everything. We know more about each other now, and we love those parts of each other. So we walk hand in hand, matching nail polish and all. We sneak kisses behind trees and underwater when we're swimming. We lie on the sand of the beach together with George and Brad and Ashleigh and Paz and tell jokes and laugh and try to explain musical theater to Hudson, who says he wants to learn because I learned all about what he likes.

"So, we only have one week left," he says, holding my hand on the beach.

"Yeah," I say sadly. "We'll make the most of it."

"Right. So, I'm going to do theater for the last week."

"What?"

"You did all my stuff for two weeks. I can go a week without the obstacle course.... Maybe I'll do some sports

after lunch if I'm feeling like I have to move around, but only if it's okay with you, babe."

"You don't owe me anything," I say.

"All right, then even if it's not okay with you. But I'm joining theater. I will move stuff around, or...try to dance, or whatever."

I laugh. "How about you stop by when you can?"

"Okay. I just want to spend time with you."

"I know." I lay my head on his shoulder. "But the last week of rehearsal is always crazy. We literally call it Hell Week."

"So I won't see you?" He frowns.

"We'll make time," I say. "I promise."

He smiles and kisses me.

That night, we roast mushrooms and more hot dogs, but it's not raining, so there's no tarp and we don't end up living in a tent of smoke. Instead, we all sing and drink bug juice and tell jokes and watch the fire until it dies down. We all seem happy. We all feel like a family.

When the sun goes down, Hudson and I go back to our tent, kissing frantically before we even zip the door closed. You'd think finally having sex would calm me down, but it's only made me want him more, and I'm down on my knees undoing his fly in less than a minute.

"Maybe tonight," I say, pulling his shorts down and kissing his thighs through his boxer briefs, "you can top me?"

He laughs. "I'd love to, but not tonight. You're going to want a real shower before that."

I think about it for a minute before realizing what he means. "Right," I say, a little disappointed.

He kneels down next to me and kisses me. "But there's still plenty of other stuff we can do."

I grin, grabbing him by the waist and slipping my hands down the back of his underwear to squeeze his ass.

"Well, I guess if you insist."

The next day, after packing up and making sure we're leaving no trash behind, we row back to camp. We stay in the same canoes we came up in, but now the canoe with Hudson, Brad, and Sam glides alongside ours, all of us shouting jokes back and forth and singing together until Connie tells us we're too close and to get some distance, and we split up, and then get close again a few minutes later.

When we make it back to camp, everyone runs to the pool to bleach our bodies with chlorine and get the river stink off ourselves, before heading up to the cabins for a proper shower and then dinner.

After dinner, maybe knowing we're all a little overdosed on nature, is another movie night (*Love, Simon*) and Hudson and I hold hands and lean on each other as we watch. Then we make out a little next to the side of my cabin before I hear Mark call, "Lights-out in five," and we say good night.

"So, you finally get everything you wanted," Ashleigh

says when I come into the cabin and run for my toothbrush. "Plan executed. Happy ending."

"Endings," George says. "He had two nights in the tent."

I roll my eyes, but I smile. "Yeah, I guess it all worked."

And it did. And I should be happy. And I am. But I'm worried, too. The only time we have left is Hell Week, and then the summer is over and Hudson goes back to his parents, the real world, where he'll be constantly reminded that I'm not the right sort of boy for him to be with. That he can do better—not in the usual sense, because let's face it, he can't—but in the way he used to mean better. More straight-acting. More approved of. Safer. Has he really changed, or is it more like a constant battle where I'm fighting for him, and one where I'm not going to be in the picture for the next eleven months?

I look over at Mark, who is standing by the light switch, waiting for us all to get in bed.

"Okay, Randy?" he asks.

"I think so."

As always, Hell Week lives up to its name. Everything needs to be perfected and suddenly two dozen new problems pop up. A lighting gel melts, Jen inexplicably forgets all the lyrics to "Rosie," the chorus becomes entirely left-footed.

"Are we cursed?" Mark asks the theater one afternoon before stalking outside to call his therapist.

And yet, I'm loving it. The chaos, the energy. Maybe I'm the kind of drama queen that thrives on the chaos. Or maybe it's that Hudson is here, and every time I start to feel stressed, it's like he senses it, and he's suddenly next to me, his hand resting on my hip, telling me he doesn't quite get everything, but it seems pretty cool, or being amazed at how different colored lights change the tone of the set. Everything is new to him, and all he wants to do is be there for me. I'm really lucky.

And we talk, between scenes, during dinner. Really talk, with me as Randy, and he wants to know everything: about my love of musical theater (all-encompassing), why I don't wear eyeliner (I poke myself in the eye), the first time I wore nail polish (at camp, first week, after asking George if he'd do my nails; outside camp, at thirteen, I stole my mom's and when she caught me she laughed and said it was kind of weird to see a boy with painted nails, "But if it makes you happy..."). We talk about Randy things, and he listens and loves everything I tell him.

I tell him about our first week, the night we talked. He doesn't remember, but he says that he remembers that night, because it was the first week he'd slept soundly. And now he knows it was because of me.

Ashleigh gives me the photos from the underwater camera. All the underwater ones are blurry, but there's one of

him kissing me on the cheek above water that I tape to the post of my bed, so I can look at it as I go to sleep.

He even starts helping out with the makeup for the actors in the show. It must be muscle memory or something, because he can apply one of the best cat's eyes I've seen, and fast, too. And he's made a few changes to the stage makeup that have everyone looking fantastic. I wonder if his grandma looked like everyone onstage at some point. If he'll see her when he watches the show, peeking out.

He even stole one of the blue eyeliner pencils and has started wearing it when he's around camp. Just a little cat's eye. Nothing too dramatic. But it makes me happy to know not only did he find his place in the theater, but it was like he was always meant to be there. Just like maybe I was always meant to direct (but not NOT act, of course. Direct in *addition* to acting).

I feel bad I don't have much time with him, though, and I feel especially bad that now that we're sleeping in cabins again, we can't get any alone time. On Thursday, he convinces me to sneak away after lunch to hike to our spot overlooking the camp, where we strip and don't spend any time at all admiring the view before rinsing ourselves off with water bottles and rushing back down to the drama cabin, where Mark rolls his eyes at us as we walk in late.

"I can't wait to introduce you to my parents," Hudson says to me over dinner, holding my hand. "I want to show them how happy you make me."

I smile so hard it hurts at that. "And you'll get to meet mine," I say.

I'm worried about Hudson's parents, though. I'm worried about what he said about how they might react to Brad's painted nails—by not letting Hudson come back next summer. I look down at our hands—still painted purple, but chipping. I love those nails, and his hands, holding them and seeing our matching nail polish. I love the feel of his hand woven into mine. But I also don't want that hand to get hurt.

After dinner, we go back to the theater to run a few more scenes. I sit next to Mark in the audience while Hudson is backstage helping put on people's makeup.

"Can I ask you something?" I say to Mark between scenes.

"It's really not the best time, Randy," Mark says. "But make it quick."

"Hudson's parents...they don't like him acting femme. Should I tell him to take off his nail polish before they get here? Should I take off mine?"

Mark snorts. "You should be yourself. And he should be himself. You've helped that boy come out of his shell, and he is clearly happier for it, and I'm very happy for you, but I don't know his family situation. My advice is to always be yourself, and not apologize for it."

I lean back in my chair. Right. That's true. That's good.

"Thanks," I say. He pats my leg, watching the stage.

"Still, you should talk to Connie. She knows his parents."

"Oh," I say, frowning that this isn't easy and decided. "All right. Can I go find her now?"

"Sure, sure, just...No, come on, the set needs to change faster than that, people! You did it twice as fast three hours ago. WHAT IS HAPPENING?"

I smile. Mark is too busy to give me much advice right now. But I get up and walk out of the cabin. The rest of the camp tonight is playing flashlight freeze tag, running around in the dark trying to catch each other in beams of light. Connie is one of the refs, so I find her standing to the side of the soccer field.

"Where's your flashlight, Randy? Or are you in the theater tonight? I hear the show is going to be good this year."

"It is." I nod, smiling. "But I wanted to talk to you about something."

"Sure," she says, turning away from the field and looking at me. "Everything okay?"

"I'm worried about Hudson."

"Why?"

"It's his parents. You've met them, right?"

Connie nods. "Yes. I've spoken to them at the end of the summer before. And I know a little about Hudson's home life from what he's told me."

"So you know Hudson and I are together, right?"

Connie laughs. "The whole camp knows, Randy."

I blush, happy the dark is hiding it. "Okay, but you've seen he's wearing nail polish and he's working at the theater."

"Yes. Young love can change a person. It's actually very sweet, I think."

"Will his parents think so, too, though?"

Connie sighs. "I was going to talk to him on Saturday," she says quietly. She sits down cross-legged on the grass and I sit down next to her. "I wanted to give him some more time being...here, you know? That's why we made this place. A place away from the world. You ever watch *The West Wing*? No, you're too young. Far from the things of man. That's what this place is. Except *man* meaning 'straight people.' It's a safe place. A place for you all to be yourselves and have a childhood that you don't get anywhere else." She takes a deep breath and exhales slowly. "But it's got an expiration date."

"Okay..."

"He needs to take the nail polish off," she says. "And if he's going to introduce you to his parents as his boyfriend, you need to take yours off, too. You need to be Del again."

"But isn't it better to just be yourself, and be proud?" I ask.

"Here? Yes. Absolutely. Out there? You have to keep yourself safe first. You're still just kids. Hudson needs his parents to feed him, clothe him, not kick him out or beat him or berate him or send him to a conversion camp. He needs them to let him come back here next summer. And that means he has to stay...what they want him to be."

"But they're his parents. They send him here."

"They don't like sending him here. I'm always happy when I see his name come in as a camper. I don't know how he convinces them, but they don't like this place." I know what it is. His grandma, guilting them from beyond the grave. "You'll see, on Sunday. Watch their eyes, like they're in enemy territory. We're not the same as them. We're not them. Maybe not even people. Hudson is, because he's their son, and because even with this one thing, he hasn't pushed himself too far outside their idea of what he should be: male, masculine . . . whatever nonsense words people put on behavior sets they approve of." She leans back against a tree, and her hands absently start pulling blades of grass. "I didn't come out until I was twenty-seven. You know that? I injured my leg, I knew my career was done, and it was a relief to me. Because now I could do it, now I could come out. Except I'd come out to my coach before that. Years before. Nineteen. He'd walked in on me one day in a hotel room, and I was wearing this skirt I'd seen and had to have. It was beautiful. Blue silk, dip dyed so it was lighter at the waist, flowed like a dream. He tore it off me. Ripped it to shreds. I tried to explain how I felt, how I'd always felt. But he told me that I couldn't be that. He said if I wanted to put on women's clothes in private, that was fine. But I couldn't do it in public. I couldn't be a woman, tell people I was a woman, do what felt right to me: longer hair, longer nails. . . . I had to show some restraint. Like an adult, he said. Everything else was . . . he called it 'bedroom stuff,' which I didn't understand at first,

but then I realized he thought it was a sex thing." She pauses. "I should not be telling that to a camper."

"Mark says worse."

She snorts a laugh. "I know he does. Anyway, my coach told me if I came out, or even started to show signs I would, he would dump me, I'd lose all my endorsement deals, and I'd be banned from the sport. My life would be over. So I kept myself safe. Until my life kind of was over because of the injury. And then I finally got to be reborn."

"But is that the same?"

"No, no...nothing is the same. No coming out story is the same as another. And you're already out, Hudson is out. And gay is different from trans. Gender non-conforming is different from trans. You know that. But what I mean is there's out and then there's the sort of out people don't want you to be. I could know I was a woman in my mind, but not act on it. Hudson can know in his head he's a guy in nail polish and eyeliner who will kick your ass on the obstacle course and look fabulous doing it. There are different degrees of out...and you need to stick to the ones that are safe. Now, what's safe changes with where you are, and who you're with. I don't have that luxury. But I'm also an adult now. I'm not saying it's safe in the world for me, but my parents can't kick me out of the house. So Hudson has to find the degree of out that will keep him safe when he's around his parents."

I nod. "That...I think that's what I'm worried about." I lie back in the grass.

"I can talk to him. Convince him to take the nail polish off."

"No, I'll do it. It should be me." I don't want to, but it should be me.

"Just remember, Randy, he's your boyfriend, not your... camper. You're not responsible for...teaching him how to be gay."

I laugh. "I'm not teaching him that. There's no one way to be gay."

"You know what I mean. To be...himself."

"I know. And I'm not, I don't think. I'm just supporting him. Even if he weren't my boyfriend, that's what we're supposed to do for each other, right?"

"That's right," she says, standing up and brushing dirt off her knees. "You're a good kid, Randy. Let me know if you need help talking to him."

"Thanks."

I walk back to the theater, going inside just in time to watch a sandbag narrowly miss one of the new kids in the chorus as it falls to the stage with a thud loud enough that the whole theater goes quiet.

"Are we cursed?" Mark shouts. "Did one of you say the name of the Scottish play out loud or say it's going to be the best show ever or 'I bet no one gets hit by a sandbag this year' or 'I bet Mark doesn't have a stroke this year'? Well? Did any of you say that?" No one answers. "Everyone go outside and turn around three times and spit!"

I try not to laugh.

I find Hudson backstage, just sort of watching the panic in everyone's eyes, not sure how to help, and I take him by the hand and I lead him outside, where I kiss him and lie down in the grass.

"You have to take the nail polish off," I say. "Both of us do."

"No way, babe," he says, like he was expecting this conversation. "I don't care what my parents think."

I hold his face in my hands. He's so beautiful. And he's more beautiful now than he ever was.

"I'm glad you don't care, but you have to. We have to. Otherwise they might not send you back next year."

Hudson looks down at his nails. "But it reminds me of you." His voice is already shaky with tears. "Of us."

"We don't need nail polish to remember us, right? We'll have texting and video chat and I'm going to send you all the musicals on Netflix you should watch, because we need to improve your dramatic education."

He laughs, but only once, and it's sort of sad. "I feel like, now that I know who I am, or more of who I am, I don't want to hide it anymore. Such a cliché, right? But…" He holds his hands out, the nail polish glinting. "This is me. Every time I catch a glance of my hands now, I feel, like, this rush, like swinging across the Peanut Butter Pit, or making a goal. Every finger is like a victory, reminding me who I am. That I'm special. So I don't want to give that up."

I nod and stretch my own hands out, taking one of his. "If there's one thing I've learned this summer, it's that my wearing nail polish doesn't make me *me*. Sure, I see myself in my hands, and I feel more like me, I feel like I'm showing off who I am, like I'm proud of who I am...but even when I took it off, and called myself Del, I was Randy underneath. I don't think I could not be him even if I tried."

"I know," he says, squeezing my hand. "I fell in love with Randy."

"So, it's not really hiding," I say. "It's a role. For an audience of two—your parents. And you only have to play it around them. But you're still you. You have nail polish on underneath your nails, and eye shadow under your lids and the fiercest cat's eye...they're just under everything, waiting to come out. Which you can do with me. With me you always get to be whomever you want to be."

He takes my hands and our fingers wrap around each other.

"Okay, but not until Saturday. And you have to take it off. Oh...and there's one thing we have to do first."

Saturday night, when we don't have rehearsals—to give everyone a chance to rest up for tomorrow—Hudson and I walk to the tree in the woods where hearts and names are carved, and there, using an X-Acto knife from A&C, we carve our own heart, and in it: *Randy and Hudson*. Not HAL, not Del.

Hudson was very specific about that. We weren't those people anymore. And then, with our hands sticky with sap and bark, we walk up to the cliff, our cliff, and look out over the camp.

"Okay," Hudson says, his hand in mine, our legs dangling over the edge, staring at the camp below. "I'm ready."

With some cotton balls and nail polish remover that George lent me, we strip each other in a different way. Then we lie down in the grass, holding hands, staring at the stars, the chemical smell of the remover hovering in the air.

"I was thinking about sneaking out and buying makeup, practicing on myself in my room. I think I'd look cool in eye shadow."

"You'd look good in anything," I say. "But do your parents go through your room?"

"Yeah," he sighs.

"Your browser history?"

"I don't think so."

"Then find some videos. Makeup tutorials. Spend the whole year picking out your favorite colors and I'll bring them next summer."

He tightens his grip on my hand in the dark, like he's afraid to let go. I get it; I am, too. Above us, real stars sparkle like glitter on black velvet. A drag queen evening gown. They're miles away, I know, but it feels like we're wrapped in it.

"I'm afraid of being without you all year," he says. "I'm afraid of losing myself. Of turning back into . . ."

"You won't. I mean it. You can't suddenly wake up and say, 'I know this isn't who I am, but it's who I should be,' when you already know everyone is trying to trick you into thinking that."

"Are you sure?"

I'm not, but I don't say that. "I'll be there, whenever you need. Text or e-mail or even a phone call."

He lays his head on my chest. "I'm going to miss you so much, though."

"Me too."

TWENTY-SEVEN

When the curtain rises, I swear I can feel all my internal organs rising with it, trying to get out through my mouth and only failing because all of them get stuck in my throat at once. Every year before, I've been backstage, waiting in the wings, rehearsing my lines in my head, going over which face went with which lyric, my body shaking as I peek out to see the audience, wondering if I'll flub a line or miss a dance step or go flat.

This is so much worse than that.

I have no control, I realize. If I miss a dance step, that's my fault, and I can take responsibility for it. But this is everyone's dance steps. Everyone's acting and singing and if even one of them messes up, I know that's on me. For not directing them well enough. For not giving them what they needed to

make it work. I look over at Mark, in the seat next to me in the front row, who is chewing on the edge of his thumbnail. A nicotine patch peeks out from under the arm of his counselor shirt.

"Is this how you feel every year?" I ask him. He nods. "No wonder you need so much therapy."

He barks a laugh and stops chewing his nail. "Thanks for that." He pats me on the leg. "It'll be fine, Randy. It'll be great."

I look over at my parents, who are watching this exchange with the usual look of "we don't understand, but we're proud of you, honey" that they wear whenever they come to camp. I love them for trying. Behind me is Hudson, and his parents, whom I met briefly and were exactly who Connie said they'd be—looking around like they were in enemy territory, their eyes always darting left and right, looking for exits, or maybe weak points. When Hudson introduced me as his boyfriend, his mother turned away to try to hide rolling her eyes and his dad's smile went hard and forced as he reached out to shake my hand. He had a tight grip, too, as he said, "Well, I guess you must be the girl, since you're shorter."

I wanted to tell him that's not how it works, but I smiled and pretended I hadn't heard it, instead. Because I didn't want Hudson to get in trouble. Hudson looked over at me, his eyes wide with amusement. It was easier than I thought, actually, the pretending to be Del again, or some variation of him, because I knew Hudson knows the real me, and I know

the real him. It's like we were sharing a secret, one his parents will never know.

His parents felt more at ease when I introduced them to my parents, and they all talked while Hudson and I found a tree to hide behind and take kissing selfies with our newly returned phones. There's a great one where behind us you can see the tops of trees from underneath, and the shadows look like space and the light look like thousands of stars pressed together, and there we are, floating in space, kissing each other. I immediately made it my lock screen. We traded numbers and texted and settled everything we needed to stay in touch the rest of the year.

And then we all walked down to the theater and took our seats.

The whole show, I can feel Hudson behind me, like a reassuring presence, just as strongly as I can feel Mark's edginess, his involuntary winces at every almost-missed cue or whenever we come to a moment we'd been having trouble with. But nothing goes wrong. The show is amazing. Seeing it all together with the lights down and a full audience makes it different somehow. Now the actors get to work with someone—the people in the audience, play to them, play WITH them. You can see it in their eyes, the way they come to life when there's a laugh or people clap. And the way Mark directed—his vision, if you will—is stunning. It is the queerest I've ever seen one of his shows. *Bye Bye Birdie* is supposed to be about the war of the sexes, maybe. Kim's right to kiss

Birdie without making her boyfriend jealous. Rose wanting Albert to honor his promise to marry her. The fact that these men don't seem to respect these women enough to do what they promised or trust them. But with the cross-casting, a few lyric changes, and playing with the acting, it's become something different. Now it's about daring to be yourself, even when the world is telling you to be something else. Sure, Albert still won't commit to Rose, but now it feels like that's because his mother might be homophobic. Hugo still doesn't want Kim to kiss Birdie, but it's about the symbolism of their relationship in a different world. And George knocks it out of the park. He's a gay man now, but a family man, and one who maybe would have belonged to the Mattachine Society—one who believes it's best for queer people to blend in...until the Ed Sullivan number when he joins the rainbow choir. That's his moment of transcendence. Sure, he comes crashing back later, not understanding the kids and their new-fangled ways of looking at queerness, but in that moment, George gets to be all of us, finding our best selves through love.

I'm the first one up to give him a standing ovation, and he spots me in the audience and winks at me, and nods his head slightly. I turn around. I wasn't the first one up. Hudson was. And Brad was right behind him and then the entire audience rose as George and everyone else bowed.

"What a show." I breathe the words out as the curtain comes down.

"I think we did pretty good this year," Mark says, hugging Crystal on his other side, and then me. "Pretty damn good. Oh! Maybe we should do *Damn Yankees* next year?"

"Might be a bit adult," Crystal says. "And it's less of an ensemble piece."

"What do you mean less of an ensemble piece?" Mark says. "It's absolutely an ensemble piece!"

I turn away from them to my parents, who are beaming with pride and confusion.

"I loved those costumes, honey," my mom says. "Did you pick those out?"

"I helped," I say.

"So great, kiddo," Dad says, giving me a hug. "I didn't understand half of it, but I know good work when I see it."

"Thanks," I say, rolling my eyes. Behind me, Hudson's parents are already headed for the door, but Hudson is smiling at me.

"That was amazing," he says. "I don't know if I got all of it...but it was special. I could feel it was special."

"That's what I said!" my dad cried, clapping Hudson on the back. "I like him." He and Mom start walking for the exit, and Hudson gives me a hug.

"Thank you," Hudson says, his arms wrapped around me.

"You don't need to thank me. Thank you," I say. I can feel the tears coming. We're about to be apart for nearly a year.

"Babe, don't cry," he says softly. "If you cry, I'll cry, and if I cry, my parents will get mad."

I take a deep breath and break the hug, nodding. No crying. Not now anyway.

"We still have lunch first, anyway," I say.

He nods, and we go backstage to congratulate everyone on the show. Mark and Crystal are radiating joy, Ashleigh and Paz are dancing to music only they seem to hear, and George and Brad are making out in the prop closet. It really is the perfect end to a perfect(ish) summer.

"I'm going to miss this," Hudson says, squeezing my hand so tightly, I'm afraid it might come off. I squeeze back even tighter. "And you."

"It'll be here next year, waiting for us. And the year after that...we'll find the place in the world that's like this. Or we'll make it."

"Yeah," he says, putting his arm around me. "I like that. I think it won't be hard to make it, either. I think...wherever you are feels like camp now."

I pull his arms tight around me and take a deep breath. I can smell the grass and the trees outside, the hairspray and wood of the theater, the sweat of the actors and Hudson, that smell that I've given up trying to name, but that I know is him. All of it blends together and I can see a life extending from it in front of me, a future. Freedom, love...no, it's better than that. It smells like home.

TRANSCRIPT OF L. C. ROSEN'S ACKNOWLEDGMENTS SPEECH FOR *CAMP*, GIVEN 5/25/2020

Oh my god, oh my god.

Rosen takes the mic on stage as applause dies down. He removes a piece of crumpled paper from his pocket.

I really didn't expect this at all.

Rosen unfolds paper, looks at the award, then looks back at the paper.

I'm going to try to go quickly, though.

To orchestra: Don't you play me off yet!

Rosen pauses, as though for laughter. There is none.

First of all, thank you to the Academy.

Rosen pauses—again there is no applause.

I'd like to start by thanking my family!

Rosen looks out at audience, in the direction of his parents.

My parents! I wouldn't be here without your support. I wouldn't even have tried writing without you. And to the rest of my family, thank you so much!

I, of course, need to thank my amazing agent, Joy, over at David Black. She's always looked out for me and believed in me, and look!

Rosen holds up the award statue and shakes it in the air. One person in the audience claps.

Look what we did! Thank you so much to the entire team over at David Black—David, Gary, anyone else I'm missing, and Lucy at APA—thank you for all the hard work you do!

And I couldn't have done this without Alvina at Little, Brown taking a chance on me and this project!

Rosen turns to Alvina in the audience.

Thank you so, so much. We make such a great team, and your constant guidance was inspirational! I really couldn't have done it without you.

Rosen turns back to the rest of the audience.

To all the aspiring young writers out there—if you get a chance to work with Alvina, do it! Best career decision you could ever make! And thank you so much to everyone else at Little, Brown: Victoria, Alex, Ruqayyah, Christy, Michelle, Marisa, Jen, Emily, Natali, Valerie, Karina, Angelie, Sasha, Olivia, I know I've forgotten some people, I'm sorry, oh no, the man in the orchestra pit is looking at me. No! Don't! Not yet! Just a few more names, I promise!

Rosen unfolds the paper again, revealing it to be even larger than it first seemed.

Thank you to my first readers! People who looked at

early drafts and told me I wasn't crazy: Robin, Adam, thank you! Couldn't have done it without you!

Oh! And the UK team! I love the UK team. They shouldn't be so far down the list!

Rosen looks up and shakes his head at this mistake, as though he hadn't written the whole thing out.

Ben! Ben, you took such a strong lead with this, and you were my rock. You helped me get through so much of this. Everyone, if you have a chance to work with Ben, work with Ben! And Simon. Simon hates it when I say nice things about him, but, Simon, working with you is always a dream. Michael, oh, Michael, you too! You're amazing. And Emma, Shreeta, Alice, and all the rest of the team at Penguin Random House UK, you are all a dream to work with, thank you!

Orchestra starts to play Stephen Sondheim's "Send in the Clowns."

To orchestra: No! Come on! We were working so well together!

Fine, I'll just talk over you, then!

Rosen yells over the orchestra.

And to my support system, my boys: Adam, Julian, Phil, Sandy, Adib, Caleb, Tom, Shaun, Cale!

Rosen beats his chest with a fist.

You are my everything—you keep me sane! And Lauren, Robin, Richard, Matt, Leslie, Theo, Staab, Skes, Molly, Laura, Desiree, Alexis, Ryan, Teri, T.S., Dahlia, Simon, Amy

Rose, Cori, and so many others! I couldn't keep doing what I'm doing without you!

The music begins to play louder. Behind Rosen, a man in a tuxedo steps forward. Rosen half turns and waves him away.

No! I still have more!

Rosen flips over the paper he's been reading from.

My mentor, Dan, and all my teachers! I know I'm forgetting people, but—

The mic cuts out. The man in the tuxedo takes Rosen by the elbow. Rosen shakes him off, but the man grabs hold again.

Fine! Fine! Just one more: Chris, for being Chris. Thank you all so, so much!

He is being pulled off stage as he shouts this. The music swells and the curtain closes to light applause.

LeoBuscaglia

Bus 9 to Paradise

A LOVING VOYAGE

Edited By
DANIEL KIMBER

Much of this material has appeared in several newspapers through the New York Times Syndication Sales Corporation, Special Feature Syndicate.

Also by Leo Buscaglia

Love

Because I Am Human

The Way of the Bull

The Disabled and Their Parents:
A Counseling Challenge

Personhood

The Fall of Freddie the Leaf

Living, Loving & Learning

Loving Each Other

Library of Congress catalog number: 85-63187
SLACK, Incorporated ISBN: 0-943432-67-7
William Morrow and Company, Inc. ISBN: 0-688-06293-8
Published in the United States of America by:
SLACK, Incorporated
6900 Grove Road
Thorofare, New Jersey 08086
In the United States, distributed to the trade by:
William Morrow and Company, Inc.
105 Madison Avenue
New York, New York 10016

In Canada, distributed to the trade by:
MacMillan of Canada
a Division of Canada Publishing Corporation
164 Commander Boulevard
Agincourt, Ontario
M1S3C7

Printed in the United States of America.
10 9 8 7 6 5 4 3 2 1
Book Design by Larry Pezzato.

Table of Contents

In Memory of

David Hall

PROLOGUE

I was in Melbourne, Australia, with my publisher promoting a new book. Such tours are usually very demanding and this was no exception. So, when we were finally granted a day of rest, we agreed to spend it out-of-doors, away from hotels, bookstores, T.V. studios and radio stations. The warm, clear day seemed perfect for a walk through one of Melbourne's quaint suburbs. Our goal was the city zoo.

On our way we stopped at a bus stop, hoping that it might offer us some indication that we were going in the right direction. The schedule, mounted on a tall pole, clearly listed times of bus arrivals and departures. We were suddenly struck with a designation that read, "Bus 9 to Paradise." How beautiful it sounded . . . Bus 9 to Paradise. We thought, "Wouldn't it be nice if we could actually ride on a bus destined for Paradise?" We wondered what it would be like; whether after we got there, would it be truly our idea of heaven.

In Dante's classic, *The Divine Comedy,* he pictured paradise as a vision of the rose, his metaphor for the purest kind of love. Mark Twain, on the other hand, created a much more down-to-earth, life-on-the-Mississippi scene. The Argentine author, Jorge Luis Borges, always imagined paradise "as a kind of library."

I'm sure each of us dreams of a paradise with visions no less idyllic than the poets, philosophers and artists. For some, paradise conjures dreams of limitless green pastures and refreshing waters reflecting skies of rainbows. For others it is a gold-red dusk over the Manhattan skyline. Some of us envision a land free of anxiety and pressures, with soothing tones of celestial angel choruses. Others would opt for fresh challenges accompanied by New Orleans jazz bands or the abandoned, joyous growl of a B.B. King. Some would wish

for tranquility and peaceful silence.

It's obvious that if there were to be an actual earthly paradise, it would be a very personal creation. There would certainly be no easy transport, no designated "Bus 9." This undiscovered territory has no common destination. (Isn't it interesting and wonderful that we don't even agree about paradise?)

We did not take Bus 9 to Paradise. I'm happy that we didn't for it seems clear that paradise is to be found only in our own immense and limitless minds, shaped by our own unique experience and willingness to continually grow and change. If there is a commonality, it seems to me to be that *life is paradise for those who love many things with a passion:* people, food, flowers, music, dance, books, art, memories, poetry, family, learning—an endless list. There is no need to seek paradise in some far-off future. The more passionately we love many things, the closer we come to living our paradise NOW.

LIFE IS PARADISE FOR THOSE WHO LOVE MANY THINGS WITH A PASSION!

A Passion for Loving

Perhaps it's time to look again at the ways and power of love. For many, just the thought that love is a real possibility gives hope to what could otherwise be an empty life. What harm can come from mutual respect, gentleness, goodness, trust and peaceful coexistence? Think about it. Only love has the power to unite without taking away another's dignity, another's self. Only love holds no jealous possession over people and nations. Only love is capable of putting humanity before ideology or race. Only love can supply the endless energies required to overcome hunger and despair.

"Love one another." These words were spoken more than two thousand years ago. Powerful though this command is, many of us have succeeded in ignoring it for these many years. We all give lip service to it but few of us expect anyone to really practice it. We leave that to madmen and saints.

In fact, we have become suspicious of lovers and either dismiss them as naive and irrelevant, or we see them as phonies. We are certain that no one could really care about anyone else without having some ulterior motive. The qualities of love such as tenderness, commitment, concern, generosity and trust are relegated to the realm of platitudes and are ignored.

Today the phrase "love one another" takes on a more urgent tone. It seems to me that we must love one another or die. Modern society shrugs off still another plea for love. It is amused by the suggestion that the world could be cemented together, not by the threat of holocaust or an arms race, but through a deep respect for life. No one will deny that we have reached a critical point in our history. In fact, there are growing numbers of fatalists who believe we have reached a point of no return. One thing is painfully obvious. Conventional methods to bring peace and understanding to our world have failed.

The more we look about us, the more we find hate, violence, prejudice and disregard for human life. We listen to newscasters and read columnists who deal out statistics about war dead, starvation, children being abused and sacrificed, disregard for human dignity and human rights. And all with about as much feeling as a report of the day's football scores. We are becoming conditioned to a whole spectrum of wasted human potential. Still, we continue to ignore love as a possible alternative.

I recall the shock I felt when I was traveling in the Soviet Union and a man I met in Odessa said to me, "Why do you

want to kill us?'' I tried to make him understand that I wanted to kill no one, that I celebrated life, not death. Somewhere buried in our respective ideologies were two people trying to relate their very real and very human concerns—not only for the world, but for each other as individuals. Through the magic of caring communication, we accomplished a victory of sorts—we forgot about all the things that separated us and were soon lost in one another. At that instant all contradictions and symbols were refuted. We both chose life.

I am sure that many would respond to this as naive and unrealistic; that love is barely strong enough to maintain most close family relationships and that beyond that, the heart is strained to its limits. So it is ridiculous for anyone to count on the power of love for a solution to international problems. I've often been told that in my zeal to love everyone I risk ending up loving no one. Nothing can be further from the truth. Universal love is not only possible, it is the most complete love of which we are capable as human beings.

But love can only work when we give up the antiquated mindsets which continue to paralyze us. We need to challenge the sophisticates who view it as romantic nonsense, idealistic bosh, unscientific and anti-intellectual. We need to accept love in our life as the most universal force for unification and good, accessible to all who really want it.

Only then will we discover that love, fully realized, has the power to lay aside the petty things which separate us and reveal the fact that our *enemy* has a face and a heart. It is at this point that all things again become possible.

There are those who are certain they can solve all the issues and problems of the day with one solution. Regardless of the

topic of discussion, they invariably return to their theories as being at the heart of the matter. I have been accused of being preoccupied with the topic of love and wanting to apply it to all life situations. Since I've been doing this for over thirty years, I am often mistakenly labeled an authority on the subject. The expectation is that I can offer guidance or solutions in all matters relating to love.

If someone were to claim to be an authority on life we would quite properly dismiss them as ridiculous. Life encompasses us, not the other way around. The topic of love in all its manifestations is also all encompassing. I have found that it invites us more to share in experiences than to strive to be exalted teachers. So when I suggest that we learn to love more each day, it's a tired cliché only if we regard the words of the message instead of the powerful challenge it presents.

I believe that we are all searching for something that will make existence more meaningful. We want to get outside of ourselves and mingle our lives with others. We hope to become better lovers and more complete human beings. Sometimes we can learn from the examples of others. My purpose as a teacher is to facilitate growth. If in sharing the thoughtful phrases of an ancient philosopher or in suggesting that we strive for a greater vision of the future, the purpose is sound, I consider it a labor of love to continue my work.

So I ask you again to consider the tremendous power of love, not simply as an abstraction, but as a dynamic, tangible force. It is an energy source that is never diminished by its use; it gives us the strength and security to challenge ourselves and others to change and grow.

And there is also a quieter power of love we often fail to recognize. Babe Ruth, immortalized for his prowess with a baseball bat, revealed this less-noted strength when he talked about the famous people in his life who never signed an autograph, but who wrote their names on just a few simple

hearts. If each of us were to recollect our sharpest, most vivid memories, I would be willing to bet that the moments of love and the people who were part of them are the most permanently etched.

Many of us still act as if we believe that the real wonder of love lies in the magical effect it has in making people lose their appetite, get weak in the knees and generally succumb to a sort of general anesthesia.

When we learn to expand our definition of love, we find that many other incredible things are possible. A single phone call out of the blue to tell people we're thinking about them can set the mood of an entire day on both ends of the line. A single compliment can accomplish the same thing. We will move mountains for people who make us feel special by their love and caring.

Admittedly, this is not the stuff of torrid romance novels. They are, however, meaningful examples of the power of love. They remind us that words such as hopeless and impossible have no meaning in the context of loving one another.

There is also a transcendent power of love, one that was working before we were born and that guaranteed us a whole army of people who would love us no matter what. And ultimately, there is the faith which, in all religions, tells us of another kind of love which lasts beyond any concept of time.

I think we'd all agree that to go through life without a true friend is to have missed one of the most satisfying and challenging of human experiences. Still, each day people live and die among strangers, alone, never having experienced a real friend.

We humans have an instinctual need to be close to one

another. We have people around us almost continually—people we know casually, see occasionally or meet in brief daily encounters. Some of them we call friends, but what we actually mean is acquaintances. To have a friend means something very different—more of a sacred thing. Aristotle described friendship as "one soul in two bodies."

Friendship involves two people committed to each other over a long period of time—through conflict, joy, unhappiness and change. Most of us take our friendships for granted. We become passive in maintaining them and lose sight of the fact that they need constant effort, care and attention.

Emerson, in his stunning essay, *Of Friendship,* said, "We take care of our health, we make our roof tight and clothing sufficient, but who provides wisely that we should not be wanting in the best property of all—friends?" He adds, "The best way to have a friend is to be one." Most of us have found this to be true. We take such care and guard so closely the things we treasure, but are so often lax with the special gift of friendship. If we really gave some thought to it, we would work harder to keep these special bonds growing and strong. There are few things in life which offer us greater rewards.

A short time ago I lost a special friend to death. Both of us had valued and nurtured our relationship for over twenty-five years. During that period we were often separated by time or circumstance, but we were determined never to allow anything to interfere with our ever-growing friendship. I've often thought of our varied experiences, of the changes each of us went through and of the bonds which made us friends for life.

My friend helped me to see myself in all my human imperfections while he revealed his own. Together, we gave each other room to make mistakes, the strength to meet frustration and even failure, because we knew that we would always have the other to fall back on, to offer support and

encouragement to start over.

We hurt or disappointed each other from time to time, but from this we learned to practice the delicate art of human forgiveness until we reached the point when we could look beyond the hurt rather than backward in anger and resentment. We stopped judging and censuring. We each knew that when the other was foolish or had lapses, it was never a permanent condition.

We shared our most personal thoughts, feelings, ideas, plans and dreams. When there was a conflict to be resolved, we discovered the real mutual benefits of friendship which we could have found in no other way. We became mirrors to one another, each reflecting the other's uniqueness from a different perspective. We were often required to test our friendship, having to see how much we would be willing to do and give to keep it alive over the years. It's an overworked adage, but nonetheless true, that you can always tell who your true friends are when you are in need.

To lose my dear friend after so many years of loving investment was terribly painful. It was difficult to part with such a positive force in my life. But nothing is forever. In reality we never lose the people we love. They become immortal through us. They continue to live in our hearts and minds. They participate in our every act, idea and decision. No one will ever replace them and in spite of the pain we are richer for all the years invested in them. Because of them, we have so much more to bring to our present relationships and all those to come.

I recently sat with a despondent friend whose husband had sought what he thought were greener fields and found them.

He left my friend and their two children with the casualness of one taking off on a holiday cruise. Echoing a recently read, self-help book, he said he had a right to happiness and his greatest responsibility was to himself. He was hoping that he could still have a friendship with his wife and, of course, unlimited visiting privileges with his children.

His wife had other ideas. She was bitter, hurt and vindictive. He had shattered her ego and broken up the family. In no way was she about to maintain a friendship with him. In fact she was quick to call him a rodent and several expletives I had never heard her use before!

She turned to me, a friend, for help. She couldn't seem to stop crying. She'd lost interest in her home and her children. Though she continued to work, she found that always being so upset and distracted caused her to be negative in her interactions with others. She snapped at friends, became inpatient with coworkers in the office and found herself shouting at the children.

She continued to find endless reasons for hating her ex-husband, but she also began to hate herself in the process. She was filled with regrets and self-recriminations. She was certain that if she had done more for him—made herself more attractive, kept a better home—she wouldn't have lost him and the children would still have a father.

How could I help her? No amount of tears or regrets were going to bring her husband back or revitalize the dead marriage. I am never one to offer advice. I gave that up years ago. I'm as confused as everyone else. How can I tell others what to do? Anyway, there was no easy solution. Damaged egos require long healing periods.

She could not continue in her present state. Prolonged despair was already taking its toll. Of course, there were many things she could do. Among them, it seemed to me, she could finally face the fact that life does go on. She was still

young, attractive and capable, and just because her husband had obviously devalued these traits, he was really just one person of many. It was not a matter of comparing herself with the other woman. There was no basis for comparison. Armed with this reality, I suggested that she might accept the situation, forgive her husband for his actions and herself for whatever part she might have unconsciously played in his decision.

We discussed that much of her pain was based on the fact that she was taking responsibility for her husband's acts. I reminded her that since she was the innocent victim it seemed unrealistic for her to take on so much guilt, so many tears. She became irate! "Forgive him!" she said, horrified. "Are you crazy? I'd die first! I'll find a way someday to get even with him. I'll find a way to hurt him like he hurt me!" Her face took on a frightening look. Fresh tears fell as she refused to let go of her anger.

Her husband was off celebrating a new life with new possibilities and a new person, none of which she had any control over. She, on the other hand, was drowning in despair. Most of us have learned from experience that not to forgive hurts *us* more than anyone else. Why do we find it so hard to forgive?

Grudges carried for a lifetime are a pretty heavy load. In addition to adding wrinkles to brows, they create much bitterness and suspicion. No one is guiltless. If we hope to be forgiven for our actions or shortcomings, we might start by attempting to forgive others for theirs. There is not always justice. Sometimes we have to forgive even when we've been wronged, for our own sake.

Perhaps my friend will one day realize that she did the best she could in their relationship at the time, and that her husband thought he had done the same. Certainly I am not condoning his actions, but in the act of forgiving we release

ourselves from bondage. It then becomes possible for us to move forward and love again, wiser for the experience.

A man once told me that his dog's love was the only love in his life of which he was sure. He explained, "He always greets me with enthusiasm, he is responsive to my touch, he's forgiving, and he's there when I need him. He loves me without conditions." This was quite a statement! Either the people in this man's life had fallen short of giving him the assurance he needed, or his idea of love needed redefining.

In human relationships we are seldom guaranteed such unequivocal love and we are often given to wonder whether we are in fact loved by those closest to us. Since our definitions of love are constantly changing as we learn more about giving it each day, it's not unusual that we question whether or not we are receiving it.

A wife says to a husband (or vice versa),

"Do you love me?"

"Of course," he replies.

"Why?" she presses for a more definitive answer.

"What do you mean why? I've been married to you for twenty years, haven't I?"

How satisfied would we be if we presented someone with a vintage wine and upon asking his opinion of it he replied, "I'm drinking it, aren't I?"

Love, as intangible, as complex, and as personal as it is, still needs expression between those who share it. No two people express their love in the same way, and it is that unique expression which makes love the most powerful and enduring of life's forces.

Love is as encompassing as life itself, and when we seek to

define it we sometimes end up imposing limits on it. We can, however, attempt to describe it, and in so doing, better understand it. One of the most beautiful descriptions I've ever read is from Corinthians I, and even as well known as it is, is still well worth repeating:

> Love is patient and kind; love is not jealous or conceited or proud; love is not ill mannered, or selfish, or irritable; love does not keep a record of wrongs: Love is not happy with evil but is happy with the truth. Love never gives up: its faith, hope, and patience never fail. Love is eternal . . . There are faith, hope and love, these three; but the greatest of these is love.

So, for the question, "How do I know when I am truly loved?" there can be only partial answers that need elaboration and the special touch that each of us brings to a relationship. Certainly, though, when we are loved, the people who love us want us to be what we are, not what they are. They rejoice in the fact that we are growing with our ideas, our dreams, our uniqueness, our future. They want us to be independent and free, not submissive and afraid. The people who love us want to simplify our existence, not by protecting us from pain, but by being there when we need them. They encourage risk because they understand that by risking we continue to grow. They help us to find alternatives for behavior, rejoicing in our success and comforting us in our failure. They are not only lovers, but friends, loyal and willing to make allowances for our imperfections. They can be counted upon for support and companionship.

Each of us has different requirements for how much and what kind of love we receive. Some of us need to hear the words, "I love you," each day, while for others, the words are contained in a look, an attitude, an unspoken communication. No matter how love is expressed, the important thing is that it be communicated freely and often.

I receive letters from a variety of people who all have a

similar tale to tell: the love seems to have gone out of their relationship. "He's not nearly as romantic as he was when we first dated." "She's not the same girl I fell in love with."

I prefer to think of love as something we *grow* into, not something we fall in and out of. I also believe that it is something that cannot be limited by one person's definition or demands of what it should be. There are always at least two sides to any love relationship.

An expression of love is the most basic of human assurances. When it is given freely and without condition, it can only strengthen and give greater purpose to a relationship.

Any number of psychology textbooks will tell us that our basic patterns of behavior are most influenced in our early years by our parents. Mom and Dad are credited (but more often it seems, faulted) for their part as role models. Some people live their lives believing that their inability to express love as they would like to stems from the fact that their parents didn't teach them to love. And so they state that the die is cast and the past becomes a convenient scapegoat to explain or rationalize their chronic loneliness and lovelessness.

We should never subscribe to any idea that even suggests that human behavior, whatever its origin, cannot be changed. There is great hope for those of us who feel that we lack the ability to love fully and joyfully without fear. That hope lies in the knowledge that we can dedicate ourselves to the process of learning to love *today*. As we attempt to live in love, we'll understand that pain, discomfort, and even rejection are very much a part of the process. Loving will require courage, resiliency and hope, and will never come to people who give

up easily. But since love is the most rewarding of human experiences, it is certainly worth the risk.

A student who attended my Love Class some years ago was inspired by one of our discussions and decided to go directly home and sweep his wife off her feet, bringing new love into their lives. Understandably, after ten years of marriage devoid of outward shows of affection, she became suspicious of his real motives.

"Why this sudden love offering after so many years?" she pondered. He had either gone crazy or he was feeling guilty about something. When she faced him with these suspicions he was thoroughly incensed over her reaction. He fully expected her to sing hallelujahs and fall into his arms. Instead he was received with doubt, suspicion, and rejection. And so, as often happens under such conditions, he retreated into the safety and habit of his unromantic self. Love had failed him. He even justified this by declaring that he had tried and that therefore it wasn't his fault. It was his wife who wasn't a lover.

This man may have been in earnest about wanting to become a more loving person, but he really wasn't prepared to encounter the complexity of feelings love can create. Nor was he willing to commit himself to the idea that learning to love does not happen overnight but requires time, effort, and patience.

Ours is a culture that offers "how to" information on every conceivable subject. Television programs, self-help books, manuals, articles, etc. are continually showing us the way to a better personality, a more beautiful body, more friends, or less fears. They tell us how to become sexual acrobats or just how to grow a better petunia. We think nothing of investing our time and money in developing a better backhand or having the greenest lawn on the block and yet we hold back at the least suggestion that the same effort might be necessary if we desire to become more loving individuals. This would be a

better world if we would exert the same amount of zeal we apply to our hobbies to the infinitely more satisfying goal of becoming better lovers.

Most of us can remember the story of Ebenezer Scrooge and his amazing transformation from a hateful and heartless old man to a kind and loving one, all in one night. That this beloved story and others like it are told year after year for generations suggests the timeless value we hold for a life transformed by love. Most of us however, barring the visitation of a helpful ghost, will have to be the architects of our own change, and accept the fact that it may not happen overnight.

If we must begin at square one, then so be it. The important thing is that we begin now. Each new moment of love experienced and learned leads to more such moments, and moment to moment we make this a better world for ourselves and for all those we encounter.

I learned long ago how profoundly disappointing unfulfilled expectations can be. The lesson has stayed with me. It happened one Christmas when I was in my teens. I remember the sudden appearance under my family's Christmas tree of the largest present I had ever hoped to see. It stood at least a foot taller than I and was twice as heavy; and, wonder of wonders, it had my name on it. For two whole weeks before Christmas, this present towered above all others and it defied any conventional attempts to learn of its contents before its time.

Those two weeks seemed an eternity. I could think of little else. My mind was filled with imaginings. Because of its size and mystery, that gift created an aura of sheer magic for me.

When the day of days arrived, my family gathered in celebration. The main attraction was to be the opening of my present. How many times in the past two weeks I had anticipated this moment. Even as I was opening it, I remember experiencing a vague sense of disappointment—the Great Mystery was about to end and I would no longer be able to engage in my soaring dreams.

It was a handmade desk that my Uncle Louie had painstakingly built. It was certainly beautiful and much needed. But by this time nothing of this world could have satisfied my expectations. I can't imagine what I had expected. Still, in that disappointment was a lesson that would last a lifetime.

Buddha once wrote that, "When we cease expecting, we have all things." If we expect nothing, we are always delighted. When we have expectations, no matter how much we get, we tend to expect more. We can hope that everyone will love us, but we cannot expect them to. In realizing this, we free ourselves and others of the burden of conforming to our expectations. When others say, "you must love me, I'm your wife, husband, mother, brother, lover, etc.," they forget that love can only be given freely. And no matter how much we demand it, it will come only when it is freely offered.

Most of us enter relationships with a set of expectations that have been steadily accumulating and waiting for just the right person to fill them. If the list is long and the demands are rigid, the wait can be a lifetime. The whole idea that we expect others to behave in a prescribed manner or conform to a preset image denies them their most precious asset, their uniqueness, and puts them into the category of a commodity.

What attracts us to others are usually the qualities that make them unique. Instead of rejoicing in their uniqueness, we attempt to fit them into neat little categories and expect them to perform accordingly. How much better it would be to

bury expectations and relate to the individual we love—as the remarkable, singularly unique person that he or she is. A person who will never come this way again.

Teachers must constantly avoid preconceived notions of their students for the simple reason that they become self-fulfilling prophecies. Students who are expected to perform a certain way because of their race, appearance, family, or background, invariably play the role in which they are cast and consequently are prevented from being themselves.

A friend of mine once told me that he was continually disenchanted with his dates. In each instance on a first date, he was certain he would meet the love of his life. Of course, no girl could meet his requirements as wife, mother, house-keeper, entertainer, sex symbol, and conversationalist. It took him years of disappointment before he discovered that it was actually more fun (and certainly more realistic) to discover each girl as an individual, and allow her to reveal herself as she was, not as he dreamed her. He was soon happily married.

To avoid the inevitable disappointment of unfulfilled expectations, we should expect only of ourselves. In this way we will free others to be themselves while we stretch and grow to our fullest potential.

A Passion for Joy

*T*he pursuit of happiness is perhaps our most basic drive. It is even mentioned in our Constitution. How we pursue it, and even how we define it, varies from person to person. Perhaps what makes it so elusive is our problem in not only not knowing how to obtain it, but how to keep it around. Our highest spirits can be so quickly conquered by adversity.

The well-known writer William S. Burroughs recently stated in an interview that for him, happiness is a by-product of "function, purpose and conflict; that those who seek happiness for itself seek victory without war."

Ancient Egyptians believed that upon their death they would be asked by the god Osiris two questions and their answers would determine whether they could continue their journey in the afterlife. The first question was, "Did you bring joy?" The second was, "Did you find joy?" These goals then become a sacred charge in life and the only way to obtain eternal happiness.

These are questions no less vital today than they were in ancient Egypt. They are ones we must continually ask ourselves. Most of us have our own strong sense of purpose to celebrate life and spread all the joy we can.

Think of the happiest people you know. They're the ones who seem to be able to find joy everywhere. If we study these people very closely and analyze just how they do it, we may find some answers far simpler than we would have believed. We've heard them before:

"There's good in every person. It's up to me to bring it out."

"There is a light side of everything if you look for it."

"I see each new day as a challenge. What I make of it is up to me."

Our search for happiness and our capacity to bring it to others leads us back to ourselves, for we start by finding joy in ourselves. The inner joy we develop becomes the wellspring from which we draw to use in every encounter.

I am amazed at the human capacity to find joy even in the harshest extremes, the cruelest of fates, the stories of people with broken bodies but whose spirit remains high. We admire their courage but seldom consider the profound example they provide for all of us, especially those of us who hide behind despair and hopelessness.

As a teacher, I used to encourage my students to keep a journal as a record of their innermost thoughts and feelings. Occasionally I would ask that they show them to me for our

discussion. I noticed a tendency in them to emphasize the negative in life. There were the, "Oh, woe is me," stories. The "Life is miserable, boring, depressing, confusing, unfair, cruel, etc., etc." stories. Each day seemed to be a test of endurance rather than an adventure.

"Why don't you write of the joy in your life?" I would ask them. "It's really your choice."

The answer was always that the bad things just seemed to have more impact than the good things. They seemed to take joy for granted. Their problems touched them more deeply than their moments of joy. That notion is perhaps what inspired a study done a few years ago to determine the dominant mood of currently popular songs. The findings revealed that about three-fourths of the songs dealt with the pain and anguish of love. You know the type:

"You broke my heart, I'm so alone,

All day long, I sit and moan."

Or a current favorite, "Love is a Battlefield." (Whatever happened to "Love is a Many-Splendored Thing"?)

Soap operas so frequently capture this spirit with their unending tales of sorrow and affliction. People say that their soaps help them endure their own problems. But we need more out of life than just physical ease and freedom from care. Our goldfish have that.

The happiness in life that we all seek so often involves what we give to others. Ancient Egyptians understood that finding joy in life and bringing it to others were one and the same. It is as Louis Mann once wrote, that "Happiness is a perfume which you cannot pour on others without getting a few drops on yourself."

Isn't it strange how suspicious we sometimes are of happiness? If we have it we are somehow sure that it can't last. We're certain that misery can't be too far off. We have a vague feeling that we'll be punished for prolonged joy.

The great author of madness, Luigi Pirandello, tells a story of a man who was so frightened by joy that it drove him mad. When he found the woman of his dreams he was so certain he'd lose her that he feigned disinterest until he almost did lose her. When he planned their honeymoon his anxiety reached the breaking point. He told everyone that they would be going to Florence and Venice. Instead he took his bride to Naples—the opposite direction. He felt he could in this way trick the misery which would be trying to find him in Florence and Venice and would not know that he was having an ecstatic honeymoon in Naples!

Most of us are not quite that pathological, but perhaps we may recognize the symptoms. We feel that there is something not quite acceptable about having things go right for us. We begin to imagine despair around every corner until we bring it upon ourselves. I have a dear friend who, when everything in her life is fine, is sure that the next telephone call will be a message of personal catastrophe, every letter will be from the IRS or someone suing her, every telegram an announcement of the death of a loved one. Experience should have convinced her by this time that her fears are not reasonable, but she's always the same. Now she has added another problem. She's worried about her worrying!

When we were children we took for granted that each day would bring us greater happiness. We celebrated everything: flowers, animals, other children, loving adults, learning—we embraced them all with open arms and growing joy. I wonder what causes this joy to give way to cynicism later in life?

Some people are really bothered by others' happiness. They may even show real contempt for other people's joy,

which they call naiveté. These are the people H.L. Mencken once described. He said that they are so pessimistic that when they smell flowers, they immediately look for a coffin. This cynical attitude is usually brought on by envy. Being a little short on happiness makes some people want to believe that it's a universal condition.

There is a great deal of compassion for the miserable and we are eager to help make their lives better. But few of us see any need to help those who are already happy to remain so. We need them and should honor them.

William Phelps was right on target when he said, "If happiness consisted of physical ease and freedom from care, then the happiest individual would not be either a man or a woman, it would be an American cow!" We make our own happiness and it takes work. If we are living a happy life and have worked at making it so, we deserve it and have no reason to feel guilty about it.

There are days when I feel so good only my rational mind keeps me from levitating. People often accuse me of putting it on. They're certain that no one could feel *that* good. They know that I have the same problems they do. My health leaves a little to be desired. I have all sorts of demands made on me. They wonder what I have to be so happy about. My response is simple. I'm still alive and there is still so much more to do, to experience, to love. Why shouldn't I be happy?

Perhaps we object so much to another's happiness because it may prove to us that living happily in our crazy, mixed-up world is possible. We'd rather think that it isn't. It gives us an excuse not to work at it. We can say that happy people are living an illusion, that they are ignorant and unaware, that they can't be in touch with reality. All this, in spite of the fact that we can know happiness if we learn to embrace it.

The despair which we believe to be lurking around each dark corner mostly exists in our minds. Everyone encounters

it but only some of us honor it. It's possible that we will know even more happiness around that same corner. Perhaps it's true that happiness begets more happiness. I know there are some who are reading this and thinking, "That Buscaglia is more naive than I thought." Perhaps so, but as we are all traveling to the same destination, at least I can say I'm making the journey with joy in my heart and a smile on my face. How about you?

One of the major problems in the world today is that we've lost our sense of humor—this seems especially true of our leaders. An intriguing fantasy for me would be a great conference of the world's nations where, instead of politicians or statesmen, each country would send its leading humorists to represent it. Instead of an aura of pomp and seriousness that would normally be dictated by such an occasion, there would prevail a lightheartedness, with an assembly of individuals bent on raising spirits instead of suspicions.

Behind it all would be the assumption that very few things in this world so instantly form a common bond among people as laughter. It's a universal language that requires no interpretation. Serious problems needn't be addressed only by serious-minded people.

I place this idea in the realm of fantasy because I understand all too well the time-honored convention of sober thought and strict decorum that exists whenever political leaders come together to iron out their differences. This is true even though we know that in interpersonal relationships, nothing can defuse a problem more readily than a good laugh. Perhaps it is my own naiveté that leads me to believe that diplomats could be guided by the same principle.

I'm sure our humorists and comedians will never be elevated to the status of diplomats but I shall always maintain that they are among our most beneficial physicians. Anyone who makes us laugh and convinces us not to take ourselves too seriously is contributing directly to our physical and mental well-being. As the most recent medical research tells us, laughter can be the best medicine. I often wonder how many modern-day neuroses are based, at least in part, on people who have lost touch with the fact that life is a wondrous joke with all of us as the gag line.

A sense of humor helps us to forget, if even for a moment, our often inflated sense of seriousness and propriety. It is a declaration of our superiority over the woes and calamities that may befall us. I know a family that serves as a beautiful example of this. From the grandparents down to the youngest members, laughter is always present when they gather together, even in the face of gloom. One of the favorite stories they tell is about the morning of the great California earthquake in 1971. After the rumbling had ceased and everyone had gone about the house tentatively surveying the damage, they joined a small congregation of neighbors in the street. One of the daughters suddenly gasped and pointed to part of the house which had crumbled, exposing the bathroom toilet. The youngest son began to laugh at this most preposterous sight and commented that this would certainly cut down on bathroom use. The laughter became contagious as the rest of the family joined in while their dumbfounded neighbors looked on. In the retelling of this story, it is the remark of an elder neighbor that still brings the loudest roars of laughter: "Laughter at such a time—they must be crazy!"

Granted there is nothing inherently funny about the destruction of property, but here was a family who rose above the despair of the moment; and even, as their neighbor suggested, by being just a little crazy at that instant, saved the day

from despair. It's a fact that all of us are just a little crazy and we are better off if we get in touch with our madness from time to time. (If you think you're not crazy—you're probably crazier than most!) This family's remembrance of that day is not just in the joy of recalling an amusing story, but also in a sense of pride they all share in this personal triumph of the human spirit.

Many people persist in suppressing the spirit of joy in the unfortunate belief that life is strictly serious business. We often view silliness or childishness as regressions in behavior instead of realizing that each of us has a ridiculous side and that the child in us is one of our most prized possessions. We cultivate refinement and sophistication at the expense of spontaneity and fun. Polite tittering substitutes for unrestrained laughter. Joyous impulses are moderated or lost altogether in deference to common sense or good taste.

In each of us there is a reservoir of joyous freedom— madness, if you will. It's a natural and splendid balance to our more serious, socially proper side which allows us to suspend from time to time our rules of decorum. Why not rejoice a bit in our foolishness? In a world that knows no shortage of nonsense, we shouldn't hesitate to happily and playfully add our own touch of insanity. It's one of the best ways I know to survive.

Americans are often portrayed as being forever busy. Tradition has it that our reverence for the work ethic is second to none. According to this image, even our leisure moments are crammed with pressing duties and obligations; things are always unfinished or in need of our attention. We seem in perpetual motion.

As with all stereotypes, there are too many exceptions to take it all that seriously. Besides, worse things have been said about people than that they work too hard. The implication, though, is that overworkers have forgotten how to relax. I do know just such a person, whom I shall call Tom. His friends call him a workaholic. His doctor advised him to take up a nice, slow-paced, leisurely hobby—anything to divert him, body and mind, from his frantic routine. It was decided that vegetable gardening would be just the thing for him.

So, with a little plot of land, a few tools and some overalls, Tom set about to cultivate a few crops and a more tranquil personality. His approach, however, was no different from anything else he ever tried: Get in there and give it all you've got—which is an admirable trait so long as it is not an all-consuming one. Well, Tom's garden was a study in horticulture. His friends and neighbors were impressed not only with the garden, but with his determination to find peace in it.

What they were unaware of was his growing obsession with garden pests which were descending on his little patch. Each evening after coming home from work, he would charge out to the back yard to do battle. Every little invader was wiped out with a vengeance. After all, if vegetable gardening was to be his hobby, there had certainly better be some tangible results to show for it. When he began to lose sleep thinking about the possibility of his tomatoes being ravaged, Tom decided that growing vegetables was not the key to his serenity. Last I heard, he was practicing meditation. I wish him luck.

It does seem paradoxical that one's leisure time could ever be a source of anxiety or stress, yet I wonder how many of us have truly learned to relax, or, as Walt Whitman wrote, ". . . to loaf and invite the soul," or to arrive at the point when we don't think of time, even when papers are stacking up on the desk, or deadlines are coming up. Of course, if we

do all this, we run the risk of being called lazy.

I remember being stranded many years ago in a town just outside of Paris. It was toward midday and I needed a mechanic to put some life back into my rented Citroen. Of course, all shops were closed and all activity was at a standstill. It was merely the customary two-hour lunch time that was being observed. Think of it! Two hours for lunch. Time to eat, to take a nap, visit, or just disengage from the day's activity for awhile. What was there to do? So I took a walk and found myself lying on a shaded hillside overlooking an old abandoned barn. I laid there trying to remember the last time I had done something like this.

When I awoke from an enchanting sleep, I felt a deep sense of calm. I walked slowly back from that hillside, thankful for the delay, and resolved not to run through the rest of my agenda without enjoying it.

One of the directions in which our technology seems to be leading us is more leisure time. Our work force is increasingly becoming mechanized and computerized, leaving us with the challenge of a whole new dimension in freedom. In meeting that challenge, I hope we may learn to seek out hidden paths of our potential. We may take the time to know ourselves and each other better, and come to understand our intimate connection with all living things. Perhaps we may also learn to have more control over our own destiny. We may learn that sometimes to do nothing is to do something.

Everyone loves to play. Playfulness is instinctive and it is universal. All forms of life play: dolphins, chimpanzees, squirrels, dogs, cats—all take time to play. They splash, chase, rough-and-tumble, tease and tickle. We love to watch

their playfulness and stand for hours envying them their fun.

Was it so long ago that we pleaded with our mothers, "Mom, can I go out and play?" Remember? But too soon we grew up. We found that grownups often looked down upon play. They saw it as a form of idleness and a waste of time. We were encouraged to give up our childish ways, be serious and get on with mature, productive behavior. We were made to see that work was good—play was somehow unacceptable. We learned that there was something not quite right about a grown person playing.

The human need to play is a powerful one. When we ignore it we feel there is something missing in our lives and attempt to fill the void. The young husband creeps quietly behind his wife and wrestles her to the carpet, tickling her and uttering loving sounds. "What are you doing? Stop it!" she demands. "You're ruining my hairdo!"

The new wife playfully ties the bottoms of her husband's pajamas so that when he hastily tries to put them on he falls to the floor. "Very funny," he says angrily. "I thought you grew up. One would think you had better things to do." So go the playful intimacies which could bring joy and spontaneity to a loving relationship. Our adult life loses its surprise, its freedom, and we grow up seriously. Then we wonder where all the fun has gone. Perhaps it has gone with the light touch and the harmless play that was once second nature to us.

I am often accused of being childish. I prefer to interpret that as child-like. I still get wildly enthusiastic about little things. I tend to exaggerate and fantasize and embellish. I still listen to instinctual urges. I play with leaves. I skip down the street and run against the wind. I never water my garden without soaking myself. It has been after such times of joy that I have achieved my greatest creativity and produced my best work.

There is a good deal of excellent research on child's play. It

has shown us conclusively that through play, with the freedom of action it allows and the stressless environment in which it occurs, children discover, relate to and define themselves and their world. It is through their play that they build their power of inquiry, vitalize themselves, and release their frustrations and negative feelings. It encourages their spontaneity, which is later responsible for their creativity. It offers them one of the few times in which they can express their personal and unique selves without outside influence. It is, therefore, paradoxical that many educators and parents still differentiate between a time for learning and a time for play without seeing the vital connection between them.

Many of us will say that we do play. We play golf, tennis, baseball, bridge, etc. But these are not play activities, they are games. They have strict rules. There are winners and losers. There are sides. There is often tension, competition, skill expectations, disappointments and criticism. I'm not saying that such games are bad. I'm merely suggesting that they are not play. In play we don't keep score. No one wins or loses. Anyone can play, alone or in a group. There are no sides—we're all on the same side.

If we make time for play, it can change our lives and it costs nothing. It has all sorts of educational, physical and psychological benefits. A happy and fulfilling adult life may even depend upon the intensity and variety of our play experiences. Of course, we will run the risk of being accused of going through our second childhood or of having lost our minds. (Where's Leo? Oh, he's out in the backyard jumping on a pile of leaves!)

It's three thirty in the afternoon on a warm Los Angeles day. The office is especially still. The only sounds I hear are the rhythmic clicks of the typewriter and the muffled, soothing sound of someone speaking on the telephone in the next office. My eyes are heavy. My mind is dull. I'm straining to stay awake. It's the perfect time for a short nap.

I know that no one naps in the United States in the afternoon except lazy ne'er-do-wells or bums. It may be the Latin in me, but when my body cries out for rest I can't help but give in. It's comforting to know that I am joined by two-thirds of the world's population.

In Mediterranean countries, the Middle and Far East, South and Central America, Africa, everything and everyone stops for a little rest in the afternoon. Shops close, streets empty, shades are drawn and millions of civilized human beings lie down for a short period before continuing with work and the evening's recreation which follows.

The afternoon nap is not new to me. I remember that Mama and Papa would send us all to our rooms each afternoon, when it was feasible, to take a short break from the daily routine. Of course we all protested loudly, but to no avail. With their Italian heritage, Mama and Papa were never able to understand how people went eight or nine hours without a break. They knew that after a short rest they were able to work or play with more vitality.

It always amuses me to see Americans wandering aimlessly and angrily through European streets during the siesta period, waiting for the shops to reopen, and cursing the inconvenience of it all. They are certain that this need to take a nap, this yielding to laziness would never happen in the United States. It seems inconceivable to them that anyone would stop a busy, important schedule to rest in midday.

Going full steam from early morning to late evening has become part of the American work ethic. We do have all night

to rest, after all. It is hammered into us from our childhood and is part of our history. Benjamin Franklin taught us, "Up, sluggard, and waste not life—in the grave we'll be sleeping enough." And somewhere in the back of our minds echoes the most sacred of business creeds that "time is money." So we continue to go against the cries of our bodies' need for rest, for getting away from it all, for regenerating, and continue to push ourselves through long uninterrupted periods of work.

I recall with amusement my first visit to Spain. Siestas begin shortly after midday and end in the early evening. At first, like so many eager travelers, I objected to spending this valuable time in my hotel room. I was restless to be on the move. But where was I to go? Museums were closed, restaurants didn't serve dinner until nine or ten o'clock, theaters opened their doors about eleven PM.

Happily (or should I say by force), I finally fell into the routine. Though I wasn't able to sleep through the entire siesta, I found that escaping the hot afternoon sun each day was a wise move and in the cool of my room I could daydream or read or just rest for the evening ahead. I found it a splendid way to recharge from the morning's activities. I repeated this routine in Greece, Italy, Yugoslavia, Austria and even in industrious Switzerland. My parents were delighted. Leo had finally achieved a higher level of civilization! Of course, when I returned home it was back to the old rhythm. In trying to readjust, I found that I had grown accustomed to splitting up my day. So I had to become very creative to be able to set aside a short period for a nap. Sometimes I stretch out on the floor of my office, my secretary holding all calls for a short period. Sometimes I lie peacefully under a tree, often having to convince my friends that I didn't find their company boring—merely that I'd learned to obey certain signals my body was sending to my brain.

When I suggest such a routine to friends as a physical or emotional necessity, their response is predictable. "I can't nap in the afternoon, it's my busiest time." Or, "If I take a nap, it makes me groggy for hours." For some it would undoubtedly be a problem. Still, it seems to me that such a universal custom, which has existed for so long, might bear closer examination. Perhaps in time even the most active or doubting among us will see the benefits of such a proposal.

Right now I'm looking at my cat, as he curls up on a mound of wet dirt in the shade, taking his fifteenth cat nap of the day. No wonder he has lived so long and remained so agile. He knows instinctively that peak performance has its requirements.

I could continue by giving scientific proof of the value of napping, but as I said earlier, it's mid-afternoon and my eyes are getting heavier by the moment. My body is crying out for those precious moments. As Shakespeare wrote, "Oh, beloved nap time, nature's soft nurse."

A Passion for Self Respect

William James once wrote, "Probably a crab would be filled with a personal sense of outrage if it could hear us class it without apology, as a crustacean, and thus dismiss it. 'I am no such thing,' it would say; 'I am myself, myself alone.'"

The human spirit is such that it will defy every effort to lump it into categories, whether it is done for convenience or by design. It is our very uniqueness, our individual identity, that transcends our short existence here and therefore must always be preserved.

One of the most memorable characters in my boyhood was a rather eccentric gentleman known to everyone simply as Carlo. When I think of that old neighborhood, a number of characters spring to mind, but the memory of him is always a happy one. I was quite young when I first saw Carlo. He was doing what he loved best—walking in the fresh air, seemingly without direction, singing opera. Oh, how that man could sing! Arias from Puccini, Verdi and Donizetti. Sometimes he would pause for a moment, reach for a high note, and gesture dramatically to no one in particular. "He's gotta be a little coocootz," Mama would say, "but he sings good and that's-a nice." We all pretty much agreed.

Since he only performed on occasion, the novelty of hearing him sing as he did has never really worn off for me. No one ever seemed annoyed or offended. People just stared and smiled. Carlo didn't seem to mind their responses. He just moved right along, doing what, for him, came naturally.

I never knew what happened to Carlo. He just stopped coming around. Maybe he's off serenading other neighborhoods. I've always suspected that many of those who found him strange also had a secret admiration for that man. He dared to share with others what most of us, out of fear of what the neighbors would think, keep to ourselves. After all, *normal* people properly confine their bellowing to the shower. Here was an individual who followed his own joyous impulse without being too concerned with reactions that others might have.

The story carries with it a time-honored moral: You have a right to be yourself. So many of us live our lives to please others and conform to their image of us. We all have a persistent voice within that reminds us of who we are and what is right for us. There is comfort in knowing that there are people we care about who will love us even if our way is a little crazy at times. What makes these people so special is the

fact that they accept us in sanity and in madness. We recognize and appreciate this when we say things like, "I can be myself around him," or, "She likes me for what I am." Sooner or later we all discover that we're really not very good at being anything else. People are always saying to me, "Thank you for being you." My answer is always, "I tried for years to be someone else and it didn't work."

It seems to me that there is an implicit condition in any relationship which must suggest, "Accept me for myself or not at all. Any other arrangement is cheating both of us."

For many of us school was the place where we first learned that there were others in this world who would not accept us for ourselves. It was a hard lesson but often taught us to modify and conform. We struggled to restrain those natural impulses that set us apart from others.

Still, there is another side of us that insists upon having an identity all our own. How we love it when someone points out those special qualities that belong only to us. No finer compliment can be paid to another human being than to recognize his or her unique contribution to the rest of us which stems from being individual and special.

True, we live in a world that requires a measure of conformity. There are conventions to be respected, precedents to guide us, and some rules we must follow. What doesn't exist is enough encouragement for those of us who are struggling to be ourselves.

My value lies in the fact that I am I. Your value lies in the fact that you are you. There are those who struggle to make everyone the same. If we succumb, there will be no surprises, no laughter, no creativity, and no opera in the streets.

I remember quite well one of my grade school teachers who assisted me in one of my first real efforts in art. The class was supposed to draw a gold miner squatting by a stream panning for gold. The teacher began the lesson by holding up her drawing of a miner and informed us that if we followed instructions exactly, ours would look just like hers. First we drew a series of circles, then some connecting lines, then we erased here, and added there and, presto—thirty cloned miners as seen through the eyes of our teacher.

There were, as I recall, a few notable exceptions, among which was my own. My miner was fatter than the rest and had mounds of black curly hair. What made this particular memory stand out in my mind is the hurt I felt when that teacher held up my drawing to the class as an example of one who did not follow directions. The point was rather harshly made that we achieve by conforming and that individual expression was to be avoided. This teacher, who I am sure was dedicated to my growth, sought to achieve it by making a common denominator of me instead of encouraging and helping me develop that which was unique in me.

Thankfully, our philosophy of education has changed quite a bit since those days. I think we are moving away from the idea of education as mass production and more toward the idea that one of the prime elements of human uniqueness is the ability to create.

I would like to believe that everything about us is unique. There are enough forces out there that will regulate us, push us around, think for us and make us into "things," but the one counter we always have is the assertion of our unique self. Even when we were babies there was undoubtedly someone declaring that we had our mother's eyes or our father's determination or Aunt Betty's dimples—and there we lay with a face like none other, with a voice that brought a brand new sound into the world, and with a mind that would be our most

unique contribution to the world.

We need to be told early and often just how special we are. We need to stop trying to make others into what we feel they *ought* to be and help them find out who they *are*. How often do we hear things such as, "Oh, it's just a stage he's going through," or, "She's a textbook case," and forget that another's experience is really unique even though it has happened before and will happen to millions of others again.

It always seems to take less energy to place people in categories than it does to know them in their own right. But when we seek out and celebrate those special qualities in others, not only do we feel closer to them, but we ourselves are enriched from the experience.

I recently talked with a woman who said to me, "I'm an ugly, unhappy, uninteresting, and lonely woman. Who can love someone like me?" I thought sadly, "Only a person seeking an ugly, unhappy, uninteresting and lonely woman."

We are almost always our own harshest critics. Very often we are the least inclined to seek out and project the positive in ourselves. It's true that our self-images largely reflect a composite of the images others have of us. If we feel unattractive or boring or inconsequential, it is primarily because we think that others perceive us in these ways. But it's also possible that they are wrong! Or perhaps we're not projecting our best selves.

This sad woman had formed a low opinion of herself and was certain others shared that opinion. She was also convinced that those who didn't surely *would* once they got to know her. Why she held herself in such low regard is difficult to say, but it was painfully obvious that her entire outlook on

life, her potential as a unique human being, was stunted by her harsh perceptions of herself. Her capacity to enrich the lives of others was all but lost.

It's an old adage, but it still holds true, that if we don't like ourselves, nobody else will. Teenagers, perhaps more than others, provide ample evidence of this tendency. Many of us I'm sure can remember our adolescence. It was mostly a time of uncertainty, of changing moods, and, to varying degrees, of self-consciousness. If our hair wasn't just so, our clothes didn't fit exactly right, or a sudden blemish was on display, the whole world became an inhospitable place. Consequently we could often be found sulking in the shadows at the least assault on our self-esteem. Others might have viewed us in this context as brooding, temperamental, and unpredictable. Actually it was simply a case of momentarily not feeling good about ourselves.

Teenagers, of course, are not the only ones to succumb to feelings and behaviors reflecting self-doubt or inadequacy. It is natural that we all fall short of being the best that we can be from time to time, but to generalize these negative attitudes can be destructive and painful.

Helen Keller once wrote, "I learned that it is possible for us to create light and sound and order within us no matter what calamity may befall us in the outer world." Those of us who grapple with our self-images might pause to reflect on this beautiful example of one who insisted on discovering an inner light even in the face of a darkened outer world.

Instead of viewing ourselves as defective merchandise, we should be willing to delve beyond the surface and get in touch with our uniquely-fashioned self. For as long as *we* devalue *ourselves,* so will others. We may actually begin, in time, to conform to our artificial image that can dim, perhaps for all time, our inner light.

We all feel rejected and unloved at times. Perhaps we feel

momentarily out of sync with the rest of the world or that we may have less value than others. Still, we must remember that we are all that we have in the last analysis. The possibilities are unlimited if we never abandon ourselves.

If we feel ugly, keep in mind that beauty has many dimensions. If we feel unhappy, remember the words of Abe Lincoln: "Man is just about as happy as he makes up his mind to be." If we feel uninteresting, keep discovering. The world is mostly a fascinating mystery. If we feel lonely, don't wait for others to come to us—move toward others! Remember that we'll starve to death unless we exert the energy necessary to put food in our mouths.

It's not easy to give up the idea of a perfect world. We want to think of our parents as being perfect, we search for perfect relationships and perfect solutions to our problems. It is indeed a constant struggle to separate the real from the ideal—to see in our imperfection an essential element of our humanness.

We can all remember the most beloved children's stories that always seemed to end with the prince, in all his perfection and heroic, romantic, splendor, galloping off with the heroine with her virtually flawless characteristics, united for all time in their perfect love.

A currently popular theory holds that from these fantasies an indelible impression is formed of true love and happily-ever-aftering—one that persists into the realities of the adult world. There follows from this a disenchantment with real-life romance, real-life experience and real-life marriage, which are usually pale facsimiles of the perfect storybook kind.

We need sequels to these stories showing the happy couple, a little older and fatter, still contented, but just a little more reality-oriented. Children of all ages might benefit from seeing that the magic of falling in love is not lost when two people become older—even if Prince Charming is balding and his princess's backside is not as slim.

We continually indulge ourselves with the notion of human perfection, whether in individuals or in relationships. Somewhere out there, we are told, there are perfect marriages, perfect lovers, and even a perfect "10" if we look hard enough. Some of us are unfortunate enough to have grown up believing that we had perfect parents—an impression that was probably very carefully nurtured by these parents, who for some reason wished to keep their human imperfections a secret from their children. Small wonder that such children often fail at any lasting relationships, in or out of marriage, in their hopeless pursuit of the perfect life.

Our history books have long advanced the notion that our Founding Fathers were individuals of godlike perfection—perfectly moral, just, humane, etc. Only in recent years have historians searched for the persons behind the monuments. The smashing of false illusions of perfection has finally made it possible for us to truly appreciate the human being beyond the greatness, and in this way better realize our potential for the same.

Occasionally, we distinguish the imperfect in people with words such as idiosyncracy or eccentric. There are professionals who even emphasize their imperfections by drawing attention to them. When we laugh with others in this way, we are reminded not to take our own flaws too seriously and can accept the idea that imperfection is very much a part of the human condition.

Robert Clarke, in his book, *The Importance of Being Imperfect,* urges us to love our imperfect selves. "Only

then," he writes, "can we afford to enjoy flawed people in peace, for we have made our peace with a flawed self; we can afford to be vulnerable in the exchange of love, for we are unafraid to give the self we love away; we can afford to become more humanity-righteous, because we no longer need to be self-righteous."

We hear it said often enough that, "I love you in spite of your imperfections," but it's probably closer to the truth to say, "I love you *because* of your imperfections."

I'd like to believe that we are by nature social creatures. Anyone who has ever experienced loneliness—and who among us hasn't—will agree with that. We need each other. But as much as we need to be with each other, we also need to be alone from time to time. The thought is expressed beautifully by Paul Tillich. In his book, *Courage To Be*, he writes, "Our language has wisely sensed the two sides of being alone. It has created the word loneliness to express the pain of being alone. And it has created the word solitude to express the glory of being alone."

One of the absolute essentials of my life is to have time to myself. Time to collect scattered thoughts, time for quiet contemplation, time to think things through, or time to just go along at my own pace. To me, it's a very reasonable demand of the body and the mind that I disengage from everything and everyone occasionally. It's amazing how often I am criticized for this trait. I, say my critics, who love people so much, have no right to be a private person.

This requirement is not new for me. I discovered it early. In my childhood there were the day-long excursions into the fields near our home, the hours of exploring whatever came

into view or grasp, completely absorbed in my environment. There were very special trees that had the most accommodating branches for climbing and for building my own little fortress of solitude, way up high. When I really needed to be alone, that was my place.

I still like to break away on my own and wander to places that invite exploration. Sad to say, I'm less inclined to climb trees these days, but the stars seem just as close and glorious from the backyard porch, and it's a great deal less strenuous.

I manage to get away by myself for a few days every now and then. It's a need that reasserts itself at appropriate intervals in my life. I divorce myself from newspapers, radio, T.V., and telephone, even though it's not always easy to leave these things behind. But for me, doing this has its rewards.

First of all, there is the absolute splendor of no static from the outside. Getting far enough away from the sounds of the city means an opportunity to listen to my own heart and mind. I sometimes forget their sound in the constant roar of daily life. Having experienced this for a week or so, the renewing effect it has on my mind and body is unmistakable. Being cut off from a week's worth of news, and the calamities and carnage that are its mainstays, is a very special kind of therapy.

It's most enlightening to discover that, like a never ending soap opera, nothing is really missed by failing occasionally to keep current. In fact, separating oneself from the woes of the world can do wonders for one's outlook and general mood. One returns refreshed and optimistic!

It's so easy to become wrapped up in a routine of people and places that we neglect the all-important time of separation. Even when we find ourselves alone we are sometimes prone to fill the empty space with the chatter of a television set or a radio, almost as if we were afraid of the quiet.

We forget that there is an inner music that's nice to listen to

sometimes. Thomas Edison said of his deafness that it was an asset because from it he learned to listen from within. All of us, to some degree, suffer from a different kind of deafness that is caused by ignoring or closing off those inner channels. Solitude is an excellent way of improving our hearing.

One of the most difficult things for the human mind to comprehend is that life moves on even though many of us don't seem to be fully aware of it. This lack of consciousness is often responsible for causing many of us to waste a great portion of our lives. We lose much of our childhood, our adolescence, our young adulthood, our middle age, simply because we spend so much time living in the future. The tragedy is that what is lost is gone forever. None of us has been able to relive the past or change our transgressions.

Most of us live for tomorrow. We have convinced ourselves that it will be better, that we will be richer, wiser and more secure. This may be pleasant to contemplate, but also costly if it means losing even a moment of our present. I know we are brought up to work hard, to save our money and invest in the future. In this way, we're told, someday we will be able to enjoy what we dream about. The sad part is that too often by the time we reach those golden years, we no longer need the same things or we're too tired, too ill, too set in our ways to enjoy them.

How many trips have we postponed until some indefinite time, only because they seemed too strenuous or stressful? How many possibilities of happiness have we missed because we waited for a more convenient moment? How many people have we failed to celebrate because we thought we'd have them forever?

I had a friend whose wife had always wanted to visit her relatives in Scotland, the country of her parents' birth. It was her only wish. Though they could certainly afford to go, my friend throught it was a rather frivolous way to spend money. There was always a less expensive place to go, the mortgage to be paid, the need for a new lawn mower or plans for the children's education.

Now, the house is paid for, he has his new lawn mower, the children have all been educated, and are married and on their own. His wife's special dream was never realized. She died last year. He's alone with his accumulated things. It pained me to hear him lament, "I wish I had . . .," as we so often do in hindsight.

I'm not suggesting that we should be spendthrifts or completely self-indulgent, or that we fail to plan sensibly for our future. I'm simply saying that we all have present needs and that too often they become permanent gaps in our lives when they are not realized. We all need a little frivolity and self-indulgence from time to time.

Though frowned upon in our culture, pampering ourselves now and then seems to me a healthful thing. Why should it cause us to feel a sense of selfishness and guilt, especially when these feelings take all the fun out of it? We all know the joy of buying that expensive pair of shoes we love so much, or having dinner in that elegant restaurant we read about, or sending flowers or gifts for no reason other than the special joy it will bring to someone.

It's sad to hear things such as—

"People only send me flowers when I'm ill, or in a hospital when I'm too distracted to enjoy them. And how sad that the day I receive the most flowers I won't even see them. Who needs flowers after you're dead?"

"I get presents on my birthday or the usual holidays, but I'd forego these for a surprise gift sometime—just a sign that

someone is thinking about me when they don't really have to."

"We should have taken that trip last year. Now he/she is in the hospital and we may never be able to do it."

"I should have told her I loved her while she was still here."

To pass up or ignore the possibilities of present laughter, to fill our lives with plans for some nebulous tomorrow is to court the possibility of permanent, irreparable loss. Time is limited, even for the youngest of us. It is something we can control and enhance with our expressions of love and caring now. Such opportunities come only so often in a lifetime. To suggest that we all have a right to be pampered now and again without the usual accompanying feelings of guilt is not asking so much.

We often spend our lifetime doing the sensible thing, mostly for the welfare of others. Common sense, self-denial, prudence—these things certainly have their place so long as they don't become constants in our life. We all need frequent doses of "I deserve this." Aside from what immediate happiness it brings to us, it is also a basic reminder that "I like me and I'm worth it."

A Passion for Food

I, like so many of us, love to eat. It's not that I'm obsessed, for I've been known to diet and fast for days without too much trouble. It's basically that I like the tastes, the textures and the aroma of well-prepared food. I love veal and lamb and carrots and barley and beans and artichokes and asparagus and pasta and chili and corn and rabbit and chicken and chocolate chip cookies and . . and . . and . .

For me, eating is also one of the last of the great rituals: we meet for a quiet lunch, we have friendly dinner parties and we linger over brunch. All of these occasions are special times when we drop the rush ethic and sit back for a few hours of sharing. Most of my happiest childhood memories are somehow connected with meals. I remember the huge piles of food on large platters, the heavenly odors, and oh, the anticipation!

Mama's minestrone soup was more than just something to eat. It became a symbol of many things. It was security, goodness, health, an economic gauge, a unifier, and an expression of love that was tangible and stuck to your ribs. Most all ethnic groups have their special soup: Chicken soup, Won Ton soup, Miso soup, Menudo, Onion are a few which come to mind.

All of us have childhood memories which refuse to die and continually cause us to relive moments of the past. One of these was the odor emanating from the soup pot. I can still see it sitting on the stove in all its enameled beauty, its contents ever-simmering, steam rising as from a dormant volcano.

When I came home from school I could pick up the aroma from the street and when I entered the back screened porch, the odor was overwhelming. Whether Mama was standing over it with a long wooden spoon, stirring, or whether she was away from the stove, I knew that I had come home.

There is really no recipe for minestrone soup. I recall that it all started with some water and a bag of meat bones which Mama usually got free from the butcher. (He later began to charge her a few pennies for them, which she thought was outrageous.) To the bones boiling away in the water she would add vegetables: onions, tomatoes, cabbage, carrots, beans, peas, garlic (of course!)—and pastas of various shapes and sizes. I always suspected that, as with all recipes Mama cooked, there was a special secret ingredient. In this case I noticed that when the soup began to lose its flavor, or became too thick, she'd add a generous splash of wine, stir it and leave it to continue its slow, gentle simmer.

There are so many things in life which link me to my past, but few have been more lasting than Mama's soup. For my family, it became an economic indicator more accurate than Wall Street. We could always judge our financial condition by the thickness of the soup. A thick brew indicated that things

were going well with the Buscaglias, a watery soup denoted meager, less plentiful times. No matter the abundance of food served in our home, nothing was ever thrown out. Everything ended up in the soup pot.

Minestrone was medicinal. It served both physical and mental needs. No matter what time of day or night any member of the family came home, it was soup time. If Papa worked late—and his job as a waiter made this more often than not—Mama would get up out of bed in her cotton bathrobe, her long brown hair falling in waves over her shoulders, and they'd sit down to a bowl of soup. She mostly listened while he ate and told her of the trials and tribulations, or joys and successes, of the day.

If we got hurt, Mama's remedy was always a Band-Aid, a hug and a bowl of soup. It cured colds, fever, headaches, indigestion, heartaches and loneliness.

How often a bowl of minestrone served to unite us and bring us together in warmth and joy! It was an act of communion. When people dropped in, strangers included, we would soon find ourselves huddled around the kitchen table, talking over a bowl of steaming soup. It took care of breakfast, a quick lunch, or a midnight snack. It was sometimes even a sign that someone needed to talk.

Mama died about ten years ago, six years before Papa. Somehow, the house was never the same. Someone turned the gas off under the minestrone pot the day after she was buried, and a whole era went out with the flame.

Oh, sure, members of the family still make minestrone soup from time to time. It's made in smaller quantities now and only on special occasions. The continual warmth and reassurance with which it once filled the house is somehow missing. In fact, the younger kids say that it makes the house smell bad, that eating it is too fattening, or that they get tired of it.

There are so few things that one can really count on these days. We need more minestrone pots in the world. I long for the security, the aroma, the taste. I'm sure there are still such soups simmering in houses all over the world.

Long may they simmer!

I'm being bombarded with the notion that we must all diet and that if we do not we'll succumb to a variety of ailments and illnesses or worse, die before our time. We are also told that skinny is beautiful, that we look best when we have a slim, sleek line. I recently attended a fashion show that was given for charity. The models all looked as if they could use a bit of the charity. Aside from the lovely faces, they appeared more like clothing racks upon which the gowns had been carefully draped.

I'm not anti-dieting and I'm very health conscious. I love my yogurt and granola and bean sprouts and wheat germ along with the healthiest of them. But I do resent the fact that I am made to feel like some sort of glutton at every meal, determined to kill myself. "You're not having another helping!" "Not that sugar-filled pastry!" "Remember cholesterol!" And so it goes.

Are we all determined to look like Jane Fonda? I like the Fonda look, but it seldom occurs to people that Ms. Fonda has a very fine bone structure. She was lucky. All of her bones are in the proper place for a classic female figure. As for the classic male, see Paul Newman or Matt Dillon. But what about those of us with larger, less classic bones? We could shake 'em and rock 'em and bounce 'em until we drop with exhaustion and still appear as if we'd had six orders of pasta in butter and a pound of Galliano cheese cake!

We seem to forget that we are not alike in many ways, and body size and shape are simply ways in which we differ. Wouldn't it be nice if we could accept this and let each other be? Still we are continually told that we must stop eating if we want all of our emotional and physical problems to end. So we starve for a few days, lose a few pounds and develop such a voracious appetite that when we give up our diet we eat everything in sight. After a day or two we're back where we started.

We very seldom ask why we are dieting. For whom are we dieting? Are we determined to make the cover of *Vogue*? Do we live for those brief moments when our friends exclaim, "Gee, you're losing weight!"? Or are we doing it for ourselves—which, in the end, is the only valid reason. I have a friend who dieted for months to please her husband, or so she thought. Her husband actually felt she looked better with the ten extra pounds!

I have friends who eat everything in sight for weeks, then pop off to the fat farm at two thousand dollars a week to lose it all. There they delight over dinners of lettuce garnished elegantly with radish and celery stick, and a small piece of mock meatloaf made with minced mushrooms. Meanwhile, their dreams are filled with Swiss chocolate and Winchell's donuts. But they stay with it. They forget that there is no law in the land that says a healthy woman cannot weigh more than 120 or a healthy man, 180.

I can't understand how people can put away enough food to keep a horse well fed and never show it, while some of us just look at a pastry shelf and gain twelve pounds. I know I must take care of my body. I want it to be the vehicle in which a healthy, productive person is housed. I love living. But I also refuse to relinquish the joy of food and the splendor of long, lovely dinners with people I care about.

I don't object to others dieting if they know why they're

doing it and as long as they don't descend on me in their crusade against eating. In the end, it will matter little whether we leave this world with a size 32 or 36 waist.

It's difficult to forget painful memories of prejudice. As a child, I was one of the few first-generation Italian Americans in my elementary school. I was, of course, called a *wop* and a *dago,* accused of being part of the Mafia, and a party to the formation of a Sacco-Vanzetti radical group. All this, Papa informed me, was the usual prejudicial nonsense of the uninformed and unfeeling. I was also accused of always smelling of garlic. This, I'm certain, was true. I was raised on Allium sativum (garlic). It was strung around my neck each morning by my determined Mama over my loud protestations.

"Mama! It stinks! Americans don't tie garlic around their necks!"

"You're right," Mama would answer, with her on-target logic. "And Americans get the flu every year! You never do. So shut up!" Of course she was right. No one ever came close enough to me to spread their viruses!

When I returned from school, there were no chocolate chip cookies or cupcakes for me. I got a giant piece of Italian bread, the crust of which was rubbed generously with several cloves of garlic, then covered with butter. I loved it! I still do.

There are so many miracles in the world, miracles to be celebrated and for me, garlic is among the most deserving. You can have it whole, minced, sliced or rubbed on a salad bowl. It's high in protein, and though it is also high in calories, it has fewer than brussels sprouts.

Since ancient times, garlic has been celebrated. The Egyptians attributed God-like qualities to it. The Hebrews

demanded its use under Talmudic rule. The Greeks and Romans put it into almost every dish, and especially encouraged their athletes to eat it in large quantities for strength. It's to be found to some degree in the cuisine of every nation and is often referred to as the universal herb. Over time it has been prescribed as an expectorant, a diuretic, an antiseptic and a rubefacient. It was even suggested at one time as an aid for sunstroke.

Though the founders of modern medicine, Hippocrates and Galen, all spoke highly of the attributes of garlic, it is only recently that today's medical researchers are discovering its many medical uses. They are finding that garlic may have special powers because it contains components which, when pressed or crushed, produce allyl. This acts as an antibacterial agent which seems to affect only harmful bacteria! The research seems to suggest that eating garlic is a natural way of lowering high blood pressure and cholesterol, and an aid against cold viruses, diarrhea, poor blood clotting, and rheumatism. Strange how Mama, who didn't know allyl from rubefacients and couldn't care less, knew all these things instinctively.

It doesn't really matter to me if the above research proves valuable or not. I like garlic! I never sauté anything without garlic popping away in hot olive oil. Lamb is fantastic with no other seasoning but garlic and rosemary inserted in the meat at regular intervals prior to roasting. Salad dressings come alive with garlic. There is even a delectable recipe for chicken which calls for *forty* cloves of garlic. Overwhelming! But don't be a coward. Try it. You'll love it. You need have no concern. The forty cloves are placed around the chicken in the roasting pan unpeeled. After they're cooked they can be removed and used to season the gravy, or simply popped into your mouth as a treat for the chef. The taste is fantastic. You won't believe how mellow garlic can be after cooking.

Friends always question how a person who advocates togetherness as much as I do could suggest something as antisocial as garlic. Easy! Once eaten, garlic becomes a wonderful unifying force. People come together out of a kind of self-preservation, then stay together.

Of course I can accept the fact that there are those who, when they come within a hundred yards of garlic, turn a deep green and move away as fast as good manners will allow. No matter. I've tried to share one of life's great miracles, which is one of my major purposes in life. If there are those who don't agree, for them there may always be the miracle of parsley!

A few years ago I was told that I would live a longer and more productive life if I jogged three miles a day, gave up red meat, limited myself to four eggs a week, stopped using salt, did away with liquor of any kind, watched my diet, took food supplements and medication to lower my cholesterol count and blood pressure. Since I have a great reverence for life, I tried to do all these things. It wasn't easy but I did make some significant changes. In spite of it all, I had a heart attack that caused me to undergo a quintuple bypass operation. Happily, I recovered.

Again I was assured that exercise and diet would do the trick. Now, of course, I became more zealous than ever. I even began to read the research literature in the health journals and medical books. The result was more confusion and new anxieties; I'm certain it didn't do my blood pressure any good either.

I'm told in a series of articles by responsible doctors, for instance, that I must lower my cholesterol level because there is a direct correlation between heart disease and high choles-

terol. This finding, I am assured, is conclusive, with mounting evidence being accumulated almost daily. Then I am presented with another set of studies which indicate that there is some doubt that these findings are accurate, that there is still much to learn about the cholesterol question.

I have been all but convinced that I should give up salt forever—that salt is a poison for some people. As a result I don't even have salt or a salt shaker in the house. Though I am certain that I fall into the group called salt sensitive, I am told that for most people a moderate intake of salt is no problem; and that, in fact, an absence of salt can actually be harmful.

Exercise has become another problem. The literature is full of articles and testimonies extolling the virtues of jogging, aerobics, jazzercise, and working out for the prevention of heart disease. On the other hand, I am flooded with material warning me to proceed with great caution in the area of exercise. Jogging, I am told, may put a strain on my ankles, back and heart.

In the same way, I have been convinced for years that drinking alcohol is the surest way of killing myself and to be avoided at any cost. Now I read that a glass of wine or a cocktail each evening can be a positive addition to a cardiac diet.

I have long since given up red meat. A big, juicy steak is mostly a memory for me. I have also attempted to do the same with other fatty foods and switched to a diet of fresh vegetables, nuts and beans. Now I am warned that this may not be providing me with adequate nourishment. I am also told by meat eaters that most vegetables today are sprayed with deadly pesticides and that even if they are not, some plants over the years develop natural toxins which are cancer-causing agents! (With names that would make one swear off vegetables forever).

There's just no winning! And though most of this is beyond

my humble understanding, it's enough to make me apprehensive about every morsel of food that goes into my mouth.

Of course, we've all heard that our water and air are becoming more and more polluted. Even our pure and cleansing rain is now full of acid, I'm told. So what to do? Where to turn? Whom to believe? I can't give up eating, drinking or breathing. It's enough to confuse and depress anyone who thinks about it long enough.

Good friends tell me that the best way to rid myself of these anxieties is to stop reading medical literature and start reading Agatha Christie instead. It's certainly far better than staring at my plate at every meal, wondering just what sort of chemicals and hidden toxins are lurking beneath the surface ready to do me in. I've never been a believer in "ignorance is bliss," but I might be willing to make an exception in this case.

My mother was a very wise woman. She always said, "Have it all—but in moderation." She lived to be 82. Not bad for a woman with high blood pressure and astronomical levels of cholesterol. Could it be that Mama was right again?

I've seldom seen a garden without rows of zucchini vines. I've seen gardens without Swiss chard, carrots, eggplant, and even tomatoes, but never without zucchini. Perhaps it's because they are so easy to grow and they're so hearty. They yield so much for so little energy.

Most people dismiss the zucchini as simply another variety of summer squash. They talk about it as if it were some sort of cucumber. But those of us who have lived under the influence of zucchini power know better.

Papa was an expert zucchini grower. He planted them year

after year. His yield was remarkable. You could count on it. Another thing you could count on, much to Mama's chagrin, was that all of the zucchini was ready about the same time. Neither Mama nor Papa were ever known to waste a thing. Papa usually picked the zucchini daily, just when it reached the length of his hand and the circumference of a thin banana. That's the time when it was most tender and delicious.

The problem was always how to use such a large crop before it spoiled. Mama would steam it, fry it, can it, mash it, put it raw into salads, make casseroles, even pickle it—but in no way could she use all the squash which accumulated daily on her kitchen counter.

Of course, Papa's greatest joy was to share what he had with others. I can still see him tenderly packing his zucchini into little sacks. He always chose the best to give away. After all, you can't give away a bruised or imperfect zucchini. Then he'd take off into the neighborhood. We would try to convince him that there might be some neighbors who hated zucchini. "You're crazy" he'd say. "Everybody likes zucchini!" And off he'd go, ringing doorbells and handing over his precious gifts. Each neighbor seemed delighted, but it was I who had to deal with the neighborhood kids who would corner me on the way home from school. "I'll kill you," they'd threaten, "if your Dad doesn't stop giving us those green things."

Mama, in the meantime, was kept busy giving out recipes to neighborhood cooks.

"They're good steamed and served with a little butter and garlic. But be sure they're not mushy—just *al dente.*"

"You can egg and flour them and lightly brown them in olive oil until they're just crisp."

"You can mash them, put nuts and bits of dried fruits with them in a casserole and bake them."

"You can just cut them up and serve them raw in a salad."

"You can hollow them out and fill them with your favorite stuffing and put them in the oven."

(And all of this, please note, before Nouvelle Cuisine made the zucchini an "in" vegetable.)

Of course the neighborhood kids would have undoubtedly added their own recipe idea:

"You can throw them in the garbage can!"

It's amazing how much interchange, conversation, sharing and controversy can come from a single vegetable.

When summer was over we thought we were through with the dreaded zucchini. No way! Mama had canned quarts of it and what wasn't canned was pickled. I hardly remember a dinner where a zucchini didn't rear its green head. My sister, Lee, even gave them a special name. She called them "zucks," to rhyme with "yucks." She never dared repeat this in front of Mama or Papa, but this name brought on knowing snickers from us every time she whispered it at the table.

Yes, zucchini has real power. It's a must for any home gardener who enjoys eating it and sharing the bounty with neighbors. And did you know that as the zucchini grows it produces a beautiful yellow flower much like a lily? After you enjoy them aesthetically for a few days, and while they're still young, you can pick them for another delectable treat. All you have to do is to bread the flowers and fry them lightly in oil. They are a rare delicacy and a treat for the palate.

Others may think I'm a little crazy for singling out a mere vegetable for such a tribute, but let's face it—something so unique deserves a little praise. Long may it grow and serve!

America is having a love affair with wine. I'm delighted. Never before have so many people given up the Martini,

Margarita or Gimlet for a refreshing glass of wine.

I was introduced to the magic of wine at a very young age, even before I was able to read and write. Papa always made his own wine and all of us were treated to small sips of the velvety reds and the lighthearted whites at birthday celebrations, dinner parties, Christmas, Easter, first communions and confirmations.

Of course, many in our neighborhood were shocked that we children were being given alcohol at such an early age. They were certain it would stunt our growth, fry our brains or make us alcoholics. Mama and Papa could never understand their concern. After all, it was part of the wedding feast at Cana, used at the Last Supper and offered at the communion rail. Mama advocated a taste of wine from time to time for medicinal purposes. She was certain that it was the natural way to cure anemia, liver problems, kidney ailments, and a perfect tonic to purify the blood. The privilege was, of course, never to be abused. All of us grew to normal size and none of us has a drinking problem.

The annual ritual of making the wine was one of the most festive of the year. It was planned months in advance. The grapes were ordered by the truckload and the boxes hand carried up the driveway to the garage where all the paraphernalia for grinding and pressing the wine were stored. All the male members of the family, shirt sleeves rolled up and clothes deeply stained with purple, moved knowingly through the wine making process.

I was the smallest, so it was I who, with clean bare feet, was put onto the pressed grapes to move them evenly around the giant barrel. While this was going on, the women were busily—and with much joy and laughter—preparing the ravioli and antipasto which would make up the dinner. What a special night! We would sit down at the table much later than usual, with voracious appetites, and devour the dinner with a

passion. There was much joyful talk and endless laughter.

Papa never took wines casually. He felt it his duty to teach us all how to truly appreciate them. Never swallow wine as you do water—sip it. Never fill the wine glass so you can swish the wine about without spilling it. He informed us of the many varieties, how to appreciate the color—the rich reds, the deep ambers, the clear purples. He taught us about the nose (aroma) and how to use the mouth and tongue to sample and judge each new wine. He taught us the vocabulary that went with it—high and low acidity, corky, dull, vigorous, and so on. The experience was much like a religious ceremony—not pretentious or phony, just sheer joy, another of life's gifts to be relished.

Papa's education in wines offered me one of my greatest triumphs. When I was in my first year of college, I visited New York City for the first time. The trip was a birthday present from my more successful friends. I was taken, as part of the gift, to one of the top restaurants at the time. The name shall remain unwritten. My friends asked me to select the wine. There was an Italian wine on the list that Papa had often mentioned fondly as one of his favorites. Though it was more expensive than some of the others, I was persuaded to order it.

The wine steward was rather intimidating, with his medals and silver cup dangling from his neck. He opened the wine and poured a bit into my glass. Though Papa was 3000 miles away, I heard his instructions. Step by step I followed them carefully. I paused. Could it be? Could the wine be corky? My friends stared at me in horror. I heard Papa say, "What has been the good of so many years of preparation if you don't speak up?"

"It's corky," I stammered. "Corky!" the steward exclaimed. "We have one of the world's great wine cellars. We don't have corky wines!" I heard myself say, "Nev-

ertheless . . ." I watched my friends cringe as the steward tasted the wine. I could hear my heart pounding wildly and wondered if everyone in the room could hear it also. My apprehension was short lived. I heard the steward whisper "I'm sorry, sir. It is corky. You're right. I'm sorry." Triumph!

I know that there are those who, for one reason or another, will not and should not touch any alcoholic beverage. I admire them greatly for abiding by their choice. For me, a glass of wine with a good dinner will always open a storeroom of warm memories and be an occasion for celebration.

We have all been given to believe that Marco Polo brought pasta from China. I cannot tell you the times I have been put down by pseudo-historians who scoffed at my pride in Italian spaghetti assuring me that its origin wasn't even Italian! Somehow, there was something not quite right about the national food of Italy having originated in China, and in my heart I have always felt that it could not be so. You can imagine my elation recently when I learned that they were wrong. Marco Polo never made the claim of bringing pasta to Italy and historians have found that Italians were already cooking semolina flour (the stuff that pasta is made of) in boiling water as a basic food as early as 27 B.C.

You're probably wondering why I should care at all about the origin of pasta. Well, I take great pride in my Italian beginnings. Pasta has always been an important part of my life. It means a great deal to the people of Italy. It is of such importance in their daily diet that the Olympic team brought its own pasta across the sea to Los Angeles, just in case.

Most of all, a recent report by the U.S. Senate Committee on Nutrition and Human Needs has recommended that pasta

be added as a daily supplement to the American diet. It seems necessary, then, that we set the record straight.

I can already see the slim-conscious among us recoiling in horror. "Pasta every day?!" they'll exclaim. "The government nutritionists have gone mad! We'll be a country of blimps and hippos." Not so! It isn't pasta that's fattening. In fact, it's very healthful. The calorie difference is between a Spaghetti Alfredo made with cream, butter and grated cheeses and a simple sauce of tomatoes simmered for hours with herbs fresh from the garden.

Is there anything more stimulating to the palate and the eye than a steaming dish of pasta covered with a sauce Bolognese heavy on the tomatoes? Primavera bright with crisp, fresh vegetables? Carbonara with prosciutto, butter and cheese? Pesto with fresh basil, garlic, cheese, pine nuts and olive oil?

There are almost as many kinds of pasta as there are ways of preparing it: thin pasta, thick pasta, tubular pasta, butterfly pasta, lasagna noodles, and on and on in every size and shape. I have just learned that Italian designer Guiliano of Turino has done a designer noodle. I can just see it in shops from Fifth Avenue to Rodeo Drive, somewhere between Louis Vuitton and Yves Saint Laurent!

Perhaps the next best thing about serving a pasta (the taste being first) is that it's so economical. For a few dollars you can stuff several dozen people. It's easy, too. Most pastas are cooked and ready to serve in 15 or 20 minutes. With a green salad or a beautiful antipasto, you have a feast.

We're so fortunate in the United States. Having developed from a cultural melting pot, the best of foreign cuisines have always been available for us to revel in—from kreplock to couscous to pickled herring to sushi to crepes to enchiladas to weinerschnitzel to fried rice to dim sum to pasta. Of course, there's nothing wrong with a great hamburger, turkey, or roast beef and potatoes; but to limit ourselves to these is sad.

So get the water boiling fast. Drop in the pasta of your choice. Wait until it's *al dente* (just a bit firm to the teeth and never allowed to get mushy). There are those who say that the best test for pasta readiness is to take a morsel out of the boiling water and throw it against the wall. If it sticks, it's done. I have never tried it that way and don't recommend it. For your wall's sake, do it the easy way—just take out a string and bite. Then toss it with your favorite sauce and sprinkle it with grated cheese (Parmesan or Romano if you can afford it, but Cheddar or Jack work well also). Pour the beverage of your choice, put Pavarotti on the record player, light the candles and go to it!

A Passion
for
Dignity

My life was completely changed by the suicide many years ago of one of my brighter and more creative students. She left no clue, no note, no explanation as to why she should take her life. From all appearances she had everything: beauty, charm, a loving family, a promising future. But, it seems to me, somewhere along the line she must have lost sight of her own individual dignity.

Only when we realize our value as unique human beings can we begin to develop a sense of dignity and a respect for our place in life. There are so few persons giving out this message. More often than not we are dehumanized and made to feel guilty because of our differences. We become convinced that we lack what it takes to deal with life. Few encourage us to try, to risk. Too seldom are we told of our specialness or challenged with the wonder of our undiscovered selves.

I have been wondering lately whatever happened to pride. Not pride in the sense of arrogance or an exaggerated sense of self-importance, but rather a feeling of self-respect, high expectations and values relating to oneself, and a reasonable sense of one's world.

Near my office there lives an elderly man. He moves slowly, totters a bit and speaks haltingly. He lives in a small apartment house in what is otherwise an industrial center. He exists on a scandalously low fixed income. Still, he's always cheery and ready to stop anything he's doing for a neighborly greeting. He can almost always be found neatly garbed in work clothes laboring over a small garden he has planted in front of his apartment. Over the years he has created the neatest and most colorful spot in the neighborhood. It's alive with roses, azaleas, mums, or whatever the seasonal flower happens to be.

I asked him once why he worked so hard on a plot of land which wasn't even his, when his landlord seemed to care so little. "Well," he answered, "he might not care about it, but I do. I live here and it's a reflection of me. And that's enough reason." I had felt that his answer would be something like that. The other apartment dwellers love him.

This past summer I was in Switzerland. As every visitor knows, it has a long tradition of national pride. The Swiss care greatly about their country. Dozens of times I watched as people of all ages stopped to pick up litter on streets and sidewalks, or reprimand others who were abusing the environment. "This is our home," they say, "and if we want it to remain beautiful, we've got to keep our pride in it alive."

This attitude is reflected in the amount of time each household sets aside to beautify the environment with window boxes of cascading flowers, and by keeping gardens neat and manicured. They do this for themselves, not to impress the tourists. The result is a country that is a visual pleasure to

experience—clean, colorful and caring. Here, in America, I look about me with sadness. I see walls and public transport smeared with graffiti. I see lovely old homes and neighborhoods abandoned to decay and often lost in overgrown weeds. Trash is often strewn on streets and sidewalks, and in public parks and recreation areas.

The attitude seems to be that anything outside one's home is not one's responsibility. It's the familiar rationalization, "If others don't feel responsible, why should I?" So we allow our public places to be converted into trash piles and we live in them. The sad part is that children who are raised without a sense of pride grow to accept, and then perpetuate, the situation. The attitude continues: "Who cares? It's none of my concern."

A friend of mine was recently planning an anniversary party. He was going over the wine list with his caterer, who suggested that he could save a substantial amount of money if he would serve an inexpensive wine. "Most people won't know the difference," he was assured. "I will," my friend replied. He wanted the best he could afford on this special occasion, to share with his friends. He paid the difference.

Too easily we judge this kind of pride as someone being a showoff. We dismiss such a person as having an excess of vanity and an exaggerated sense of importance. In reality, it may be that such an individual is making an effort which we might be simply too apathetic to make. How much easier it is to criticize in such a situation than it is to follow such an example.

When I was growing up we were very poor. I had to constantly wear hand-me-downs, often patched and visibly worn. Our home was an old frame house which had been around for years. Still, we were always immaculately clean, our clothes carefully washed and ironed. Our home was always freshly painted, the grass neatly trimmed and mowed,

and surrounded by flower beds and vegetable gardens. "We don't have much," Mama told us, "but it's ours. We're proud of it and we're gonna take care of it." Heaven help us if we forgot!

I have heard from many sources that pride in oneself is not of itself a virtue. Well, that may be so. But I feel certain it's the embryo of many much-needed virtues. Long may it continue to grow.

As soon as someone wins a sweepstakes, the first thing they decide to do is quit working. To many of us, that sounds like the ideal state. Few of us realize how much happiness is dependent upon our work. We complain that we have too much work, that it's just so much drudgery, but we fail to realize that it's our work that keeps us alert, growing, and helps us to maintain our dignity.

During the recent layoffs in the automobile industry, I talked with a man who had worked all of his life. This was his first experience with idleness. At first, the newness of the situation and the requirement of receiving and reporting for unemployment compensation kept him going. But he soon discovered that the hours, days, weeks, and months of idle time were getting to him. He began to lose interest in everything, including his family. He had no incentive for getting out of bed in the morning. His life, though lacking nothing but work, seemed out of focus. Time, which he had barely been aware of before, now weighed heavily upon him. He became irritable, shouted at his children and resented his working wife.

You might say that he had everything—health, friends, a loving family, possessions and sufficient money to see him

through this crisis. But there was something very seriously missing. It took time before he realized that it was the lack of productive work that gave each day meaning. It was this realization that resulted in his throwing himself into painting the house. It saved him until he was called back to his job.

Work of any kind offers many rewards even if we don't much care for what it is we're doing. It keeps us in human company. It brings us into life. It requires us to experience new things and gives us a sense of reward. Thinking, feeling, planning have little value if we know there is no practical benefit to be gained by it.

A few years back I visited my relatives in a small provincial town in northern Italy. It was apparent what an integral part work played in their lives. Aunts, uncles, cousins—all rose at dawn and went out into the fields raking, hoeing, plowing and planting, sometimes late into the evening. There, actively moving under the warm Italian sun and over the fertile earth, there seemed to be no time for boredom. There was always something which needed doing.

In the evening, after they had washed the earth from their bodies, the festivities began. Good fresh food from the garden, cool wines from the cellar, animated conversation, laughter, joking, teasing and general rejoicing. Before too long they were all peacefully sleeping, ready for the next day's work.

I realize that many would ask, "Is that enough?" For some, perhaps not. But I never saw such smiles. Their lives had meaning, and at the heart of it was work and the rewards they received from it. They knew a congenial occupation, something into which they could enter with abandon, which offered them emotional and physical peace.

I know that there are many who criticize and come down brutally hard on the Puritan ethic that has made work such a vital part of our mentality. They will point out that for many,

work is dull, demeaning and offers no greater reward than a small paycheck at the end of the week. They will argue that there is little good that can be said for time spent at a job which we abhor, and of course I would agree. But these situations may also serve as an incentive for bettering ourselves and our skills.

We have all had many jobs—some routine and others challenging. We know that work, well done, is rewarding and even necessary for human well-being. Our lives change when we stop looking at our work as a necessary evil and begin to see it as a privilege. We may then start executing it with more gusto, excitement and dignity.

I recently watched some World War II footage on television which showed several military men being honored with medals for various feats of valor. It was all very impressive. Amid the cheering crowds and fanfare were heads of state and generals pinning on the medals and, in some cases, even kissing the recipients on both cheeks. One man was being recognized for having risked his life to save his buddies. Another one was honored for having blown up tanks or downed enemy planes.

We love to pay tribute to our heroes, perhaps for what it inspires in all of us—to reach above and beyond the everyday pattern. Certainly, I'd not be the one to deny anyone his medal, but suddenly it occurred to me that there are so many who deserve recognition for what they do, but who will more than likely never get it—no medal for distinguished service, no Pulitzer prize, no Nobel prize, no public recognition.

Medals should go to parents who successfully raise children through teething, tantrums, braces and broken hearts,

and all the growing pains in between—and in spite of it continue to love them without expectation or reward.

I'd like to bestow an award on grandparents who, after years of giving of themselves, are not content to live their lives in their children's shadows, but continue to grow and work independently and enthusiastically.

I'd like to reward all the political leaders who are sincerely engaged in the endless struggle for a better quality of life for us all.

Likewise, I'd like to give a medal to the professionals in our society who maintain their ideals, practice their skills with pride and dedication toward a healthier, more sane, more livable society.

Recognition would be no less deserved for our blue-collar workers who help keep our cities safe, clean, and running efficiently, whose work we all take so much for granted, and without whose daily contribution we would surely fall apart.

I would like to give medals to educators who, despite low salaries, difficult classroom conditions, and often low public esteem, continue to educate our young people year after year and, for the most part, succeed.

I would like to single out researchers in all fields who spend most of their time in laboratories, with little or no financial support, seeking secrets with patient devotion— secrets which will enhance life and human well-being.

There are so many artists, writers, musicians, singers, and entertainers of all sorts who deserve medals for the hours of joy, inspiration and beauty their creativity brings to all of us.

All of the these people make our society work and they should be recognized for it.

Of course, we know that there are less than ideal parents and grandparents, as well as dishonest and self-serving politicians, teachers, public servants and professionals. Strangely enough, they are the ones we seem to notice the most, often to

the extent that we lose sight of or take for granted the good that the majority does.

Most of the latter will never appear on television or in newspaper headlines. Very few of them will ever receive medals. In fact, they never expect them. Still, I think it's a great idea and I guess it's up to us to find the means of honoring each other.

It doesn't take much—an encouraging, complimentary word to a good mother, father, an honest professional, fine teacher, or to a hard-working fire fighter or policeman. I don't think they'd care so much about a formal ceremony. A simple expression of thanks, a positive gesture or a brief telephone call can have great value, also.

Aristotle wisely made an important distinction when he wrote, "Dignity does not consist in possessing honors, but in deserving them." Good work and steady devotion to one's principles do have their own rewards, but a little recognition now and then certainly doesn't hurt.

I saw a futuristic movie that gave another one of those bleak accounts of life in the 23rd century. There was hopelessness everywhere; lives were lived mechanically against the background of a sterile and colorless, often violent, world. People were vacant, pressed into a painful uniformity and seemingly without personality.

There have been a number of books and films in recent years that give a similarly bleak account of the future. It's interesting how they share this stark vision of tomorrow. One supposes that it's based on an appraisal of the present—that authors feel we are, in fact, headed down such a road now. Depersonalization, they suggest, seems to be one factor that

points us in that direction, because it has become more and more a part of our present.

I have a friend who regularly points out the grim and unmistakable signs of our dehumanization. He loves to use the government as an example. "We're nothing more than an index card or a speck on some microchip," he tells me. "We're a statistic that gets counted and catalogued every 10 years, and only noticed when we fail to pay our taxes.

He recalls when there was a bond between producers and consumers. Then quality and reputation meant something, when people were more important than profit. There is, no doubt, some truth in his observations. There are times when all of us feel swept up in a mass culture; a modern society that places increasingly less emphasis on person-to-person intimacy. Perhaps it is part of our love/hate relationship with a technology that takes us to the limits of our imaginations, but often abandons us there, to feel more isolated than ever.

My friend works in an office where he spends the better part of his day inside a cubicle with a computer. His daily regimen is imposed upon him by his machine; he is supervised by it, even disciplined by it. His interaction with other people at work is pretty much confined to coffee and lunch breaks. Under these circumstances, one can understand his feeling of alienation.

But I believe he is more the exception than the rule. It seems to me that companies and corporations that employ people in repetitive and tedious work, especially work that is done in isolation, have, more than ever, rediscovered the importance of meeting human needs. They've learned that people who are made to feel less like people don't perform well in any kind of work situation. They acquire attitudes of apathy and boredom. They develop ulcers and nervous habits. They're more often ill, need medical attention more frequently; they tend to burn out earlier.

It's very simple. We need each other. In our day-to-day living there is no substitute for the human touch. We need other people to appreciate our accomplishments and encourage our creativity. No matter how much we automate our lives or learn to substitute wires and circuits for people, that message is clear.

At the supermarket, a checker told me that her job will soon be automated. "I won't be needed at all," she sighed. I tried to reassure her that her friendly smile and warmth were irreplaceable, but she seemed resigned to giving way to speed and efficiency. I certainly hope she's wrong.

In 1970, Alvin Toffler wrote *Future Shock*. In this book, he talked about how we were becoming a modular society. He warned about people in our lives whom we treat like components—plugging them in and out to suit our needs. He used the example of a modular shoe salesman: "Consciously or not," he said, "we define our relationships with most people in functional terms. So long as we do not become involved with the shoe salesman's problems or his more general hopes, dreams and frustrations, he is fully interchangeable with any other salesman of equal competence."

I am not afraid of the implication that people will become replaceable or are indeed interchangeable. I am certain that however great are the changes in store for our future, the human being will triumph. But in working to build a better future, that is something we cannot afford to take for granted.

A Passion
for
Plants and
Animals

I was astounded to read that Americans own somewhere around one trillion pets. That's TRILLION, not billion. I suppose that number includes hamsters, guppies, bunnies and the like. Still, we are second to none in our consuming interest in maintaining animals in our domestic environments. There have been some very interesting studies recently about pets and plants and the effect they have on their owners in terms of stress reduction, lowering blood pressure and even of lengthening their lives. Researchers have discovered that patients who nurture pets and plants actually have a more successful rate of recovery from illnesses and disease than those without them. It seems that they tap a nurturing instinct that is life-enhancing and common to us all.

I realize that coming home from a hectic workday and sitting down to look at your fish or pet turtle (instead of more traditional ways of relaxing) may sound pretty crazy. But experiments have shown that different interactions between pet and owner can be quite therapeutic. The intimacy of petting, stroking, hugging, even talking to an animal, for instance, has measurable effects on blood pressure and stress reduction. The unconditional love which seems to be so difficult to find among humans appears to be automatic with pets. In addition, they inspire our more playful nature. They make us laugh.

I'm not suggesting that these things are available to us only through our association with the animal kingdom. Anyone who has ever spent a sleepless night listening to the howling and screeching of neighborhood pets might want to argue the point vigorously, especially about animals and stress reduction. I do find it interesting, though, that what we sometimes observe in animal behavior is what we would like to see in humans.

It's not often that we find a person who will love us without regard to age, fortune or physical condition. How many people always greet us with enthusiasm and are acutely sensitive to our moods? Small wonder that we often treat our pets like people, sometimes even better. I know of a certain poodle that is fed only the choicest cuts of beef (cooked medium rare), has its own wardrobe, a birthday party once a year with cake and only pedigreed guests in attendance, and even has a prepaid plot in a local pet cemetery.

There are obedience schools that issue diplomas to dogs wearing mortar boards on their heads during the graduation ceremony. Some churches will bless your animal, while one in California even performs marriage ceremonies for pets that have mating on their minds. And isn't it interesting how we have become to a degree desensitized to T.V. violence and

torture where people are involved, but when an animal is in any way victimized, become indignant and write letters of protest.

I don't pretend to know much about animal behavior—I'm still too puzzled by the human kind. I do have my cat, Cocktail, and between us there is a sort of understanding. We're both very independent creatures who need a place to call home and the freedom to get away once in a while. He likes his catnip and I like my California Chardonnay '82. We both like classical music and dislike visits to the doctor/ veterinarian.

Quite frankly, I've never really thought of my cat in any therapeutic sense. He does make me laugh sometimes when he falls on his back, legs in the air, and snoozes in the warm sun. I'm sure he thinks I'm funny too.

If raising and caring for pets helps us learn how to be more loving and caring friends, lovers, parents, etc., then we are fortunate in having them. If they put us more in touch with all living things and our responsibilities to tend to them carefully and lovingly, then we can indeed be thankful that trillions of them are around.

I know that everybody thinks their dog or cat is the most beautiful, has the most wonderful personality, or is the most intelligent. Well, let me tell you about mine. He doesn't have pedigree papers but he's certainly not just an ordinary alley cat. He appeared at my doorstep one rainy night—frightened, hungry, alone and wet. He couldn't have been more than three inches from the ground—a tiny pack of bones. (No way did I imagine that he would grow to be the size and weight of a baby hippopotamus.) At any rate, from his first pleading

meow, though I had many times sworn that my busy schedule was not conducive to pets, I knew he was mine.

After a good feeding, I examined him carefully: lovely gray coat, large green eyes, perky ears and a cocked tail. His name came easily—Cocktail (no reference to the gin and tonic variety).

It soon became apparent that Cocktail was no ordinary cat. Yes, he had the usual traits: independence, a certain aloofness, a natural knowledge of human frailty. But there was something more—something deeper, mystical, all-knowing. My friends called it *cat psychosis,* but Cocktail and I knew differently.

One day I was looking through a psychological journal and found an interesting classified ad. It stated that a researcher was seeking cats who seemed to have behavior patterns which revealed the possibility of high intelligence. He was in the process of creating and standardizing a cat I.Q. test.

Always eager to aid in the advancement of science, I answered the ad. Within a few days I received a box containing a ball, a string, a bell, a pencil and an instruction sheet. I could hardly wait to begin the experiment. Of course Cocktail had his own ideas and it wasn't until a week or so later that he wandered over to me, ready for the game.

Each item was scored according to function such as approach, activity, planning, execution, attention span and so on. For instance, when you rolled the ball to the cat, did he play with it? How did he play with it? Did he lose interest after a moment or did he remain with the task at hand? Did he retrieve the ball? Did he seem to enjoy the game?

These activities, plus general traits, were written on the scoring sheet and put into a self-addressed envelope to go to the researcher. A response was promised shortly.

Cocktail didn't object to the many activities. In fact he seemed intrigued with the attention and the diversity of the

problems presented to him. I must admit, I lost interest before he did. The test included a questionnaire that I found rather disturbing. It asked, "Does your cat recognize you as its keeper and choose to come to you rather than others in a group?" I couldn't honestly say that Cocktail selected me particularly out of a group. In fact, it seemed as though he selected that person most allergic to cats. Does that mean he is wise? nasty? intuitive? or what?

After a few weeks I received an excited letter from the experimenter. Cocktail had the highest I.Q. score of any cat tested so far—a cat genius!

It's not easy living with a genius—even a cat genius! There is no way of knowing what he's thinking, what he's about to do or when he'll do it. Cocktail seemed to sense the triumph. He seems to move with more grace, spends more time preening himself and eats only the more expensive cat foods.

We spend millions of dollars each year on cat food, vets and flea collars. Our cats are oblivious to their expense. They reject a mackerel dinner with the flippancy of a princess abandoning paté with truffles. They do what they want when they want and are ready to scratch you without a qualm if you interfere with their needs. Still, we love them, care for them, worry about them, plan their food and take them to the vet at any sign of a disorder. It's a cat's life, indeed!

Cocktail is sitting on an embroidered pillow I picked up in Korea and to which, over my protestations, he's become attached. He is partially awake, knowing, I'm certain, that I'm writing about him, but feigning total disinterest.

Sometimes I wonder who needs the I.Q. test!

It took me a long time to understand Papa's enthusiasm for growing things. Not until I was on my own did I find any satisfaction in scattering a few seeds and watching them grow. But I still remember Papa's excitement every spring, anticipating a new crop of flowers in the backyard. Actually I regarded it as some sort of seasonal madness that overtook him. What else could account for working fertilizer into the soil with such elation?

It was just a small suburban plot that we had then, but Papa always made use of every square inch of it. He was continually going outside to look things over. He'd pull a few weeds between the corn stalks, give a little support to the peas, and gently pat the zucchini vines, pleased to be a part of it all. Papa was a true nurturer. Not a year went by that he didn't cultivate that little patch. He used to bring me out and show me, with great enthusiasm, when the seeds first broke through the soil.

"You see what a miracle this is, Felice?" he would exclaim. "You get so much with just a little care and love." For my part, however, knowing that a small green speck would in time grow into a cauliflower was hardly my idea of a miracle. Still, I'd muster my enthusiasm and humor him with, "Yes, Papa. It's wonderful!" Later I would come to understand.

Papa fully agreed with Luther Burbank, who said that, "Love is the secret to improved plant breeding." It's quite an amazing statement from a man of science, but devoted gardeners, indoor and outdoor, know it to be true. It's only part of another truth which says that all life, not only human, is affected positively by love.

It has become fairly well accepted now that, like human beings, plants respond to the warmth of the human voice, have feelings, can sense moods, and may even have musical preferences. Perhaps the reason I don't have too much luck

with house plants is that they don't like my music. A constant dose of opera, after all, is not everyone's cup of tea. Puccini and Richard Strauss and Wagner may admittedly get the best plant down.

We have developed plant hotels and plant sitters, both available to offer care and company when we are away. There are plant doctors and even plant psychiatrists, I am told, for the really temperamental types. There are plant probes that can be inserted into the soil and actually hum when conditions are just right. My favorite is a plant stand that says, "Thank you," whenever you tend to the plant that sits on it.

There is some interesting work being done right now in mental institutions and drug rehabilitation centers. Patients are being given seeds or small cuttings of plants and encouraged to tend them. It is their plant; and its well-being, in fact its very survival, is in their hands. The results from these studies have been quite exciting and very positive. Whatever the reasons, these activities seem to bring back meaning into otherwise confused lives. It also brings a sense of creation, a sense of having accomplished something positive and good, and the reinforcement which comes from the knowledge of a job well done. This same finding has been supported among the elderly in convalescent homes. Nurturing seems to tap essential feelings of dignity and inner peace.

I have friends who have pots of African violets in every room of their house. Regardless of their setting, they seem to flourish. They develop gigantic, rich green leaves and an assortment of strikingly colorful blooms. I have never seen the likes of them anywhere else. I continually ask my friends for their secret. Their answer is always simply and matter-of-factly the same: "Just water, a little light and some love." The statement is more profound than it sounds.

Plants ask for little more than light, water, fertilizer, and some kind attention now and then. Perhaps people ask for a

bit more, but the dynamics are essentially the same, whether it is a prize-winning squash, a little pot of grape ivy, or a human being. In fact, it may be one of the answers to the question of what life is all about.

A Passion for Change

The human mind is a miracle. Once it accepts a new idea or learns a new fact, it stretches forever and never goes back to its original dimension. It is limitless. No one has even guessed its potential. Still, so many of us spend a lifetime marking boundaries and defining limits. Young children in their innocence have not yet learned their limitations and so joyfully and instinctively stretch to learn, and so should we all!

I remember a wooden plaque that hung on the kitchen wall in the house where I grew up. A simple proverb in Italian imparted the wisdom of the world in capsule form: "Siamo vecchie troppo presto, e troppo tarde intellengente." (We get too soon old and too late smart.) It wasn't until much later in life that I allowed the significance of that familiar message to settle in my mind. It reminded me that a human life is indeed short, especially when we attempt to reach its full potential. It told me that each moment of our lives was esssential in bringing us closer to realizing that potential. Yet to arrive near the end only to reflect on how much was missed along the way is one of the greatest of human tragedies.

Each day we should learn something new about the world, and in so doing we will never again be the same. If we feel inconsequential or that our lives are becoming stagnant, we should celebrate the limitless capacity we have to experience more.

To place proper value on learning, we need to recognize a basic law of nature: *That which does not grow, dies.* Children who watch television for six hours a day (which is the norm) will probably develop a passive attitude toward their world. Indoors, they will miss the birth of spring or the first soft snows of winter. A life that is lived within fixed limits and that travels only the well worn paths of habit and routine is diminished greatly by failing to recognize that we live in a constant state of change. *That which does not grow, dies.*

We often grow up to comments such as, "I had to learn this, so will *you*," with the flip side being, "If it was good enough for *me*, it's good enough for *you*." Adults often adopt this line of reasoning when they must confront the whys and wherefores of children. In the process they deny them their precious need to know. Think of the possibilities for learning when we say to another, "I don't know the answer but let's find out together. Together we can unravel some of the mys-

tery and explore the wonder that is everywhere about us."

Too many of us settle on the notion that education is something that took place at a fixed period in our lives. We mistakenly classify people's intelligence according to the number of years that they attended school. Rather we should regard education as a never ending pursuit and see that the truest measure of intelligence is a dedication to continue the process throughout life. Some of the most ignorant people I know have advanced degrees to show for their education while some of the wisest people I know never made it past high school. It's not really a paradox if we keep in mind that learning is not confined to a classroom and is not imparted solely by people whom we designate as teachers. We are all teachers and we are all students. I believe that it is the mark of true wisdom to appreciate and profit from both roles.

Each day is a fresh beginning, a little life unto itself. Most of us have struggled to live up to this moment, to come to this time. Opportunities for growth, a chance to learn something new—some things in life come along only once, and it is our choice alone whether we seize them or not.

The old advertising slogan, "So simple a child can do it," has taken on new meaning for me.

For a long while I've been intimidated by the specter of a computerized world. Everyone tells me how simple computers are. I've been to seminars showing me the unbelievable time-saving possibilities of these electronic marvels. They are especially helpful, I am told, for anyone who writes as much as I do. I can no longer fight this fact. I know that it's true; I've seen it work. They use little space and can do things in moments which require me, a pair of scissors, and a roll of

tape, many hours to accomplish.

I am not fighting against our entry into the computer age. Far be it from me to resist the inevitable. The future is here and it comes equipped with a keyboard, a key pad, a viewing screen and a printout.

The fact is that the future arrived in my office a few weeks ago. There is now a personal computer sitting on the table where I used to spread out my legal pad and pens. (I should add that I am advanced enough to use a felt tip pen, not a quill.) My secretary operates the new machine. She has taken to it like an Italian baby to spaghetti. I stand over her shoulder marveling, as if she were doing sleight of hand or card tricks.

Since this computer is here and ready to be used, or, ready to be accessed, as they say in the computer world, I thought it wise to make use of its fullest potential. But how do I get access to this marvel, since anything more complicated than a dependable old wall-mounted pencil sharpener exposes my mechanical illiteracy?

I know that children have no fear of the future, so that seemed a good place to seek help. I have a nephew, Ronald, in elementary school, who has a near total mastery of anything mechanical, and this includes computers. I told him this thing was in the office and I needed help.

"Does it have a dual disc drive?" he asked without hesitation. "They're better if they're built in." I was unable to answer him, not knowing what a disc is, let alone whether my new acquisition has one. He produced a box of floppy discs from his room. I recognized that the computer in my office does indeed have slots for them.

We continued to discuss, in somewhat mystical language, my system. When I asked if it would be possible for the computer to do certain things, I was corrected. "Computers don't 'do things'; they 'perform functions,' " he said. "They don't 'hook up' to other computers; they 'interface.' You

don't call it 'that little thing with the two cups that the phone fastens to,' the proper term is 'modem.' "

I had no difficulty being tutored by my twelve-year-old nephew. He never spoke condescendingly to me. He took the machine for granted and has simply accepted the fact that computers are now a way of life. He plays with them and does his homework on them and even creates programs for them.

I, on the other hand, am awed by what this equipment can do. It can interchange paragraphs, switch words around and even correct my spelling. It informs me of its limitations, takes commands and asks questions. It even seems to have a sense of diplomacy. Rather than accuse me of making an error, it prints "One of us has made a mistake!" It never gets tired and is always patient and ready to go when I am.

I think it was somewhat normal for me to be leery of computers. They represent a break with some very familiar habits and traditions. It is only human to instinctively avoid anything that shifts radically from the acceptable, comfortable past. But the world is governed by ceaseless change and we must therefore establish links with the present and future as well as the past. Computer technology is an excellent case in point, as the newest systems grow obsolete in only a few years, or even months.

This ability to see, experience and accept the new is one of our saving characteristics. To be fearful of tomorrow, to close ourselves to possibilities, to resist the inevitable, to advocate standing still when all else is moving forward, is to lose touch. If we accept the new with joy and wonder, we can move gracefully into each tomorrow. More often than not, the children shall lead us.

I was recently introduced to one of those talking cars—the ones that have little recorded messages for people: "Excuse me but you forgot to close the door completely." "Turn off the lights, please." "Oh! Oh! You've left the key in the ignition." When I first heard of this innovation, I remember shaking my head in amazement and wondering, "What next?" Of course, I wouldn't mind a car that would slip in an occasional "Hi, Leo, you look terrific today!"

It's interesting how we sometimes approach, with mixed emotions, the benefits of modern technology. Instinct makes us a little cautious in the face of change, especially when it threatens our established traditions or habits. Take watches, for example. The fact that my friend's multi-function digital watch tells time is not nearly as important to him as the thrill of the intergallactic war game that it includes and he can play whenever he's bored. On the other hand, they tell me that in the not-too-distant future our wrist watches will be mini-centers of communication, receiving televised transmissions, even serving as telephones.

There are predictions that we will become more visual and less verbal in the coming century. Video discs will supposedly replace books to a large extent. My first reaction to that is NEVER. It conjures a vision of our libraries being converted into learning arcades with people somehow electronically wired, each in his or her own little cubicle. I suppose in each of us there is an irrepressible traditionalist. But I also remember from a history lesson long ago that Gutenberg's invention of movable type was met with great resistance because it threatened the tradition of orally passing along information and telling stories.

Medical advances promise to extend lives well beyond present expectancies; and, of course, this raises many questions for us all. As with any revolutionary change in humankind, there is a fear of tampering with natural order. Caroline

Bird in her book, *The Good Years,* sees something positive in the wealth of resources which a large population of older people would bring. She writes, "They will become the innovators, drawing on their lengthening historical perspective to see a wider canvas of the human experience."

It's truly difficult to keep a perspective when we deal with the unknown. But again, it's helpful to draw from past experience to judge more reasonably where the future is leading us. The Wright brothers were told repeatedly that if God had intended men to fly, He would have given them wings. Only sixty years later, men were walking on the moon.

I'll always be skeptical of the idea that in any aspect of our lives we will require less human contact—all technological innovations to the contrary. Case in point: A few years ago a good friend received one of those questionnaires from a computer dating service. "Just fill it out and send it in and we'll get back to you," it said. He decided that a little experiment was in order.

He was not exactly truthful in his answers. In fact, he made himself sound more like Attila the Hun or Jack the Ripper than a prospective date. He did this only to see if a computer could find a match for the completely unlovable person he invented. He was not surprised, but a little wary, when a reply came within days informing him of the dozens of individuals on the computer's compatibility index who were possibly right for him!

I know that computer dating has indeed helped bring people together, but being the hopeless romantic that I am, I'm more inclined to believe that the real magic still lies in two people personally discovering each other and not in the mating of two data processing cards.

I don't believe that modern technology is somehow foreclosing on our humanity. It's comforting to know that there are human constants like truth, beauty, love, laughter—so

many complex and also amazingly simple aspects of our makeup that will always be irreplaceable because they will always be uniquely human.

The only certitudes I've found in life are death and change. One is an end, the other a beginning. Change is life. Without change there would be no growth, no understanding, no relating and no surprises. We are by nature changing beings. Still, we seem to fear and resist it more than any other aspect of life.

Healthy human beings welcome the opportunity to adapt to new experiences. In fact they're quite comfortable in a constant state of change. They are alive to the possibility of becoming someone new each moment. Only habit and apathy prevent the rest of us from having the same outlook.

When we don't care, or resign ourselves to patterns and routines, we begin to stagnate. We are prone to accept the comfortable illusion that life is a series of habits and conditioned responses. In actuality this is a comfort more like a disease, which leads to a kind of intellectual and emotional death. We can allow ourselves and a dynamic world to go to waste. Ellen Glasgow, an American novelist, said, "The only difference between a rut and a grave are their dimensions."

To accept new ideas and give up old values and habits is not always comfortable. It is often easier for us to deny that there may be more appropriate, more creative possibilities for our lives. We fail to understand that when we resist these potentialities, life becomes at best a continual struggle; at worst, it passes us by and we are left alone and lonely.

We constantly hear that there are people who will never change, that they can't change for one reason or another. It's a

familiar litany and utter nonsense! Change is always possible unless our brain has stopped functioning. It is a choice that need not be wrenching or threatening. Adapting to life's currents is a natural process, and, in the final analysis, the path of least resistance.

A few years ago my next door neighbor, who was in his seventies, was served an ultimatum by his children: his desire to find a new life after the death of his wife of many years was an impossible dream and must be abandoned. "You're too old and set in your ways to change now," they told him. Perhaps they felt it was time for him to collect his memories instead of charging ahead to make new ones. Happily he was wise enough not to listen. His family was shocked when they heard that he had gone dancing at the local recreation center. They were appalled when he met a lovely lady and decided to remarry! "There's no fool like an old fool—you're going to know nothing but misery," they all told him. This man died three happy years later while on a wonderful trip to New York, a city he'd never seen but always wanted to. He fell peacefully smiling into the arms of his new wife.

Of course the new, the untested, the uncertain cause their share of anxiety. But any change is better than none and most change is for the better. It has the power to uplift, to heal, to stimulate, surprise, open new doors, bring fresh experience and create excitement in life. It elevates us from mediocrity and saves us from false security. Certainly it is worth the risk! We must also keep in mind that it is only through change that we can continue to experiment with ourselves and our lives.

Change also causes us to alter our perceptions so that we are never locked into our opinions and feelings about each other. We may find that cousin Fred, who has always been a crashing bore, or our neighbor who is standoffish, are one day changed. Or perhaps it is *we* who are changed in how we perceive them.

When we find that life is a bore, that existence is a chore, that the wonder and magic of being alive is vanishing, it is possible that it is because we are resisting change. If we have become trapped in a dull, lifeless rhythm, we must resolve to give up our resistance and dance to a new step. When we do, we will surely rediscover that change is our greatest source of happiness, stimulation and continued growth.

A Passion for Overcoming Frustration

Of all the living creatures in our world, only humans accumulate problems and wear them like a yoke around their necks. Some of us even have a remarkable facility for embracing the frustrations of others. We love making other people's frustrations ours! As if our own were not enough! There is no question that conflict does darken the world around us, and it is entirely human to recognize and try to avoid it. But in meeting conflict, we need to understand that the process doesn't end once we solve a problem; there will be more ahead. The positive aspect of this is that in those experiences there also exists great potential for growth.

My car sometimes decides to make noises, but only for my ears. When I become fearful that it will fall to pieces, I take it in to be checked. I tell the mechanic about the problem and we listen together. Magically, the noises disappear. So we take it for a spin around the block and it purrs more quietly than on the day I bought it. I make an utter fool of myself trying to recreate the noise and assure him it's real. The mechanic scratches his head and says he has never heard any such sound. So I leave and there is the noise again!

Phones are also sources of frustration. I am constantly getting busy signals. If I do get through, I'm put on hold or get that tinny sound of piped-in music which drives me mad. After five songs someone comes on the line and asks, "Are you being helped?" "What can I do for you?" I re-explain what I want. "I'll put you through," they say, and in an instant there is an emptiness and silence—we've been disconnected. I redial and go through the whole process again. This time I'm informed that I need to be transferred to another department. Back we go to the switchboard operator, who directs me to someone else. Now I get another chance to tell my story. Of course, this is only the third time.

The very ultimate in frustration for me comes in the form of instruction manuals. I try to avoid them, but once a year or so I'll get something that comes in a box with two of the most dreaded words in the English language written on it: Assembly Required.

Nothing can reduce me to a jibbering idiot faster than a set of instructions with a bunch of parts, cryptic diagrams, and a jargon that defies rational explanation. For example: "Insert rocker arm assembly over carriage bolt while releasing preset selector wheel (See Figure A)." Inevitably, at the end of the whole operation, I discover an extra part, or worse—a part is missing, which tells me that this thing that I've put together is going to be defective; it's going to shake or fall apart and do

something it shouldn't.

While I'm on the subject of frustrations, why is it that every time I open the utensil drawer, the first thing I see is the nutcracker? That is, until I want to crack a nut—then it has gone into hiding. And why is it that the section of the newspaper I most want to read has crash landed in the shrubbery where it's torn or wet beyond salvation?

And what about when the dessert cart is wheeled over to your table at a restaurant and you see desserts that were made in heaven but you know that one more bite will bring on indigestion. Of course, you order it anyway. Who can resist? And you spend the rest of the night reading a book because of that one additional bite.

Does anyone else feel these frustrations or is it that I am more neurotic than most? I only know it makes me feel better when I air them out, and especially when I find that other people feel them too. In fact, they will often share very helpful suggestions for coping that I hadn't thought of.

For instance, it was suggested that I take the dictionary and learn a new word when I'm put on telephone hold. Someone else suggested that for an extra few dollars most stores will assemble items which need putting together. The dessert problem can be solved by looking at the dessert cart before ordering dinner and planning accordingly.

It's nice to learn that I am among millions who share petty frustrations. We all have them. They are as much a part of life as death and taxes. It does us good to recognize them for what they are, have a good laugh and let them go. When we do, they seem to fall into perspective. After all, I know it's frustrating, but what other choice is there?

I don't know about you, but I can't throw anything away. I still have neckties that are five inches wide and sport coats with one inch lapels. I have term papers I wrote in elementary school on the effects of the Industrial Revolution, and postcards I received from Aunt Pina when she visited Venice, Italy, in 1940.

I keep promising myself that I am going to have a monumental cleaning one day and get rid of it all. But just as I get about doing it I start feeling the romantic pangs which I attach to these inanimate objects. My memories give them heart and in no way can I throw out things of the heart.

My mother gave me that tie on my twentieth birthday. I traveled around the world in those pants. That term paper was my first truly researched literary masterpiece. Perhaps someday someone will reprint it as part of a biography: *Leo—The Early Years*. So the boxes get more plentiful, the bags take up more space and the house gets smaller. I even have cancelled checks and income tax forms from 1942.

When I was deeply involved in the study of Zen, I remember that my teachers had nothing more than the clothes on their backs and a small bag full of their belongings which they flung over their shoulders. In a few moments they could pack and be off, free to roam where they willed. I can't imagine what I'd do if an emergency made it essential that I leave my home. How many moving vans would I require?

I know people who rent space in order to store possessions for which there is no longer any room in their house. They have the crystal they were given on their wedding day still neatly and safely packed in its original box. They are even saving the white ribbons. They are stored next to the bone china which they have never used. They are not quite sure what they are saving these things for, or why. They just sit there. I am certain that heaven supplies its own crystal and bone china. It doesn't need the few pieces they've been

saving for so many years.

We are part of a society that loves obsolescence. We never totally wear things out. We just store them somewhere. After all, we say, it's still good and we may need it someday. If we keep it long enough, we rationalize, it may even be worth a great deal of money as an antique! We collect used pipe, odd pieces of rugs, battered suitcases, broken ironing boards, picture frames, old 45 and 78 rpm records—you name it, there's a collector for it.

Philosophers for centuries have reminded us of the uselessness of collecting. They have warned us, as Buddha did, that the more we have, the more we have to worry about. I have never seen a statue or painting of Jesus of Nazareth, Lao Tzu, or Buddha with mounds of travel gear, or carrying huge packs of belongings. It is always we simple humans who have loaded elephants, camel trains, or trucks.

As time passes we often become the slave of our things. We are fearful of taking a holiday because we're concerned about our belongings being left alone. A friend has a new Mercedes which he never parks in a parking lot or on a crowded street for fear of someone scratching it. But he is equally worried about leaving it on a side street for fear that it will be stolen. It's interesting to ponder whether he owns the car or the car owns him. But we are all in some way as guilty as he.

I wish I had a solution to the disease, but it just seems to get worse. The more we have, the more we seem to want and need, and the more we have to be concerned about.

A poet, D. Johnson, recently wrote to me and included a work which deals with the horrors of collecting. It's nice to know that others are in this quandary, too. The poem is called, *Collecting: A Modern Paradigm.* The conclusion sends chills through me. It says,

"So, you're either a collector or something collected or both.

And who knows
When we're displaced by our own junk
We might meet at the top of the heap."

I don't know whether I'll succeed, but the next time I pass a closet I'm going to try to throw out all the things in it which I've not used for three or more years. That means more than half the closet. I promise to let you know if I succeed!

I'm not a total disbeliever in ghosts, goblins or mysterious phantoms. In fact, I must confess that there are certain occurrences in my house that defy any rational explanation. For instance, one of the great and perpetual mysteries is where my socks disappear. I can't seem to keep a matching pair. I am continually having to buy new socks. After the first wash, some of them simply vanish.

They never go in pairs, which wouldn't be so bad. The annoying thing is that I am left with one green sock, one blue and one black. I have accumulated a huge pile which I dare not throw out lest a matching sock reappear as mysteriously as it disappeared. So far this hasn't happened.

They certainly can't just walk off. Or can they? I have become slightly neurotic about seeing that socks go into the washer and dryer in pairs, but still they vanish. I've checked the machines for teeth, for escape hatches or mysterious tubes that might eat up or siphon off my socks. This would account for the mystery, but there are no such things in either the washer or the dryer. Check your machine if you don't believe me. I have come to believe that this is just another one of life's frustrations. I still suspect a phantom somewhere in the laundry room just waiting for the rinse cycle to end.

Every bit as strange as the disappearing socks is the myster-

ious appearance of clothes hangers. I have hundreds in the house and I can't imagine where they come from. I can't ever remember buying a wire clothes hanger, and no matter how many I return to the cleaners, give away or put into the trash, the closets remain full of them. If I had a choice, I'd rather have socks magically appear than hangers.

Speaking of household mysteries, how is it that cookies vanish even when I don't eat them? Especially the chocolate chip-macadamia nut clusters? I fill the cookie jar on the kitchen sink at great expense. (Do you know that at some cookie stores the cookies are now weighed and sold by the ounce?) Within days they're gone!

This is especially true on weekends when they seem to vanish faster than ever. I know it's not me. I steadfastly ration myself to one or two a day. No one else in the house, including the cat, who loves chocolate, will accept the blame. Still, when I crave a cookie most, the cookie monster, or whatever it, he, or she might be, has been there before me.

I've tried giving up cookies, but before long, I go into withdrawal. So I fill up the cookie jar and resign myself to ending up with only a portion of them.

I'm convinced also that certain cooking ingredients go the way of the cookies. As much as I love cooking and creating gourmet dishes, I'm at a loss to explain how just the ingredient I need is always missing. Where has the vanilla gone? The curry? The cumin? The oregano? I buy these things in giant cans and bottles. In fact, an entire kitchen wall is covered with exotic herbs and seasonings—but where is the one I need?

I once believed that I was alone in these mysteries, but the more I risk talking about them the more people admit to having had similar experiences. I have a friend who constantly loses underwear, another who can't keep shampoos in the house, another who never sends anything to be ironed or

cleaned and still has enough wire hangers to make mobiles, planters, wall hangings, back scratchers, or hundreds of other exotic things.

I often wonder if the green sock that's disappeared ends up in someone else's wash. And there's something very strange about the fact that my neighbor never runs out of vanilla!

I think that most people would agree that, though a bit eccentric, I am basically a rational man. I can't help but feel that there must be a good explanation for all of these phenomena. It's obvious that I, for one, have not yet found it. So the mysteries continue.

However, I have found that the sock problem has reached epidemic proportions all over the United States. I am not alone. Friends and family, men and women alike, from all over the country, have offered comfort and helpful suggestions.

There were the practical people who suggested that I simply pin, staple or use string to keep socks together. I've even been told of commercially made clips which guaranteed that the socks would come out as they went in, two by two.

Other practical suggestions included going through the sock drawer at periodic intervals to check on mismatched or escaped single socks.

An entrepreneur came up with a sure-fire plan for selling one-of-a-kind socks, or arranging for mismatched socks to be traded on the open market.

An artist suggested that being fearful of mixing colors is a cultural hangup. She encouraged me to wear mismatched socks fearlessly. "The more outrageous the color combinations the better," she said, "like flowers in a garden."

A less daring person solved the problem by purchasing all his socks in the same color. In this way, he assured me, ". . . I'd not solve the mystery, but I would do away with my problem. After all, isn't life just a series of compromises?"

It's surprising how many people wash their socks in a nylon mesh bag like the ones one gets in the produce department of a grocery store. This way, people say, you wash socks apart from everything else, yet keep them together.

A scientist assures me that it has been scientifically proven that socks disappear and coat hangers keep proliferating because socks are the larvae of coat hangers.

A believer in reincarnation offered that those of us who have a sock problem are paying for some heinous crime we committed in some previous life. Perhaps, he suggests, we were foot muggers who purloined footwear to satisfy some fiendish fetish.

In 1975, even Jules Feiffer, the cartoonist, expressed his puzzlement about missing socks. In his cartoon, his pathetic figure gets down to his last two pair of socks, when his washing machine sends him a message which reads "Quit trifling with the laws of nature and bring the machine more socks!"

Perhaps the most astounding story came from a husband/father who does the family laundry. He was hounded by his family about their missing socks, but to his great frustration was unable to find a solution. One day a disappearing blue sock, another day a materialized green sock. The problem reached its peak when his wife confronted him and in suspicious tones demanded to know about a strange piece of lingerie which had mysteriously appeared in the laundry. It certainly wasn't hers! As the ensuing battle raged and reached a peak, the mystery was solved when their dog casually came into the laundry room bearing a sock from their neighbor's wash!

There is a psychological theory which suggests that we become less frustrated with problems when we learn how common they are. There is a companion theory which states that the more alternatives we have for solving a problem, the

less will be the frustration in trying to solve it. I am therefore grateful to my wise and caring friends and family who took the time from their busy and significant schedules to help me. Although the mystery remains, I shall sleep better now, knowing what good company I keep!

I rarely allow things to irritate me anymore, but one thing that always succeeds in doing so is waiting. Time is so precious, I can't imagine how some people can feel totally unconcerned about squandering it for us. Now, if we want to waste our own time, that's up to us. But I object to others thinking their time has more value than mine.

I have a very wonderful friend. In almost every way he's a delight, but I've never known him to arrive anywhere on time. If he arranges an appointment with you for ten o'clock, you can be certain that you'll be hearing from him at ten-thirty with a frantic telephone call letting you know that he's running a bit late. It's doubly annoying when you've struggled to get up early to have breakfast with him, at his enthusiastic suggestion, only to sit around for an hour awaiting his convenience.

I fully believe that annoyances should be verbalized immediately before they grow into monsters that threaten loving relationships. I have spoken to my friend repeatedly about this lateness. Each time he has a perfectly legitimate excuse: his car wouldn't start; he didn't get his wakeup call; he was winding up a most important meeting with a client; his telephone lines failed. I have no reason to doubt him—perhaps he is prone to catastrophes. But I begin to question all these things happening so consistently. It always upsets me that this man has caused me to waste so many precious hours

of my life when I could have been active and productive. This never seems to have occurred to him.

Of course I could decline his invitations. That would certainly stop the problem. But he's such a stimulating, generous and amusing person (when he's there), I would hate losing him as a friend.

I have this same problem with doctors. My appointment is for 1 P.M. I miss lunch to get to his office on time through crowded freeway traffic. I arrive a comfortable ten minutes early and am informed casually that the doctor is running a bit late. I am asked to take a seat and told that he'll be with me as soon as possible. One hour later I am ushered into a small visiting room and again made to wait, this time in a state of uncomfortable undress for another fifteen minutes. The doctor finally appears without so much as an apology and asks, "Well, now, how are we doing today?" It's no surprise that he finds my blood pressure elevated!

I always seem to be the person who arrives on time to meetings, dinner parties, or whatever. I am also always the one who must sit and wait while the others straggle in.

So many people are casual about time that I'm beginning to think I must be the neurotic one. They tell me that being punctual is a sign of obsessive-compulsive tendencies. But I can't feel good about being late. It seems to me to be very presumptuous of those who think that their time has more value than another's.

Naturally there are occasions when it is truly impossible to be punctual. We're caught in an emergency, tied up in traffic, or a myriad of other situations. But for me, it becomes pathological when it happens with almost predictable consistency.

I know that there are many like myself who can identify with the problem. Perhaps we should join forces and simply refuse to wait, or take off on our own after a considerate

fifteen minutes of waiting.

The Swiss are among the most punctual people in the world. Perhaps it is because they learn from childhood that trains arrive and leave as scheduled, theatre curtains rise as indicated in the program and no one is admitted late, and stores close at their appointed hour. Maybe that is why people without a time sense are so often upset when dealing with Swiss society, and those of us who care about time are so delighted and relieved to be there.

Time waits for no one. I wonder if the day will ever come when we'll be brave enough to do the same.

A Passion for Giving

The great Chinese philosopher Lao Tzu wrote that "Kindness in words creates confidence, kindness in thinking creates profoundness, and kindness in giving creates love."

I've witnessed this scene in restaurants many times. Two men prepare to leave and one grabs for the check. The other attempts to snatch it away from him and the familiar tug of war commences. Each is determined to make his gesture, even if it means straight-arming the other all the way to the cashier. I know the situation, I know the feeling.

The giving and receiving that is a natural part of any relationship often becomes an epic struggle of "whose turn is it now?" Certainly no one wants to be perpetually on the receiving or giving end, but when two people give freely there shouldn't be any need to keep score. That's true whether the giving comes from the pocketbook or the heart.

Children are most often associated with a perpetual "give me" attitude and we tend to be more tolerant of it because they are children. We sometimes forget that they also love to give—a drawing, a favorite rock, a clay impression. Remember what a joyful discovery it was when we first learned that we could make others happy by giving. It was a joy that never grew old. Still, there was always a temptation to equate giving with buying, which was a notion not easily discounted in a society that is so *thing* oriented. With so many occasions for gift giving, we can easily attach more importance to the gift than to the occasion for which it is given.

One of my students told me of a different tradition that is shared by her family. Rather than exchange gifts every 25th of December, they do it at random times throughout the year. Instead of the hectic seasonal shopping experience, each family member waits for the right gift to come along and then gives it as a Christmas present even if it's in June.

If that all sounds like it's not in keeping with the spirit of things, quite the contrary was true in this family. We should be reminded every Christmas that presents are but a token symbol of a far more significant gift. This spirit should be with us the year round. My student felt that the traditional day

was made more wondrous, less commercial, and the focus was more highly spiritual. Their way, the spirit of Christmas extends throughout the year and it becomes something they want to do instead of something dictated by custom.

But the spirit of giving comes in many forms, and in this country there's certainly no shortage of selfless contributions of time, money and caring wherever it is needed. Last year over 40 million people worked an average of nine hours a week as volunteers in hospitals, schools, convalescent homes, health agencies, international relief organizations, etc. So often statistics are misleading, but in this case there is a positive commitment to give where it is needed and where only tangible rewards are offered.

Receiving is another part of giving and it's not always the easiest thing to do with grace. A friend of mine is thrown into a dither every Christmas, mailing out cards as she receives them from others. Getting an unexpected present without reciprocating is a particular horror for her to contemplate. Everything must be entered in a ledger and a balance must be struck for her own piece of mind. It seems that she came from a family where very meticulous attention was always given to equality in all things. Giving to one meant having to give to all. What was no doubt intended to be a system of fairness probably ended in promoting more pettiness and jealousy than anything else.

One who gives in love, whether it is a dazzling present or a thoughtful compliment, is always repaid when it is received in the same spirit. Just as listening is at least half of the art of communicating, the art of receiving with joy, appreciation and sensitivity is every bit as important as the giving.

Sometimes we need to be reminded just how important it is that we participate in the welfare and growth of others. It's all too easy to fold our arms and ask, "What can *I* do?," or make the all-too-familiar statement, "Sorry, no time." For many, this can become a way of life.

When I was teaching in the public schools, I can remember the many teachers' meetings and seminars we were obliged to attend. The purported purpose was to come together in order to focus more clearly on the main goals of education. Always, no matter how we worded our objectives or devised our formulas, the one recurring theme year after year was the need for total involvement. From the policymakers to the implementers and the recipient students, the key ingredient in a successful education program was the active participation of everyone.

Anyone who has ever studied successful business practices knows that one of the main requirements is that of working together, from the administrative level, to each worker. Where this is accomplished, the result is invariably a successful business with high achievement and production levels. There is a definite correlation.

I remember a retired doctor who came to one of the schools where I taught. He told the prinicipal that he lived nearby and that he wanted to volunteer his services in whatever capacity he was needed. He wanted to help out in the classroom. He had no relatives in attendance or any vested interest in making the offer. He simply wanted to help, as an aide or a tutor, to share some of his knowledge and experience. In retirement he finally had plenty of time and had chosen this place and this time to extend himself. He was determined to continue to be a positive force in the lives of others.

Naturally, the principal and the teaching staff were a little overwhelmed. That sort of thing doesn't happen very much, not anywhere. The doctor soon became invaluable. He gave

much. His specialties were health education and math, but more important than what he contributed to those subjects, was his example to the children. They loved him. His warm presence and desire to become involved was a beautiful object lesson in human relations: to give of oneself without expecting anything in return is one of the finest things one human being can do for another.

Stories such as this inevitably bring on the skeptics. After all, there must be an angle. We are constantly told that nothing is free, that every investment must have a return. Certainly our doctor friend was greatly rewarded for his selfless involvement with those children, but in intangible ways. Whether or not we care to admit it, he was a model for the kind of people we most need and appreciate.

Even if we are suspicious of anyone who would give of himself to strangers, we can perhaps give some thought to our commitments closer to home. In my neighborhood there is a daycare center which I pass everyday. I see young children waiting, often into the evening, for a parent to reclaim them. Once having done that, I sometimes imagine that it's a quick dinner, a little time in front of the television set, then off to bed, ready to be packed off the next day.

I don't mean that to sound like an indictment of the many families who find it necessary to participate in such a routine. For better or worse, having two parents working is a present reality for many children. Whether by choice or economic necessity, the result is less involvement within the family.

This means that a more concentrated effort is required in seeing that the time they do have together is of the highest quality. They will have to try to be more intuitive in deciding when to stop everything and take time to listen, or give support, or just be there to love.

Each of us sooner or later realizes that our relationships with others require giving of ourselves—not only of our time,

but our sincere and caring involvement as well. Too often we close the book on the many who need us by allotting just so much of ourselves, and end by being miserly with what should be the easiest and least expensive thing to give— ourselves.

It was years ago when I first saw Hong Kong. I was told that it was the Jewel of the Orient. It's true. I was enthralled by its beauty. The vista from Victoria Peak is awesome, no matter the nature of the weather or the time of day. It's so peaceful there, high above the city, and strangely quiet, considering the explosion of activity that is just below. But I also loved the hustle and bustle of humanity around the Star Ferry, which connects the Kowloon part of the city with the Hong Kong side. Throngs of people pack the ferry boats at every hour.

I loved sitting there under a lamplight at dusk, watching on one side the changing colors of the harbor and on the other the rush of hundreds of commuters going home.

On one such evening, I noticed a very young man who sat not too far from me on the same bench. He was engrossed in a book and seemed oblivious to the noisy passengers and the deepening sunset. In the week that followed I discovered that no matter how frequently I went to my bench in the evening the same studious young man was always there.

One night he turned to me and queried, in very halting English, "Could you help me to say this word?" I found that the book which had so entranced him was an English-Chinese dictionary. After I had helped him with the word, he told me that his name was Wong and that he was trying to teach himself English. He did this so he could get a good job and make a better life for himself and his large family.

Wong and I became fast friends. We met almost nightly after that at the Star Ferry. He became my tour guide and helped me to find my way around Hong Kong. I became his English conversation teacher.

Wong's story was a poignant one. He and his family, though proud and willing to work, were existing at a level just above desperation. Wong was the eldest son of a family of eleven, and the only one working. Armed only with a dictionary, his prospects for a better life seemed a distant dream. Though I was traveling on a very limited budget, I decided that I could help. Before leaving Hong Kong, I arranged for his tuition at an English language school.

I was gone from the United States for a little over two years. When I returned there was a note from Wong. He was on his way to mastery of English. He had found a new, better-paying job and was able to raise the standard of living for everyone in his family. Enclosed in his letter was a bank note for a few dollars to repay what he saw as his debt to me.

I returned the money with a note which read something like this: "Wong, please take the money down to the Star Ferry and when you find a young man sitting there under a street lamp, trying to learn English from a dictionary, give him the money from both of us, with love." Wong got the message. I can only hope that he passed it along, and that each one touched will have touched another.

For longer than we can remember we've been reminded that love isn't love until it's given away. All over the world I've found this expressed with more and more frequency. Despite language barriers, I discovered that an expression of true love could never be misinterpreted. There were many who shared their food even though it was in meager supply. There were individuals who went miles out of their way to escort me to my destination, concerned about my getting lost. There were strangers who shared their lives, with touching vulnerability.

These were all expressions of love given freely.

Though individually we may not be capable of affecting world peace and understanding, it is a cause served by each single act of love and kindness, whenever and wherever they happen. One of our best hopes continues to lie in the individual—the small acts of kindness we can each perform, the infectious cheer we can spread, the generous act we can perform without expectation of reward, the show of tenderness, the moment of nurturing, the time given in support.

Recently I received a letter from a reader who wrote, "You are always so positive about life, so hopeful about loving and about people's behavior that it was an inspiration for me to get out of myself a bit more. I wanted to explore the art of giving which you so often encourage. I'm rather young and don't have much to give, so I decided to buy a bunch of daisies, stand at a local intersection, and hand them out with a simple, 'Have a beautiful day.' I thought it would be fun and might help to make others a bit happier. It ended by being a very enlightening experience—not exactly what I expected, but I learned a lot about human nature."

"It surprised me how few people would accept my gift. Many just passed me by, avoiding my smile. Others actually pushed my hand away. Some simply uttered a curt 'No thank you' and moved on their way. Others reluctantly took the flower and waited for some pitch, wondering what they had to give in return. The saddest thing I learned was that people are suspicious of giving. It's as if they're afraid that taking will commit them in some way. I wasn't even able to get rid of all my daisies. I went home with some of them drooping in my hand. What a strange world this is!"

It's unfortunate but nonetheless true that we live in a world of skeptics. Some individuals are constantly on their guard, unwilling to accept the possibility that there may be an honest person around, or that acts of kindness and goodness happen all the time. In a real sense, we're all responsible for this attitude and in small ways perpetuate it. We are products of our experiences. If someone has offered us a rose and immediately followed up with a plea for a donation, we naturally form a mindset against such future occurrences. From that time on, every rose offered may be suspect.

There are few of us who are without some experience which has left us disillusioned and feeling duped. We are pounced upon at airports and supermarkets by people offering all kinds of things in seemingly good faith, only to be followed by a plea for donations or support for some special cause. We are sent free samples of products, supposedly only in the spirit of good public relations and our valued opinions, but later find that we've been coerced into buying something out of a feeling of obligation.

This sort of behavior can even be seen among lovers. We are convinced of another's love, only to find later that it has been given with expectations and conditions. It is natural, then, that we become a little more doubtful, a little less receptive. In a society where one doesn't often encounter selflessness and real generosity, it's not surprising that we build defenses against them.

I have a good friend who loves to participate in swap meets. Once he created a small area in his booth where he placed objects marked "free"—things he simply wanted to give away. He was surprised to find that no one took them. Finally, he attached a low price to each of the items and they quickly disappeared, leaving him a few dollars richer, but a great deal more confused about human behavior. This was another example of people's conviction that "everything has its

price," that "nothing's free in this world."

It seems to me that there is an important lesson to be learned from all this. If we enjoy giving and see what a desperate need our world has for it, if we want to disprove the skeptics, we must be willing to take a few rejections and be tolerant of eccentric behavior. Giving without expectations is a very positive action, which must not be extinguished because of occasional negative and thankless responses.

My suggestion to the young girl was that she continue to offer her flowers if that is her way of expressing herself and it gives her pleasure. Perhaps others will eventually see that she is indeed sincere. They will then be richer—if not with a total change in attitude, at least by a flower given freely in the spirit of love.

According to a recent Gallup Poll, 55 percent of Americans are volunteers who contribute their time to improving society. This is a very interesting statistic. I've heard that people have a tendency to shade the truth in polls. We like to think of ourselves as being actively engaged in helping others, so who's going to feel comfortable responding to this poll negatively?

Helping others is one of the most rewarding experiences we can share. In fact, it is usually the helper who is helped through helping! Studies show that owning pets or plants promotes a longer and healthier life simply because they require the owner's helping hand. It gives meaning to existence—something to get out of bed for.

We come from a long tradition of helping each other. Americans were brought up on barn raisings, bucket brigades, quilting bees and cake sales. We are known for our

positive and immediate response to those in need. Our tele-thons and fund-raisers bring in thousands of dollars for Olympic teams, the physically impaired and hunger victims in many parts of the world. The problem, however, is that these causes are one-shot deals—we give, then forget. Some-how we lose sight of the fact that need is ongoing. It's all too easy to sit back and say, "I've done my bit," as if giving is done in quotas.

There are many deterrents to giving. Some say they don't know how to help or where to direct their services. We don't have to *know* how—we can be taught. And we don't have to *know* where—we just need to look about us.

We say that we don't have time. This is perhaps the weakest of all excuses. The greatest expenditure of free time in the United States is spent watching television. The average is about six hours a day, and that produces little more than boredom, passivity and extra fat where it isn't wanted. If each of us were to surrender just one night a week, there would be millions of free hours to give others.

We sometimes take a narrow view of what it means to give. We associate giving with money. Of course money is impor-tant, but there is no amount that can buy the value of someone who will sit with a dying person who would otherwise be alone. Or someone who will deliver a warm meal to an elderly house bound individual, or volunteer to teach read-ing, or just listen to a person who is afraid, lonely or rejected.

I recently boarded a flight to New York. The stewardess shouted with delight when I entered the plane. "I've wanted to meet you for such a long time. May I talk with you later?" she asked. When she got a break, she sat next to me and frantically told her story—a cheating husband, a disturbed child, a feeling of despondency and helplessness, a fear of being unable to cope. After a long while she stopped in mid-sentence and sighed deeply with relief. She wiped her tears

and sat up in the seat. "Oh, Dr. Buscaglia," she said, "you've helped me so much." I hadn't said a word. Sometimes helping can mean just listening, without judgment or advice.

We never become more visible or meaningful than when we help someone else. What we do, after all, is a tangible statement about who we are, what we value and how we feel about ourselves and our world. Author Helen Colton says the way to find what we can best do is to ask ourselves what we love or hate with a passion and then do something about it.

The world is in great need of helpers. We who inhabit it cannot survive without them. Our growth and our survival depend upon our willingness to give to each other. It's a well-worn adage, but nonetheless true, that "love isn't love until it is given away." Until it's manifested through some caring act, love is nothing more than a very good idea—only an idea, a simple word, a notion in the abstract.

There is something for each of us to do. We become truly human at the moment when we reach out to help someone.

A Passion for Growth and Acceptance

I agree that there is perhaps no greater joy in life than to find ways of overcoming our weaknesses. We know all about the thrill of victory and the agony of defeat. We seem to encounter obstacle after obstacle. Still, with hope, dignity, a little madness, and some belief in the self, we can make great strides toward achieving our goals. The greatest failure is to fail to try. Many of us have probably given up just when, with a bit more persistence and patience, we would have made it. So often when all seems lost everything points to failure, then comes the breakthrough.

Loneliness is fast becoming the great American malaise. It seems to ignore age, gender and socioeconomic levels. Surveys tell us that one quarter of the population suffers from chronic loneliness. It is among the leading causes of suicide. Books and magazines are consistently full of information and advice for the lonely—be more aggressive, step out and meet people, you have a right to be you, get out of that shell of your own making, celebrate life, count your blessings. Though sometimes good advice, these remedies seem to be of small comfort to the lonely.

No one need be told that loneliness can be very painful. In fact, it can cause us to feel almost totally devastated. It produces counter-productive feelings, discourages risk and saps emotional resources. It is not surprising that people will even select to remain in completely unfulfilling relationships rather than risk being alone.

We all know that loneliness has little or nothing to do with being physically alone. In fact, some of the most lonely among us are constantly in crowds, surrounded by people. No matter what our situation, most of us will at one time or another experience loneliness.

Few of us prepare ourselves for these possibilities. We carefully save our money for the future, we insure ourselves against economic reverses and prepare for countless unpredictable occurrences, but we do little about the time when we may have to face things alone, or find ourselves disconnected from others.

I have hundreds of letters from such individuals. They tell me they have suddenly been forced through loneliness to struggle with feelings of emptiness and unworthiness. They discover themselves on their own—some for the first time in their lives—and have no resources to call upon to contend with it. They seem to find little inner reserve or strength, or more important, no real sense of self.

It has been found that what people do in such a situation depends more upon how they feel about themselves than any other single factor. It is not so much a matter of fighting loneliness as it is using the strength that comes from self-knowledge to put it into its proper perspective.

Loneliness is never pleasant. It will always require us to actively work through a period of adjustment or healing. But this time can also to be one of learning and growth, for it compels us to examine and reevaluate ourselves and the world we've created, to get to know ourselves better.

It is a pity that we often wait until loneliness is strangling us before we try to understand its complexities. Still it's understandable, since we are brought up to avoid being alone, as if it were some type of antisocial behavior. Our young lives are often spent filled with planned social activities and interactions. We are encouraged to join clubs, teams, classes. We often become so busy that to find ourselves alone, faced with some nonscheduled time, is to many an almost devastating experience.

Heaven forbid that we should have an unplanned weekend! No one tells us that it's perfectly normal to want to be alone, to have private times when we can tune in to our own needs and desires, guided only by our own resources, or carried away by our spur of the moment impulses and dreams. We all need our separate worlds, apart from others, where we can quietly retire for regrouping, for getting back in touch with ourselves. We need this personal solitary place as a pleasant alternative to our more public lives. We must treasure this part of our existence as much as we do the more social part. Then, when loneliness comes, we will have that special place to fall back upon.

It is wonderful to have significant and loving people in our lives. We cannot live in complete happiness without them. But we must not allow ourselves to depend so completely

upon them that we lose our sense of separateness. There should always be an inner place we can count on that is solely ours.

To conquer loneliness we shall each have to assume the sacred responsibility of becoming a complete person. And most of all, to define ourselves without always including someone else in the definition.

The brochure we receive in the mail is all about victims. Along with a frightening picture of a battered woman is a very calculated message that it's high time we realize that we're all potential victims of violence. The brochure does not calm our fears, rather it capitalizes on them—we had better insure ourselves against possible crime. The statistics this ad cites are indeed alarming: a crime is committed every two seconds in the United States; in the past five years the number of violent crimes has increased more than twenty percent; nearly one-third of all households will be victimized by violence at some time.

How easily we can become intimidated not only by such statistics, but by the vague feeling of impending disaster that they create in our minds. More disturbing is the fact that we can become victims of our own fears, and fear can dominate our very lives. What statistics tell us is often what the researcher or advertiser interprets. For example, the chances of being killed in an auto accident is nearly ten times greater than being the victim of a violent crime. It can happen just as suddenly and just as brutally, yet how many of us cower in our homes afraid to drive?

There is unquestionably too much violence in America. No one doubts that each tragic instance is deserving of our

strongest condemnation. But when it causes us to retreat in any way from full enjoyment of life, it is time to bring such fears into perspective.

Consider just a few examples of how quickly and completely we are seized by fear:

After several episodes of sabotaged candy given out at Halloween in recent years, many children throughout the country have been kept indoors on that very special night. There is even a growing sentiment that we phase out the holiday in order that we may protect our children.

A box of Girl Scout cookies was found to have a straight pin wedged in one of its cookies. On the same day, every local T.V. station headlined this newest danger to our children's well-being. X-ray centers were even set up for any who were fearful of biting into their cookies. Isn't it amazing how readily we sensationalize the demented schemes of a few twisted individuals and how they can dominate our lives?

Increasingly I hear of parents who live in constant fear that some calamity will befall their children. One young mother I talked to would not allow her children to play in front of their home, let alone go to the playground, for fear that they would be kidnapped. One cannot guarantee her that such a thing will never happen any more than she can be assured that a plane will never crash into her house. If we choose to live our lives fully, we must be willing to encounter risks along the way. One necessarily involves the other.

Fears and anxieties also have an unfortunate way of putting masks on people. Strangers are viewed for the potential harm they may cause instead of the growth and joy they might offer. Trust gives way to suspicion. Caring involvement with others is replaced by watching out for number one.

We are told repeatedly that one of the greatest deterrents to crime is a sense of community, of neighborliness, even of watchful concern for one another. I remember an old gen-

tleman who lived on the street where I grew up. He was, as far as the block was concerned, a one-man Neighborhood Watch. With the least activity anywhere on the street, he was reliably present at one of his windows, peering through his curtains. We regarded him as something of a busybody, but at the same time were comforted by his vigilance. Nothing escaped his watchful eye.

I'm not suggesting that we all become sentries and watchdogs. Instead, we might consider coming out of our houses a little more often, if for no other reason than to feel more connected to our neighbors. Sometimes our fears are magnified simply because we feel alone in facing them. While the inner sanctums of our homes do provide a sort of insulation from the world, they can also isolate us from it. Surely our streets and neighborhoods can become more hospitable places when we are more together with the people in them.

How much more manageable our fears become when we learn to expand our definition of family and recognize that we're all in this together. We need each other. Fear is said to be the primary disease of the twentieth century. As we approach the end of this hundred years, perhaps we will come to learn that a caring involvement for each other might be a cure.

I don't imagine there is anyone fully alive who has not felt discouraged. The word *discourage* is defined as to deprive of courage, hope or confidence. Phrases such as, "It's not worth it," "I can't," "I give up," "I've failed," are standard. None of us is a complete stranger to feelings of hopelessness. It is usually because we feel disappointed or trapped or have lost our sense of direction and hope for the future.

Discouragement is a very human attribute. We need not censure ourselves for feeling it. But it is important to know that no matter what the circumstances that have brought us to this point, they are not insurmountable. The world is full of possibilities; and, as long as there are possibilities, there is hope. Even the most successful and happiest people can tell you about having spent time questioning themselves, their values and their abilities. But they have never lost the capacity to hope.

There is a man whom we all know. His history goes as follows: Twice he failed in business. He ran for the state legislature and for Congress twice and failed. He was defeated twice in Senate races. He worked hard to become Vice President of the United States with no success. The woman he loved died when she was very young. Eventually he suffered a nervous breakdown. Through all of this he had the self-knowledge and strength to overcome adversity, continue with life and become President. His name, of course, is Abraham Lincoln.

We are inspired by such a message. But we are not all Lincolns. Still, there is much to be learned by his example and the examples of other survivors. Because something goes wrong does not mean that it's the end of the world. In fact, it may be the challenge we need to awaken us to our strengths. The real dilemma is the feeling that there is no way to turn, no place to go, no one to help us. What is important to remember is that there are many solutions to every problem. We are not perfect and may make mistakes but all things come to an end. Armed with this knowledge we are halfway to a solution.

There were many times when I was growing up that could have been devastating for the entire family. Times when Papa had lost his job, when there was no money even for the bare necessities, when things truly looked hopeless. In spite of, or perhaps especially because of those times, Mama and Papa

never allowed us to lose our sense of humor, sense of self, or the assurance that we'd find a way. Somehow, we always did.

I was fortunate to have learned this early in life. I know that after experiencing discouragement, the first thing I try to do is keep in mind that nothing lasts forever, that only I can decide what I can do to make things better. With this hope and faith in the future I'm off and running, again seeking new solutions.

I believe that the truly healthy person is the one who has the greatest number of alternatives for any behavior. We are limited only by our willingness to discover these alternatives. Let's say that we find ourselves in tears. There is nothing wrong with tears. They often sharpen our ability to see. We then need to ask ourselves if crying forever is what we want to do. If not, we must consider what else we can possibly do to help ourselves and solve our problem.

We can consider possible alternatives. It may be helpful to find what others have done in similar situations. With a list of alternatives in hand, we will feel less trapped and more in a position to decide what is best for us.

Finally comes the greatest step: We must *do* something. In action comes true knowledge and a wonderful sense of freedom. We are never really trapped. Discouragement at times seems inescapable. But, to remain in this state is a waste of time, energy and life. We can learn to put discouragement aside. When we do, we can get on with life.

There is a park near my home where I used to jog every evening. These days it invites me to take a brisk walk. In slowing down I've become more attuned to the surroundings that I was pounding and panting my way through before.

A few months ago, I noticed more and more parents practicing baseball in the park with their children. One youngster told me that tryouts for Little League were approaching and, "You gotta be good if you wanna make the team." Being the institution that Little League is, I understand the anticipation that goes along with "making the team."

Once in a while I'll see a father and son throwing and catching and batting long after the sun has set. The father is patient with his son's clumsiness, yet he also seems determined to make a ballplayer of him. The son wants to please Dad, but it's painfully obvious, in some cases, that baseball may not be the way. Given a choice, he may wish he were home with his chemistry set or exploring the woods—anything but this struggle with bat and ball and glove.

Most of us have seen this drama played out before. Certainly some of these youngsters will learn the game and gain much from the experience, but I'd guess that some will also feel frustration. Their talents may lie elsewhere and, therefore, go unnoticed.

Each of us possesses gifts that make us distinct. These qualities only await recognition and development. The problem is they may not always be what others expect. For instance, Eddie is sitting on the end of the bench waiting to get into the game. He can't hit a ball, but he has marvelous musical talent. And there, buried in the third row of dancers, is Beth, stomping her way through her tenth ballet recital. She'd rather be learning about animals, a subject that has interested her for a long time.

Eric is a stargazer. Like Einstein, who hated formal schooling, he dreams of distant corners of the universe and faraway planets. His teachers say he is inattentive and a daydreamer. His parents don't understand why his grades are poor. One day he is given a telescope and a new world opens up to him.

Now the universe is limitless. Perhaps his future is better focused.

I remember a student (I'll call him Rodney) who was classified as a below-average student. He had behavioral problems and a poor academic performance. Nothing we did seemed to have any effect on him. He was continually late to class and always had an unusual excuse: A sparrow had fallen to the ground and needed to be returned to its nest; a five-car accident happened in front of his house and he had to get the ambulance. All sorts of calamities and strange occurrences seemed to delay Rodney, especially on his way to school.

One morning, in desperation, I assigned him a one-page composition in which he was to explain in detail what happened to him that day. He had no trouble writing several pages. In fact it was an unusually fascinating piece of fiction. It was easy to see Rodney's uniqueness—he was a born storyteller. Before the year was over, Rodney was turning out tales about all sorts of things. He became interested in ideas and was inspired by other authors. He read avidly and was far more interested in his education. He even started coming to school on time.

Our educational system often fails to identify individual talents that make each student unique. Instead we place greater emphasis on long-term, specific objectives and standards that must be met by all. This often creates the boredom and apathy that causes spark and creativity to wane and die.

We hear from time to time about some individuals who have conquered the system. There is no doubt that when this occurs everyone benefits, for it is from this that art is created, mystery understood and dreams are made real.

It is interesting how often we look back at our past with fondness. We talk about the good old days when life seemed less complicated and more carefree. (Was there ever really a time that was not complicated?) It may be that complex images of our past simply become glossed over by time and memory. But the most significant aspect about this yearning is our deep desire to uncomplicate our lives. It isn't that we're asking to retreat to some rural outpost and spend the remainder of our days in quiet meditation and communion with nature. It simply means that most of us seem overburdened with responsibilities, worry, and a belief in a continual need to strive for more.

However, I believe that most of us would go mad if we had to give up much of our complicated life patterns. I have a friend, for instance, who sets out each year for a week of camping alone in Yosemite National Park. All year he gives lip service to the importance of this escape for maintaining his continued sanity and physical well-being. When the appointed time comes, he leaves his wife and children; and, with tent, canteen, hiking boots, air mattress and sleeping bag in tow, sets off for the valley and his much sought-after solitude. It never fails that he returns after only a few days, having had his fill of peace and quiet.

We sometimes hear affluent people recall the early days of their relationships when they had little of monetary value, a small one-room apartment, an old car and a slim bank balance. Yet they refer to those days as among the happiest they have ever known. Still, as we mature, we don't seem to strive for the simple lives we claim to want. In fact, we work to increase our gains because we never seem to have enough.

We fail to recognize that the more we own, the more we are possessed by what we own—that more is not necessarily better. In time we even begin to define ourselves by the number of things we possess. Perhaps it is well to remember

that the only things we can take with us are those which will fit into a coffin.

Prior to their marriage, two former students of mine learned the value of simplicity. They nearly broke their engagement over the trials of planning the ceremony. The printer, the caterer, the florist, the dresses, the tuxedos, the rental agencies, the reception hall, the band and you mustn't forget the monogrammed matchbooks!

Then there was the guest list with each side questioning the other and worrying about who might be offended. And the registration of china, crystal and silverware patterns, and bath towels and linens, ad infinitum. The staggering number of decisions, the frayed nerves, the frantic anticipation were almost too much. Here were two people very much in love. The only wish they had was to declare their love in a formal way before friends and family. They had looked forward to their special day all of their young lives but were barely on speaking terms before the ceremony.

On the other hand, I recently watched a little girl flying a kite in the park below my house. There she was with a few sticks, paper, string, a little wind and a great expanse of sky—the simplest of activities. She didn't have to go far from home. She was totally caught up in the moment, mesmerized by the gentle movements of the kite. She stayed in the park for a long while, totally at peace.

Really, life is simple. It is we who are complex. Of course, when I say this I am challenged with the naiveté of such a statement. The retort I most often hear is "Well, that may be true of your life, but there's nothing simple about mine!" I am tempted to say that if life is not simple, we may be responsible for its complexities. And if we desire it to be otherwise, it's never too late.

Of course we should strive to become all that we can and do all that is possible to make the world a better place in which to

grow in joy. We should strive to obtain those things which we feel we need to make our lives more comfortable and satisfying. But we must never allow those things to dominate.

When the clutter, anxiety and complications threaten to hem us in, we should bring to mind the words of Thoreau, "Simplify! Simplify!" And if even this fails, we might learn from the children and go fly a kite!

Everyone is out there these days finding themselves. No one is left minding the store. It's a growing epidemic. Never in our history have so many people become obsessed with the need to know themselves, and never in our history have so many become lost, confused and despairing in the process.

Happily, the past three decades have been times of changing attitudes, values and roles. We are finally able to admit (some still reluctantly) that women are as wise, creative and able as men. We have finally been forced to recognize that they have the right to succeed, grow and contribute to the extent of their abilities; that for those who so desire, there must be no limitations placed in the way of becoming all that they are able to be.

Things are changing for men, too. They are discovering at last how much better it is to have an efficient, capable and interesting woman around than the somewhat empty role model of *wife*. Men are finding new joy in sharing full responsibility for the social, economic and psychological climate of their homes and families. They have found that in sharing tasks, for instance, both husband and wife are released for more productive, special and personal time.

These discoveries have forced many to redefine roles, to decry the loss of so many years and to set out with determina-

tion to rectify this by dedicating themselves to the task of seeking their true selves.

I know a couple who were happily married for eleven years. Then the wife took a psychology course in personal growth. Through it she was convinced that she was missing life being *simply* a wife and mother. She learned the jargon about waste of human potential, the value of the individual, the search for identity. Somewhere out there, she decided, was the woman she wanted to be. Before the class ended she left her husband and their four children in the *search for self.*

I'm not condemning her actions. In fact, I was equally as eager in my own search. It led me around the world twice. I left family, friends, a promising career and wandered the mountains of Nepal and Valleys of the Moon. I listened to the great gurus, I read the mystical texts, I joined monasteries and ashrams. I studied yoga and meditation techniques. I admit that there was value in this. A search is always exciting and full of newness. But along the way I found that my search was not bringing me any closer to finding that elusive *me*.

Eventually I returned. I had experienced wonderful things and had made many new and lasting friends. I had acquired a great deal of knowledge, but once home found that there was nothing I had discovered on my trip that I could not have found in my own backyard. Of course, it would not have been so exotic or dramatic, nor would it have made such exciting dinner conversation. But what I had needed to discover—myself—was always with me.

Understanding oneself is a worthy and commendable goal. But it is not necessary to leave everything and everyone in order to do it. My friend's wife, for example, found that singles bars, sexual freedom, loneliness, and mystical teachings afforded her a no more conducive environment to knowing herself than would a sympathetic husband, an understanding family, friends and a secure home.

Change is always difficult. People who feel that they have been denied experiences or made wrong choices and have consequently missed life can become frantic about their sense of loss. Rightfully so. There is no greater loss for all of us than a life unlived. But we should keep in mind, before we leave on a search, that even the philosophies most dedicated to knowing ourselves tell us that self-knowledge and enlightenment can come through making a loaf of bread, growing a beautiful garden, or hearing a piece of music.

Oscar Wilde said that, "Only the shallow know themselves," and he was right. There can be no end to the process of self-discovery if we are continually learning, growing and changing. Knowing oneself is a process, not a goal. No one person or place is more conducive than any other in helping this process along.

The tools are not out there somewhere. They are inside of us. Only we can assume the challenge of our voyage. The experience becomes more valuable and meaningful when we take those we love with us along the way. The search for ourselves takes on real meaning when each day becomes a Bon Voyage party.

Any serious human relationship takes work. Not so much in the sense of learning the right rules or formulas that govern all relationships (if there were such things), but in two individuals working together to find what is best for both of them. How people compromise, for instance, says much about the kind of relationship they've worked out together.

Two very dear friends have been struggling with a compromise of sorts in their marriage. It all has to do with a motorcycle. The husband has owned one from the beginning of their

marriage, much to the displeasure of his wife. She has pleaded all along that he search for a safer way to experience the freedom and exhilaration of the outdoors, as he likes to put it. So he has given in a little bit over the years by riding it only occasionally. She in turn has stopped nagging and only says a quiet little prayer for his safe return each time he goes out on it.

This has worked well for twelve years. Recently, however, he was in a very serious accident from which, miraculously, he emerged unscathed. Nearly realizing her worst fears, his wife revived her campaign, this time insisting that he get rid of the motorcycle once and for all. As she sees it, he has a family and future to think about, and continuing his, "Sunday on the road with the wind in my face," shows a lack of responsibility.

He countered, now somewhat less forcefully, that his motorcycle represents freedom for him. On this he was adamant. He was the rock of Gibraltar. He would not move.

Friends and family were brought into the argument. I was present when it was being discussed around a dinner table and when it appeared that things were heating up a bit, someone suggested that a compromise might be worked out. Surely there was some way to handle this situation to the satisfaction of both parties. After all, they were intelligent adults. All sorts of alternatives were offered. Some were absurd, some were practical, but they had all of us, including the main actors in this little drama, seeing some sign of compromise in the whole thing, providing a ray of hope. It was finally agreed that all future motorcycle riding would be confined to off-road trails where the chance of injury was far less than on city streets. The husband acquiesced to this. The marriage was saved.

I wonder how many of us stake out areas in our relationships where we refuse to budge. "It's a matter of princi-

ple," we say. Or sometimes we just fold our arms with an air of finality as if to say, "That's just the way it is." Right or wrong, we take our stand. We put on our granite faces and use phrases such as "over my dead body" or "not until hell freezes over."

Certainly there are some things in life that are not easily compromised. Where serious principles are concerned, we may be less inclined to meet someone halfway. But often we maintain that it is our pride or honor that requires us to hold to a position when actually our own self-interest may be the hidden reason.

I am reminded of a woman who called in to a radio talk show I guest-hosted recently. She had worked herself into quite a state over her husband's near total obsession with watching football. She was particularly distressed by a huge radar dish he had put atop their house to bring into their home virtually every football game telecast in this hemisphere. "He parks himself in front of the television set and watches game after game, day after day, from September through January. When I complain, he tells me I might try to develop a little interest in football." He even offered to take her to a football game.

When I mentioned compromise she was stunned. "I hate football with a passion," she hissed. "Never!" That was that. It sounded like a stalemate that they were just going to have to live with. Still, I'm certain that with some serious, honest communication, just a little movement *toward* instead of away from each other, there would be a solution—and if not a solution, at least a little better understanding.

There is indeed an art to compromising. It's such an important part of any relationship. Perhaps it would do us all some good to consider the "nevers"—all the unequivocal no-way-am-I-going-to-change attitudes that we develop and lock into our personalities. Meeting someone halfway does involve

giving in, although too often we hesitate because we look upon it as giving up something. A good compromise is one of the simplest ways to affirm and grow in the love and mutual respect that is so vital to any lasting relationship.

You'd love Peter. He's a real charmer. He speaks with a wonderful Hungarian accent and lives in beautiful comfort high on a hill overlooking his adopted city of Vienna. He is now in his eighties and as alert and challenging as a teenager. He has a most fascinating philosophy. He observes that people seem to live life in three states: the state of *must*, the state of *should*, and the state of *want to*. Happiness according to Peter is determined by how much of our lives is spent in the state of *want to*.

We all know the state of musts. Most of our lives are full of them. They are the many day-to-day necessities of life which must be taken care of whether we like them or not: earning a living, eating, cleaning—tasks which take most of our time.

Don't misunderstand. Peter is not suggesting that these activities are bad. He simply feels that they are *must* things and often fill our lives with dull routine that we'd enjoy being rid of.

Our life also has its share of *shoulds*. These are the things which, unlike eating or sleeping, are not essential for our survival, but are expected of the average person—the little niceties we engage in because we want to be socially accepted. People we visit or have as guests because we feel we should. Cards, thank-you notes, presents we should send. We should take mother to dinner. We should write to our uncle. We should have a dinner party—it's our turn. We would certainly continue to exist without actualizing these shoulds

but we pressure ourselves into doing them. They require time, energy, and will.

The third category, according to Peter, is that of *want to*. These are the choice activities of life, those things we are seeing, doing, accomplishing because they amuse us, enhance us and build our sense of self. They vary, of course, with each person. But what they have in common is that they are volitional and result in bringing us joy and fulfillment.

One of the most exciting challenges is to attempt to create a life full of the *want tos*, a life as free as possible from *musts* and *shoulds*. We all can do this if we really want to.

For example, let's say that we are shopping for food, certainly a must for all of us. We detest supermarkets: the crowds, the lines, the carts which keep getting in our way. We anticipate each trip with dread. When we finally get there, we push our cart with determination, rush frantically through the aisles in search of the items we require, and rush out.

In order to change this activity to a *want to,* we might try approaching the market with a new, more open view. We can see it as an adventure, a journey into a blaze of color, texture, odors and design. Oranges, bananas, grapefruit, cherries, tomatoes, lettuce, radishes, leeks, eggplant—all glistening in rows of color and pattern. Canned foods, boxed foods, all in an amazing array of creative packaging. It is easy to see how a trip to the market could be a ticket to a journey into sensual enjoyment. Even the long wait in the checkout line can be made into a pleasant experience. We can try to imagine that each cart we see is an expression of a human personality. The woman with the cart overflowing with steak, ground meat, hot dogs, diapers, gigantic boxes of dry cereals and gallons of milk. What does that tell you! Then there's the man with one lamb chop, one tomato, one frozen dessert and a copy of *Sports Illustrated*. How can these experiences be viewed as *musts*?

As to the *shoulds,* we might try to make shoulds, *why nots*? If that note to your uncle will bring him joy, why not? If the dinner party has the power to please and delight, why not? If it has to be done, why not in joy?

It should be enough to remember that each of us has the power to please, to make the world a better place. Why not?

The greater the number of *want tos,* the more wonderful and happy the life. It certainly is worth a try. Let's start by attempting to drop the words must or should from our language. When we do express them, let's find new ways to make them turn into *want to*. Why not?

A Passion for Life

Life is a dynamic process. It welcomes anyone who takes up the invitation to be an active part of it. What we call the secret of happiness is no more a secret than our willingness to choose life.

As we all know, there are those many very scholarly people who say that the unicorn is a mythical animal and never existed. Many years ago, the Irish Rovers suggested, in a song, the reason for their disappearance. The song says that unicorns did exist but they were too busy playing and having fun to heed Noah's warning and were drowned in the Great Flood.

Let me begin by saying that I don't buy either explanation. I've seen unicorns—I know they exist. They are sleek, fleet of body and mind, mild-mannered, trusting and easily tamed. I understand that by saying I know unicorns I will be accused of being empty-headed or an undying romantic, and I will admit there is some truth in both accusations. But, you may ask, why risk this and discuss unicorns at all? Because I feel that our world is much in need of them.

They are creatures characterized as unique, mystical, pure in heart and mind, pensive, innocent, trusting, wise, possessing great strength and certain fearlessness when fighting evil. They have also been considered a fragment of divinity. In other words, they represent all of the virtues to which we should aspire as human beings. Unicorns are good, kind, sensitive and loving.

It's so strange that such an incredibly lovely creature has always been an object of the hunt. From the start of recorded history to the twentieth century we have been intrigued with the idea of seeking them out, wounding them, caging them, or worse, killing them. No matter—they refuse to die. Unicorns remain a subject of opera, ballet, poetry, novels and paintings. They appear in the art of every continent and culture, from the scratches on walls of prehistoric caves to the gold-framed paintings on silk-lined corridors of contemporary museums. Hardly anyone visits New York City without making a pilgrimage to the Cloisters to see the glorious tapestries of the "Hunt of the Unicorn." Modern writers such

as Günter Grass, W.H. Auden and Tennessee Williams use the unicorn as a symbol to illuminate the problems of our modern world. The spirit of the unicorn refuses to vanish.

Many value the spirit and keep it alive within themselves. They try to be caring, forgiving, trusting, pure of heart, vulnerable and dedicated to the sharing of joy and beauty. These people are often seen as living in the past (the good ol' days) when things were simpler. We are told that in our modern, enlightened society there is no place for unicorns. So when people do encounter them, they are hunted, caged, or killed.

Strange that we always kill our saints. They seem to represent something extremely threatening. They offer a challenge that goodness can exist and it is easier not to have to accept the challenge. We would rather accuse them of being simplistic, naive, unrealistic. We convince ourselves that they are insincere, suspect and phony.

Why is it so difficult for us to express and accept positive human values? When will we stop tormenting our unicorns? It is my feeling that unicorns are not extinct at all—they have simply gone underground. They hide in big cities, quiet forests, deserted beaches and country lanes. Occasionally they come together for a brief time for mutual encouragement, but they soon disperse out of fear of being ambushed.

It is my dream that one day, in the not too distant future, thousands of unicorns will come forward from all over the world, unafraid, to share their warmth, their strength and their love. I know they are to be found, for some days I encounter as many as twenty—in shopping centers, at theatres, on crowded streets. Some days I find only three or four and I must admit that there are times when not one appears.

Appearing as a unicorn is a great risk. I understand that. The hunters are still there with bow or gun, ready to kill. But I'd like to remind unicorns that their horns are strong, per-

haps stronger than they know. Goodness, beauty and love have survived since the beginning of our time on this earth. A free spirit can never be caged. As Anne Morrow Lindbergh said in her poem about the unicorn, even in captivity it is free.

I am still finding unicorns. I know that they are not extinct. They are to be found almost anywhere. By the way, if you know of any, would you please let me know?

We all have weaknesses. I don't think any of us knows too many perfect people. Actually, I'm not sure I'd want to. Of course, I know people who constantly tell me about overcoming their weaknesses and the joy of approaching the ultimate peace and enlightenment. I'm happy for them, but I have a long way to go. My life is a history of continually dealing with weaknesses and attempting to overcome them. But I've found that life doesn't demand perfection of me—only I do.

For example, I'm a terrible speller. There are times when my secretary can't even guess at the word I've managed to butcher. I recall writing a term paper in high school about the legendary Scheherazade. I titled it "The Tail of Scheherazade." My English teacher commented on the paper in horror, "Really!"

I'm also rotten at sports. I can neither hit nor throw a ball. I was always the bane of my coach's existence, not to speak of my teammates whose groans, each time I went to bat, sounded like the rumbling of Mount Etna.

I have too many weaknesses to list, but the two mentioned always have seemed the most visible. I still can't spell and the older I get the less of a threat I pose to Pete Rose or Abdul Jabbar. But I've managed to survive. I've managed to write seven books and several articles for professional and popular

journals and magazines. It's been great to have editors who do know how to spell. As for sports, I once was a decent jogger and am now a devoted long-distance walker, neither of which has required me to hit or throw a ball.

I've learned to live with these weaknesses happily ever after. In fact, they've taught me humility and how to handle ridicule. And in the process they have rid me of illusions of perfection.

Helen Keller, the great lady who lived her life in deafness and blindness, said, "I thank God for my handicaps, for through them I have found myself, my work, and my God." Certainly this statement is worth pondering as a challenge to us all, each of us having our own handicaps and weaknesses.

Most of my professional life has been spent working with the physically and mentally disabled. I owe much to this experience. These individuals have taught me about will and determination. There were those who were blind who learned to *see* with their fingers and their imaginations. Others were deaf and learned to use circumstances as signals. They used what they had to compensate for what they lacked—strengths to compensate for weaknesses.

All of us have this power. It is a way of achieving a victory over ourselves. Whether we have it naturally or acquire it, it is always there. Some of our weaknesses can be overcome with willingness to learn the necessary skills to do so. Some can't, even when we try. It's impossible for me to understand why I never learned to spell. I'm an avid reader. I enjoy writing. But, oh those words! Still, I get by. I discovered how to use a dictionary. If I couldn't spell the word well enough even to look it up, I learned not to be too proud to ask.

I was not as fortunate with learning to play ball. I was often ignored by teammates and coaches who were far too busy trying to win to take the time to help a loser. Still, with jogging or walking, I can get the exercise I need without the

ridicule. I may not win any trophies, but I often get free marathon T shirts!

I was raised on "Try, try again," and discovered that my successes were often in direct proportion to my persistence. "To strive with difficulties and to conquer them is the highest form of human felicity," Samuel Johnson told us. But if we can't overcome some of our weaknesses, all is not lost. As long as we've tried, there was something to be learned in the effort. For example, I've learned a lot and have had a happy life, even if I did give Scheherazade a tail and my gym coaches ulcers.

On February 15, 1984, the world lost a great human being. The wonderful performer Ethel Merman died. Her life was a breathtaking adventure. At 21 she was already a star—a status she never lost. She sang and danced her way through fourteen hit musicals and countless movies. She married four times, suffered the loss of a daughter, and went through surgery to remove a brain tumor. Nothing but death stopped her. She gave life her all until the last. "Always give them the old fire," she was often quoted as saying, "even when you feel like a squashed cake of ice."

The old fire Ethel Merman gave us will be missed. The world is much in need of her vigor and enthusiasm for life. She was a pro as a performer as well as a human being. She kept reminding us throughout her life that anything worth doing is worth doing full speed ahead. Of course, it's not always easy to stay up, especially when you feel more like squashed ice—damp, cold, alone, misunderstood. There is nothing wrong with these feelings, of course. They are a part of life. But there are those who wear them like medals of

honor. They can't wait to share their unhappiness, laying their chill upon even the most innocent strangers. They are forever illustrating the old adage, "Misery doesn't only love company, it demands it!"

We all know people whom we love dearly; but as much as we care for them, we always face our encounters with a sense of dread. The moment we ask "How's it going?" they start with a deluge of horrors: Their bursitis is acting up again, they're being abused by their neighbors, nobody really cares about them, they're not long for this world, they think they have cancer, their dear friend Sally is dying, and so it goes. Then they ask why we don't see them more often!

I don't know if Ethel Merman had bursitis or was abused by neighbors, but whatever she was feeling on the evenings I saw her perform, I always left the theater a lot happier, much stronger, and a great deal more positive because of being in her space.

We all enjoy being around enthusiastic people. They have a way of avoiding the usual automatic stimulus-response pattern and create their own script as they go along. It isn't that these individuals are more problem-free than we. I saw Ethel Merman in *Gypsy* three times over a span of a year. Each time her performance was almost too big for the limitations of the theater, but there was always a subtle difference, too. Each audience had unique expectations, responses and reactions. Ethel always played the moment, recognizing the audience's needs and satisfying them, despite her personal feelings at the time. She always acted as if she was there for our pleasure, that this was her first and most important performance. Though doing seven shows a week surely must get tiresome, I never saw a bored Ethel. Like all of us, she must have had times of illness, times of loneliness, even times of despair, but I never saw her down. You might say, "Sure, that's true, but that's her job," and you'd be right. But it tells us that

staying up is something of a choice. The great thing about a positive approach to life, a desire to show our best self, is that it produces wonderful side effects. It not only creates a happy space for those in our presence, it encourages others to be more positive themselves.

I recall as a freshman in college perceiving myself as a budding poet. I have since abandoned this vision, much to the relief of the literary community, as well as, and more specifically, my English professor. I was especially proud of a phrase I wrote that poses no threat to T.S. Eliot or e.e. cummings, but it said something for me and still does: "I quietly live my Autumn and joyfully share my Spring." Granted this thought may be appalling to the existentialists and those who demand one hundred percent authenticity all the time, but it has made a great difference in my life, and also, I think, in the lives of those around me.

Personally, I want to thank Ms. Merman (and all the Ethels with fire) for bringing Spring to a world too often in the throes of Winter.

I just finished reading a fascinating history of Alcatraz Island entitled *The Rock*. It is written by Pierre Odier, a California high school teacher. Along with a group of his students he spent a week on that island to learn something of its past and to bring into focus a subject that has been, from the beginning, shrouded in mystery.

He describes quite vividly their experiences in poring over the completely deserted prison facility, sifting through what evidence remained of human beings who existed in the starkest of conditions. Imagine being in this place of ultimate confinement where all human contact, including speaking,

among inmates was forbidden, all communication with the outside world was virtually nonexistent.

Odier writes that even in the midst of this hellish place there survived some very noble examples of the human spirit: prisoners who devised an entire language of hand signals for conversing, debating, even for carrying on chess games; a guard who risked his job by secretly slipping candy bars to the prisoners on a regular basis—incognito. No one, including the prisoners, ever discovered the identity of that caring individual. Another unidentified guard dressed up as Santa Claus one Christmas to bring some little joy to a place otherwise filled with hopelessness and despair.

The human spirit! As long as we have inhabited the earth, we humans have taken immeasurable pride in our nobler instincts. No matter how often people or societies have attempted to put them down, they rise again—in concentration camps, in prisons such as Alcatraz, and in many places where one would expect to find precious little evidence of this spirit.

Recently a documentary was done on California farmworkers. They were asked where they got the strength to return to the fields day after day in an endless struggle for survival. Their answers revealed individuals determined to maintain dignity and purpose in their lives: "We are accustomed to the soil and have faith in God." "I work with my thoughts constantly on my children and a better future." "We have learned to do our jobs well and in that we gain satisfaction."

These are people who work long, hard hours. Their tasks are back-breaking and very repetitive. Their rewards are meager. Yet in spite of this, there persists a spirit of dedication, not to some higher work authority, but to their own self-respect as human beings.

All of us were schooled in the tradition of learning admira-

ble traits by studying inspiring examples of courage and persistence. When we did this we found that as long as there has been war, there have also been peacemakers; as long as we have been plagued with disease, there have also been healers. As long as there was pain and confusion, there were scientists and other researchers laboring to find solutions; and as long as there was ignorance in the world, there were always willing teachers to help guide us toward greater enlightenment.

These examples taught us to have courage in facing our own obstacles by learning that the human spirit has the power to rise above all odds. We discovered that we can direct history, shape our environment and mold our lives, and not the other way around.

I believe that wherever and whenever this human spirit is in evidence—whether it is a prisoner striving to be heard, someone in a concentration camp determined to live, or a laborer executing tasks with hope and confidence in the future—it is cause for celebration of life. Whenever we are striving to remold a misshapen world to our higher visions, or simply living in dignity in spite of circumstances, we are at our very best. The human spirit, dedicated to life and beauty and good, is not dead, in spite of all that we hear to the contrary.

When I was first teaching, I was determined to promote in my students an active imagination. I remember in particular an activity that we all loved which we called "Balloons to the Moon." This is what we did. Each child received a balloon which was filled with helium, then tied, and had attached to its end a postcard with a message on it. It read something like, "Whoever finds me, please put me into a mailbox. I'm part of a very exciting experiment and need your help to

complete it. Thank you for your kindness."

The balloons were all released in the air and the children watched as each lifted and disappeared from sight. The postcards were stamped and had a return address so that any that were found could be returned. It was sort of a contest to see whose balloon would go the farthest, and while the children's imaginations were given flight, we talked of weather patterns, local geography, and faraway places. We talked of the kindness of strangers—how people completely unknown to us might help out just to be nice. Most of the children imagined fantastic possibilities.

"Mine will catch a wind and make it to China," said one.

"Mine's going to sail over the highest mountain," said another.

"My balloon is caught on a telephone wire." There was always one!

"Well, here's another one, Johnny. Set it off!"

Imagination is the place where we keep the things that cannot be and yet we know they *are*. We sometimes assume that only children are especially in touch with this magical place, that adults have shed their innocence for a more tangible world. There are the vague recollections of a time in our lives when all things were possible, when the real world, with all its logic and restraint was not yet upon us. Still, there are those occasional flights of fantasy, the daydreams, the journeys to faraway places. I've often wondered about the mystery of so much of the brain that lies fallow. Perhaps it is through our imagination that we awaken some of its unknown potential. It is the one quality that is invariably attributed to our most inspired, creative people. George Bernard Shaw once wrote that "Imagination is the beginning of creation. You imagine what you desire; you will what you imagine; and at last you create what you will."

With just a little imagination we can shake loose from the

commonplace and make memorable some of those moments that are habitually the same. More and more it seems that life is a creative achievement, something more than just security and comfort. Imagination is being able to envision limitless possibilities and alternatives. It is seeking new solutions to old problems. Each day offers new opportunities, new experiences—no day has ever been like any other, and neither should our approach to it.

Find as many exciting ways as you can of doing mundane tasks. Make cleaning house a symphony of movement for keeping trim. It could be anything from Mahler to Michael Jackson to Sinatra. A well-choreographed samba might be just the trick to bring a little flair and excitement to doing the laundry. Try creating a spectacular pasta of your own, rather than playing it safe with the usual packaged noodles. It takes the same amount of time and it's a lot more fun. Tap your creative instincts as often as possible lest you begin to believe you have none.

From the accounts of prisoners of war who suffered years of deprivation inconceivable to most of us, stories are told of individuals who imagined an outer world in every detail that they could summon. Dreams were born, art was created, poems were written—all under the stark and barren circumstances of their confinement. What an incredible example of the power and liberating force of imagination.

We have to take responsibility for our own boredom and delve into the limitless opportunities that our imaginations afford us. Whether in fashioning a masterpiece of art, or seeing a problem from a new perspective, the creative instinct is uniquely human and waiting within you to be tapped. So when your life seems emptier than it should, when it needs a healthy transfusion of vitality, use your imagination and tap your dreams. And, by the way, if you discover a lovely, light balloon one day, with a card attached, please send it on. I still

dream of the wonderful places mine might have gone. And if I find yours, I promise to send it back posthaste!

I know it is close to heresy these days to admit to this, but I don't think it's any fun getting old. Yes, it's true that age has its privileges, and so it should, but let's face it, it has its share of disadvantages too.

I, for example, can't kick up my heels as I used to without getting a swollen ankle. In past years I could move through my home and office in a matter of seconds. Now it takes at least a third more time, and when I've finally arrived where I am going, I sometimes forget what I've come there for. I'm more absent-minded and more frequently rely upon others to tell me "what's-his-name's" name, or the title of the book I read last week, or the telephone number of my sister whom I've been calling for years.

I can't eat as heartily as I used to. The three servings of pasta that were generally preceded by a giant antipasto and followed by a huge piece of rum cake are now distant memories. Even a single serving takes hours to make its uncomfortable and noisy way through my digestive tract.

I can't see or hear as I used to. Without glasses, reading material needs the full extension of my arm to be deciphered. I'm noticing too that when I am listening to music alone in a room, the person entering always lowers the sound slightly.

I get more tired than I used to. An eight-hour day cries out for periods of rest; and, when I don't get them, I pay the price. I nod off sometimes during very important moments.

Of course, getting older does have its advantages. I was having a prescription filled the other day and the pharmacist offered me a ten percent discount. Movie theaters cut their

admissions in half and the local eatery has special meals at one-third off after five and before seven. These little niceties are most gratifying, but I'd easily forego them for a few less aches and pains, a faster, more steady gait, or 20/20 vision.

It's difficult for me to honestly celebrate getting older. I know there have been many examples of people who never seem to age. George Bernard Shaw broke a leg while still fully functioning in his nineties—he fell out of a tree while pruning it! Grandma Moses did her best painting after she was one hundred years old. Our President, who is well beyond retirement age, seems to revel in the pressing duties of his office. It annoys me when I watch a fantastic-looking woman on T.V. expounding the joy of Oil of Olay on her wrinkle-free face, or a sprightly-looking gentleman telling me that he owes his vitality to Ex-Lax and has lived by it for lo these many decades! I have nothing against these products, but the implication for me is that we shouldn't show any signs of aging. I've tried that. It doesn't work for me.

We are told to forget that the human body does not function in top form forever. As with anything which has lasted 60, 70, or 80 years, there will be gradual wear and tear. Things will function less efficiently, they'll get clogged or stiff in the joints, or simply atrophy. This is a normal process and there is nothing wrong with it. Problems arise when we deny the process and become trapped in wishing it otherwise.

We now have a "Senior Citizen Month." It is proper that the aged should be so recognized and celebrated, but it seems odd to me to celebrate age. Perhaps it would be more fitting to honor those individuals who are still growing, productive and glowing *in spite of* their age.

I, for one, am determined to live as fully and as long as possible, despite the creaks and limitations. I may move more slowly but I'm determined to move. I may not be able to eat as much, but I refuse to relinquish the joy of food. I may develop

any number of limitations, but I'm determined to keep my eyes and ears wide open, making room for every new experience.

I have great admiration for all those who have made peace with aging, accepted it as inevitable and risen above it. It takes strength, stamina, determination, and a keen sense of humor. That's what deserves celebration and recognition, not a birth date!

It is said that Methuselah lived to be 969 years old. This may be, but historically the maximum known life span for a human being has remained pretty much the same. We know of no one who has lived to be 150 and statistically few make it to 100.

There's always someone seeking a fountain of youth or ways of extending the life span. People have made millions from gadgets, vitamins, creams and special surgery—all of which hint at having the eternal secret. It is a fact that the average life span continues to increase. Scientists are diligently at work discovering ways of engineering our genetic or hormonal clocks, regenerating tissue and transplanting vital organs.

We seem to be more health conscious than ever, with the bottom line being a longer life. We have learned that if we exercise, eat intelligently—and give up smoking, we can live beyond our former expectancies.

Many of us would question whether life extension is a good idea. We're aware of the risks of uncontrolled population growth, finite food resources, and prolonging life for people who are no longer able to live it actively.

Other questions come to mind. Will greater longevity

really improve the quality of our lives? Will it relieve a growing sense of discontent, loneliness and frustration? Will it help quiet our basic fears? Does a longer life necessarily mean a happier one?

Life is a fantastic gift, but I find few among us who are truly living it with dignity. Too many people bemoan their mortality and so few fill the time they have in life with joy.

I had many students in my years of teaching—young, attractive, intelligent and often with considerable wealth—who, when I would extoll the wonder of being alive, would roll their eyes as if to say, "What's so great about life?" They saw it, even at their young age, full of boredom, predictability, frustration, and problems, problems, problems!

At a recent talk I gave, I was confronted by a very angry person who said he just couldn't believe that I was sincere in the enthusiasm for life which I reflected in my television shows, my books and my columns. He suggested that one would have to be mad or a simpleton not to see the pain, despair and general sickness of our society. "What's there to be happy about?" he asked. "The world is full of pain and disillusionment and you're deluding us all by suggesting that one can rise above it."

The inference was clear that **there** is something not quite right about people who openly profess a love of life. We must be either lacking in intelligence or in sincerity.

Again and again we hear life being put down. Rodney Dangerfield suggested that "Life is just a bowl of pits." Edna St. Vincent Millay said, "It is not true that life is one damn thing after another . . . It's one thing over and over." Kathleen Norris said, "Life is easier to take than you think; all that is necessary is to accept the impossible, do without the indispensable and bear the intolerable." Often quoted are the words of Thoreau, who said, "The mass of men lead lives of quiet desperation."

I hear these sentiments repeated in countless situations, as if life were a test of endurance. My question then is, "If life is such a drag, why are we so determined to extend it?" Sometimes I feel like an endangered species—so unique that I seem to continue to find inspiration in words such as those of Anne Frank: "In spite of everything life is good," and naively maintain that waking up each morning is a miracle.

Lest anyone think me hopelessly lost in my own wonderland, I recognize also that there is a darker side to life. For those who choose to view it mainly from this perspective, life may well seem like one overlong ordeal. Why indeed would we work so hard to prolong an existence of pain and fear and disappointment?

Certainly no one lives free of these things, but they represent only one side. There is also another side, a lighter side, of joy, hope, trust, laughter, beauty, wonder and love. Perhaps the good life is in learning to balance the two, remembering to let go of the darkness as soon as we have learned from it, while we continue to welcome the light.

I'm all for extending life, but I wonder if it might not be more important to first find ways of living our lives with more quality and dignity before we become obsessed with extending them.

A Passion for Learning

George Bernard Shaw said it best when he wrote, "Life is no brief candle for me. It is a sort of splendid torch which I have got hold of for a moment, and I want to make it burn as brightly as possible before handing it on to future generations." Each of us bears a torch. We must keep it lit. The hope for tomorrow is to pass on blazing torches now!

I can't tell you how many graduations I've sat through in the last three decades of being a teacher. I've seen thousands of students receive their diplomas. I've listened to hundreds of speakers encourage them to "sail off into the challenge of tomorrow." I've watched as celebrities were given honorary degrees and alumni enthusiastically extolled the virtues of the "good ol' Alma Mater." I've observed parents desperately trying to locate their children among the assembly of young people, and swelling with pride as their child's name was pronounced (or mispronounced) by the President.

I've listened attentively as the valedictorian has given the class commencement speech, assuring the audience with trembling but practiced tones that this class would "make the world safe for democracy and find solutions to the economic and social ills endangering this greatest of all countries."

After a few hours of such continuing excitement, the ceremony comes to an end. The professors turn in their borrowed robes and wish their students well for the last time. The graduates have their pictures taken and are whisked off to homes and restaurants for festivities, and the custodians are alone on an empty campus. Left to fold the chairs, disassemble the platform and clean up the dropped programs and confetti, they grumble that the next commencement is just a few months away.

Graduation ceremonies certainly fulfill a very important function. Aside from being a mark of achievement for the graduates, they are also an assurance to the society about to receive them that they have acquired certain basic skills.

What continues to disturb me over the years is that we are not in agreement about what constitutes an educated person. Should we assume that the curriculum we prescribe for our young people prepares them not only for a complex and changing world, but also how to relate to other human beings?

What about faith and inner calm? What about happiness and enjoyment of living? What about courage and the conquest of fear? What about peace of mind, the ability to give and receive love? What of confidence, self-respect and self-discipline? What about hope for the future and contentment in later years? Where does this learning fit into the definition of the intelligent human being? Perhaps we have for too long believed that such things are not in the domain of public education, that people come by them naturally and develop them on their own time in their own way.

Declining achievement in our nation's schools has pointed up the need to reinforce basic skills. It is an understandable reaction to a very real problem. The danger lies in our overreacting and promoting efficiency and competency as the only true objectives of our educational system.

Somewhere along the way we need to reinforce the idea that we make decisions based on feelings as well as facts. Education's ultimate objective—that we grow and become the best person we can be and help others do the same—is only partially served by teaching the three R's. This requires us to expand our definition of education, not constrict it.

Sometimes after a graduation I leave alone, after the custodians, a bit concerned for our young, *educated* graduates— those who, I am told, will become our leaders. Have we done them justice if we've prepared them only to be skilled scientists, doctors, lawyers, teachers, engineers, and computer experts? Will the education we've given them sustain them in an insecure economy, a world on the brink of annihilation, a society charged with intimidation, suspicion and uncertainty? If not, we may have presented them with a degree which will serve them for little.

I'm still not sure what the truly *educated* person is, but I'm certain it's not dependent upon years of formal schooling. We will have been only half educated unless we have acquired

survival techniques, a sense of human dignity and worth, an appreciation of life, the ability to give and receive love, the knowledge of how to use our limited time wisely, and the determination to leave the world a better place for our having been in it.

In 1973 I wrote a book which has remained my favorite published work, *The Way of the Bull*. The title was taken from a Zen Koan which told of a young man who went in search of the bull of wisdom. When he found him, he tied the bull to a tree in the backyard, thinking that in this way it would be his forever. Of course, in the morning the bull was gone. Wisdom is not so easily obtained. The book deals with my search, the people I met, the philosophies I encountered and what I learned from it all.

To each of us, at certain points in our lives, there come opportunities to rearrange our formulas and assumptions— not necessarily to be rid of the old, but more to profit from adding something new. Anthropologists tell us that we are indelibly marked and easily identifiable by the culture in which we are raised. We carry this imprint in the way we talk and walk, even by our posture. But we are distinguished also in our human ability to adapt to new ways and learn new things—to synthesize the familiar with the unfamiliar.

Much of what I was taught in the Eastern world has stayed with me. Aside from what personal value it has for me, like all learning, its greatest value is in being shared. For instance, happiness, in the Eastern world, has little to do with acquiring material things which we so often use as a measure of a person's worth in our culture. Asians find happiness in the recognition of what one already has, and the development

and full appreciation of it.

They believe that each person is perfect as is, but must work to reflect that perfection. They believe that a life lived fully is one that is being lived in the present. Most of us live too far into the future, or weigh ourselves down with regrets about the past. The only true value is to be found in the here and now. Much of our unhappiness stems from our tendency to live in the past or future, both of which are illusions.

Living fully each moment, at the moment, means living with enthusiasm and spontaneity. It is not only learning the exciting possibilities available to us in each moment, it is learning to create them, as well.

To believe in oneself is also an essential aspect of Eastern philosophy. It's not an unfamiliar idea in our part of the world either, though my experience has been that many of us don't really value ourselves as much as we should. We think that life would be better if we were someone else. We undervalue our talents and question our worth. We are hesitant about accepting a new challenge because we convince ourselves that we haven't the resources to meet it.

We see time spent on self-understanding as useless, even selfish. We are more frightened than challenged by our potential. We understand that we are only able to share the resources we have, but continue to feel guilty about spending the time necessary to develop them.

Asian wisdom suggests that we live in attentiveness, always open and fully aware. This requires us to listen without preconceptions, watch through unprejudiced eyes, recognize, as the Buddhist says, that a frog lodged in a well cannot ever understand the limitless expanse of sky.

New learning and perceptions come from many surprising sources. Our personal world may seem vast, but within the perspective of a universe we are all like the frog in the well— so small, so limited, so unaware of the whole. Our challenge

is to break out of our limitations, self-imposed or otherwise, and accept the fact of our limitless self, vitally interacting in a limitless universe. How sad is the story of the caterpillar who looks up at the butterfly and exclaims, "You'll never get me up there!"

There is so much of value that we as Westerners can learn from Eastern thought. We are seeking the same things— self-knowledge, personal growth, inner peace—things which are attainable in many ways.

Our attitudes and philosophies fan out in an unlimited number of directions and so affect many thousands during our lifetimes. We truly have an obligation to become the best possible human beings we can. Any new learning which will aid us to attain this goal is a benefit to everyone. It may be our only hope of rising out of the well and joining the butterflies.

One of my happiest childhood memories is going to the local library after school on Thursdays for story hour. Our library had a small garden patio. There we kids assembled in a semicircle on the grass. Promptly at 3:30 P.M., the children's librarian appeared with a handful of books under her arm. She would sit on a small chair, greet us happily and begin her readings. What a magical time we had. It was there that I first became acquainted with Hans Christian Anderson, the Brothers Grimm, Lamb's *Tales of Shakespeare,* Swift's *Gulliver's Travels;* and of course, wonderful episodes of Lewis Carroll's, *Alice in Wonderland.*

I would never have known these great works if it had not been for Miss L. She was a trained, professional librarian. She loved books. She shared them as treasures.

As I grew up, it was this same person who dissuaded me

from attempting to read every book from A to Z in the library. She taught me the difference between poor and great literature. She convinced me that libraries housed trash along with masterpieces; and, if I tried to read all the books, there would be no time for the truly great volumes.

For a start she gave me Mark Twain, Charles Dickens, Pearl Buck, Agatha Christie and Edgar Allan Poe. I'll be eternally grateful for her guidance and concern. For me, she opened worlds of words in which I've remained forever mesmerized.

Her method was a perfect example of teaching through modeling. Her abundant love of books was contagious and passed on to hundreds of us.

Recently, I was shocked to read that library schools are fast disappearing. There seems to be no longer any need, or perhaps not enough money, for trained librarians—especially children's librarians. Replacing them are computer experts and information scientists. Many libraries are closing their doors or having to restrict their buying due to severe budget cuts.

School libraries often have resources so inadequate as to be almost useless. This is so even though there is proof that early and easy access to books turns children into avid readers. Having interesting books at hand and reading them aloud to children makes readers of nonreaders. It's that simple. The American Reading Council has demonstrated that they have had close to 100 percent success among low income children in getting them to read and love books if they are provided with daily access to enjoyable books and magazines.

Another depressing step toward the inevitable is that our libraries will soon be run by computers. Certainly we will then have easy access to the books and information we desire in just a few seconds. But I wonder what will happen to the magic of storytelling in the garden, the sense of criticism and

taste which can only be encouraged and passed on by a discerning, sensitive, knowledgeable person.

Meanwhile, the fact remains that we are adding one million illiterate teenagers each year to our already shocking number of nonreaders. Julia Reed Palmer, the executive director of the American Reading Council, recently wrote in *Publishers Weekly,* "Lack of access is a fact today for millions of American children who live in communities with no bookstore and who go to schools with no libraries."

There are some traditions we cannot afford to see eroded or economized. We hear enough about a future which is more and more hopeless without contributing in yet another way. A society which minimizes the value of reading or limits the accessibility of good reading materials is doing just that.

My childhood library still stands in an East Los Angeles suburb. It's a bit worn with age. The number of volumes hasn't increased greatly over the years due to continued financial cutbacks. The garden where so many of us first learned about the wonder between book covers is now being left to weeds.

A few weeks ago I had dinner with a very dear friend who is a public school principal. On this particular Friday night she appeared to be without her usual glow and bounce. Her gaze was distant and the sparkle was gone. She fell into a chair and let her head fall back and her arms dangle. "I'm beat!" she moaned. "What happened to you?" I questioned. "The usual." Then it all came out.

"One of the children fell and broke his leg. His parents are threatening to sue. Another parent came in screaming that I was prejudiced against her child because we hadn't placed

him in a gifted class. There was a rabid squirrel on the school grounds, and the custodian has threatened to quit unless the children stop messing up the restrooms. He wants them policed. How can I ask teachers to do toilet duty?"

I thought to myself "This is the usual!?"

We live in a time and place in the world where there is education for all, regardless of income, social status or ability. Schools are set up to educate—to transmit the accumulated knowledge of the past while encouraging independent thinking, creativity and joy. Somewhere along the line we have also entrusted our schools with the teaching of values, physical and mental health, and even sex education. This we insist must go on, year after year, in classrooms of 30 to 36 students.

The only way we can relate to that would be to imagine having 36 children in our home and be expected to keep order, maintain interest, motivate them to read, write, spell, do arithmetic in order to become computer experts, gain a knowledge and appreciation of history, literature, music, art, and social and moral values! How many of us would take on that task? And if we would, could we do it eight hours a day, five days a week, for ten months a year? I constantly hear parents sigh after only three months of summer vacation, "Thank heaven they're going back to school."

I can recall very vividly the frustration I felt for the many years I taught second graders in a public elementary school. I loved my work. My only real problem was a feeling of isolation. I felt a real lack of appreciation for my needs—almost abandoned. The school board had more problems than they could handle. The superintendent was constantly being attacked by one concerned group or another. My principal was over her head in Band-Aids for parents and children alike. I could hardly expect these individuals to have time for a simple second grade teacher. And there were the parents. I

remember working for weeks preparing for parents' night. I put up their children's work. I created all sorts of audio-visual aids to illustrate what we were doing to create a learning environment. I decorated the classroom, even arranged for coffee and cookies at my expense. This, in addition to a twenty-minute presentation which I had worked on for weeks. On the evening of parents' night three mothers showed up. Always the same ones.

Educating everyone is a difficult task because *everyone* includes children with educational limitations, low motivation, and social and emotional problems. Still, the educator plows ahead with a confidence bordering on naiveté. Perhaps that's what is needed.

I remember teaching in Asia where there is a no more revered profession. My students even stood at attention when I entered the classroom. Of course, I neither wanted nor expected such a thing and most of our teachers would agree. Nevertheless, the necessity to recognize and appreciate the role of educators in our society remains a vital consideration.

My friend and I discussed these things, and I'm pleased to report that after a quiet dinner with wine and good conversation, she was ready to go again. Her enthusiasm was back. Her eyes were alive.

But just a few days ago I heard that one of her teachers slipped on a toy and broke a rib. A child ran away. Her already bare bones reading program budget was cut. The roof was leaking. I hope, at least, that her custodian didn't quit, that the parents didn't sue, and that it won't rain. Then perhaps she can get on with what she was hired for—the process of education! May God bless the Educator.

Mark Twain once wrote that, when he was a boy of 14, he thought his father was so ignorant that he could hardly stand to have him around. But, he added, "When I got to be 21, I was astonished at how much he had learned in seven years."

Happily, as we grow and change, some of our most basic perceptions change as well. So it is with our images of father that we refine and focus as we grow wiser.

Unlike Twain, many people see their fathers as images of perfection, and soon learn that even pillars of strength have their vulnerabilities—that along with all their right answers and assurances, dads also have doubts and uncertainties; they are only human. We discover that our fathers are no more capable of perfection than we are. This might be a disappointment initially, but seems to bring us closer together in the long run.

When I was growing up, most fathers were out of the home much of the time. Children caught only glimpses of them in the morning or evening as they came and went to work. Father's role was mostly that of the strong, responsible, even punitive force in the family. "Just wait until your father gets home," was heard often. When father came home, he would mete out the required punishment. Seldom were fathers seen as warm, caring, nurturing parents—that was mother's role. Many children grew up hardly knowing their father as an individual. "I never see him," I'd hear from friends. "He's always too busy."

When I was a child, my father didn't fit this mold. Though he worked hard and was a good provider, he was also a real presence in our lives. He had no macho image to maintain. He was tender, warm and affectionate. Of course, he could also be firm when he needed to be. In fact, there was a look that came over him when he was disappointed or angry with our behavior that was our most dreaded punishment. We learned from his example, and were encouraged by his con-

cern and involvement with us. We felt his active caring and love in many ways. These were his gifts to us, made all the more precious because they have stayed with us through the years.

Today's roles and attitudes are changing, and so is the image of Dad. Having worked with children and young people for all of my professional career, I have noticed striking differences in attitudes regarding fathers. It has been interesting, and heartening, to observe that over the past few decades fathers' primary roles have changed from determined providers to loving nurturers. We've finally learned that fathers have intuition and instincts toward being parents just as strong as those of mothers.

Happily for fathers and their children, the notion that real men leave the raising of children to Mom—that too much involvement in the upbringing of one's children somehow compromises one's masculinity—is becoming less and less a reality. There is a growing emphasis these days on the vital bond that develops between fathers and children. Studies indicate that this bond begins to form far earlier than we once imagined—even before birth. It has been demonstrated that babies in the delivery room show a decided preference for their father's voice over the voices of strangers. This suggests that in the previous nine months Dad was already making his presence known to his child. In addition, the old image of expectant fathers pacing nervously in a waiting room is being replaced by an image of two proud parents working and sharing in the profound joy of childbirth.

Men are realizing that they have a responsibility to provide for their children not only in material ways, but in emotional ways as well. They are also more than willing to make this commitment. Even fathers who are unable to spend as much time as they would like with their children are finding that the amount of time is not nearly as important as the quality of

time they share. Warm, unhurried, joy-filled time together stimulates the mutual bonding and love so important to any relationship.

My father was a part of my life for over fifty years. He's gone now and though life goes on, no one can ever fill the void his death created. There can never be another Papa. It wasn't easy to say goodbye, but in a very real sense he'll always continue to live, through the joy of life that he taught me—his generosity, sense of humor and the many ways he made us feel so important, unique and loved.

I'll never be able to pay him back for all his years of giving, but he'd never expect to be repaid. It's good that we have a special day to honor fathers, but I'm happy I didn't wait to thank him until it was too late.

A Passion for A Better World

*T*oo often our sensibilities are assaulted and bludgeoned by all that seems bad in the world—the T.V. bulletins of the day's horrors, the full, graphic story we get by watching the eleven o'clock news.

Why do we allow ugliness to assume such an overriding importance in our lives? If we don't cast it out with determination, it will surely blind us to all the bright reality around us. If only we could step out of our perceptual traps and see that beauty and goodness comprise at least an equal part of what there is. What a miracle would unfold in this world of negativity if we all subscribed to this one simple idea!

The man called the public library. The librarian reported that he sounded hesitant and frightened. He didn't want to give his name. After an awkward pause, he told the librarian that he'd heard about a program for nonreaders. He said that he was calling for a friend. The librarian gave him all the information regarding the National Program for Adult Literacy. She encouraged him to help his friend to enroll at once, but as they talked, he admitted that he, and not his friend, was illiterate. He told her that his father had deserted the family when he was a child. His mother was sick and on welfare. He hated school and dropped out when he was twelve. Since that time he had worked at odd jobs to help support himself and his family. He never learned to read. Each time he tried to improve himself he was faced with a job application or impossible reading material. He was too embarrassed to admit he couldn't read and was forever relegated to coming to the same dead end street. He's reading now.

R. was in the eighth grade when she dropped out of school. She couldn't read a word. To support herself, she started with baby-sitting, followed by work as a maid at a local hotel and finally was promoted to the hotel supervisor. She was so efficient that she was soon offered a much better paying job at a local hospital, but was afraid to apply because of her embarrassment at not being able to read. That's when she decided to respond to a T.V. ad regarding the local reading program. She was highly motivated and learned quickly. Larry, her program coordinator, told me recently that she is doing astoundingly well and presently she has a special goal: to be able to read her family Bible.

These are true success stories. They are only two of the 23 million American adults who are classified as functionally illiterate. That means that they do not have sufficient reading and writing ability to complete a simple job application or pass a driver's test. This is a problem that is being seen more

and more as a crisis. The fact that 2.3 million individuals are added to the ranks of the illiterate each year justifies a certain alarm.

Unknown to many, there are actively successful programs to help alleviate this serious problem. They are offered free of charge and made possible through the efforts of volunteers throughout the country. The responsibility to administer these programs is passed on to each State by the U.S. Office of Education through the Governor's offices. The program is labeled, The Adult Literacy Initiative. It's designed to make each individual community responsible for its illiterate population. Generally, the program emanates from local libraries.

At a ceremony recognizing the program's inception in 1984, President Reagan said, "Let us today resolve to roll up our sleeves and get to work, because there's much to be done. Across this great land, let those of us who can read teach those who cannot. Let the light burn late in our classrooms, our church basements, our libraries, around kitchen tables, wherever we can gather to help others to help themselves to the American Dream."

Volunteers all over the country have responded to the call. Diagnostic programs supervised by professionals are matching the needs of the nonreader with willing volunteers. This program is functioning, even within the walls of local prisons. Anyone is eligible.

Reading is essential for growth. It gives a whole dimension to our lives. It has been so since the first reading material was made available to the masses. It helps us to know and understand each other and our world better, to see beneath exteriors, to wipe out boundaries and distances. Thankfully there are those among us who are determined to achieve literacy for all.

Overcoming illiteracy in our country is a crusade that concerns us all. It deserves our support. Ignorance,

especially as it applies to this growing segment of our population, is only served by our complacency.

Like so many other statistics that frighten or appall us, the trend toward greater illiteracy is seen as one more sign of our decay and disintegration. But while the doomsayers are marking our time, there are those who are stepping forward to reverse the trend—because they care.

What would we do without our dreams? How would we get through even one day without them?

Of course, I'm told that healthy individuals face reality head on, that to live with illusions is a very dangerous thing, that the world is a serious business and doesn't have room for dreamers. Well, I don't believe it. It's not a problem as long as we know the difference between illusion and delusion.

For many of us, reality can frequently be a bit too real. In fact, we are often tossed about by the whims of an incomprehensible, often cruel reality. We may be forced to face poverty, danger, illness, impending death, lack of love, loneliness—the list seems endless. Illusions can be a great help in handling these situations.

All of us live with illusions. They abound in places like Atlantic City or Las Vegas. I'm not referring to professional or compulsive gamblers, just the thousands of individuals sitting hopefully, hour after hour, at the one-armed-bandits, dreaming of hitting the jackpot. We know full well that the odds are against us, but we're sure the prize is just one more nickel, dime, quarter or dollar away. When asked why we do it, we say that it's just a form of recreation, that gambling is fun. But in the back of our minds is the newspaper story about the person who last year hit the million dollar jackpot. So we

stay in the noisy, smoky room and try to stick it out. No real harm done—in fact, we are quite ready to do the same on our next visit.

It is often the hope of finding that certain someone that keeps the single people going to special bars, church socials, community events. Without these activities, which suggest that someone may be waiting at the very next turn, they might never break free from their past. That kind of illusion can't be too wrong.

I have a good friend who has a terminal illness. Not long ago she was told that her condition would worsen progressively. She has a dream, not a delusion, that getting back to her friends, family, job and old lifestyle would give her the additional momentum she needed for life. So far she's been right, much to the amazement of her physicians.

As a poor kid growing up in a Los Angeles ghetto, I had dreams of going to college and becoming a teacher—a seemingly impossible desire considering our financial condition. Mama, who had her share of dreams, was always more of a realist when it came to the dreams of her children. She wanted me to become a barber. "People will always have hair," she'd argue logically. "It keeps growing. They'll always need a good barber. You can't fail."

I was a stubborn kid and refused to relinquish my dream. I found a way to realize it. After five years of higher education, I became a teacher with the monumental salary of six thousand dollars a year. Mama was quick to point out that, figuring the price of haircuts, I'd have made a lot more than that and after much less preparation. Are mamas ever wrong?

I can't even imagine a world without those dreamers who have the feeling that things will be better tomorrow. In that feeling becomes a sort of self-fulfilling prophecy and causes us to work actively to make things better.

I'm not suggesting that we all start living an illusion, but

it's an interesting psychological finding that one hundred percent realists are often among the most depressed persons in our society. I'll take healthy illusion any day. If our dreams cause us to become active seekers and partakers of life, setting up the necessary contingencies for making things happen, then they can be positive forces which are conducive to happiness and growth.

We might learn a lesson from Snow White. She dreamed that someday her Prince would come. But in the meantime, in place of moping around, she had a good life with the Seven Dwarfs!

I had a student who is severely physically handicapped. She was born with cerebral palsy, which has affected all four of her extremities. Her muscles are tense and require an inordinate amount of energy to control. She has a wheelchair over which she takes command and pushes around with determination as often as she sits in it. She's an attractive girl. She has a brilliant mind. Without asking for any special advantages she has managed to climb the educational ladder to a graduate program in special education with a top grade point average. She is determined to dedicate her professional life to making the world a better place for the many individuals like herself.

During the day she works full time as a high school teacher. At the end of the day she drives herself to the university in her specially equipped automobile and takes evening classes. She then goes home and prepares for her next day's classes as well as does her homework. Never have I heard her complain or ask for any special considerations.

She is only one of many such impaired individuals I have

worked with during my thirty years of interacting with the disabled. It has always seemed to me that, benevolent as we claim to be in our society, we should want to make life as easy as possible for such individuals, recognizing the almost insurmountable physical and emotional problems they must deal with in their daily lives. But every time I speak with my student she relates another horror story, which indicates that prejudice, ignorance and avoidance of the handicapped as a group are still rampant in our society.

For example, when she told a rehabilitation counselor that her professional goal was to earn a Doctorate in Education, he told her that for her to strive for such an exalted goal was unrealistic. "Why," he added, "even I don't have a Ph.D. . . ."! We have a long way to go.

Another time when she was being interviewed for a teaching position, even though she had scored in the top ten percent on the written examination, had completed all the requirements with honors, and had proven her ability in her practice teaching and field work assignments, one of the interviewers took her aside and asked, "Why are you so determined and stubborn about getting a job? With the seriousness of your handicap you could apply for total disability and never have to work a day in your life!"

Most recently she caused quite a stir when she entered a gourmet restaurant with some friends. Even though, with elbows planted firmly on the table, she can get food to her mouth without too much mishap, the maitre d' was totally taken aback. His attitude reflected his disapproval that such a person should consider defacing his elegant establishment. She had to patiently assure him that all he had to do was to bring food and drink—she would do the rest.

A day seldom passes when she is not submitted to such demeaning, condescending experiences. Often, it's true, people mean well. Still, it's amazing to me that she is able to

survive these situations and still maintain a sense of human dignity as a woman, and an unyielding sense of determination.

She is only one of the many thousands of handicapped—some blind, some deaf, some paraplegic—who must deal with this attitude daily. We sometimes seem to forget that they are people too. They vary as much as the nonimpaired. Some are efficient, strong and self-reliant. Others are careless, frightened and dependent. It seems that we should at least be able to allow these individuals to make their own statements without having to deal with our preconceptions. Few of them ask for special considerations. They ask only for the same understanding, caring and compassion we would give to any human being.

Many of us still react negatively to differences, physical or otherwise. We avoid those individuals who do not meet *normal* standards, who move differently, who look different, speak differently, use canes, wheelchairs, or braces. We forget that these are only external things and are the least important facets of the individual. We fail to get beyond the cosmetic and directly into the heart. When we do allow ourselves to do this, we find a person there like ourselves—who loves, cries, laughs, knows frustration and loneliness and desperately wants to be appreciated for what he or she really is. It is at this point that the human connection, a connection which goes beyond the impairment, becomes possible.

Each year we read about or see television coverage of natural disasters: floods, tornadoes, hurricanes, earthquakes. We are appalled by the devastation they create and are amazed

by the ability we human beings have to rise above them, to re-energize, to reassemble our resources and go on living.

For instance, each summer California dries up. Those of us who are natives prefer to call it California's "golden period," a time when the state's rolling hills become golden and beautiful because of the tall dried grasses. Of course, the slightest spark can bring on a roaring inferno of seven foot high flames which, when fanned by the summer winds, can devour anything in its path. Gallant fire fighters battle the flames for weeks on end, often successfully, but at times helplessly, while the fires explode trees and houses, kill animals and plant life—anything in the way.

Recently I spoke with some friends who live in one of these dry rural areas and were still shaken as they described "that night the fires came." They stood outside their home watching the flames surround them in the night sky, moving closer with each moment. They told of the intense heat and ashes, and of the oppressive winds taking their breath away. There was the dreaded sound of the police and fire vehicles sent to blare out the news of a necessary evacuation, and then the numbing scene of friends and neighbors gathering up their families, pets and valuables, abandoning their homes to the approaching flames.

They described how in the midst of this tragedy and pain there was also a common concern and understanding among the neighbors. Volunteers came from everywhere to evacuate houses, search the neighborhood for each other's children and do what they could to save property.

Everyone and everything seemed to move silently and quickly through the darkness as the roads filled with vehicles heading for safe ground. The warnings continued through the night as the sky blazed a darker red.

Finally my friends followed their neighbors. They gathered their two dogs, two cats and two horses. They went into their

home for what might be the last time, trying to decide what to take with them. They looked about them at the things they'd collected and loved and cared for all these years: works of art, furniture, mementos—no time to take any of them. A lifetime of accumulated memorabilia, and nothing to do but shut the door and leave it all to fate. There was only time to gather up some valuable papers, rush out the door and not look back.

It was interesting to hear what people took as they frantically escaped to safety. One woman took her grocery discount coupons. A man took a box of tools (he was determined to build again). Some took family albums, kitchen utensils, antique furniture, letters. One man even took his television set. Another took his daughter's favorite toys—the teddy bear she couldn't sleep without and her Cabbage Patch doll. This, he felt, would give her some continuity amidst all the uprooting.

It would be an interesting exercise for us all to ask ourselves what we would salvage if we had only a few moments to gather things. We would certainly learn a great deal about ourselves.

If such disasters have any value, it must be in causing us to look deeply into what is truly important in life. Too often our worth as individuals is determined by how many things we possess and what their monetary value is. We can become so attached to our things that we sometimes find ourselves controlled by them. We forget that things are usually replaceable.

I recall time after time, while on my world travels, visiting lands where natural catastrophes were a way of life and had taught the local people well. Why build big houses in places where monsoons would likely take them into the sea? Why accumulate things which will only have to be packed and moved? How much wiser to invest in more permanent and vital things such as family and friendships.

People in the aftermath of catastrophic events often seem to have a strange sense of exhilaration. Perhaps it is because they find they can survive a threatening situation, or perhaps it is the realization that they are not alone—that there are those who would stand by them in time of need. Whatever the insight, it's a pity that we must sometimes suffer tragedy in order to learn the real values.

"Don't ever waste," Mama would say. "Think about all the starving people in the world." Was there ever a mother who didn't say that? I must admit that thinking of starving people in the world didn't help my appetite. In fact, with my dish full of food, I couldn't imagine what she was talking about. It was not until years later when I traveled the streets of the world that I began to understand a little about the effects of poverty and hunger.

We in America are among the best fed people in the world. We return mounds of uneaten food in restaurants, throw out great quantities in our garbage cans, and allow it to go to waste in our refrigerators. We seldom permit ourselves to feel hunger pangs. Why should we?

We have short-order food stands around every corner, well-stocked supermarkets everywhere, and restaurants of every degree of splendor specializing in varieties of cuisines. Most of us have some money in our pockets to purchase these things when we choose. Why should we concern ourselves with hunger?

The World Bank estimates that a quarter of the human race in the world today is chronically undernourished. One out of every four human beings will go to bed hungry tonight and more than half of these are children. We don't have to go out

of our country to find hunger. All we need do is look in at any food kitchen from Los Angeles to New York, from Detroit to Dallas. If we study the greater picture, we find that half the population of all developing countries is hungry. One out of every two people in Benin, Cape Verde, Gambia, Mali, Somalia, Niger, and many other countries is starving. Remote places . . . almost unreal . . . not very pleasant . . . easy to forget.

There is no shortage of food in the world. There is sufficient food, I've read, to provide two pounds a day for every living person on earth—surely enough for the maintenance of life. But having food available is just not the whole problem. If it were, there wouldn't be any hungry people in the United States.

I recall my wisecrack answer as a child when I was told that I had to eat everything on my plate because of the starving children in Africa. I'd mumble over my plenty, "Well, why don't you wrap it up and send it to them." I can't tell you how brilliant I thought my solution to be. If it were only that easy.

World hunger is not like an immediate crisis to which we respond once and it disappears. It is an ongoing problem. Our role in attempting to alleviate it raises moral, political and practical questions—questions that governments, as well as individuals, are not always willing to face. Although it's not difficult to reach the conscience of anyone who has seen the anguished faces and the distended stomachs of starving children, it is sometimes too remote a problem for others to concern themselves about.

Few can question the humanitarian tradition in most of the world. An article or news broadcast about a family in need always produces immediate and positive responses. No one truly desires anyone to suffer or starve. After all, we are all members of the human family and we exist together on a very small planet. The pain, desperation and agony brought on by

hunger cannot be ignored. Hunger continues to initiate the most violent wars. It has been known to topple the strongest governments.

Franklin Delano Roosevelt reminded us that, "True individual freedom cannot exist without economic security and independence. People who are hungry and out of a job are the stuff of which dictatorships are made."

There is no simple solution for ending poverty and hunger in the world. It seems shocking to me that it has been with us for so many centuries and still many of our our great educators, scientists, physicians and religious leaders still do not accept this horror as a number one priority and humanity's most immediate challenge.

There is something that each of us can do if we are willing. Finding ways to become involved is a good beginning.

A few years ago I was invited to a local high school for a very special day that had been weeks in the planning. It was called International Day and everybody—students, teachers, administrators and parents—participated. It was a school which had a very diverse ethnic enrollment and this was to be a day to celebrate that diversity. In a central area of the campus, foods from around the world were prepared and proudly displayed. Many students wore clothing that was traditional for their native country. There was latin music in one area, sitar music from India in another, rock in another, music from the Middle East in another, and taking their turn on a makeshift stage were four very elegantly dressed Korean girls doing a traditional dance. There was a special magic in the air that was beautifully reflected in the smiling and proud faces of all who participated.

The teachers and administrators were glowing as they observed their student body milling together, watching, learning, celebrating—such a contrast to the tight-knit ethnic groups that usually dominated the scene. The objectives of this event were clearly to increase the students' awareness and appreciation for other cultures, but as I observed and joined in the spirit of this day, I felt a far more important cause was being served. There was a sense of togetherness that was felt and spread by all. Prejudices and animosities were momentarily forgotten. Perhaps for the first time, some of these young people could emerge from their stereotypes and truly sense the pride that comes from varied heritages rich in tradition.

I'd like to believe this day was something more than just a diversion from the classroom. From the interaction I observed, I would judge it was a total triumph for human relations. I'm enough of a realist to know that ingrained habits and prejudices are not so easily changed. The distance between these groups could not be spanned in a single day. More days like it would certainly help, however. Many of the students no doubt reflected the concerns of their adult models. After all, the school was only a microcosm of the larger community, which had been, and still is, struggling to adjust to its growing ethnic diversity.

Enjoying friends and getting along with others is one of the most basic of human needs. I have never known a time when qualities such as friendship and consideration for others were not considered among the greatest of human virtues. H.A. Overstreet stresses this in his statement that, "A person is not mature until he has both the ability and the willingness to see himself among others and to do unto those others as he would have them do to him."

Yet, often when we are confronted with change or unfamiliar situations or people, our instinct is to withdraw, or

even in extreme cases lash out against them. The constructive, dynamic potential that change can bring seldom occurs to us when we place such a premium on familiarity and conformity. The things which make us different should be cause for celebration. Think of it! Each of us is unique among all the varieties of life, and in so many vital ways.

When Robinson Crusoe discovered Friday, though they had vast and varied differences, the joy of their shared company removed any barriers that might have come between them. They became understanding friends. I believe that we sense the truth in their story. It is the same sense that tells us how beautiful it is to see young children who have not yet learned the *importance* of things like skin color, shape of eyes, or a different language.

A good friend recently told me of a case in point. Her daughter is presently attending a first grade class which is predominantly black. She loves her school and her friends. Recently she was sitting at the dinner table with her parents. Out of the blue she said, "Can I have a baby sister? And please, can she be black?"

Once we all were children. What happened?

A Passion for Celebrations

Life is meant to be a celebration! It shouldn't be necessary to set aside special times to remind us of this fact. Wise is the person who finds a reason to make every day a special one.

Traditionally the start of every new year is a time for letting go of the past, wiping the slate clean and renewing our hope in a future, both immediate and distant. We are of course most receptive to anything that strengthens our faith in tomorrow. After all, that's where we will spend the remainder of our lives. Our tradition of forward thinking also includes a vision of a better life for generations yet to come.

So for the sake of continuity and posterity we invest the future with our best intentions. We try to remain hopeful for tomorrow's children and their children. But we are continually reminded from many sides of dark clouds on the horizon. Hope and apprehension for the future are forever in a running battle. We are told that the future will not be a very nice place in which to live; but a different impulse tells us that where there is life there is still hope.

I've often thought that we allow our past to speak too loudly in its implications for our future. Though very often accused of being too optimistic and even Pollyannaish, I am always more willing to look for positive signs than for inexorable doom.

There's a lot of pessimism out there and I'm not buying it. In fact, I'm sick of it. It's hard for me to understand people who say things like, "I'm not bringing a child into this troubled world"; or, "Better we should end it and start over again."

From my vantage point, the world still has just as much chance at Utopia as it does at Armageddon. Besides, like William Faulkner, if I must choose between a life of pain and suffering and no life at all, I'll take the pain and suffering anytime. No matter how miserable people tell me that existence is for us, I'll never be without hope. I haven't learned how to lose it yet.

When I so often say that we all have unlimited potential, I mean exactly that. I feel certain that the most stunning novel

is yet to be written, the most awesome building has yet to be built, the greatest symphony is yet to be composed, the tastiest dessert is yet to be dreamed of. There are planets and stars to be investigated and visited—a whole, as yet undiscovered, universe will continue to stagger the imaginations of a thousand more generations. There are breakthroughs still to be accomplished in virtually every field of human endeavor.

From my perspective, I plan to learn from the past and not suffer because of it. Like many before me, I see a renaissance just ahead and I want to be part of it. It's only natural that I wish to join those whose main purpose is to pass along to another generation the accumulated knowledge and inspiration of the past.

It's really not a lot to ask. We have witnessed so many fantastic things and we know with our hearts and our minds that miracles do happen. I ask only that we believe in the simple proposition that it is continued hope which sustains life. And hope arises from the knowledge that we are living in a time of abundant new beginnings. That's enough cause for celebration.

All of our holidays have one thing in common: a sense of gratitude we share for something or someone. We are thankful to God, to Mom or Dad, or to those who were dedicated to a principle or a cause greater than themselves. The celebration of national holidays was impressed upon me early in life. I especially loved the ones that earned me time off from school. I had a guilty feeling, however, that I should observe these special days by celebrating and by commemorating what they stood for. Too often they became a cause for

a vacation instead.

The Fourth of July was always given special significance in my home because my parents were immigrants. To them, all the clichés about coming to the land of opportunity and freedom were true. Mama and Papa often told us of the long ocean voyage that brought them to a new life; of the Poles, Russians and Greeks who were crowded together with them; of the mixture of hope and fear written on all their faces; and of the joy of first viewing the Statue of Liberty. They clearly remembered spending anxious hours at Ellis Island, then being ushered into a rush of human activity, which, to their amazement, was a typical day on the streets of New York. From here it was many days on a train through the heart of the country to the West Coast—a place that only a year earlier was as distant and unreachable as any spot on earth could be.

Reliving those days were Mama and Papa's way of celebrating a dream of a better life come true. The Fourth of July always seemed a fitting occasion to recall their great adventure—there were enough twists and turns, and interesting people to make it a grand story every time we heard it. Mama and Papa insisted that their children give thanks for being able to live in a land of such freedom and abundance. They seemed more patriotic than the parents of my friends who were born in America and often took their freedom for granted. My parents' gratitude was deeply felt, and they wanted their children to feel the same.

Today patriotism has become something to snicker at. But I continue to remember the human values and principles that are very much a part of our daily lives, even though they are often taken for granted.

We live in a country, for example, that has a tradition of welcoming newcomers to its shores. We regularly attribute America's greatness to the diversity of its people and to the piece of the world they brought with them.

We've also managed to maintain a sense of humor in our country. It's wonderful to be able to take time off from the serious business of living in the real world to find so many things to laugh at. We hold an undying affection for the people who make us laugh, especially in our darkest hours when laughter is most needed.

On one hand, we celebrate the world's oldest living Constitution and, on the other hand, we are ever restless for change and for finding a better way. We continue to honor the wisdom and foresight of those before us, but we also never forget that we are no less responsible for maintaining the principles of the Constitution. We are far closer now, for instance, to "All men are created equal," than when the Declaration of Independence was written. And we have every reason to believe that future generations will perfect the idea further.

I love the fact that Americans aren't afraid of criticism. We make no effort to hide our shortcomings. Neither do we try to close the book on our past so that we may forget a few of its sorry chapters. We always seem ready to challenge and re-examine the values that we hold out to ourselves and others. We do this as individuals and, no less, as a nation. In taking stock in ourselves, it's fitting that we celebrate our Fourth of July with the cheers, accolades and superlatives that we deserve. We have much to be grateful for.

I love the Fall. I think it's my favorite time of the year. There is a wonderful nip in the air. The trees become rainbows and the feel of soft wool sweaters is reassuring against the cold winds. It's a dormant time, a time for all things to rest for awhile—except for humans. We go on and on. But even *we* are asked to sit back and take a moment to reflect, to review

our labors and celebrate what is completed before Spring starts the process all over again. It's that time again for expressions of thanksgiving.

There's something wonderful about the celebration of Thanksgiving. It's such a uniquely American holiday. We hear repeated the stories of Plymouth Rock, Pilgrims and friendly native Americans. We talk about counting our blessings and make lists of those things for which we are thankful. We stop lamenting for a moment things we don't have and celebrate the things we do have.

I can still remember vividly, as many of us can, being in elementary school and preparing for Thanksgiving. We cut out turkeys and colored pictures of the first Thanksgiving feast. Then, happily, with feathered headdresses firmly set on our heads and our turkey cutouts in hand, we were released from school for a four-day holiday. For that, we were truly thankful.

I am amazed how well I remember our Thanksgiving preparations in Miss V.'s third grade class. Miss V. was a very special teacher—one of those you appreciate more in retrospect than at the time. The students thought her an oddball, but no one objected to being in her class. Not only did we do all the usual things for Thanksgiving, but Miss V. had some very special ideas of her own. She requested that we all make a list of the things we were personally thankful for. She told us that we'd be sharing these things with the class just before the holiday.

Though none of us expected much from this assignment, we all did as requested. When the day came we all sat down in a semicircle with Miss V. at the center. She asked for volunteers. Silence. Even in the third grade we had already learned that only fools volunteer. Finally, after an anxious silence, F., the class star, offered to share her list. She was grateful for her doll, her bicycle, her stuffed bear, etc.

Miss V. was furious. "Trivia!" she shouted. "Those are all unimportant things. It's nice that you have them and you should be grateful that you do. But think of the important things we have to be grateful for!" We were all confused. What more important things could there be than our dolls, bicycles, and stuffed bears? Silence. One of our less brilliant classmates ventured a guess. "Turkey?" he asked. Miss V., not renowned for her patience, turned bright red and went into a tirade. "That's just another unimportant thing," she said shaking her head. "Now think!" Silence.

"Why do we really celebrate the day called Thanksgiving?" We all sat quietly, afraid to speak. "Because the Pilgrims landed on Plymouth Rock," the class genius volunteered again. "That's part of the reason but that's the historic reason. What should we be thankful for now?" she sighed deeply. Another silence.

"Well, I guess I'll have to help you. I'll start." We were in rapt attention. She started: "I'm thankful for my eyes that see, my ears that hear, my legs that let me walk, my arms that hold, my mouth that speaks, my mind that thinks. I'm thankful for all the beautiful things in the world and my ability to enjoy them. I'm thankful for hope and dreams and love." This was all too much for the class. We thought it was hilarious. Of course, no one dared look at anyone else for fear that we'd break up, but we heard a snicker here and there. Our fun was not long lasting, for it was now our turn to complete the assignment.

It was natural that most of us echoed Miss V.'s list. With serious faces, stifling laughter, we told each other that we were grateful for our eyes, nose, ears and so on. Some of the more daring class members even began to add things like pets, mothers and fathers, brothers and sisters, and God. But it was J. who changed the day. He was a very small, rather undernourished, shy, and quiet Latin boy. He had hardly been

heard from during the year. In a rather quavering voice he said, "I'm thankful I can go to school and learn. Then, when I grow up I can get a good job and help my mother and father and sisters. Maybe then we can have a nice house and my mother won't be sad all the time and won't fight with my father." I remember that he stopped and looked at Miss V. for approval and added, "And I'm thankful for my ears and my eyes, too."

In a moment, Miss V. had him in her arms. She gave him the longest loving hug I had ever seen her give—she wasn't usually much of a hugger.

I can't speak for the other class members, but that scene stays vividly in my memory. I learned a little more in those few seconds about the real significance of Thanksgiving. It had a little to do with history but it was mostly about now.

Even today I know that my friends and family think I'm crazy, but like Miss V., I use the Thanksgiving meal as a special expression of thankfulness and encourage everyone else at the table to do the same. There are so many things we take for granted in our daily lives. Why must we wait until losing them to realize how thankful we should have been for them? I'd like to present a partial list of what I'm thankful for.

The miracle of life. The privilege of being alive, of waking up in the morning ready for a new day to be experienced with enthusiasm and vitality, the challenge that is mine to make the world a better place, both for me and for everyone else.

For people—each one unique, no two alike. Each with something special to contribute—those who agree with us and help us to grow, as well as those who disagree with us, challenge us and help us to see new possibilities.

For food—wonderful food, each morsel differing from any other. The odors of chicken soup simmering on the stove, or a roast cooking in the oven. The taste and smell of basil, rosemary, crisp apples, ripe peaches, freshly gathered tomatoes and green peppers, onions and garlic.

For gardens—grass, vegetables or flowers. Roses, orchids, daisies and forget-me-nots. Carrots, potatoes, radishes and corn.

For optimists, for they make all things a possibility.

For pragmatists, for they keep us in balance.

For romanticists, for they keep our dreams alive.

For a future, and what is called progress, in the hope that it might lead us to solving the world's problems: hunger, war, fear, suspicion, loneliness.

For the past—the fond memories of how things were. Pre-television days when we took time to talk to each other. When things were made to last. When there were real butchers, bakers and candlestick makers in place of people who appear only when we "ring the bell for service."

For our country, for the United States of America, imperfections and all, which is still the freest land in the world. Where we can worship freely, choose our own leaders and live an existence mainly of our own choice.

For good health: the superb feeling of having full power to use our mental and physical resources to the maximum. And if we aren't as well as we might be, to use what we have and make it do.

For family and friends, for they offer us the needed consistency and loving support that makes it possible for us to continue to risk, and fail, and keep trying. It's good to know that there is someone close by who cares, forgives and accepts.

Our society has provided us with a multitude of things to be thankful for. At the same time it has made some of us too sophisticated for a simple, heartfelt expression of gratitude. A strange paradox.

The original Thanksgiving was a celebration of abundance made more meaningful by memories of scarcity and hardship only a short time before. We tell and retell the Pilgrims' story to carry foward the spirit of that celebration. We do this in the hope that each Thanksgiving we will open our hearts and our minds, even if only for the day, and appreciate the miracle of our existence—and appreciate especially having each other to share it with.

Each year we set aside one day for the celebration of love. We send cards and make phone calls. We buy candy and flowers as offerings for those we love. Even these token gifts we sometimes choose grudgingly. I'll never forget an experience I had in a stationery store once just prior to Valentine's Day. I was among many people looking through

cards covered with hearts and cherubs and red bows.

A woman squeezed herself among us and started groaning about what a nuisance Valentine's Day is. The whole thing was just another commercial exploitation to her, yet she felt compelled to get a card for her lover. Then the cards were either too sentimental or too stupid. When I suggested she might write her own she replied, "Are you kidding? Who has the time for such . . . . . .?"

This heartwarming experience was almost immediately followed by another. A young woman was complaining that she had been sent by her boss to buy a card for his wife. "If my husband couldn't take the time to personally buy me a card, I'd kill him!" she said angrily. There I was, surrounded by hearts, cupids, and loving sentiments, and suddenly the place was a war zone.

We seldom give any serious thought to human love on this special day. I've often thought that we should spend at least as much time studying the dynamics of loving each other as we do in acquiring any other skill. For various reasons, though, we don't do this. We say that love is indescribable. We say that it's unattainable; or, as with so many other things, we take it for granted. Some of the following might be considered, not in any definitive sense, but as simple expressions of a very complex subject.

> The next time I have the urge to speak negatively or rudely to you, I'll swallow and be silent. Loving you doesn't give me license for rudeness.

> If I can't be generous and supportive, I'll at least try not to stand in your way. Loving you means wanting you to grow.

> I won't put my problems onto you. You have

enough problems, I'm certain, and you don't need mine. My love should simplify your life, not complicate it.

I don't always have to be right. I can accept the fact that you are right as often as I am. Loving is sharing with each other. If I already know I'm right, I'll never profit from your insight.

I don't always have to be running the show. Loving is an ebb and flow. Sometimes I'll need to give in. At other times I'll need to take control.

I don't have to be perfect, nor do you. Love is a celebration of our humanness, not our perfection.

I can give up wanting to change you. If I want you in my life, the best thing for both of us is for me to accept you as you are. After all, love is moving forward together in mutual growth.

I don't need to place blame. Since I'm an adult who makes decisions based upon personal experience, there is no one to blame for a poor decision except myself. Love puts the responsibility where it belongs.

I can give up expectations. To wish is one thing, to expect is another. One brings hope, the other can bring pain. Love is free of expectations.

To love is the greatest of human experiences and sooner or later we all realize that without it life is empty and mean-

ingless. Love is always worth the effort, even if it brings confusion, uncertainty and pain in the process. A loving relationship should be a celebration all its own. Let's use this special day as a reminder of that, and then continue celebrating throughout the year.

A Passion for Communication

*O*ne of the surest expressions of love is the sharing of thoughts and feelings. Loving others is to want to understand how they think and how they feel about themselves and the world they live in. Where words fail, it's comforting to realize how many other vital and eloquent ways we have of communicating with each other.

One of our mightiest human possessions is the word. Words have the power to build, to store and create, as well as tear down and destroy. We think with words, we organize our world with words, we communicate with words, we inform with words, we build relationships with words. Our worlds are very much limited by the words we use. Sometimes we become so caught up with words that we forget that they are just symbols for things, and we begin to see them as a substitute for the things they are meant to represent.

It's important to remind ourselves that words are just phonetic symbols put side by side. By themselves they're nothing. Most of the words we know were learned before we were six or seven years old, too early to fully analyze or understand them. These words were defined for us and we accepted them as presented. For example, if the significant people in our lives felt strong hate toward a particular person or thing, the words they taught us concerning these things became a part of our attitude as well. The words soon represented a constellation of thoughts and feelings surrounding those things. Soon we found that we were thinking and responding negatively to them. Of course, this couldn't be helped. Nevertheless, it was in this way that we learned what to hate or fear or avoid.

Just as we acquired the words for goodness, hope, optimism, joy and love, we learned also to attach negative symbols and discovered early the power of directing them where we pleased. We found that words could hurt. As a child, I can remember the standard retort for word bullies: Sticks and stones may break my bones but names can never hurt me! Occasionally this brought a rock or a stick my way, but it was more difficult not to feel the sting of such words as *dirty wop, skinny freak, dumb retard*. I wonder how many of us still feel the pain of labels that devastated us long ago.

Perhaps one of the great human tragedies is that few of us

even stop to ask whether the words we think with and which cause us to feel so strongly are ours or simply echoes which continue to reverberate in our minds. If we stopped to redefine these words, we might discover that many of them are no longer relevant to the present. Words we learned as children may have prevented us from truly experiencing and understanding other persons or things as they really are. For many of us these words continue to serve in their capacity to reject, exclude and judge.

The great humanitarian-scientist, Buckminster Fuller, said that one of the most significant events of his life was when he stopped everything and wrote his own dictionary. He redefined words according to his experience, as what they represented in *his* reality, not that of others. This effect forced him to re-examine his values and reassess his attitudes. It gave him a far deeper appreciation of the power of words for the remainder of his life.

As adults we know that certain behavior is discarded early in life because it is childish and inappropriate. As wise adults we learn that certain words and labels should be discarded as well because they are hurtful or destructive, and if that means passing up the opportunity to tell the latest ethnic joke, then we are all the more fortunate for that insight.

There can be no word large enough to encompass the wonder of a human being. To judge others by a single label is to miss them entirely. As a child I may have been poor, or skinny, or Italian, or a number of things, but I was much more than each one of them. Thank goodness for those special individuals who learned to look beyond the labels and to know me as a whole person. It's not surprising that they turned out to be the people most worth knowing.

Words so often desensitize us. They can paralyze our senses as well as our better instincts. Words are powerful things which we too often take casually. They were created to

help us give organization to chaos. But, unless we are careful, they become traps which lead us to apathy, hate and loneliness. We mustn't allow words to control us. They are our tools to enlarge, not narrow, our lives.

We all need to touch and to be touched. In his book, *Touching,* Ashley Montagu warns us that we cannot fully function and grow without being touched. Volumes of literature attest to the crucial importance of tactile stimulation in a newborn baby; in fact, studies indicate that brain damage, even death, may result from a lack of it. Dr. Montagu writes that this need for being stroked and fondled does not diminish with age. If anything, it increases.

This brings to mind a friend whom I shall call Cliff. He is a wonderful man, a devoted and loving father, and in the usual tradition of the American male, very restrained in any open display of affection. Though no one can question the love he feels for his five sons and they for him, it has not been their custom to be overtly expressive of their feelings for each other. When they greet each other they do so with a "Hi" and a handshake.

About a year ago Cliff suffered a severe stroke. The damage was extensive and irreparable. In addition to physical and mental impairment, there was an amazing change in his emotional makeup. A lifetime of developing a tough exterior was stripped away in the moment of extremity. In fact, the first time I visited him after the stroke, he gave me a tremendous hug. His eyes filled with tears. He no longer seemed to care about convention or what others might think of a man who would openly embrace another man. Even though he was left without speech, that one tender moment spoke volumes.

For the sons, much of what they cherished in their father was lost. But what they now discovered was a new, more gentle, loving person, one that had been hidden from them for all their years. Those who knew Cliff were saddened to see him incapacitated but touched also by this change that had come over him. From the oldest son who is forty-five to the youngest who is thirty-four, their father was still an important role model, but now teaching them that showing affection is a sign of strength rather than of weakness.

So many of us hesitate to touch and be touched. We have learned to substitute a peck on the cheek or an impersonal handshake for a warm embrace, a caressing hand. I taught a class entitled Love 1A, in which I freely advocated that my students be more physically expressive with their families and friends. Some of them felt this was a slightly unorthodox activity and were noticeably uncomfortable with the idea. They couldn't even hug their parents!

We found that many of us really needed to develop a more demonstrative way of expressing our affection, and that, for whatever reasons, people do find the prospect of physically reaching out to others to be difficult. Yet we learned that for those who are reticent, there is always the joyful discovery that their reticence can be easily overcome. There are so many willing individuals who would gladly be recipients.

Most of all we came to the conclusion that where words fail us in our efforts to understand and be understood, reaching out with a hug or gentle touch is often the most direct and eloquent form of communication we have. There is something very unambiguous about one person surrounding another in a warm embrace. It's difficult to misinterpret a loving touch.

I received a letter once from a husband who learned the value of this kind of communication from the recurring arguments he had with his wife. "Our arguments tend to follow a

similar pattern," he wrote. "It's always logic versus emotion. I try always to be perfectly rational while she tries to communicate her feelings. We get nowhere. I know deep inside that sometimes all I have to do is take her into my arms and if it doesn't end the argument, it at least helps us to talk *to* each other instead of *at* each other."

One of our most basic goals in life should be to become better friends and lovers, to draw ever closer to each other in all ways. Touch is the most intimate of our senses and in reaching out to others, the message is clear: I'm here, I'm close, and I care. What a pity that many of us wait a lifetime to discover this miraculous power.

The other day I received a very kind invitation to a dinner party. It came during a period when my life seemed particularly frantic. I attempted to explain this to the caller, but she was unable to understand. She insisted. She assured me that the evening wouldn't be strenuous and would include only a few other guests. I suggested that because of the pressures I was dealing with, I'd probably be very poor company, but she was determined not to take "no" for an answer.

To say no is difficult. But so is accepting no for an answer. Why is it that "no" always seems to infer a rejection or imply rudeness? We seem obliged all too often to say "yes" when we should be saying "no." But how to say it gracefully? More often than not our attempts are inadequate, so we participate in activities from which we receive little pleasure, spending hours at receptions we detest, with individuals who exhaust us. We do this to avoid seeming impolite, ungrateful or exclusive. We forget that we have the right to say no to anything that concerns our own person or time.

It seldom occurs to us that a no answer can be the most considerate and positive one we can give. Saying yes from a sense of obligation, fear of rejection or guilt makes no sense. It's degrading to us and unfair to others. To be present anywhere in body only, without will or spirit, wishing to be elsewhere, is an insult to all concerned. A "no" in such a situation is certainly a blessing to everyone.

I recently talked to a friend who told me that she has come to dread her daughter's invitations to dinner. She senses that her daughter sees these evenings as unpleasant chores. Rather than confront her with it, she pretends to be more gracious and enthusiastic than she usually feels. She says she does this to keep peace in the family even if it means continuing to play out this little charade. Though there are times when a no answer seems out of the question, it is also possible that the alternatives are worse.

For example, it seems wiser to risk a possible misunderstanding than to spend useless hours in boredom or resentment. If there is one thing we don't owe to anyone, it is our reluctant presence. If we are only saying yes from a sense of duty, the other person is always better off without us. It's certain that others can and will survive without us if we're not available. We're more replaceable than we think.

Children illustrate this daily in their play and it would be well for us to learn from them. Mary runs to Pete with great joy and enthusiasm and asks him to play. Pete doesn't share her joy and tells her so. Mary doesn't become despondent or fall into a deep state of gloom. She asks Joe. Instinctively she knows that there are others available somewhere who will meet her needs. Her life doesn't revolve around Pete. She seeks out other friends who would love to play with her. They think she's great.

When others produce feelings of guilt in us when we say no it might be well to let them know at once what we are feeling.

Generally, pointing it out in a kind manner that we are feeling manipulated or hemmed in will usually be enough to get them to reconsider their behavior if they truly care about us.

It's apparent then that saying no can, in many cases, become an act of loving. In fact, relationships grow best within certain limits and structures, and a "no" now and then helps to clarify what these limits are. "No" at the right time can help others to better understand us and our special needs. It's something we have a right to expect from one another.

Life is too short for us to spend great chunks of our time doing things we'd rather not be doing. We should be less fearful of saying no. In the end, it may be the most loving thing we can say.

It seems to me that if there is ever going to be peace among humans, we can't wait for total agreement—we're going to have to settle for coexistence. Since truth is so often perceived differently by each of us, it can be no other way. For all those who have good reasons for a nuclear freeze, there are as many who feel it would be political suicide. Thousands feel that one candidate for public office is a savior, and as many are certain that he or she will lead us to ruin. I am certain that if someone were to ask us the color of a red rose at which we were all looking, there would be some who would see it not as red, but wine or purple or magenta, and be willing to argue the point to the bitter end.

Such minor disagreements can be responsible for losing friends, breaking up marriages, and on a more frightening scale, bringing on world conflicts. Why do we have to fully agree with people in order to continue to love and respect them? After all, an opinion about something or someone is

simply an opinion, a unique way of viewing the world. Each of us has a very personal world view; but no matter how we see something, we as people have more intrinsic value than any single opinion. In fact, I make a point of seeking friends who have diverse opinions. They are the ones who are most often responsible for my changing attitudes. They keep me continually evaluating my beliefs. They are the ones who most challenge my mind and encourage my growth.

It is well to remember that a loving relationship need not be an agreeing one. We can continue to coexist in love as long as we keep dialogue going. Perhaps if you see something as white and I see it as black, there is a meeting point, a gray area, upon which we might begin to agree. From this point we can extend the parameters of agreement. In the end we might never fully agree but we can come to understand that there are many ways of seeing things.

One of the traps we frequently fall into is the idea that arguments are either won or lost, that right and wrong can always be clearly defined by force of argument. When we dig in and argue *the* truth, we are mostly looking only for confirmation of *our* truth. Uncertainty becomes weakness and saying that the other guy might be right becomes unthinkable when we are convinced of our own rightness.

We tend to adopt fixed attitudes in certain areas. We cling to the rightness of our views as if they were inscribed on tablets; and in the process, confine ourselves to the limits of our own experience. I've heard arguments between people escalate to ridiculous proportions simply because they refused to acknowledge the possibility of being wrong—as if such an admission would compromise their worth as human beings—as if the maintenance of a healthy ego required constant vindication of their views. Ironically, the opposite is true. People who work hard at being infallible will inevitably learn the price of their insistence.

When we unburden ourselves of the responsibility of being right all the time, we are free to learn from others. Just the simple admission that "I might be wrong," or, "You might be right," can work wonders in communication. Instead of standing alone in our rightness, we can draw closer to each other by discovering common beliefs and looking for a basis for agreement. Having the strength of conviction ceases to be a positive attribute when it interferes with people trying to find truth in their common experience. Besides, what does it profit you if you are right and you have won, but have lost a friend?

Complex disagreements may not be easily settled, but it is well to start negotiations free of assumptions of right and wrong. Better to start with the possibility that there is a little wrong in the most right of us and a little right in the most wrong of us.

There are some important words and phrases we seem to have great difficulty with. They're everyday words that get caught between our good intentions on one hand and our inhibitions or fear of rejection on the other. Take for example those two seldom heard but highly effective words, "I'm sorry." For many of us "I'm sorry," is a painful admission of a fault or imperfection. They imply, "I was wrong," and that's the part that seems to activate our defenses and keep us from speaking.

But "I'm sorry," doesn't need to be a vindication for one side or another. It's far more effective in making things right again than in showing who was wrong. Still, the words come hard, as if saying them reveals some weakness, some vulnerability.

Just a little thought on the matter tells us the opposite is true. Being vulnerable and able to say, "I was wrong," is one of the surest signs of strength. It informs others that we are sensitive to their pain or to their mood. It's far better than putting up walls and trying to maintain the myth of being perfect. The magic words, "I'm sorry," have unlimited power to heal and restore.

There are other phrases with which we struggle now and then such as, "Help me." This implies a need for someone else's strength right now. A need to be together right now. No matter how independent and self-reliant we become, we will always need others. They are a source of confidence when ours is faltering. By offering us another perspective, they can help us to see more clearly. But these things are not always freely given and must often be asked for.

We learned early in life that, "I can do it myself," was very rewarding. We were encouraged to be self-reliant and told that asking for help was a sign of weakness. We therefore find it difficult to say, "I need you." We still like to feel that we are in total control and hesitate to reach out for help.

"I don't know," is another little phrase that comes hard to some of us. It's a curious thing the way we often need to project an image of infallibility, of always having an answer for everything. We've all encountered people like that. For whatever reason they regard, "I don't know," as a personal defect, as if each question or problem in life represented a challenge to their reputations.

In a poem entitled, *The Rock,* T.S. Eliot tells us that, "All our knowledge brings us nearer to our ignorance. Where is the wisdom we have lost in knowledge?" Some of the wisest people I know have the fewest answers and the least amount of certainty. Perhaps they have found that true knowledge is not in the knowing but in the seeking. I'm always a little suspicious of any organization or philosophy or creed that has

the answer for every question. I think it is more likely that others are struggling with the same problems and asking the same questions, and some questions may have no answers. As each of us seeks to find our own answers in life, "I don't know," might be the best place to begin.

The last of our underused phrases is really contained in part within the other three. It says what the others can only imply. The words are, "I love you." Why is it so difficult for some of us to say these three simple words? Why do we leave this phrase behind and regard it as a vestige of our earlier, more romantic selves? We come to believe that after a time love speaks for itself, that it is something implied by a relationship: "We've been together for twenty years. If that's not love, I don't know what is." And so, sadly, the words go the way of flowers and moonlight drives and holding hands at the movies.

We forget that even the most secure among us needs reassurance from time to time. We don't realize that sometimes the other person may be feeling more remote or disconnected, or that we ourselves are becoming more complacent in our relationship. Saying, "I love you," implies that "I don't take you for granted," that the force which brought you together still keeps you together.

The space that so often expands between people is so easily bridged with the right words at the right time. As relationships and the people in them inevitably change, it's important that we reaffirm that some things are constant. "I'm sorry," "I need you," "I love you," are powerful ways of reinforcing this affirmation.

Every culture shares a common repertoire of visual signals. Each time we make contact with others, whether for the first time or in a daily setting, body language can establish instant rapport. A whole array of clues and cues are on display.

Take smiles, for example. Such a simple yet telling act. There are some people who seem to think a smile is a major investment in human relations. They seem to be saying that a smile is risky business indeed, considering that it might not be returned or be misinterpreted.

Still, there is an interesting dynamic at work when two strangers encounter one another. Often one or the other briefly struggles with the decision of whether or not to dare a smile. It seems a rather pointless dilemma when one considers the possible consequences: He/she may not reciprocate. So what? You did what was natural for you and so did the other person. It doesn't take too much effort since more effort is involved when one frowns. Also, there is a 50-50 chance that your smile will be returned. In this case, two people have become just a little less like strangers, a little less alone.

A smile can say many things in many situations. Without it we would be greatly restricted in our dealings with other people. Anyone who would doubt that might want to try going through a day without a smile. If it turns out to be an easy thing to do, I'd be a little concerned. For most of us, our smiles come naturally and are an expression of being fully alive. William James wrote that we are happy *because* we smile, not the reverse. That's something to think about.

It's interesting that our very first smiles appeared shortly after birth without any prompting from anyone. Psychologists have learned that the smile is a prerequisite to later positive relationships. Paul Eckman, a California psychologist, once conducted studies among various cultures to determine which facial expressions were universally recognized.

In literate and preliterate cultures, the one image that was consistently identified was the portrait of a smiling face.

I'm partial to all kinds of smiles which come directly from the heart and end in a full laugh. I love the kind of smile that comes to a person who is quietly remembering a beautiful moment in the past or anticipating joy to come. And there is the magical smile between two people which is the perfect complement to meeting for the first time. It's the most direct way of saying, without words, "I'm truly glad to know you." And I love that wonderful smile on parents' faces when their child has done something especially well.

If you'll study your own face, you'll discover that the lines which extend from the corners of the nose to the sides of the mouth are the ones formed when we smile. They are the first and usually most pronounced lines that appear on the face. They seem to follow a natural contour. If William James was right about our being happy because we smile, we are all blessed with an abundant source of happiness.

We are in the midst of a communication revolution and the emphasis these days seems to be on speed and efficiency. But I can't help wondering whatever happened to the art of letter writing. We seem to have forgotten how to do it. Words are taped, transcribed and processed these days. Letters are considered passé as long as a phone is handy; we say it saves us time and energy. So we lose yet another personal touch.

On the other hand, businesses and corporations have rediscovered the value of the personal letter in their dealings with the public. Think of all those form letters we receive which try so hard to sound personal. They even call us by our first name. The illusion is almost perfect. We are supposed to

believe that someone in some distant marketing firm cares enough to write us a personal note.

I'm sure that the people who send these letters know they're not fooling anyone. But they also understand a little basic human psychology. People are more apt to pay attention to a message that acknowledges them personally. It certainly beats "occupant," "homeowner," or "to whom it may concern."

We are naturally drawn to a letter, especially one which comes to us in a handwritten envelope. They seem so rare. We recognize that a letter takes time and effort, and that's why it's so well received.

The problem is that we think we need to be a Virginia Woolf or a Marcel Proust when we communicate something in writing. We worry about poor grammar, bad spelling and all the rules that guided us through school essays and compositions. We think we must be literary or poetic or terribly clever when we say it in writing. We forget that it is sufficient to know that someone cared enough to send a personal message.

I get cards and letters written on the strangest things. They're very often scribbled notes with no literary pretensions, just something to keep in touch, share love or say hello. Not long ago I received a postcard with only three words on it. The salutation: "Leo," the body: "Ugh," and the closing: "Me." The "ugh" was an opinion of a Broadway play I had asked my friend to send along after he had seen it. A lengthy description would not have been nearly as eloquent as that one-word message.

And there's another advantage to letter writing that we don't often think about. It allows us the opportunity to say exactly what we feel. We have time to reflect and put things just the way we want them. I'm all for face-to-face communication, but for whatever reason, we don't always say in person

what we really feel. Sometimes it helps to sort out our feelings in quiet, then capture them on paper. Even if no one else appreciates it, it has value in helping to clarify things in our own mind.

Have you ever thought about why we save letters we've received over the years and count them among our private treasures? Why else do we read and reread them, each time letting the words impart their meaning as if for the first time? What else could account for mail carriers' popularity except their bringing such letters to us. Certainly they bring other things too, but I'd venture to say that one personal letter from someone we care about is worth five of any other kind.

My sister Lee has saved all of my letters from my many travels, going back nearly thirty years. I only discovered this a few months ago while sitting around a dinner table savoring one of her great dining experiences. "Remember all those letters you used to write me from Europe and the Orient?" she asked. "Well, here they are." And with that she placed a box full of memories on my lap. The collection was a living narrative of places and people and experiences that up to now were only dimming memories. I was reminded of an old and very wise saying from the Orient: The strongest memory is paler than the weakest ink.

How few modern lovers will know the joy of rereading that bundle of letters, tied with ribbon, preserved over the years as a lasting narrative of a growing love. We have so many ways to communicate with each other. Sometimes it seems as if putting pen to paper is the most neglected one. There's so much we can accomplish with the right words at the right time. Why not put it in writing?

One of the most interesting communication problems I've heard of was between two individuals who had been married for twenty years. After all those years the husband seemed to consciously turn off his wife's statements. He never seemed to hear her. She would ask him to do something, and he would sit there sphinx-like, even when she became noticeably perturbed with him for not answering. I wondered about this behavior. His explanation was fascinating.

"I don't ignore her. My doctor told me that I'm deaf to high frequency tones. When my wife is angry, her voice registers about a half an octave higher. I can't hear her. Of course she doesn't believe a word of it."

Indeed his wife was not easily convinced that when he turned a deaf ear to her (so to speak), his listening problem was physiological. I suspect, along with her, that he took full advantage of his condition to screen out all sorts of unpleasant communications. Happily, their love is strong enough to overcome the problem.

Really listening to others is an art—one that we must be continually cultivating. It is so much more than just hearing words and reacting to them. I believe the very best in us is brought out when we truly listen to others, because to do so requires some of the noblest of human traits. "I listen to you because I respect you. I want to know you. I want to understand you better." "I listen to you because I feel with you, knowing that I will need your compassion one day, too." "I listen to you because I love you."

So many of us are working so hard at making ourselves heard, that we forget that the better half of communicating is *listening*. We have all experienced the distress of talking to people who are so self-absorbed that they are not hearing a word we say—all the while preparing dazzling responses of their own. Diogenes might have had just such people in mind when he wrote over two thousand years ago, "We have two

ears and only one tongue in order that we may hear more and speak less." If you keep talking, you just hear yourself say what you already know.

Then there are those whose attention may be won for only brief periods. As you talk, they will glance in every other direction but your eyeballs, which is where they should look when you are talking to them. Sometimes they will even engage others in the middle of a conversation and you are left talking to yourself. They seem to be suffering from the delusion that their attention is so precious that it can only be given in limited quantities. Whatever, it is one of the worst insults one human being can give to another.

A story of one of my college students illustrates just how critical listening can be. She had been battling a severe depression and was trying to communicate her problems to her parents. More than once she spoke to them of her world caving in around her, and her parents, for whatever reason, chose not to hear. She even went so far as to tell them that she had contemplated suicide, and still her parents did not listen. When she finally did attempt suicide, and fortunately failed, the mother and father were dumbstruck. You can imagine this young woman's frustration when they asked, "Why didn't you tell us you were having problems?"

It is ironic that where good communication is the most critical, it is often in its sorriest state. The people who are the closest to us in life are very often assumed to be the most predictable and therefore are often the least listened to because of it. When we close people out, so much more is neglected than just good conversation. There is the greater harm in being indifferent to the growth and change that constantly takes place in each of us. We must remind one another that every day finds each of us a little changed from the day before. If we fail to listen, we are one day likely to be faced with a stranger. Each day there is a new you waiting to

unfold and be discovered by anyone who will take the time to listen.

It was on the day the Russians informed the world that they were boycotting the Los Angeles Olympic Games. That same evening I happened to see an interesting confrontation on television between representatives of the Soviet and American governments. The subject, of course, was the boycott. The atmosphere was quite tense.

First the gentleman from our State Department launched a scathing attack on the Russian government. He brought up every negative thing it had done for the last five years. Not a hint of conciliation in his approach. It was a cardinal opportunity to take the offensive and it was seized with determination.

The rebuttal from the Soviet representative returned in kind what was hurled at him. He dredged up every complaint and example, real or imagined, of American wrongdoing that he could manage in the few minutes allotted him.

It was a standoff. Both men apparently did what habit and tradition dictated under the circumstances. Each had a position to advance or defend and it was done forcefully and without compromise. What made this exchange a memorable one for me was the presence of a third participant in the dialogue. After the partisans had dug their trenches, the president of the U.S. Olympic Committee, Peter Ueberroth, was asked to comment.

At that time, his sole concern was the full participation of *all* countries in the Olympics. He seemed to better understand the need to steer a middle course, so he artfully directed the dialogue toward the question of what could be done to

everyone together. It had a much nicer ring than, "Look what you've done wrong lately."

After this there was a noticeable change in the atmosphere. The adversaries seemed to relax their posture a little and even though neither was willing to see things differently, at least the harshness was gone. All it took was a little tact. One would think that diplomats, as we like to call them, would be a little better practiced in this skill.

We'd like to think that the people in whom we place so much faith will understand the power and the effect of their words and use them wisely, for all our sakes. We come to realize, however, that our leaders and our spokespersons are capable of the same miscalculations as the rest of us in our communications with others.

We're daily given the choice of trampling on people's feelings, or being a little considerate. The latter usually requires nothing more than thinking before we speak. It's really not a very demanding proposition, but as we all know, some people have difficulty in this area.

We all like to be straightforward in our dealings with others, but we realize also that honesty sometimes requires a measure of kindness. Still, we have those who are of the opinion that their perception of the world is the stuff honesty is made of. They'll tell you when they don't like the tilt of your hat or the consistency of your noodle casserole. If they disagree with you, they'll always let you know because not to do so, in their view, is to violate the truth. They would never preface a comment with "The way I see it," rather, they explain, "Well, to be perfectly honest . . ." and follow this with a brutal frankness that nobody could appreciate. As children these individuals were no doubt treasured for their candid nature and natural innocence. But as adults they can be pretty difficult individuals to be around.

Frankness is not necessarily honesty. Happily most of us

learn to cultivate a sense of reserve out of simple consideration for others. True honesty includes a measure of goodwill
because we recognize that truth may be hurtful or malicious. I
don't believe that among lovers and friends there should be no
reserve. Even the most loving couple must be careful. Some
undeveloped or spontaneous remarks are often better left
unspoken. Thoughts verbalized in moments of despair, suspicion, anger or condemnation can often be permanently
damaging to a relationship.

Tactfulness, on the other hand, is being careful to pick the
best time for all concerned. Even saying nothing may be the
sort of tact that is just right for the situation. Of course, that
may mean holding back that perfect retort or saving the, "I
told you so," for another day.

Those who can temper frankness with thoughtfulness are
to be admired. We need more of that kind of honesty in our
relationships, as well as in the political arena. We all benefit
from honest communication, but especially when it is mixed
with a little tact.

Once someone is labeled, it's difficult to change the image
it creates.

Three years ago *Time* and *Newsweek* did profiles on me. In
the headlines I was described as *Dr. Hug* in *Time,* and *The
Prince of Hugs* in *Newsweek.* These tags were not meant to be
derogatory, just the usual eye-catching media hype. It
worked. Since then I have never appeared on television or
radio, or been written about in a newspaper article without
being associated with the *hug* label.

The sad part of such labeling is that it suggests I am a
gimmicky individual who, by hugging everyone in sight, is

not to be taken seriously. This is hardly what a person, who has dedicated his life to the better understanding of human love, would hope for. It's true that I value hugs. In fact, I feel they are essential to good health and a long life. People feel isolated and lonely without them. Hugging is natural and I have never thought of it as any big deal.

I was raised in a large Italian family where a hug and a kiss on both cheeks was expected. In fact, it was a punishable offense not to hug grandma, grandpa and the long stream of friends and relatives who regularly passed through our home.

It didn't take long to discover, however, that not all the world loves a hugger. I was reprimanded by teachers and shunned by many of my peers who thought me weird. It seemed sad and puzzling to me that I had to be cautious of whom I hugged and under what circumstances I hugged them. It also made me unhappy to think that many were missing the joy and contentment a hug produced.

In my travels outside the United States, I became delightfully aware that in most countries people hugged and kissed in greeting. In Asia, for example, men and women alike walk hand in hand, arm in arm.

However, in my media tour of England when my book *Living, Loving & Learning* was published there, hugging caused a minor sensation. The media announced my arrival by saving that "Dr. Hug" from the United States was coming to change Britons' habits. One London newspaper even sent a group of attractive women through the city to hug people at random and make notes for what the paper called a scientific survey. The results were surprising—even to them. Most people interviewed said they loved the human contact and wished there were more of it in their country. There were, however, those who felt it infringed on their space or that it was appalling.

Year after year we are presented with interesting and ver-

ifiable research that suggests hugging is healthy. *Touch Therapy,* by Helen Colton, teaches how touching can enhance one's life. To my knowledge no one has claimed that a warm, caring hug can be detrimental to your health. Wherever I speak, people line up and wait for hours to share a friendly hug, often decrying the fact that they get so few and need them so much.

Isn't it interesting how we reserve our embraces for such intense emotional occasions as sexual acts, moments of extreme elation, tragedy or catastrophe? We rush into the security of another's arms after earthquakes, floods, and accidents. Men, who might never do so otherwise, pat and hug each other with wild abandon after winning a game or accomplishing a successful athletic feat. Family members gathered at a funeral find special comfort and tenderness in each other's arms, even though it is not customary for them to be affectionate with one other.

It is natural for us to want to show affection, but for some mysterious reason we equate tenderness with sentimentality, weakness and vulnerability. We are often as hesitant to give a hug as to receive it.

So what's the big deal? Hugging is a very human affirmation of being valued and cherished. It feels good, costs nothing and requires little effort. It's healthy for both the hugged and the hugger.

So have you hugged your wife, husband, father, mother, child, grandmother, grandfather, mother-in-law, father-in-law, neighbor, coworker, priest, minister, psychologist, boss lately?

A Passion for Empathy

Papa used to tell me, "Felice, it costs nothing to be nice," and after waiting for the wisdom of that to settle in my mind, he would always follow with, "And you get so much in return."

"Put yourself in my shoes." It's a familiar request. Perhaps the phrase is derived from the native American Sioux who said never to judge another until you had walked for two weeks in his moccasins. We usually say it because someone doesn't understand what we're feeling and we'd like them to identify with us. It reassures us that we're not alone in facing our problems. In short, we need their empathy.

The dictionary defines empathy as, "having the capacity to participate in the ideas and feelings of another." It's a very special human quality that allows us to step outside of ourselves and try to understand another person from within. Often, no words are necessary. Feelings are conveyed even when we don't have the ability to describe them.

From one of Grimm's tales comes a poignant example of just how important empathy (or lack of it) can be. Some of us might remember "Grandfather's Corner," the story of an old man who lived with his son and his son's wife. The father was almost deaf and blind and had difficulty eating without spilling his food. Occasionally he would drop a bowl and break it. The son and his wife thought it was disgusting and made him eat in a corner behind the stove. They gave him a wooden bowl which couldn't be broken.

One day the little grandson was working with some pieces of wood. When his father asked what he was doing, he replied, "I'm making a trough for you and mother to eat out of when I'm grown up." From that moment on, his grandfather rejoined the family at the table and no one ever said another word about it.

The realization that, "I, too, may be there one day," is a splendid teacher of empathy. Surely we can all foresee a time when our needs will be different and we just may require a little extra care and compassion. Of all the human qualities which make us feel connected to each other, I believe it is the ability to empathize that draws us closest.

All of us have known rejection and failure in one form or another. From these experiences we understand just that much better the disappointment or the despair of others. Part of the strength that comes with adversity is the forming of empathy. Not only do we learn to feel with others, but we're also less apt to judge them.

One of the most interesting examples of empathy I've ever heard comes from George Orwell, writing about his experiences during the Spanish Civil War in, *Such Were the Days*. It was in the heat of battle when he had his gun trained on a soldier of the other side who, in that instant, was quite literally caught with his pants down. Seeing him in such a vulnerable position Orwell writes that he was unable to pull the trigger. The enemy suddenly appeared all too human.

Perhaps it would be well for us to pause from time to time before speaking or doing something and ask ourselves, "How would I feel if this were said or done to me?" We have been taught to follow the Golden Rule all our lives, not that we may become shining examples of behavior, but that we realize one more way of better understanding one another. So put yourself in my shoes, or anyone else's who needs your understanding and compassion.

When was the last time that you were complimented for anything? I recently spoke to a mother of seven who told me that she hadn't heard the word *thanks* for over five years. Expressed compliments and praise are rare these days.

Not too long ago I was asked to speak to a group of sorority girls. I was overwhelmed with the kindness, the poise and loveliness of these young ladies present. I freely shared my delight. I commented about the wisdom of one girl's state-

ment, the lovely color of another's dress, the brightness of another's smile, and the thoughtfulness of still another. As the evening progressed, one of the girls suggested that I seemed to compliment a bit too freely.

"Don't you?" I asked.

"Why should I" she was quick to respond. "No one compliments me!"

"I compliment because I feel that it makes me feel good and it makes others happy. Isn't that reason enough?" I asked her. "It's such an easy thing to do."

She wasn't convinced. She was certain that I must be phony or have some ulterior motive.

On the other hand, I have noticed that people are often embarrassed when they are complimented. They become suspicious and get that, "What's he after?" look on their faces.

"What a lovely outfit!" I say.

"Oh, this old rag!" they answer, "I've had it for years." It's difficult to understand that anyone would wear an old rag they'd had for years unless they still cared enough about it to be seen in it. An ordinary, "Oh, thank you. I like it too," would seem a healthier response.

But it is understandable that living in a society in which we feel awkward giving compliments would not prepare us for receiving them. Yet, most of us need to be praised from time to time. Compliments are a needed expression of affirmation, of being seen and approved. We emerge from such experiences feeling more complete, more joyful, more confident. After all, there is nothing wrong with desiring approval. It's a natural trait of being human. If we don't desire recognition, why do we spend hours grooming, primping, deodorizing, selecting our clothes and hairdressers so carefully?

It seems to me that we need never fear saying something kind to someone, even a stranger. Perhaps the reception will

not always be what we had hoped, but never mind, in the long run, it will be appreciated. We experience so few compliments that when we do get them it is like most unexpected happenings; it puts us off balance. Think about many parents, for example, who are so often ready to criticize but less apt to comment on the good their children do. They forget that constant faultfinding does little but produce hate and avoidance reactions. But when there is an equal amount of praise offered for things well done, then the criticism becomes more tolerable and has a more lasting effect.

Certainly there is something good, something beautiful, something positive in everyone. I recently saw an elderly lady with a beautiful wine-colored, velvet hat perched saucily on her graying hair. She sat buried in a newspaper in the waiting room of a doctor's office. I decided to respond to my instinct and leaned over to her. "You look lovely in that hat. It's a wonderful color." She put down her paper and smiled warmly. "I love hats!" she said. "I'm glad you noticed it." This was the start of a long, animated conversation. She became radiant and even more lovely. Our wait seemed so much shorter. It cost me nothing. It helped us both to feel more joyful. When I left, I wondered how many people there had admired the hat, but had said nothing. It takes so little energy and everyone gains. Try it and experience for yourself the pure magic that is in a word of praise.

Every generation has had its critics of teenagers. In ancient Greece, Socrates lamented their bad manners and contempt for authority. St. Paul, writing about five hundred years later, described the youth of Rome as "filled with wickedness, rottenness, greed and malice." The very word teen comes

from an old Anglo-Saxon word (teona) which means vexation.

No doubt many generations have felt slightly vexed by adolescent behavior and attitudes, but there's also that abundance of energy and exciting sense of beginning that are so much a part of this time of life.

Teenagers. What are they up to now? Pink and orange hair, outrageous clothes, bizarre music, a language all their own, a lack of respect for established values—in other words, nothing really out of the ordinary. Not that all teens can be identified with this image, but they do seem to cause a good deal of concern for the present generation of adults.

Recently I visited an old friend whose daughter is in her middle teens. The last time I had seen her she was in pigtails and missing some front teeth. Now she wore a plastic hand grenade as an earring and a bondage belt around her waist. Her clothes were disheveled and the colors clashed horribly (or from her standpoint, perfectly). To complete this ensemble, she wore combat boots.

She had indeed changed from the cute little munchkin I remembered; but after talking to her for awhile, she seemed a typical teenager.

Much has been written about this so-called difficult period—gallant attempts to help confused parents better understand what is going on in the teenage mind. We are told that adolescents are going through an identity crisis, a hazy area between childhood and adulthood. it is a time of identity confusion, of peer pressure, of sexual awakening. It is a period to begin developing a philosophy of life, questioning truths and seeking heroes and answers. These can be unsettling things which cause us to throw up our arms to heaven, shake our heads and wonder, as every generation has, just where this is all leading us.

Letters I've received express a sincere concern with, as one woman put it, "young people's preoccupation with the

devil." She illustrates her belief with "their song lyrics, their sacrilegious jewelry, and those shocking performances." Though not to such an extreme, I must confess to being a little bewildered by some of these things myself. Up to now, my idea of a wild outfit has been a plaid, multi-colored sport coat with yellow pants. Musically speaking, I don't suppose I'll ever understand a group with a name like Johnny Rotten and the Sex Pistols.

But then that's not the sort of understanding teenagers need anyway. I think the very least we can do is try to remember our own adolescence and even if we were models of stability, we can certainly recall what a volatile period it was. Surely it's possible for us to attempt to understand and offer guidance without too much criticism.

Teenagers are people involved in their own kind of struggle. Just like the rest of us, they sometimes need to work them out in their own way, at their own pace. What they need is support and understanding, not put-downs.

No doubt today's teenagers will be the next generation's critics, and it seems to me there's a natural order to it all. They'll know they've made the transition when they begin to preface statements with, "When I was your age. . ." and then proceed to explain a better way. We can easily forget that it's possible for others to benefit from our experience without their having to duplicate it.

Some of the most conservative, proper people today were children of the 60's and 70's. They were called hippies. I remember so well how they stirred up the more settled members of society with their appearance, their music and their philosophy. I would venture a guess that most of yesterday's hippies find themselves in very different roles today, none the worse for the shocking experiences of their youth. Those of us who view the excesses of today's teenagers with a sense of alarm might consider yesterday's "love children," the major-

ity of whom are living with home mortgages, and raising sons and daughters through measles and braces.

Personally, I can't think of anything more exciting than young people coming to grips with their own uniqueness as individuals. We all did it, and happily, most of us survived. Adolescence is the natural time for this. We can do no less than help them to do the same.

A Passion for All Stages of Life

I remember quite clearly an old photo of Papa that was pasted with care in our family album. It was his earliest picture as a young boy and the only likeness of him that survived his childhood. More than anything, I remember those vital and gentle eyes shining through the old and weathered picture. It was a look that he carried throughout his life.

When I feel age encroaching, I remember those eyes and think of the things about Papa that defied time. I am again reminded that what is essential in all of us is ageless. Beginnings and endings are united when we understand that aging may be simply a continuous process from innocent childhood to sophisticated childishness.

It is painfully apparent to anyone who knows me or my work that food happens to be among my greatest passions. For me, it's one of life's immense pleasures. When I was a child, I hated food. It saddens me to think of the wonderful meals Mama and Papa cooked that deserved a great deal of appreciation. I ate only to stay alive. I was a skinny kid, though this may be difficult to believe for anyone seeing me now. Everyone coaxed me and pleaded lest I fade away or die of malnutrition.

Eating became less a problem as I grew into young adulthood, but my weight remained the same. Times and styles change and what was formerly seen as the cure of *thin* had become a blessing. Diet-conscious friends were more than a little envious of me as I ate with abandon without any observable effect. As others struggled with the battle of the bulge, I approached every dining experience with the assurance that it would never happen to me.

"It will in time," I was told by more more pudgy friends. "Wait 'til you hit thirty. You'll see." I did.

At about thirty-five, I began to expand. I was appalled to find that the body is actually inflatable. For the first time in my life it became obvious that I needed to exercise some discipline over what I put into my mouth. By this time, of course, I'd formed a passionate love affair with food. Meals had become a special delight rather than just a pause to refuel.

The endless varieties of fish, meat, vegetables—all smothered in rich hollandaise, bechamel and assorted cream and butter-based sauces had become an anticipated source of pleasure. Breakfast, lunch and dinner were much-waited-for-rituals, all of which were punctuated with coffee cake, sweet rolls and outlandish desserts. It was like having finally discovered one of life's true miracles only to have it torn abruptly away.

The irony of it all! In the ensuing years people began to comment that I was looking "especially healthy." I was hearing words such as *paunch* and *pleasingly plump.*

Many can no doubt identify with this depressing happening: the sudden discovery that your trousers or skirts have shrunk and seem more like tourniquets than clothing. We soon became a part of a whole fraternity involved in a similar awakening. We also become even more painfully aware of those not yet affected.

We assure ourselves that the boyish or girlish figure can be regained with just a little sacrifice. We become determined to adopt a healthful regimen of diet and exercise. We begin to jog and/or lift weights. We skip desserts. Chocolate becomes something to dream of but never to consume. Late night snacks are a definite taboo. A new concept of eating gradually sinks in. It's called moderation.

But to our horror, all seems to no avail. Very little seems to affect the expanding bulge. We call on humor to salve our pain. We begin to refer to our excess inches by endearing names, like love handles. We buy clothes a size larger and blame it on the cut of the items. We pass mirrors more swiftly than before.

One of my nephews just turned thirty. He tells me that he's joined a gym, that he'll never lose his lifeguard physique. For his sake I hope he won't, but I have my doubts when I watch him put away food. (How many miles must one run at thirty to work off five calories?)

I guess the only comfort lies in the fact that a spreading mid-section happens to most of us. It becomes, therefore, a common bond and as far as I'm concerned, anything that brings us together can't be all bad!

Years ago, when I was teaching my Love Class at the University of Southern California, I asked my students to write a short history of the lives of their parents. They stared blankly at me. "A history of our parents!" They were incredulous. "What do you mean?"

A short history, I explained, about where they came from, how they met, their special moments of joy or pain. A history.

It became quickly apparent that they knew nothing about their family histories. When challenged, the majority of the students didn't even know the exact color of their parents' eyes. It hadn't occurred to them that Mom and Dad had ever courted and loved! It was impossible for some of them to accept the fact that their mother had ever received a first kiss or had gone on dates that may not have included their father!

This lack of awareness is not confined to my students. Most of us take those we love for granted. We assume that they are there and will always be there when we need them. Not so!

I recall the after-dinner talking time in our home when I was a child. I can't tell you how many times we asked Mama to tell us about her years as a young servant girl to the Padrone. The indignities. The insults. The inhumane treatment. How vivid were her descriptions of the crowded immigrant ship on which she came to America, her long stay on Ellis Island with her sick child, the train trip to Los Angeles—unable to speak English, shy and afraid.

Papa's stories of his work at the factory in Italy, of his first job in America, times of extreme poverty, times of genuine joy were of equal interest. We children sat in rapt attention, full of admiration and wonder that our parents had achieved so much. I learned that things didn't start with me. I was a part of an ongoing history full of pride, survival and love.

We do not exist in isolation, we are a part of a greater story, some of it having been written, some which we will write, and some which we will pass on to others to complete.

At a recent book fair I found a most interesting soft cover book. As I recall, it was called something like, *Father Was Quite a Boy.* A companion book was called, *Mother Was Quite a Girl.* These books were simply a series of open-end questions for mama and papa to fill in. Describe your parents. What was the name of your first boyfriend? Who took you to your prom? Etc. When completed, these books were to be given to the children as part of their legacy. What a splendid idea! What a long-lasting and valuable gift.

So often we are too concerned with tomorrow to recognize the significance of yesterday. Yet that represents the thread of explanation which guides us to who we are now.

I can't tell you the joy my students felt when they completed their assignment. For some, it was the best time the family had experienced together in years. "Did you know my dad first worked on a railroad?" "My mother waited tables when she was in high school." "My mother was my father's buddy's girlfriend. Dad won a wife but lost a friend." "Mama had a miscarriage which still brings her sorrow." "Dad married his first wife when she was only seventeen." "I had no idea my mom was such a hellion when she was my age!"

We all agreed that it would have been a tragedy to have missed the experience of the past. "It scares me," one student said, "when I think that my parents could have died and I wouldn't have known them at all!"

We owe each other a knowledge of the past. It's a shared bond from which we gain the knowledge and strength to face our tomorrows!

Just a few years ago I found myself in a hospital intensive care unit. I awakened in a large, noisy room with a number of other patients lying about in various stages of devastating ailments. There were respirators, intravenous tubes, bottles, catheters, a host of monitoring devices suspended from everywhere. Being there myself was trauma enough—I had no desire to inflict this scene upon friends and relatives. I gave specific instructions that I was to receive no visitors. I was told that I would be out of intensive care, if all went well, within twenty-four hours. Then I would see people.

That room was a lonely place. I know it seems strange that in a place where you are never long out of sight of a trained, watchful eye one can be so lonely, so frightened, so confused and alone. But so it was. I didn't realize how much I needed the people I knew and loved. I needed to see a friendly face—not an efficient one, but a loving one. I needed to feel a warm touch—not a professional touch, but a tender one.

At that point I was awakened by the sound of the door opening quietly behind me. Not the door which led into the cluttered room, but the one that opened to the corridor outside. I thought I might be having a dream, or that perhaps the drugs I'd been given were bringing on a hallucination. But there he was. My very dear friend. He walked cautiously between the respirator, the I.V. tubes and other equipment, smiled down at me and took my hand. It was a moment of sheer magic. I forgot the horror of the room—the tubes, the bottles, the noise. It didn't matter how he had gotten in or whether he would soon be asked to leave. A human being whom I loved was near and sharing my experience. I'll remember this moment forever.

It is ironic that when people need us most we are often least able to give. This is especially true at times of serious illness or impending death. I'm certainly as guilty as everyone else. It happens every time when someone in my family or a

dear friend is ill or in a hospital. I am torn between wanting to be near them and a strange feeling of wanting to avoid having to see them. Emotionally I feel this confusion, even though I feel strongly that no one should suffer alone or die alone.

Things were different in generations past. The critically ill were kept in the home and lovingly nursed and attended to. It was a family member who tenderly closed their eyes for the last time. Only death could separate them. Perhaps what has happened is that we have allowed ourselves to be intimidated by medical jargon and hospitals. The result has been understandable feelings of inadequacy and fear. We feel that we have no part in our loved ones' recuperation, that we may indeed be jeopardizing their health by keeping them at home. So we have relinquished our potential roles in the healing process.

It is natural that when people feel ill or are dying they want to be at home. They want to be near those they have loved for so many years and who have loved them in return. They want to be in the home and in the bed where they feel most at ease. Yet the moment they most need this loving support system, they are ambulanced away to isolation or intensive-care wards, often to spend their last hours alone or among strangers. So many of us have lost loved ones without ever being able to say goodbye. It can leave us with lasting feelings of sadness, a painful lack of closure.

We must never forget that the person behind the pale face, the pained countenance, or the emaciated body is still the person we love. We must never forget that the need for affection, touching, reassuring, communication and love is still there—only now, intensified.

We all need each other. Perhaps one day we will become ill or incapacitated and require the warmth and tenderness of others. The only way we can be assured that our needs will be

fulfilled is to overcome these unrealistic but very human fears, and try to change the process now.

The phrase, old age, aside from being meaningless, more often than not carries with it a negative connotation. Instead of viewing it as a stage of human development, we often look upon it as a disease, characterized by rocking chairs, stooped and ailing bodies, and people who can no longer fend for themselves. Behind it all is the assumption that our later adulthood is something to be dreaded.

In past years there seems to have been a more definable role for the elderly of our society. In many present cultures apart from our own, older members are accorded great deference and are revered *because* of their age and not in spite of it.

With our fetish for youth and all its charms, we are consumed with the idea that there is a prime of life which exists only within certain fixed limits and that it is a fleeting thing. Then, at the first sign that we have gone beyond those limits, we are cast aside and expected to make room for the new generation.

Small wonder that more and more people with the means to do so are settling into retirement communities where they are accepted. For others less fortunate, there are convalescent (why this misnomer?) homes aplenty, which may provide a quiet place in which to live out one's life, but which will never be a substitute for being among loved ones and feeling needed.

When we see reflected in a furrowed and lined face simply a lifetime that is being used up, and nothing more, we disregard a lifetime of accumulated wisdom. We fail to appreciate the imprint of time and the rich tapestry of experiences that is

reflected in it. Think what a magnificent storehouse of memories are contained in a full life—the moments of passion, of contentment, of despair, of joy—things that the most sophisticated computer could never retain in its most complicated program. It's interesting that of all the human faculties, long-term memory often remains intact while recent memory fails with age. There is a natural order suggested by this if we consider the priceless treasures that are preserved in the minds of those who have lived long and have so much to pass along to the rest of us.

Our attitudes toward older people will surely determine the world we will know when we ourselves age. If we continue to think of chronological age as an indication of an individual's productivity and capacity for growth, then we effectively mark our own boundaries. Life becomes a succession of closing doors and we begin to say things like, "I'm too old for that," and "Those were the good old days." We agonize over each new gray hair, each wrinkle, as portents of the end.

One of the most common stereotypes of the elderly is that they are bitter or cranky people who have withdrawn from others and often from life in general. The more likely possibility is that we have withdrawn from them.

It is funny to me when I meet young people who see fifty as old. I recently attended a birthday party for a six year old (remember six?). Some of us older folk were trying to give the birthday boy a concept of birthdays and the aging process. He at one point turned to me and asked rather disarmingly, "How old are you?" I responded, evading the question, "How old do you think I am?" "A hundred?" he answered without a moment's hesitation. I'll know better next time.

It's interesting how our attitudes change as we become older. Each stage of life seems to bring with it new needs, beliefs, attitudes and responses. I especially became aware of this when I passed fifty. It is as dramatic as when we pass from childhood to adolescence, or adolescence to adulthood, but we seem less aware of the growing older part of it. There are, however, compensations.

It takes us at least fifty years to finally learn that our life and happiness are not dependent upon any single situation or person. We learn that we don't have to have everything our way, that we don't need to be loved by everyone, and that the world doesn't end if we are rejected.

What a relief finally to know this. We still remember the pain of those first rejections, the feelings of emptiness that seemed to surround us. But after fifty years of living we learn that life will go on, that rejection is merely a part of life and not the end of it. With the perfect vision of hindsight, we wonder why we didn't learn this sooner.

After fifty it seems easier to be ourselves. We realize at last that it takes too much energy to play the game—the game of being what others think we should be. Our priorities change too. For one thing, we don't mind being a little less social. Not having something to do all day Saturday, especially Saturday night, has long ceased to be the tragedy it once was.

Having two or three nights a week booked in advance seems more like obligation than recreation. After fifty we find ourselves looking for excuses to have more time at home to read, watch a good T.V. program or just do nothing. We've even accepted the fact that doing nothing can be doing something. We can say no to an invitation without spending hours planning excuses.

After fifty, our eating and drinking habits seem to change radically too. Our idea of a late dinner out is 6:30 P.M. and we begin to look at our watches in order to start home by nine.

We switch to decaffeinated coffee and light drinks. We give up salted Margaritas and very dry Martinis. We request soda with a twist of lime instead.

Where once we never thought about our health, we now find our cabinets full of multiple vitamins; we swear by our juicer and stock up on high fiber foods. We become aware of our heart beat (where on earth had it been before now?) and know the exact reading of our systolic and diastolic blood pressure. We become more concerned with our vision, our hearing, our skin care, our digestion and our muscle tone. We get practical hairdos, see our dentist more often and go back to Ivory soap.

Our idea of entertainment changes. We tend toward activities which bring us peace, rather than nonstop excitement. We become more choosy about what books we read and what films, plays or television programs we watch. "Let's go to a movie," becomes far more specific and more often means, "Let's go to the local revival theater and see an old Humphrey Bogart or Bette Davis film." We are less tolerant of imperfection in our entertainment and find ourselves more often leaving at intermission. Double features, of course, are out!

I'm certain that as we become 60, 70, or 80 we'll acquire new needs and values, but so it should be. We can look back with fondness at what once was, but also in gratitude for where it has led us. I like to think that these changes are part of the wisdom which comes with age, rather than being a condition that is part of aging.

One of the assignments I gave my counseling students each year always brought on a good deal of controversy and mixed

feelings. I would ask my class what they would do if they found they had only five more days to live. Assuming they would be in good health and could do anything they chose, they had to decide how and with whom they would spend their last moments.

Some would wax quite poetic: "I'd go to my favorite spot in Yosemite with my husband/wife/lover." "I'd share my love of nature and die under the stars in my lover's arms." "I'd take a trip to India and spend my last days studying Asian philosophy." Some said they'd seek out the great adventure, gliding free above the earth, diving in the bluest lagoon, climbing where only few have gone. Some wanted to spend their remaining time in quiet introspection or meditation to make final peace with themselves or with God.

But most answers were simple statements: "I'd want to die among those I love." "I'd go home and tell my family I love them." "I'd try to explain my death to my children." "I'd want us to have a big party and see all my family and friends one last time."

Most had in common a strong desire to do something that would make their lives feel more complete, and all with a sense of urgency that always caused me to ask, "Why must you wait for your last five days for doing these things? Why not now?"

Our discussions would often turn to the subject of death and dying and inevitably they became sessions of questions that have no answers. Many had experienced death in one form or another; most had witnessed thousands of deaths on T.V., but all with a remoteness that left them very curious about this great mystery. Though we were unable to agree upon any answers to our questions, I felt there was value in the fact that we openly discussed a subject that is usually shrouded in mystery and fear.

We have more euphemisms to say that someone has died

than for anything else in the English language. People pass on, expire, slip away, or move into the Great Beyond—a thousand other things besides dying. Our avoidance of the word gives us the feeling that it's something to fear. And so we develop inordinate anxieties even to the point of interfering with our happiness now.

Erich Fromm writes, "The whole of life of the individual is nothing but the process of giving birth to himself; indeed we should be fully born when we die." We can think of death as something that stalks us all our lives or we can see it as a reminder that our time is precious. We can put in time until the end comes, or we can use the time we are given to give birth to our potential which is our human trademark.

We often think of death in terms of the tragic circumstances that surround it. We grieve especially for those who are taken prematurely, less I think from a sense of personal loss than from a life that was incomplete. Indeed the greatest tragedy of any death is to reach the end without ever having really lived at all. Why must it take a lifetime to come to this realization? How sad it is to see people who, fearing that the end is near, try frantically to cram all the living they can in the short time left to them. All the things they've ever wanted to do, all the places they've ever wanted to see, all the words that have been left unsaid, suddenly, or rather finally, it dawns on them how precious is their time and how much more they want to really live it.

Our hearts go out to these individuals who must hurry up and live but it seldom occurs to us that there is a message for us all. Whether we think of death as the gateway to the great beyond or as the grim reaper, it still reminds us to give all that we have to the here and now.

Looking back over her incomplete life, Emily, in Thornton Wilder's *Our Town*, laments, "Good-bye world . . . Good-bye to clocks ticking . . . and Mama's sunflowers. And food

and coffee. And new-ironed dresses and hot baths . . . and sleeping and waking up. Oh, earth, you're too wonderful for anybody to realize you."

A lifetime is just too short for us to spend it accumulating regrets for what we might have done. We need to remind ourselves and especially our children, that death is nothing to fear as long as we understand that each moment has a life unto itself with as much possibility for joy and happiness as we are willing to bring to it.

In our time no one is immune from the possibility of violence. No matter how cautious we are, how law abiding, how aware, violence is a very real possibility in our lives. Recently I felt its pain. One of my dearest friends was murdered in a California parking lot. The killers—I am told there were three—ran off and as of this writing have not been apprehended. No matter. My friend is dead. His family, a gentle wife and four children, are suddenly without a husband and father.

The church service was crowded with friends and co-workers, all stunned, angry and bitter. Of course the talk, all in whispers, was about why this should have happened to such a great person. It doesn't make sense that he should have been in the parking lot at the same time as the killers. Why? Idle questions. Conversation without closure. Who on earth knows why?

The priest, rather young, certainly sincere, eulogized my friend. He talked about his important position as vice president of a large department store chain. He talked about his spirituality, his family, his good work. He pointed out that all the truly important things about him were hidden behind a

newspaper headline. He said that we live in a headline-oriented society where we read the captions and seldom think about what is behind them—the human element—the only thing which gives the headline meaning. He challenged us to remember the man who will live through our love.

One of his professional colleagues also spoke of Ed. He told of his creativity, his gentleness, kindness and concern. Through his recounting of actual incidents and memories, he awakened in all of us vital experiences we had shared with Ed. For example, it brought to mind his enthusiasm for a family weekend he was initiating, a whole weekend of being together with his son and daughters and their families for meals, golf, talk and general rejoicing. He wanted to be the sole architect of the weekend. He loved them all very much and wanted to demonstrate this in a tangible way.

I saw a strange thing occur as the service progressed. We all became aware of how the family was facing the ordeal with obvious togetherness and love. Interestingly, the congregation was beginning to do the same. Husbands and wives who had entered the church separated were now closer together in the pew, holding hands, crying together, embracing. Children who had raced in ahead of parents were now being cuddled and held. Families were sitting nearer each other. Tears still flowed but more as a reflection of human strength and survival than of pity.

Strange how death and reflection on violence can bring people together as never before. Perhaps death, rather than being a force for separation, is a force for unity. It reminds us of our shared mortality. It tells us that all is temporary. It assures us the time for life is the moment we are living. It ties us together in a common plight and shows us that there is comfort to be had in shared experience.

I have been told that funerals are for the living. Perhaps my experience in the church substantiates that statement. I know

that when we got together afterward with the family and friends, there was a closeness, a caring, an expiation of pent-up pain and sorrow as is seldom felt anywhere when people assemble. Watching my friend's wife actually comforting all of us and knowing that her pain was great was a profound experience. Certainly it was an ending of one aspect of her life, but one could sense that she had already experienced other endings, none more tragic or violent, but nevertheless final.

On my way home from the services I had time to reflect. I wondered how many of those who attended the funeral had felt the overwhelming, saving quality of love and community at such a time. I wondered how many would grow from the experience. I also wondered how soon we would all go our separate ways and forget.

No matter how well we program ourselves for death and dying it always seems to fill us with dread and fear. We are rarely prepared to deal with it. As Woody Allen so aptly put it, "I'm not afraid to die. I just don't want to be there when it happens."

This seems to have been a year for partings for me. Three deaths in just a few months. Three wonderful people, creators of memories and generators of love, are no longer living.

Death is certainly no stranger in my life. Both my parents died several years ago, my grandparents are dead, my elder brother and several dear friends are all gone. As I get older I lose more and more loved ones. A friend of mine who is getting up in age recently recounted the fact that she has outlived all of her family and most of her close friends. She lamented that in her rather frail condition it was becoming too

difficult to make new friends. It was not death that she dreaded as much as the possibility of ending alone, among strangers.

In the past few years much has been done to bring the subject of death out of its shroud. Knowledgeable and caring individuals such as Elisabeth Kübler-Ross, Raymond Moody, and several others have helped us to face the inevitability of death more boldly. The growth of Hospice has further helped us face death and dying with dignity and to part from each other with strength.

Several years ago I wrote a very short book titled, *The Fall of Freddie the Leaf.* The message was intended for all ages, but it was written especially for children, to help them understand death as another story in life rather than an abrupt end. I did this because I found so little in the literature that helped me to see death as a positive life force rather than an experience to be dreaded.

The response of book publishers was very enlightening. It revealed one of our prevailing attitudes at that time regarding death. Usually, I was sent form rejection notices without even a personal note. When one was included it was usually to inform me that I must be some kind of a fiend to shock the minds of the young with thoughts of death—what children aren't exposed to certainly can't harm them. My experience with young people told me a different story. After thirty years of teaching, I can't think of many students who didn't experience some kind of loss through death. Their comfort came mostly in the form of condolences instead of any attempt at a rational explanation. My book was written with that need in mind. It took years before I found a publisher who was willing to take the risk. Since then, happily, books relating to the subject have multiplied.

It seems odd to me that we should spend most of our lives avoiding thoughts of death. We convince ourselves that oth-

ers die, but we prefer not to think of such a thing happening to our loved ones. We act as if we are immortal. We resist accepting our mortality. Even those who believe that only death will bring eternal peace seem to dread the reality.

I believe that it is only acceptance of our mortality that makes us free to live and appreciate the wonder of life. It is death after all that reminds us that we don't have forever, that if we are going to make our statement, express our love for one another, or truly experience life, it must be done now. Death is no respecter of age, social status or economic level. It comes to us all.

I've learned much from those who have died before me. They've taught me that there is no holding on, that we must let go, that there is nothing wrong with tears of parting or the pain of mourning. But the tears eventually must be dried.

Naturally, any death will leave a void in our lives. After all, there are no two individuals the same. But these spaces will be filled with different people, new experiences and new loves.

The Buddha said that every hello is to be seen as the beginning of a new goodbye, that nothing is permanent. But I like to think that every end can also be a beginning, that every goodbye can also be a new hello.

It is not death that we should fear. Rather it is the possibility of a life unlived that is the real tragedy. Perhaps the closer we come to understanding this, the more easily we will come to accept death, and the more fully we will learn to live here and now.

EPILOGUE

Creating and living our personal paradise is not always easy. In a society that is often suspicious of happy, caring and loving individuals, one runs the risk of being dismissed as ridiculous, naive or, as once happened to me, even irrelevant. But what does that matter? It simply suggests that we will have to develop the courage and strength to stand before the critics and cynics and say, "I don't agree with you. Life IS wonderful, joy IS our birthright, and love IS what it's all about," and continue to live life with a passion.